Eucharistic Epicleses, Ancient and Modern

T0326716

Founded in 1897, the Alcuin Club seeks to promote the study of Christian liturgy and worship in general with special reference to worship in the Anglican Communion. The Club has published a series of annual Collections, including *A Companion to Common Worship*, volumes 1 and 2, edited by Paul F. Bradshaw, a new edition of the classic text *Christian Prayer through the Centuries*, by Joseph Jungmann (SPCK 2007), *The Origins of Feasts, Fasts and Seasons in Early Christianity* by Paul F. Bradshaw and Maxwell E. Johnson (SPCK 2011) and, by the same authors, *The Eucharistic Liturgies: Their Evolution and Interpretation* (SPCK 2012); and, most recently, *The Cross and Creation in Christian Liturgy and Art* by Christopher Irvine (SPCK 2013). The Alcuin Liturgy Guide series aims to address the theology and practice of worship, and includes *The Use of Symbols in Worship*, edited by Christopher Irvine, and two volumes covering the celebration of the Christian Year: *Celebrating Christ's Appearing: Advent to Christmas* and *Celebrating Christ's Victory: Ash Wednesday to Trinity*, both by Benjamin Gordon-Taylor and Simon Jones. The Club works in partnership with GROW in the publication of the Joint Liturgical Studies series, with two studies being published each year. In 2013, the Club also published a major new work of reference *The Study of Liturgy and Worship: An Alciun Guide*, edited by Juliette Day and Benjamin Gordon-Taylor (SPCK 2013).

Members of the Club receive publications of the current year free and others at a reduced rate. The President of the Club is the Rt Revd Michael Perham, its Chairman is the Revd Canon Dr Donald Gray CBE, and the Secretary is the Revd Dr Gordon Jeanes. For details of membership and the annual subscription, contact The Alcuin Club, 5 Saffron Street, Royston SG8 9TR, or email: alcuinclub@gmail.com

Visit the Alcuin Club website at: **www.alcuinclub.org.uk**

Eucharistic Epicleses, Ancient and Modern

Speaking of the Spirit in Eucharistic Prayer

Anne McGowan

Alcuin Club Collections 89

Published in Great Britain in 2014
Society for Promoting Christian Knowledge
36 Causton Street
London SW1P 4ST
www.spckpublishing.co.uk

British Library Cataloguing-in-Publication Data
A catalogue record for this book is available from the British Library

SPCK ISBN 978–0–281–07155–5
eBook ISBN 978–0–281–07156–2

eBook by Data Standards Ltd, Frome, Somerset

Produced on paper from sustainable forests

Contents

Acknowledgements

The author gratefully acknowledges the permission granted by the following copyright holders.

Every effort has been made to seek permission to use copyright material reproduced in this book. The publisher apologizes for those cases where permission might not have been sought and, if notified, will formally seek permission at the earliest opportunity.

Portions of Chapter 4 and the Conclusion were originally published in *A Living Tradition* © 2012 by the Order of Salut Benedict. Published by Liturgical Press, Collegeville, MN. Used with permission.

Excerpts from the English translation of *The Roman Missal* © 2010, International Commission on English in the Liturgy Corporation. All rights reserved.

The author also gratefully acknowledges the many people who devoted their kind and critical attention to this project at various stages, especially Maxwell E. Johnson, Paul F. Bradshaw and Nathan D. Mitchell at the University of Notre Dame; members of the Problems in the Early History of Liturgy seminar of the North American Academy of Liturgy; and the editorial teams of Alcuin Club and SPCK, particulary Benjamin Gordon-Taylor, Ruth McCurry, Yolande Clarke, Louise Clairmonte, Joanne Hill and Mollie Barker.

Tables

Abbreviations

ACC	Alcuin Club Collections
Adv. Haer.	Irenaeus, *Adversus Haereses*
ANF	*Ante-Nicene Fathers*
ASB	*Alternative Service Book*
AThR	*Anglican Theological Review*
BAS	Anaphora of Basil
BCP	Book of Common Prayer
BCP	*Book of Common Prayer* of the Episcopal Church of the USA
BCW	*Book of Common Worship*
Byz-BAS	Byzantine Anaphora of Basil
CHR	Anaphora of John Chrysostom
COCU	Consultation on Church Union
E-BAS	Egyptian Anaphora of Basil
EL	*Ephemerides Liturgicae*
ELCA	Evangelical Lutheran Church in America
ELCIC	Evangelical Lutheran Church in Canada
ELW	*Evangelical Lutheran Worship*
ET	English translation
ICEL	International Commission on English in the Liturgy
ILCW	Inter-Lutheran Commission on Worship
ITQ	*Irish Theological Quarterly*
JAS	Anaphora of James
JTS	*Journal of Theological Studies*
LBW	*Lutheran Book of Worship*
LQ	*Lutheran Quarterly*
MARK	Anaphora of Mark
NAAL	North American Academy of Liturgy
OCP	*Orientalia Christiana Periodica*

OrChr	*Oriens Christianus*
OrChrAn	Orientalia Christiana Analecta
PG	J.-P. Migne (ed.), *Patrologia Graeca* (Paris 1857–66)
PSB	*Princeton Seminary Bulletin*
RefLitM	*Reformed Liturgy and Music*
SC	*Sacrosanctum Concilium*
SL	*Studia Liturgica*
SLR	Supplemental Liturgical Resource
ST	*Studia Theologica*
SWR	Supplemental Worship Resources
TS	*Theological Studies*
UMBW	*United Methodist Book of Worship*
VC	*Vigiliae Christianae*
WCC	World Council of Churches

Introduction: seeking the Spirit in a eucharistic context

Speaking of the Spirit has been a consistent challenge in the Christian tradition. A long-standing lack of clarity about the precise role of the Spirit in Christian theology is not surprising, given that references to the status of the Spirit are rather vague in its foundational text. From his first appearance, brooding over the waters at the dawn of creation (Gen. 1.2), the Spirit occupies a rather nebulous place in the Christian Scriptures.[1] In the beginning, the Spirit of God creates a primordial 'space' between heaven and the unformed earth which represents the possibility of Creation's unfolding; later it recurs as wind or breath which variously inspires life (Gen. 2.7), gently marks God's passing before human persons (see, e.g., 1 Kings 19.12–13) or violently seizes the prophets (cf. 1 Sam. 10.6). The Spirit is also symbolized as fire, either highlighting the absolute *otherness* of God, as in the theophanies of the Hebrew Scriptures, or the nearness of God's self-communication to humans, as in the outpouring of the Spirit upon the gathered disciples at Pentecost in Acts 2.[2] The Church Fathers were well aware of the pervasive *presence* of the Holy Spirit in the Christian Scriptures, always pointing the community towards the remembrance and revelation of Christ, but at the same time they noted the elusive character – the *absence* and distance of this same Spirit – in the biblical record. For example, Gregory Nazianzus observed that, 'The Old Testament preached the Father clearly, and more obscurely the Son; the New preached the divinity of

---

1 Not all Christian theologians, ancient or modern, agree that Gen. 1.2 contains an implicit reference to the Holy Spirit.
2 These three images of the Spirit – vital space, wind/breath and fire – are discussed in detail by Louis-Marie Chauvet in his book, *Symbol and Sacrament: A Sacramental Reinterpretation of Christian Existence*, trans. Patrick Madigan and Madeleine Beaumont (Collegeville, MN: Liturgical Press 1995), pp. 511–14.

the Son and insinuated that of the Spirit. At present, the Spirit lives in us and manifests itself to us more clearly.'[3] It took several centuries to articulate the distinctiveness of the Spirit within a Trinitarian framework of God's immanent and economic relationality, and this may, at least in part, explain why attention paid to the Spirit in his own right has traditionally been more diffuse than that afforded either the Father or the Son.

Many centuries later, this present age is likewise one in which both the presence – and absence – of the Spirit in Christian theology, life and liturgy has become increasingly apparent. The twentieth century saw a remarkable convergence of 'movements' in the Western churches – among them the liturgical, patristic, ecumenical and biblical movements – which were interested in applying insights recovered from the early Church to enrich contemporary theological reflection and pastoral practice.[4] Another significant 'movement' has transpired in recent decades – the movement of explicit references to the Spirit's role in the eucharistic encounter into the eucharistic prayers of several Western churches, many of which had never before articulated a distinct pneumatological component at this point in their liturgies.[5] This new emphasis on the Spirit very frequently took the form of an epiclesis – a prayer petitioning God to send the Spirit upon the eucharistic bread and wine and/or the community gathered to celebrate the Eucharist, sometimes specifying that the presence and activity of the Spirit was invoked in this context so that the elements and/or the community might be transformed, and possibly requesting further benefits that would flow from this transformation as 'fruits' of eucharistic and ecclesial communion (e.g. unity, eternal life, etc.).

Between the pneumatological controversies of the fourth century and the ecumenical reawakening of the twentieth century, however, the Spirit's place in the threefold divine economy was sometimes overlooked – or at least suffered relative neglect in comparison with the emphasis put

---

3 Gregory of Nazianzus, *Discourse* 31.26 (Sources Chrétiennes 250); quoted in Chauvet, *Symbol and Sacrament*, p. 515.
4 James F. Puglisi, 'Introduction' in James F. Puglisi (ed.), *Liturgical Renewal as a Way to Christian Unity* (Collegeville, MN: Liturgical Press 2005), p. vii.
5 One notable exception to this general trend can be found in the Church of England. The first edition of the Book of Common Prayer (BCP) (1549) prepared by Thomas Cranmer asks that God 'with thy Holy Spirit and word vouchsafe to bless and sanctify these thy gifts and creatures of bread and wine'. This epicletic petition, located before the institution narrative, was not included in the 1552 BCP but later resurfaced in Scotland and the USA.

on Christ's role in salvation history. The Western tradition in particular has often been critiqued for its deficient pneumatology or 'Christomonism'.[6] Turning to scholastic theology in general and sacramental theology in particular, it does seem that the Trinitarian pattern of sacramental worship was at least partially subsumed into a christological framework, with the unintended consequence that scholastic and neoscholastic theology tended to overlook the vital role of the Spirit as a transformative agent both of Jesus' humanity and of human persons who participate in the sacraments.[7]

The past several decades have witnessed a shift in this trend. Since the mid-1960s, a veritable deluge of scholarly attention has been focused on the role of the Holy Spirit in the modern – and now increasingly postmodern and 'post-Christian' – world. Teresa Berger and Bryan D. Spinks, in their Introduction to *The Spirit in Worship – Worship in the Spirit*, highlight three ways in which a '(re-)turn to pneumatology' has become manifest in constructive theology during the past several decades.[8] First, if recent publications are any indication, there has been a resurgence of interest in the pneumatology of past eras, whether it be searching out the Spirit's role as depicted in the Scriptures and other early Christian writings,[9] retrieving older metaphors for the Spirit that have fallen into disuse[10] or investigating anew the pneumatology of particular

---

6 On this topic, see Yves Congar, 'Pneumatologie ou "Christomonisme" dans la tradition latine?', *Ecclesia a Spiritu Sancto Edocta: Mélanges Théologiques: Hommage à Mgr. Gérard Philips* (Gembloux: J. Duculot 1970), pp. 41–63. Congar does caution, however, against positing this critique without sufficient qualification. Neither biblical nor dogmatic approaches will permit an approach to pneumatology in which the Spirit operates independently of his relation to Christ and to the Father; there *is* a distinct mission of the Spirit, but the Spirit, of course, has no distinct hypostatic incarnation (p. 42).

7 R. Kevin Seasoltz, *God's Gift Giving: In Christ and through the Spirit* (New York and London: Continuum 2007), p. 137. Others have also noted, however, that tendencies in modern theology may have contributed in their own right to the relative lack of attention given to pneumatology in the Christian West in the past several centuries. Charles C. Hefling, for example, has remarked that the concept of divine self-gift, especially since Hegel, has often been considered solely from the standpoint of Christology. See Charles C. Hefling, '*Gratia*: Grace and Gratitude: Fifty Unmodern Theses as Prolegomena to Pneumatology', *AThR* 83.3 (2001), p. 476.

8 See Teresa Berger with Bryan D. Spinks, 'Introduction' in Teresa Berger and Bryan D. Spinks (eds), *The Spirit in Worship – Worship in the Spirit* (Collegeville, MN: Liturgical Press 2009), pp. xiii–xv; the phrase '(re-)turn to pneumatology' is from p. xiii.

9 See, e.g., the essays in Graham N. Stanton, Bruce W. Longenecker and Stephen Barton (eds), *The Holy Spirit and Christian Origins: Essays in Honor of James D. G. Dunn* (Grand Rapids, MI: Eerdmans 2004).

10 See, e.g., Elizabeth A. Dreyer, *Holy Power, Holy Presence: Rediscovering Medieval Metaphors for the Holy Spirit* (New York: Paulist Press 2007).

theologians.[11] Second, studies of the Spirit from a Pentecostal and charismatic perspective have entered the mainstream of contemporary theological discussion and scholarship, expanding the conversation and creatively engaging traditional doctrines.[12] Finally, interest in the Spirit has intersected with feminist, liberationist, ecological, global and interfaith concerns, among others, to produce a multitude of new constructive theological proposals in which the Spirit plays a prominent part.[13]

Recent modern and postmodern formulations of sacramental theology have also devoted more attention to the place of the Spirit in general and to the Spirit's shaping of the sacramental encounter in particular.[14] Unfortunately, extensive attention to the *liturgical* role of the Spirit has not figured prominently in most general treatments of theology or pneumatology published in recent years.[15] Therefore, 'in this theological turn to pneumatology, the study of worship as a site of the Spirit's presence and work remains, for the most part, marginal'.[16] Nonetheless,

---

11 For an overview of such investigations of individual theologians, see F. LeRon Shults and Andrea Hollingsworth, *The Holy Spirit*, Guides to Theology (Grand Rapids, MI: Eerdmans, 2008), Part I, pp. 15–95.

12 For a representative sample of such research, see *Pneuma*, the journal of the Society for Pentecostal Studies, which was launched in 1979.

13 For examples of such studies, see Berger and Spinks, 'Introduction', pp. xiv–xv and the annotated Bibliography in Shults and Hollingsworth, *Holy Spirit*, pp. 99–150.

14 From a Roman Catholic perspective, works which incorporate pneumatology in a significant way include those of Edward J. Kilmartin, particularly *Christian Liturgy: Theology and Practice, Vol. 1: Systematic Theology and Liturgy* (Kansas City, MO: Sheed & Ward 1988); David N. Power, esp. *Sacrament: The Language of God's Giving* (New York: Crossroad 1999); and Chauvet, *Symbol and Sacrament*.

15 As a notable exception, Geoffrey Wainwright does include a fairly extensive discussion of the Spirit, including some attention to the Spirit's role in liturgy, in his work of systematic theology based on the premise *lex orandi, lex credendi*. See Geoffrey Wainwright, *Doxology: The Praise of God in Worship, Doctrine, and Life: A Systematic Theology* (London and New York: Epworth/Oxford University Press 1980), esp. pp. 87–117. Nonetheless, a distinct section on the Holy Spirit is still sometimes lacking in theological works of a general scope. As an example, Paul Bradshaw cites the two-volume collection *Systematic Theology: Roman Catholic Perspectives*, ed. Francis Schüssler Fiorenza and John P. Galvin (Minneapolis: Fortress Press 1991). See Paul F. Bradshaw, 'The Rediscovery of the Holy Spirit in Modern Eucharistic Theology and Practice' in Berger and Spinks (eds), *Spirit in Worship*, p. 80.

16 Berger and Spinks, 'Introduction', p. xv. The collection of essays that Berger and Spinks edited, *The Spirit in Worship – Worship in the Spirit*, represents the most extended consideration of this neglected topic to date. Previous discussions of worship which do give extended treatment to the role of the Spirit include Susan K. Wood, 'Participatory Knowledge of God in the Liturgy' in James Joseph Buckley and David S. Yeago (eds), *Knowing the Triune God: The Work of the Spirit in the Practices of the Church* (Grand

the place of the Spirit in the liturgy in general and certain sacraments in particular has not been entirely absent from recent ecumenical discussions and theological reflection.[17] The fruits of this exchange provide important context for understanding the epiclesis question.

THE HOLY SPIRIT IN CHRISTIAN WORSHIP AND LITURGY

The place of the Spirit in Christian worship and liturgy is intimately connected to ecclesiology, as the worship of Christian communities in the Spirit is the worship of the Church as the body of Christ.[18] Therefore, a liturgical pneumatology is also connected to Christology and ultimately to theology, insofar as it reflects the historical unfolding of the Trinitarian economy in the life of God's people. The inner dynamics of the liturgy reflect those of salvation history; God the Father inaugurates the offer of divine love to Creation, and the redemptive response of Christ makes union with God in the fellowship of the Holy Spirit possible. In this time between Pentecost and the parousia, the Spirit is God's gift to the Church (cf. Rom. 5.5), bringing believers into relationship with God and one another and making it possible for them to love the Father through the Son.

A Trinitarian pattern of worship – directed *to* the Father *through* the Son *in* the Holy Spirit – can be found in many Christian prayers.[19]

Rapids, MI: Eerdmans 2001), pp. 95–118 and Lorelei F. Fuchs and Lawrence C. Brennan, 'The Spirit in the Worship and Liturgy of the Church' in William R. Barr and Rena M. Yocum (eds), *The Church in the Movement of the Spirit* (Grand Rapids, MI: Eerdmans 1994), pp. 51–73. Wood considers the experiential, 'participatory knowledge' of God that comes through being in relationship with the triune God in a liturgical context. Fuchs and Brennan focus more specifically on the Spirit in the Western liturgical tradition.

17 For examples of ways in which ecumenical dialogues have explored the work of Christ and of the Spirit in relation to the Eucharist in particular, see Edward J. Kilmartin, 'The Active Role of Christ and the Holy Spirit in the Sanctification of the Eucharistic Elements', *TS* 45.2 (1984), pp. 226–33. Perhaps the best fruit so far of such discussion has been the agreed ecumenical statement, *Baptism, Eucharist and Ministry* (1982), produced by the World Council of Churches (WCC). See World Council of Churches, *Baptism, Eucharist and Ministry* (Geneva: WCC, 1982). The text is also available online: <http://www.oikoumene.org/en/resources/documents/wcc-commissions/faith-and-order-commission/i-unity-the-church-and-its-mission/baptism-eucharist-and-ministry-faith-and-order-paper-no-111-the-lima-text.html>.

18 On the distinctions that can be made between worship and liturgy, see James F. White, *Introduction to Christian Worship* (Nashville: Abingdon Press 2000, 3rd edn, revised and expanded), pp. 22–30. Unless otherwise specified, these terms will be used interchangeably in this work.

19 For the biblical basis of this Trinitarian pattern of Christian worship, see Fuchs and Brennan, 'Spirit in the Worship and Liturgy', pp. 65–73.

Collects typically commence with praise of the Father, continue with a request made through the Son and conclude with a reference to the Holy Spirit. Many eucharistic prayers praise and thank the Father, remember the redemption won through the Son and invoke the Holy Spirit upon the present activity of the gathered church.[20] Doxologies offer a condensed summary of God's saving activity on humanity's behalf as well as of the movement of Christian worship – to the Father through the Son and in the Holy Spirit. J. D. Crichton contends that this Trinitarian orientation of Christian worship 'serves to remind us that the aim of the whole liturgy is entrance into communion with God, a communion in the divine life and love that constitutes the Trinity'.[21]

Although many liturgical rites contain an explicit epiclesis, the presence of the Spirit in the liturgy should not be confined to such overtly pneumatic moments, as if the Spirit injects himself into the liturgical action only after a specific invitation for his presence has been extended. Historically, prayer for the coming of the Spirit has taken diverse forms in the liturgical rites of Eastern and Western churches. Geoffrey Wainwright has identified three distinct 'pneumatological patterns' in post-biblical Christian worship.[22] The first pattern entails 'the broad understanding whereby the affinity between the divine Spirit and the human spirit allowed communication between God and human beings and, consequently, the shaping of human character and conduct according to the divine model and purpose'.[23] Examples of this pattern can be found in confirmation and ordination prayers, in which the Holy Spirit is called upon to strengthen and affirm the gifts of the Spirit in the recipients of these rites for the benefit of Christian life and/or ministry.

According to the second pattern, the Holy Spirit is construed as the enabler, source or medium of worship.[24] The Spirit is seen as the basis of the Church's unity, and it is *in the Spirit* that proper worship of God occurs. One could even contend that, in the absence of the Spirit,

---

20 J. D. Crichton, 'A Theology of Worship' in Cheslyn Jones, Geoffrey Wainwright, Edward Yarnold and Paul Bradshaw (eds), *The Study of Liturgy* (London and New York: SPCK/Oxford University Press 1992, revised edn), p. 19.
21 See Crichton, 'A Theology of Worship', p. 20.
22 The first two of these patterns are already found, at least in nascent form, in the New Testament; only the third (worship explicitly directed towards the Holy Spirit as a distinct member of the Trinity) seems to have originated at a later period. See Wainwright, *Doxology*, pp. 88–93.
23 Wainwright, *Doxology*, p. 93.
24 See Wainwright, *Doxology*, pp. 94–5.

worship of God could not occur at all (cf. Rom. 8.26).[25] The Spirit is not perceived, in this pattern, as a recipient of worship in his own right. Prayer directed to the Father through the Son and in the Spirit would fit into this category and, by extension, most eucharistic epicleses would as well (since, in the majority of extant texts, the eucharistic epiclesis is framed as a request for the *Father* to send the Spirit rather than a direct appeal to the Spirit).

The third pattern consists of prayer or worship which *is* directed to the Spirit, either alongside the other members of the Trinity or in isolation. Doxologies and baptismal confessions of faith are the most common liturgical instantiations of the former scenario. Direct invocations to the Spirit can be found in some early Christian texts, such as the *Acts of Thomas*. However, among orthodox (and proto-orthodox) groups, such prayers are found only rarely and have usually been viewed as fairly late developments.[26] Hymnody also provides a number of examples of prayer and worship addressed directly to the Spirit, ranging from *Veni Creator Spiritus* (attributed to Rabanus Maurus (776–856)) to a flock of Spirit-hymns from the nineteenth century to contemporary compositions.[27] Isolated examples can be found elsewhere, such as in this prayer from Matins in the Byzantine Orthodox liturgy: 'O Heavenly King, Comforter, Spirit of Truth, who art everywhere and fillest all things, the treasury of blessings, and giver of life, come and abide in us. Cleanse us of all impurity and of thy goodness save our souls.'[28]

---

25 Drawing inspiration from Karl Barth's conception of the relationship between the Holy Spirit and worship, Matthew Myer Boulton adopts such a 'negative' view of the Spirit's intervention: 'In other words, worshiping Christians properly call on the Holy Spirit not so that she may come and supplement or enhance their already excellent, beautiful, and just proceedings, but rather so that she may creatively oppose and remake their profoundly destitute, malformed proceedings into something excellent, beautiful, and just.' See Matthew Myer Boulton, 'The Adversary: Agony, Irony, and the Liturgical Role of the Holy Spirit' in Berger and Spinks (eds), *Spirit in Worship*, pp. 59–77 (here at pp. 59–60).

26 Gabriele Winkler's recent studies of the epicletic invocations in these texts suggest that the apocryphal *Acts* should be taken more seriously by liturgical scholars as providing possible evidence for mainstream (as opposed to merely marginal) liturgical practice in second- and third-century Syria. Her research is discussed further in the next chapter.

27 For examples of hymns addressed to the Spirit, see Wainwright, *Doxology*, pp. 101–2; for more recent examples, see Berger and Spinks (eds), *Spirit in Worship*, p. xix and James Steven, 'The Spirit in Contemporary Charismatic Worship' in Berger and Spinks (eds), *Spirit in Worship*, pp. 245–59.

28 From *A Manual of Eastern Orthodox Prayer* (Crestwood, NY: St Vladimir's Seminary Press 1983), p. 2; quoted in Simon Chan, 'The Liturgy as the Work of the Spirit' in Berger and Spinks (eds), *Spirit in Worship*, p. 54.

The eucharistic prayer recapitulates the dynamics of the economic Trinity, especially the prayer in its Antiochene or West Syrian form that, for practical or theological reasons (or perhaps a combination thereof), assumed a Trinitarian structure that focuses attention on the salvific action of the first, second and third persons of the Trinity in turn. The praise and thanksgiving given to God in the opening sections of the eucharistic prayer leads to a remembrance of the saving acts of Christ, now risen and glorified, and this memorial culminates in – and even demands – the invocation of the Spirit, implicitly or explicitly. In this manner the Eucharist *makes* the Church and its members what they are as Spirit-filled entities and enables their communion with the Father and the Son.[29] From this perspective, the epiclesis can be seen as 'the fulfillment of the Eucharistic action, just as Pentecost is the fulfillment of a divine "economy" of salvation'.[30]

Traditionally, the presence of the Spirit in the eucharistic context has been viewed as transformative, impacting not only the bread and wine but also the celebrating community and even extending to the entire universe, as exemplified in this token but real transformation of earthly elements which hints of greater transformation of all things to come.[31] Eucharistic sharing is a communion in the body and blood of Christ (1 Cor. 10.16–17), and this too is dependent upon the participation of the Spirit, who vivifies the church (1 Cor. 12.1–31) and bestows gifts for the benefit of all (1 Cor. 12.7). The gift of the Spirit given through baptism and Eucharist (cf. 1 Cor. 10.16–17; 12.12–13) realizes Christ's priestly prayer for unity (John 17.21). For sharing in the life of the Spirit *is* to share in the communion of divine life experienced by the Father and the Son.[32] This is also the hope of the eucharistic liturgy, which manifests the

---

29 See Chan, 'Liturgy', p. 53 and Paul McPartlan, *The Eucharist Makes the Church: Henri De Lubac and John Zizioulas in Dialogue* (Edinburgh: T. & T. Clark 1993), esp. ch. 4.
30 John Meyendorff, *Byzantine Theology: Historical Trends and Doctrinal Themes* (New York: Fordham University Press 1979, 2nd edn), p. 207; quoted in Chan, 'Liturgy', p. 53.
31 See Geoffrey Wainwright, *Eucharist and Eschatology* (Peterborough: Epworth 2003, 3rd edn), pp. 130–7. This concept has been articulated more explicitly in some recent eucharistic prayers. For example, the concluding sentence of the epiclesis of Eucharistic Prayer 4 of the Church of Canada (1985) is: 'Pour your Spirit upon the whole earth and make it your new creation. Gather your Church together from the ends of the earth.' Bridget Nichols and Alistair MacGregor identify this as a 'terrestrial' epiclesis with allusions to the *Didache* and Joel 2.28. See Bridget Nichols and Alistair MacGregor, *The Eucharistic Epiclesis*, Ushaw Library Publications 4 (Durham: Ushaw College Library 2001), p. 31 (for prayer text and commentary) and p. xiv (for their definition of a terrestrial epiclesis).
32 Fuchs and Brennan, 'Spirit in the Worship and Liturgy', pp. 72–3.

dynamic relationships operative in the Trinitarian life, recalls the paschal mystery and orients participants towards the eschatological banquet.[33]

REVISITING THE EPICLESIS QUESTION

Although the Trinitarian undercurrent in Christian worship and eucharistic praying is widely accepted, determining how exactly (if at all) to articulate the Spirit's role in the eucharistic action has proved considerably more contentious, especially in Western Christian traditions. The title and opening paragraphs of John H. McKenna's article 'Eucharistic Epiclesis: Myopia or Microcosm?' draw attention to the controversy and promise surrounding the so-called 'epiclesis question' from the vantage point of the year 1975.[34] In 1968, J.-M. R. Tillard stated that the epiclesis – the petition for the presence and activity of the Holy Spirit upon the eucharistic elements of bread and wine and/or the assembled community – was a matter of only secondary importance which, when raised, tended to stifle theological reflection and make people myopic in their views of the Holy Spirit and the Eucharist.[35] Around the same time, however, the ecumenist Lukas Vischer declared that the epiclesis question was crucial for the progress of ecumenical dialogue on the Eucharist, while the Orthodox theologian Paul Evdokimov judged the epiclesis more important than the *Filioque* as a point of dialogue between Eastern and Western churches.[36]

Much discussion ensued in the intervening years in Western churches. As many systematic theologians adopted a more consciously Trinitarian approach to their projects, renewed attention was paid to the place of the Spirit and his role in Christian life, and, to some extent, in Christian worship. Ecumenical dialogues and liturgical revision efforts both within and among these churches contributed, in some cases, to eucharistic prayers which included explicit pneumatic epicleses. Many of these 'new'

---

33 Wood, 'Participatory Knowledge', p. 113.
34 See John H. McKenna, 'Eucharistic Epiclesis: Myopia or Microcosm?' *TS* 36.2 (1975), pp. 265–6. This comparison also begins the Introduction to his dissertation, published that same year; cf. John H. McKenna, *Eucharist and Holy Spirit: The Eucharistic Epiclesis in Twentieth-Century Theology (1900–1966)* (Great Wakering: Mayhew-McCrimmon (for the Alcuin Club) 1975), p. 11 and the second edition recently published under a different title: John H. McKenna, *The Eucharistic Epiclesis: A Detailed History from the Patristic to the Modern Era* (Chicago: Hillenbrand 2009, 2nd edn), p. xv.
35 J.-M. R. Tillard, 'L'Eucharistie et le Saint-Esprit', *Nouvelle Revue Théologique* 90 (1968), pp. 364, 379, 387.
36 Lukas Vischer, 'The Epiclesis: Sign of Unity and Renewal', *SL* 6.1 (1969), pp. 30–9; Paul Evdokimov, 'Eucharistie – mystère de l'Église', *La Pensée Orthodoxe* 2 (1968), p. 62, n. 33.

expressions of the Spirit's role in the eucharistic encounter were grounded in the search for traces of the Spirit's presence in past tradition – either the ancient tradition of the Church that had formed the common heritage of Eastern and Western Christians, or among the theological principles and writings set forth by the founders of new denominations in the sixteenth century and beyond.

In recent times, the pervasive presence of the Spirit in *all* Christian liturgical celebrations has been increasingly emphasized. Theological treatments of the Holy Spirit and Eucharist observe that, just as Christ is present and active in the eucharistic celebration in multiple ways, so too is the Spirit.[37] It is impossible to consider the risen Christ who gathers the church together as his body without remembering the Holy Spirit, for the community which assembles in Christ's name is bonded together in the fellowship of the Spirit. It is the Spirit who makes God's word, proclaimed in that assembly, a living and active one in the lives of the faithful. The presider praying for and with the community is inspired, as are all ministers, with the gifts of the Holy Spirit. The body and blood of Christ received by the faithful that they might be one was given life and gives life through the Holy Spirit.[38] To limit the role of the Holy Spirit in the Eucharist to a particular element of the anaphora or to consider the role of the epiclesis only in terms of its 'consecratory' function vis-à-vis the role of the words of Christ in the institution narrative would indeed be, as Tillard proposed, myopic. Sadly, insofar as many discussions of the epiclesis have been narrowly preoccupied by the 'problem' of its consecratory role (or lack thereof), Tillard's assessment of the epiclesis has proved prescient.

However, as John McKenna concludes, when the epiclesis is considered in a broader context, it becomes a microcosm with a multifaceted nature that holds the potential to illumine fundamental issues of Christology, pneumatology, ecclesiology and sacramental theology. McKenna underscores the theological resonance of the eucharistic epiclesis when he notes that

> any thorough treatment of the epiclesis forces us to confront theological issues such as the role of faith, of the praying assembly,

---

37 For example, see the Introduction to Patrick McGoldrick, 'The Holy Spirit and the Eucharist', *ITQ* 50 (1983), pp. 48–9.

38 The Second Vatican Council spoke of the flesh of Christ as 'given life and giving life by the Holy Spirit'. Decree on the Ministry and Life of Priests, *Presbyterorum Ordinis*, n. 5; cited in McGoldrick, 'Holy Spirit and Eucharist', p. 48.

of the ordained and universal priesthood, and of the Holy Spirit in the realization of the Eucharist, as well as the question of the Eucharistic 'real presence.'[39]

When considered in this way, Vischer and Evdokimov were right to highlight the epiclesis as an important and ecumenically significant lens which can bring a number of major theological issues into clearer focus.

Nevertheless, if recent comments on the status of the epiclesis in contemporary eucharistic praying are any indication, the issue is by no means settled. The argument over the importance of articulating the Spirit's activity in contemporary eucharistic prayers has given rise to statements just as polarized as those mentioned above. In the conclusion of a recent work on the Anglican eucharistic epiclesis, for example, David Kennedy affirms the vital importance of the epiclesis in eucharistic prayers

> because of its significance theologically and devotionally in articulat-ing a eucharistic spirituality for the twenty-first century, a spirituality which witnesses to the eternal and transforming presence of God in his world, in which humanity and all creation is being restored.[40]

From Kennedy's perspective, then, a eucharistic epiclesis is an explicit recognition of an implicit truth – that the Spirit mediates Christ's grace and God's love to human persons, enabling them to worship God as their origin and destiny and to minister with hope to the needs of a wounded world here and now.

On the other hand, the past 40 years have seen some resistance to embracing a greater emphasis on the epiclesis. It has been noted that attestation of the eucharistic epiclesis occurs early, but not so early as to be apostolic. In addition, some theologians have raised concerns that current interest in the epiclesis may simply reflect a passing Western infatuation with Eastern theology. As such, Donald Macleod is much more hesitant to support the incorporation of an epiclesis into the eucharistic prayers of his own Scottish Reformed tradition. The virtues of Eastern theological insights notwithstanding, he is wary of giving liturgical expression to what are seemingly (as yet) only 'the tentative results of an uncompleted ideological shift'. Furthermore, like Tillard,

---

39 McKenna, 'Eucharistic Epiclesis: Myopia or Microcosm?', p. 284.
40 David J. Kennedy, *Eucharistic Sacramentality in an Ecumenical Context: The Anglican Epiclesis* (Aldershot and Burlington, VT: Ashgate 2008), p. 245.

Macleod expresses concern that focusing on the epiclesis theologically or liturgically can only serve as an invitation to become mired in the question of *how* Christ is present in the Eucharist, at the expense of the more essential belief that Christ *is* present. 'The proposed answers [to the former question] are a liturgical distraction (as well as a temptation to intellectual apoplexy).'[41]

Is the eucharistic epiclesis, then, a warning symptom of some sort of theological pathology – or a microcosm that draws one into a grace-filled world where Trinitarian dynamics are at play? This study seeks to explore the theological and textual ground underlying such tensions, primarily through analysis of a selection of epicletic texts in contemporary Western eucharistic prayers and the theological principles that shaped them – principles derived in part from perceptions of the role played by the Spirit inherited from traditions ancient and modern. To that end, the purpose of this study is twofold: (1) to investigate how liturgical scholarship on the Spirit's role in early liturgical prayers and texts conducted during the twentieth century contributed to the language and pneumatology of contemporary eucharistic prayers in the Western Christian tradition, and (2) to explore how more recent studies of these ancient sources may suggest ways to articulate and incorporate a more expansive understanding of the connections between the Holy Spirit and the Eucharist into the euchological repertoire of various ecclesial traditions in the future. Just as scholarship on early liturgical texts led to the inclusion and/or expansion of the pneumatic dimension of contemporary eucharistic praying, a reassessment of the Spirit's place in early eucharistic celebrations may contribute to a still broader appreciation of the Spirit's activity and presence in the Eucharist, which in turn could help address present points of theological tension.

The first part of this book, focusing on ancient epicleses, will provide an overview of current scholarship on the epiclesis (much of which was not available to those engaged in liturgical reform efforts in various denominations during the second half of the twentieth century) and a sense of development in content and theology from the first allusions to the Holy Spirit's role in early eucharistic praying to the emergence of the fully fledged eucharistic epiclesis by the second half of the fourth century. The second part will examine the historical and theological rationale undergirding the incorporation of explicit pneumatic eucharistic

---

41 Quotes from Donald Macleod, 'Calvin into Hippolytus?' in Bryan D. Spinks and Iain R. Torrance (eds), *To Glorify God: Essays on Modern Reformed Liturgy* (Grand Rapids, MI: Eerdmans 1999), pp. 266 and 267, respectively.

epicleses into modern Western rites and consider how, in many cases, the *lex credendi* of particular traditions concerning the role of the Holy Spirit in eucharistic praying has shaped the *lex orandi* of the epicletic formulations in their worship books. Before commencing, however, a note about terminology is in order.

TERMINOLOGY, THEOLOGY AND THE EUCHARISTIC EPICLESIS

The Greek term *epiklesis* ('invocation', from ἐπικαλεω – to call upon or invoke) came to describe a prayer calling the Holy Spirit on an object (e.g. baptismal water, bread and wine) to sanctify that object and make it fruitful so that it might achieve its intended purpose, affording those Christians who would interact with this blessed object a sacramental encounter with God. In the narrower sense, 'epiclesis' can refer to the section(s) of the anaphora in which the presider asks God the Father to *send* the Holy Spirit or Logos – or, without addressing the Father as an intermediary, invites one or both of these persons to *come*. Typically there is some further expectation that the Spirit and/or Logos will imbue the eucharistic offering so that it might realize the purpose for which Christians believe it was instituted.[42] While the epicleses in contemporary eucharistic prayers are nearly always addressed to God (the Father), this is not invariably the case in early prayers. Thus one way epicleses can be categorized is by grouping them according to the divine person(s) addressed (e.g. the Spirit, the Logos, Christ, God the Father, or some combination thereof, such as the whole Trinity).

A second way of classifying epicleses is according to the orientation of the content of the requests they make. Some early epicleses consist exclusively of a petition for divine presence with no additional qualifications. A further distinction can be made (at a later stage of theological precision) between a 'communion' epiclesis and a 'consecratory' epiclesis. The former type requests that the communicants might receive salvific benefits as a result of their consumption of the 'eucharistized' bread and wine over which the Spirit's presence has been invoked. The latter type explicitly requests the sanctification of the eucharistic gifts through the Holy Spirit, i.e. that the bread and wine might become Christ's body and blood. Often – but not always – consecratory and communion dimensions occur together in the same prayer. As Robert Taft noted, the fully fledged composite form of the

---

42 Robert F. Taft, 'From Logos to Spirit: On the Early History of the Epiclesis' in Andreas Heinz and Heinrich Rennings (eds), *Gratias Agamus: Studien zum eucharistischen Hochgebet: Für Balthasar Fischer* (Freiburg: Herder 1992), p. 489.

epiclesis typically consists of (1) a petition for the Holy Spirit to be sent upon the gifts and the community, and (2) a request for the consecration of the gifts, so that (3) they might effectively contribute towards the salvation of those who receive them in communion.[43]

However, distinctions between 'communion' and 'consecratory' forms of the epiclesis should not be drawn too sharply, especially in terms of their ultimate theological importance. While some early epicletic forms seem to include only elements (1) and (3) above, Taft notes that *any* prayer that requests God's power 'to come upon something in order that it be unto salvation for those who partake of it or participate in it as God intended, necessarily implies that God *do* something by his coming to make that object salvific'.[44] Thus the terms 'communion' and 'consecration', when used in connection with the epiclesis, ultimately have more to say about the *structure* of liturgical texts than the intent or theological presuppositions of those who might have prayed them.[45] Furthermore, from what can be discerned of the early theology of eucharistic 'consecration', the change in the elements was viewed along the lines of 'transfiguration' or 'manifestation' of Christ's body and blood rather than in the sense of a conversion that entailed an ontological change in the elements.

Recently, Gabriele Winkler has questioned the aptness of semantic distinctions between consecratory–communion and Logos–Spirit forms of the epiclesis based on her studies of early Syrian baptismal and eucharistic texts such as the apocryphal *Acts of Thomas*. She posits that the most primitive form of the epiclesis was a simple request for the Lord's coming (e.g. *'Maranatha'*) which eventually became a petition for the

---

43 Taft, 'From Logos to Spirit', p. 490.
44 Taft, 'From Logos to Spirit', p. 493, emphasis added.
45 See Taft, 'From Logos to Spirit', p. 493. Further nuances could be raised about classifying epicleses according to their structure, both in terms of the consecration–communion continuum and in terms of the location of the epiclesis relative to other elements in a eucharistic prayer. In their survey of ancient and modern eucharistic epicleses, Bridget Nichols and Alistair MacGregor identify 13 different kinds of epicleses. These include an open epiclesis, whose wording 'leaves a certain leeway in interpretation concerning the operation of the Holy Spirit on the bread and wine'; a receptionist epiclesis 'which prays for the transformative consequences and benefits of receiving communion; but which avoids any direct invocation of the Holy Spirit to sanctify the eucharistic elements'; a congregational epiclesis, which prays for 'the descent of the Holy Spirit upon the members of the congregation about to receive holy communion'; and a sacramental epiclesis, which asks 'for the operation of the Holy Spirit to descend on the whole sacramental action of the Eucharist'. See Nichols and MacGregor, *Eucharistic Epiclesis*, pp. xiii–xiv.

coming of the Messiah and the Spirit – without explicit consecratory or communion dimensions. Furthermore, early Syrian texts typically do not make clear distinctions between the Messiah and the 'Spirit of holiness', thus complicating the scholarly tendency to identify 'Logos epicleses' and 'Spirit epicleses' based on the identity of the addressee of the invocation. With this caveat in mind, the terminology of consecration–communion and Logos–Spirit will be maintained here insofar as it is useful.

ECUMENICAL CONSENSUS IN EPICLETIC PRAYING: THE STATE OF THE QUESTION

When different denominations speak of the Spirit in their eucharistic prayers today, the experience is more akin to the unified experience of language that amazed those present at Pentecost (cf. Acts 2) than the polyglot confusion of languages at Babel (Gen. 11). In some cases the words printed in official worship books and invoked by the celebrant during the liturgy's great prayer are identical or nearly identical across ecclesial boundaries – because churches drew common inspiration from ancient texts such as the *Apostolic Tradition* or the Egyptian version of the anaphora attributed to St Basil. In most other pneumatic utterances the resonance remains strong enough that members of different denominations can easily understand one another.

Some uncertainty regarding the balance of Christology, pneumatology and Trinitarian theology emerges, however, upon a closer consideration of the epiclesis in contemporary eucharistic prayers. Major issues include location of the epiclesis within the eucharistic prayer as a whole (particularly in relation to the institution narrative) and the language used to articulate how the community requests the Holy Spirit to act on the people, the gifts, or both. Whereas most early prayers situated the epiclesis *after* the institution narrative, some Western traditions now place the epiclesis – or at least one part of it – *before* the institution narrative, while other traditions locate the epiclesis differently in different prayers. All of the Roman prayers composed since Vatican II, for example, feature a 'split epiclesis'[46] with a prayer for the Spirit's

---

46 This arrangement is also sometimes referred to as a 'double epiclesis', emphasizing the fact that prayers of this type feature two distinct petitions for the Spirit's presence and activity in the eucharistic context. The term 'split epiclesis', on the other hand, draws attention to the perception that the consecratory and communion aspects of the epiclesis are really two dimensions of a single reality, whether the invocations for consecration and communion are conjoined or separated in the prayer. Prime examples of 'split epicleses' include the prayers of the Roman Catholic Church (in addition to the Roman Canon) and Eucharistic Prayers A and B of the Church of England's *Common Worship*.

action on the gifts preceding the institution narrative and a prayer for the Spirit's action upon the communicants after the anamnesis. Aside from lacking a clear precedent in ancient texts (unless the Roman Canon is taken as evidence for this form[47]), at least two theological issues arise from this arrangement. The 'consecration' and 'communion' dimensions of the epiclesis are always separated, and this arrangement consistently makes the institution narrative appear as *the* (or at least the *primary*) moment of consecration.

All of the prayers from *Lutheran Book of Worship* (*LBW*) (1978) and *Evangelical Lutheran Worship* (*ELW*) (2006) place the epiclesis in the traditional West Syrian location after the institution narrative and anamnesis, and the dominant focus in most of these prayers is on the 'communion' dimension of the epiclesis. Even when the gifts are mentioned in the epiclesis, the Holy Spirit is never implicated explicitly as an agent of eucharistic consecration. The eucharistic prayers of the Episcopal Church in the USA's *Book of Common Prayer* (*BCP*) (1979), with one exception (i.e. Eucharistic Prayer C), also locate the epiclesis after the institution narrative; however, these prayers typically invoke the Spirit's specific action upon *both* the eucharistic gifts and the people. The Methodist Great Thanksgivings in *The United Methodist Book of Worship* (*UMBW*) (1992) similarly favour locating the epiclesis after the institution narrative and do this consistently in almost all of the prayers. The basic epiclesis text is quite comprehensive in terms of requesting the Spirit's action on the people and the gifts in the eucharistic *action* broadly conceived – including its ethical dimension to live as the body of Christ in the world and its ultimate eschatological orientation. The Presbyterian prayers locate the epiclesis after the institution narrative in all instances in which the institution narrative is part of the prayer. As with the Methodist prayers, most of the Presbyterian prayers are quite concerned about the Spirit's impact on the gathered people as well as the gifts and take a broad view of the eucharistic action.

Of the eight eucharistic prayers in the Church of England's *Common Worship* (2000), all possible patterns of the epiclesis are represented. Two of the prayers (A and B) have a 'split' epiclesis with a consecratory petition before the institution narrative and a 'communion' petition afterwards. Two of the prayers (C and E) mention the Holy Spirit before the institution narrative but not afterwards (outside the concluding

---

47 The Roman Canon does not have an explicit pneumatic epiclesis. On the question of whether the Roman Canon should be viewed as having a proper epiclesis at all, see Chapter 3.

doxology). The rest of the prayers (D, F, G and H) situate both the consecratory and the communion dimensions of the epiclesis after the institution narrative.

In terms of the content and language of the epiclesis, John McKenna identified four components that regularly appear in ancient epicleses. First, there is typically a petition for some sort of change or transformation of the gifts of bread and wine so that the community might receive them as Christ's body and blood. Second, eschatological references are often present that place a particular eucharistic celebration in the broader framework of God's saving activity. Third, some additional fruits of communion are frequently requested. Finally, there is usually some reference to sharing in, partaking of, or otherwise consuming the eucharistic gifts.[48] While these components are often found in contemporary Western epicleses, the review of these texts in subsequent chapters demonstrates that this is not always the case in modern prayers; common absences include eschatological references and mention of change in the bread and wine in connection with the Holy Spirit's action on the gifts.

Some contemporary epicleses address elements not prevalent in ancient ones, such as the partial realization of God's kingdom on earth here and now; the idea that fruitful communion should overflow into Christian mission, such that those who have received Christ's body and blood manifest Christ's ecclesial body in the world; and a unity that entails communion not just with fellow Christians (within and across ecclesial boundaries) but with all people as members of God's family. For example, Presbyterian Great Thanksgiving J, intended as a guide for extemporaneous prayer, includes a comprehensive résumé of reasons for invoking the Spirit at the eucharistic prayer, encompassing Christ's presence, participation in Christ's body and blood, unity (with Christ and the faithful across time and space), nourishment, maturation in Christ, ecclesial fidelity, strength for ministry, and eschatological anticipation of the kingdom of God.[49]

While one would not expect any single prayer, ancient or modern, to touch upon all of these elements thoroughly, the complete *absence* of

---

48 John H. McKenna, 'Eucharistic Prayer: Epiclesis' in Heinz and Rennings (eds), *Gratias Agamus*, p. 288. For a presentation of these elements in early eucharistic texts, see 'Table 1.1: The Epiclesis in Ancient Anaphoras' in McKenna, *Eucharistic Epiclesis*, pp. 40–1.
49 Presbyterian Church (USA) and Cumberland Presbyterian Church, *Book of Common Worship* (Louisville, KY: Westminster John Knox Press 1993), p. 156. This text is discussed further in Chapter 7.

certain of these dimensions from *all* of a tradition's prayers could be theologically telling. This brief survey should be sufficient to indicate what the subsequent analysis will demonstrate more thoroughly, i.e. that the role of the epiclesis in a specifically eucharistic context is not understood in the same way in every tradition.

OVERVIEW OF THE STUDY

The modern eucharistic prayers analysed here are drawn from a selection of official prayer texts in current use in the Roman Catholic, Lutheran, Anglican, Episcopal, Methodist and Presbyterian churches. This set of texts will include:

• Eucharistic Prayers I–IV, Eucharistic Prayers for Masses with Children I–III, Eucharistic Prayers for Masses of Reconciliation I–II, and the Eucharistic Prayer for Various Needs and Occasions from the 1970 *Roman Missal*;
• Eucharistic Prayers I–IV from the *Lutheran Book of Worship* (1978) and Great Thanksgivings I–XI from *Evangelical Lutheran Worship* (2006);
• Eucharistic Prayers I and II and A–D from the Episcopal Church in the USA's *Book of Common Prayer* (1979);
• the Great Thanksgivings from the *United Methodist Book of Worship* (1992);
• Great Thanksgivings A–J from the Presbyterian Church (USA)'s *Book of Common Worship* (*BCW*) (1993);
• Eucharistic Prayers A–H from the Church of England's *Common Worship* (2000).

Limiting the focus of detailed analysis to a subset of contemporary prayers developed and/or used by churches in the English-speaking world allowed sufficient variety of epicletic structure and content for such a study to be valuable but also a small enough sample size that the scope of the study was still manageable.

This work employs the methodology of comparative liturgical scholarship to analyse the development of pneumatic language and theology in early liturgical texts and in modern eucharistic prayers.[50] The eucharistic epiclesis is a liturgical 'unit' – a structural building block of

---

50 This method was thoroughly articulated by Anton Baumstark in his study *Vom geschichtlichen Werden der Liturgie*, Ecclesia Orans 10 (Freiburg and Breisgau: Herder 1923) and developed more extensively in *Comparative Liturgy* (Westminster, MD and London: Newman Press 1958). It has since been extended and modified by other scholars. See, e.g., Fritz West, *The Comparative Liturgy of Anton Baumstark* (Bramcote: Grove

eucharistic prayers. Therefore, applying the comparative method provides a means 'of rendering intelligible through systematizing'.[51] Examining the structure and content of eucharistic epicleses will contribute to a nuanced 'intelligibility framework' that provides some clues as to how and why ancient and modern epicleses developed the structure preserved in their extant forms, acquired new meanings over time, and got introduced into new contexts.[52] The aim of this study – to explore the traditional basis of modern prayers in dialogue with historical scholarship on ancient epicleses in order to make some modest suggestions about insights which might profitably be applied to the practical construction and use of such texts in the future – accords well with Taft's vision of liturgical history pursued according to the comparative method:

> Liturgical history … does not deal with the past, but with tradition, which is a *genetic vision of the present*, a present conditioned by its understanding of its roots. And the purpose of this history is not to recover the past (which is impossible), much less to imitate it (which would be fatuous) but to *understand liturgy* which, because it has a history, can only be understood in motion, just as the only way to understand a top is to spin it.[53]

In addition, this study will seek to adhere to the principles of what Robert Taft calls 'ecumenical scholarship', which he defines as

> a new and specifically Christian way of studying Christian tradition in order to reconcile and unite … Its deliberate intention is to emphasize the common tradition underlying differences, which, though real, may be the accidental product of history, culture, [or] language rather than essential differences in the doctrine of the apostolic faith.[54]

Books 1995), and Robert F. Taft and Gabriele Winkler (eds), *Comparative Liturgy Fifty Years after Anton Baumstark (1872–1948)* (Rome: Pontifical Oriental Institute 2001), pp. 377–406.

51 Robert F. Taft, 'The Structural Analysis of Liturgical Units: An Essay in Methodology', *Beyond East and West: Problems in Liturgical Understanding* (Rome: Pontifical Oriental Institute 1997, 2nd revised and enlarged edn), p. 188.

52 Cf. Taft, 'Structural Analysis', pp. 188–9.

53 Taft, 'Structural Analysis', pp. 191–2.

54 Robert F. Taft, 'Mass without the Consecration? The Historic Agreement on the Eucharist between the Catholic Church and the Assyrian Church of the East Promulgated 26 October 2001', *Worship* 77.6 (2003), p. 487. He articulates several evangelical and Catholic principles of ecumenical scholarship on pp. 487–8; points (1) and (5) are most directly relevant to the project pursued here.

From this perspective, a legitimate diversity in epicletic forms is to be expected in both ancient and modern times; variation in epicletic patterns is not a threat to the united pneumatic witness of the universal Church. Furthermore, the fact that most Western churches historically did *not* adopt an explicit pneumatic epiclesis until quite recently implies that contemporary advocates for the inclusion of an explicit epiclesis in Western eucharistic rites must recognize that neither the presence nor absence of such an invocation impacts the validity of the Eucharist celebrated in these traditions or the capacity of these churches to be Spirit-filled witnesses of the actions of the three divine persons working in the world for the sake of human salvation.

Since this study will be concerned not only with the epicletic language preserved in liturgical texts, but also with the living context (i.e. history and tradition) which produced them, liturgical and theological analysis of the contemporary eucharistic prayers will be supplemented by an investigation into the history and historical liturgical scholarship which shaped them, particularly those theories which proved influential in the subsequent reform of eucharistic prayers in the latter half of the twentieth century.[55] This will provide a sense of the scholarly consensus on the Spirit's role in eucharistic praying in general (and eucharistic praying during the Church's formative first few centuries in particular) which would have been available to most of the groups and committees charged with composing and revising eucharistic prayers during the past few decades. Additional insight into the specific decisions made by framers of the new eucharistic prayers will be sought from published secondary sources.

The theological and liturgical analysis of modern liturgical prayers considers how the Spirit's presence and activity is given voice in various eucharistic prayers. The position of the epiclesis (where present) is noted in relation to the structure of the eucharistic prayer as a whole, particularly in terms of the location of the epiclesis relative to the institution narrative. Other questions posed will include: To whom is the epiclesis of this prayer addressed? What does the prayer ask of the

---

55 *Apostolic Tradition* 4 and the Egyptian form of the Anaphora of Basil are especially pertinent in this regard. It is widely acknowledged that revisers and composers of eucharistic prayers in the twentieth century did look to models of eucharistic praying found in ancient liturgical texts. For example, the opening sections of the chapter on eucharistic prayers in Annibale Bugnini's *The Reform of the Liturgy, 1948–1975* (Collegeville, MN: Liturgical Press 1990) discuss how the Consilium sought to draw from the universal Church's authentic tradition when composing 'new' anaphoras for the Roman rite (see esp. pp. 448–60).

addressee? Upon whom or what is the Spirit specifically invoked – the community, the eucharistic elements, neither, or both? What (if anything) is the Spirit asked to do relative to the gifts of bread and wine? What benefits (if any) are requested for the community as a consequence of the Spirit's presence and action? The answers to these questions yield a theological 'typology' of the epiclesis as it is currently expressed within the prayers of the various denominations examined in the study.

Although questions of structure, theology and language are not the only sorts of questions which might be addressed to prayers intended for use in the complex environment of eucharistic celebrations, they do seem to be the ones most immediately pertinent to analysing a body of texts whose context of use might vary considerably in ways which are not necessarily predictable. The physical environment in which a community gathers to celebrate the Eucharist, the musical settings which may accompany the eucharistic prayer, the postures and gestures of the presider and members of the assembly, and even aspects of the intonation of the prayer may well convey a great deal about the implicit operative theology of a praying community that would not be readily apparent from its prayer texts, if these texts were viewed in isolation. While it has been recognized that such elements are of crucial importance for the inspirited and embodied participation of human persons in the eucharistic liturgy,[56] providing an account of elements such as these lies outside the scope of this project. Even though ritual components such as the gestures and postures of the presiding minister surrounding the epiclesis may prove quite significant in forming the theological inter-pretation of a particular community gathered for prayer, these gestures are, for the most part, not standardized either at the level of rubrics in official liturgical books or with respect to the manner in which different individuals might perform them. Therefore, while the mention of gesture and posture in official texts, where present, is noted, the texts of the eucharistic prayers themselves (rather than the myriad circumstances in which they might be prayed) serve as the dominant subject of analysis.

The theme underlying this chapter has been one of convergence regarding the desirability of attending to the pneumatological dimen-sions of eucharistic celebration and caution regarding the most appro-priate ways to do this in actual pastoral practice. Despite considerable

---

56 See, e.g., R. Kevin Seasoltz, 'Non-Verbal Symbols and the Eucharistic Prayer' in Frank C. Senn (ed.), *New Eucharistic Prayers: An Ecumenical Study of Their Development and Structure* (Mahwah, NJ: Paulist Press 1987), pp. 214–36.

theological convergence across and among traditions regarding the role of the Holy Spirit in eucharistic celebrations – a convergence which has been articulated in the language of recent ecumenical statements and in the texts of revised or newly composed eucharistic prayers – the current practice of eucharistic praying in the major Western Christian traditions adopts diverse approaches to the epiclesis in terms of both euchological structure and content. Structurally, some prayers situate a preliminary or 'consecratory' epiclesis before the institution narrative (sometimes accompanied by further reference to the Spirit for the fruits of communion after the anamnesis). Other prayers locate a single epiclesis following the anamnesis. The content of the epicleses in contemporary prayers is similarly diverse. Some prayers include an invocation of the Spirit solely upon the eucharistic elements of bread and wine, others request the gift of the Spirit only for the worshippers without reference to the gifts, and still others request the presence and/or action of the Spirit in connection with both the gifts *and* the worshippers. There are even a few recent prayers which invoke the Holy Spirit upon the eucharistic action in its entirety.[57]

Closer examination of contemporary eucharistic prayers, however, suggests a certain degree of 'studied ambiguity' in epicletic language which may belie an underlying theological ambivalence about the purpose for which the Holy Spirit comes when the community requests, in its eucharistic prayers, that the Spirit be sent.[58] Furthermore, despite the diversity of eucharistic language concerning the epiclesis, the vast majority of newly composed Western eucharistic prayers locate the epiclesis (or a portion thereof) in the 'Antiochene' or 'Syro-Byzantine' location – after the anamnesis – even though ancient prayer texts suggest that other models of epicletic praying were available.

---

57 The Great Thanksgiving approved by the General Conference of the United Methodist Church in May 1984 is one example of this type. Following the institution narrative, the epiclesis reads: 'Pour out your Holy Spirit on us, gathered here, and on these gifts of bread and wine. Make them be for us the body and blood of Christ, that we may be for the world the body of Christ, redeemed by his blood. By your Spirit make us one with Christ, one with each other and one in ministry of all the world, until Christ comes in final victory and we feast at his heavenly banquet.' Cited in John H. McKenna, 'The Epiclesis Revisited: A Look at Modern Eucharistic Prayers', *EL* 99 (1985), p. 321.

58 David Kennedy observed this 'studied ambiguity' (his phrase) in relation to what and whom the Spirit is invoked upon in various eucharistic prayers. See David J. Kennedy, 'The Epiclesis and the Role of the Holy Spirit in the Eucharistic Prayer' in David R. Holeton (ed.), *Revising the Eucharist: Groundwork for the Anglican Communion: Studies in Preparation for the 1995 Dublin Consultation* (Bramcote: Grove Books 1994), p. 43.

This last point hints at yet another dimension of the so-called 'epiclesis question', namely, the influence of ancient patterns of eucharistic praying (expressed in early anaphoras and patristic writings and critically examined by liturgical scholars) on the revision and composition of eucharistic prayers in the latter half of the twentieth century. The liturgical reforms of this era were influenced by the broader movement of *ressourcement* – a deliberate attempt to draw inspiration for the present from Christian sources of ages past, with a particular focus on sources dating to the first few centuries of the post-biblical age. When viewed from this perspective, the question of the place of the epiclesis in contemporary eucharistic praying becomes entwined with the broader issue of the role played by tradition – and the perception of tradition – in shaping the language and ritual structure of contemporary worship. Turning to ancient epicleses, the next two chapters will explore how scholarly studies of early eucharistic praying have shifted and extended paradigms for understanding the Spirit's role in a eucharistic context.

Part I

Ancient epicleses

Chapter 1

A reassessment of early evidence for the eucharistic epiclesis

Many of the epicletic texts formulated in the latter half of the twentieth century were constructed on the basis of certain suppositions that have been challenged by more recent scholarship on the epiclesis which has emerged in the last few decades. Christian eucharistic prayers were thought to have some direct connection with Jewish meal prayers – prayers which blessed God, offered thanks to God, and sometimes called upon God's name when blessing objects like bread and wine. Accordingly, second- and third-century texts presumably either took their inspiration from such Jewish prayers which offered God a sacrifice of praise, implored God's blessing on the communicants and perhaps invoked the name of God (sometimes conceived as the Logos or Spirit) on the elements, or were alternatively influenced by the sort of invocations then prevalent in Greco-Roman mystery religions. The drastic social and theological transitions experienced by the Church in the fourth century promoted the development of standard texts with a greater degree of theological precision than had been perceived as necessary previously. In the East, anaphoras with fixed prefaces generally conformed to a Trinitarian pattern paralleling the emerging creeds, featuring an explicit pneumatic epiclesis in the third section of the eucharistic prayer. In contrast, Western prayers contained variable parts, which, over the course of the year, expressed a similar range of themes in salvation history to the Eastern prayers. While references to the Spirit were not always as explicit as those in Eastern prayers, the twentieth-century reforms were seen as emphasizing more explicitly a pneumatological orientation that was at least implicitly present in early Western prayers.[1]

---

1 For a concise overview of the consensus scholarly opinion on the epiclesis *c.*1980, see Marion J. Hatchett, *Commentary on the American Prayer Book* (New York: Seabury Press 1980), pp. 349–53.

Current scholarship on the epiclesis, however, views the line of development of early epicleses as considerably more complex and has paid more attention to geographical and linguistic variants in the epiclesis. Based on recent studies of terminology and form by Sebastian Brock, Robert Taft and Gabriele Winkler, the following hypothesis of epicletic development in the eucharistic context has been proposed:

1 The precursor of developed epicleses may be found in early Christian appeals for the eschatological return of the risen Lord, along the lines of the *maranatha* invocation found in 1 Corinthians 16.22, Revelation 22.20 and *Didache* 10.6.

2 As eschatological expectation diminished, the urgent appeal directed to the Lord for his imminent return evolved into an invocation for the risen Christ and/or his Spirit to be immediately present to Christian communities in the context of their worship – to 'come' and be present to the worshipping assembly.

3 Over time (and as awareness of the distinct identity of the Spirit grew), such direct requests to the Lord and/or the Spirit to 'come' became requests that God (or Christ) might *let* the Logos and/or the Spirit come or rest upon the eucharistic elements – likely without further specification about what was expected to transpire in the elements and/or the community as a result of this coming.

4 Finally, such requests took the form of a petition addressed to God (the Father). The community asked God to 'send' the Holy Spirit upon the eucharistic gifts that they might be consecrated – and typically also upon the community that, in their reception of the pneumaticized gifts, the communicants might be sanctified as well.

While not seeking to resolve the question of the ultimate origins of the eucharistic epiclesis (an undertaking which deserves a dedicated study of its own), this chapter will review recent scholarship on the epiclesis that contributed to the paradigm outlined above. It will then make a modest attempt to assess the significance of variant forms of the early epiclesis, with a view towards what implications these differences might have for confirming, challenging or critiquing the current developmental framework.

THE HOLY SPIRIT IN (VERY) EARLY EUCHARISTIC PRAYING

Although Ephesians 6.18 advises Christians to 'pray in the Spirit at all times in every prayer and supplication', ancient Christian authors have relatively little to say about the place of the Spirit in Christian praying in general (or eucharistic praying in particular). In the third century Origen of Alexandria could advocate prayer to the Father, through the Son and in the Holy Spirit, but there is no evidence to suggest the existence of any standardized prayer forms during the first three centuries. There is, however, some evidence for prayer *through* the Holy Spirit before the fourth century.[2]

Robert Taft has claimed that, prior to the appearance of the eucharistic epiclesis in anaphoras of the fourth (or possibly the third) century, trying to decipher its earlier history amounts to 'sheer speculation'.[3] Although this may be the case, briefly reviewing some of these theories here is worthwhile as they have some possible connection, however tenuous it may be, to the clearer testimony to the epiclesis that survives from later centuries.

The idea that Christian eucharistic prayer is derived from the Jewish *birkat ha-mazon* and that the epiclesis in particular may have its origins in the third supplicatory section (i.e. a prayer for the restoration of Jerusalem reformulated into a prayer for the coming of God's kingdom) enjoyed wide currency a generation ago but is met with greater scepticism today.[4] Even if these prayers do not share a common lineage, they do feature a concern for God's decisive eschatological intervention – a theme which permeates many early epicletic texts as well.[5] In their development, they also share a flexible approach towards expanding the range and scope of supplicatory elements to suit the occasion and expectations of the congregation. This aspect led Paul V. Marshall to claim that 'the growth of the epiclesis of the Spirit can be seen as a developing tendency within a broader scope of supplica-

---

2 See Paul F. Bradshaw, 'God, Christ, and the Holy Spirit in Early Christian Praying' in Bryan D. Spinks (ed.), *The Place of Christ in Liturgical Prayer: Trinity, Christology, and Liturgical Theology* (Collegeville, MN: Liturgical Press/Pueblo 2008), pp. 55ff.

3 Robert F. Taft, 'From Logos to Spirit: On the Early History of the Epiclesis' in Andreas Heinz and Heinrich Rennings (eds), *Gratias Agamus: Studien zum eucharistischen Hochgebet: Für Balthasar Fischer* (Freiburg: Herder 1992), p. 491.

4 For an explanation of this hypothesis see, e.g., Louis Ligier, 'From the Last Supper to the Eucharist' in Lancelot C. Sheppard (ed.), *The New Liturgy: A Comprehensive Introduction to the New Liturgy as a Whole and to Its New Calendar, Order of Mass, Eucharistic Prayers, the Roman Canon, Prefaces and the Sunday Lectionary* (London: Darton, Longman & Todd 1970), pp. 140–1. For a discussion of problems with this theory, see Paul F. Bradshaw, *Eucharistic Origins* (London: SPCK 2004), pp. 116ff.

5 For examples of eschatological references in early epicleses, particularly focused on the theme of gathering the Church into one in the kingdom of God, see William R. Crockett, *Eucharist: Symbol of Transformation* (New York: Pueblo 1989), pp. 55–6.

tions'.[6] While the actual situation may have been somewhat more complex, the idea that the epiclesis developed in a broader context of supplication might lend at least indirect support to the recent theories of Gabriele Winkler on the origins of Christian epicleses (discussed further below). The sort of epicleses found in the apocryphal *Acts* of the apostles Thomas and John, which Winkler considers important witnesses to an early stage in the evolution of Christian liturgical practice, are likewise characterized by extensive use of supplications.

While not necessarily specific to early Christian *eucharistic* celebrations, the Aramaic invocation *maranatha* is another possible precursor of the epiclesis.[7] The phrase may be read either as an imperative (*marana tha*, 'Our Lord, come!') expressing future hope in the Lord's return or as a perfect indicative affirming a coming that has already been inaugurated (*maran atha*, 'Our Lord has come'), although the former option is more likely.[8] This expression is found in 1 Corinthians 16.22 (transliteration of the Aramaic), in Revelation 22.20 (in Greek translation – ἔρχου, Κύριε Ἰησοῦ)[9] and as part of a thanksgiving prayer after a meal in *Didache* 10.6. The *Didache* text reads:

---

6 See Paul V. Marshall in Gregory Dix, *The Shape of the Liturgy*, with additional notes by Paul V. Marshall (New York: Seabury Press 1982, reprint of 2nd (1945) edn), pp. 771–2.
7 For further discussion of this phrase in early Christian thought, see Carl Judson Davis, *The Name and Way of the Lord: Old Testament Themes, New Testament Christology* (Sheffield: Sheffield Academic Press 1996), pp. 136–9; Matthew Black, 'The Maranatha Invocation and Jude 14, 15 (1 Enoch 1:9)' in Barnabas Lindars and Stephen S. Smalley (eds), *Christ and Spirit in the New Testament: In Honour of Charles Francis Digby Moule* (Cambridge: Cambridge University Press 1973), pp. 189–96; Walter Dunphy, 'Maranatha: Development in Early Christianity', *ITQ* 37 (1970), pp. 294–308; and Klaus Thraede, 'Ursprünge und Formen des "Heiligen Kusses" im frühen Christentum', *Jahrbuch für Antike und Christentum* 11/12 (1968–9), pp. 137ff. I wish to thank Clemens Leonhard for drawing my attention to the last three of these references.
8 Sebastian P. Brock, 'Invocations to/for the Holy Spirit in Syriac Liturgical Texts: Some Comparative Approaches' in Robert F. Taft and Gabriele Winkler (eds), *Comparative Liturgy Fifty Years after Anton Baumstark (1872–1948)* (Rome: Pontifical Oriental Institute 2001), pp. 379–80. Brock notes that 'enough is now known about the likely form of the first plural suffix in Aramaic dialects of the period to be fairly certain that in first-century Palestinian Aramaic it would have been –*ana* and not –*an* . . . [thus] the Greek transcription should be broken up as *marana tha*'.
9 Concerning this passage from Revelation, which reads: 'The one who testifies to these things [i.e. Christ] says, "Surely I am coming soon." Amen. Come, Lord Jesus!', Kevin Montgomery remarks, 'Here an unambiguous present imperative responds to the former statement of future activity. The author is calling for Christ to come and be present on earth.' See Kevin Andrew Montgomery, 'When Sacraments Shall Cease: Toward a Pneumatological and Eschatological Approach to the Eucharist', MA thesis, Graduate Theological Union 2006, pp. 7–8.

May grace come, and may this world pass away.
Hosanna to the God of David.
If anyone is holy, let him come;
if anyone is not, let him repent.
Maranatha! Amen.[10]

The three texts just mentioned are diverse enough in their origins that they may underscore a widespread trend of early Christian prayer that could have influenced, directly or indirectly, later prayers.[11] Furthermore, they do share with some later eucharistic epicleses 'a petitionary dimension with a strong eschatological request',[12] although such connections could be coincidental rather than intentional.

By the second century, early Christian writers clearly distinguished between the Father and Son, but only rarely identified the Spirit as an entity distinct from the Son (cf. *The Shepherd of Hermas*, *Acts of Paul*, *2 Clement*, Pseudo-Hippolytus, Melito of Sardis, Justin Martyr and Irenaeus). While the Spirit might appear in Trinitarian formulae, there was as yet little sense of the Spirit's distinct personhood. Rather, the Spirit could be conceived as the Spirit of God or of Christ, and thus to mention Christ implied, by extension, mention of his spirit as well, and vice versa.[13] By the dawn of the third century, this begins to change (cf. the development apparent in the thought of Tertullian and Clement of Alexandria).[14] However, prior to the emergence of an explicit Spirit epiclesis in the second half of the fourth century, the status of the Spirit in pre-Nicene sources tends to be rather nebulous. Thus it cannot necessarily be presumed that discussions of the role of the Spirit in the

---

10 R. C. D. Jasper and and G. J. Cuming (eds), *Prayers of the Eucharist: Early and Reformed* (New York: Pueblo 1987, 3rd edn, revised and enlarged), p. 24. Based on his studies of the *Didache*, Arthur Vööbus claimed that the most primitive epicletic layer, witnessed in the *Didache*, was a petition for the consecration of believers which was later expanded to include other concerns. He states that 'the idea of the consecration of the elements is nothing else but an accretion to an original form of the epiclesis. In other words, it is a fallacy to project the development of later centuries into primitive Christianity.' Arthur Vööbus, *Liturgical Traditions in the Didache* (Stockholm: ETSE 1968), pp. 98–9, as quoted in William E. Thompson, 'The Epiclesis and Lutheran Theology', *Logia* 4.1 (1995), p. 33.
11 Bradshaw, 'God, Christ, and the Holy Spirit', p. 60.
12 Montgomery, *When Sacraments Shall Cease*, p. 8.
13 Bradshaw, 'God, Christ, and the Holy Spirit', p. 62.
14 For example, in *Quis dives salvetur?* 42.20, Clement of Alexandria gives God 'glory and honor through the servant Jesus Christ, the Lord of the living and the dead, and through the Holy Spirit'. Reference from Bradshaw, 'God, Christ, and the Holy Spirit', p. 62.

Eucharist refer to the *Holy* Spirit, that the term ἐπίκλησις had already acquired the technical sense that it would come to convey later, or even that early writers were concerned about pinpointing either the precise agent or moment of eucharistic consecration. These caveats must be kept in mind when considering the following evidence.

Justin Martyr, writing his *First Apology* in the mid-second century, attests to a prayer after which the eucharistic gifts were no longer ordinary food and drink but the flesh and blood of Jesus. Drawing a connection between the eucharistic action and the Incarnation, Justin serves as a potential witness to a primitive theology of eucharistic consecration involving the Logos – and perhaps even something akin to a Logos epiclesis. Justin writes:

> For we do not receive these things as common bread or common drink; but just as our Savior Jesus Christ, being incarnate through the word of God, took flesh and blood for our salvation, so too we have been taught that the food over which thanks have been given by a word of prayer which is from him [δί εὐχῆς λόγου τοῦ παρ᾽ αὐτοῦ], (the food) from which our flesh and blood are fed by transformation, is both the flesh and blood of that incarnate Jesus.[15]

The Greek phrase δί εὐχῆς λόγου τοῦ παρ᾽ αὐτοῦ has at least five possible meanings, including: 'by a word of prayer which is from him', 'by a prayer of the word which is from him', a prayer *for* the Logos (and thus perhaps a Logos epiclesis), a reference to the words of institution, or an allusion to the eucharistic prayer in its entirety.[16] However, even the theological conviction that Christ is the consecratory force behind the Eucharist – a conviction that would be quite amenable to Justin's overall

---

15 Justin, *1 Apol.* 66.2. ET from Jasper and Cuming (eds), *Prayers*, p. 29; the Greek text can be found in Anton Hänggi, Irmgard Pahl *et al.*, *Prex Eucharistica* (Freiburg: Universitätsverlag 1998), pp. 68–74. The contents of the prayer are not known, although Justin remarks in ch. 67 of the *First Apology* (as part of a description of the Sunday Eucharist) that the president 'sends up prayers and thanksgivings to the best of his ability', implying an extemporaneous rather than fixed form of prayer. The description of a baptismal Eucharist in that same text states that the congregation 'bless[es] the Maker of all things through his Son Jesus Christ and through the Holy Spirit over all that we offer' (*1 Apol.* 65.3).

16 See John H. McKenna, *The Eucharistic Epiclesis: A Detailed History from the Patristic to the Modern Era* (Chicago: Hillenbrand 2009, 2nd edn), pp. 44–6 and the references cited there. See also Geoffrey J. Cuming, 'ΔΙ᾽ ΕΥΧΗΣ ΛΟΓΟΥ (Justin, *Apology* i.66.2)', *JTS* 31.1 (1980), pp. 80–2; Anthony Gelston, 'ΔΙ᾽ ΕΥΧΗΣ ΛΟΓΟΥ (Justin, *Apology* i.66.2)', *JTS* 33.1 (1982), pp. 172–5; and Michael Heintz, 'δί εὐχῆς λόγου τοῦ παρ᾽ αὐτοῦ: (Justin, *Apology* 1.66.2): Cuming and Gelston Revisited', *SL* 33.1 (2003), pp. 33–6.

theology with its concern for the Logos – does not necessarily imply that this belief was articulated liturgically through an invocation to or of Christ. Furthermore, it does not mean that this consecratory emphasis was confined to any particular part of the prayer, even if such an invocation did exist.[17]

Irenaeus of Lyons may deserve credit for introducing the Greek term *epiklesis* to the context of the Christian Eucharist. He employs this word in a passage of *Adversus Haereses* (*c.*180) that makes an analogy between the sanctification of the Eucharist and bodily resurrection:

> For as the bread, which is produced from the earth, when it receives the invocation [ἐπίκλησις] of God, is no longer common bread, but the Eucharist, consisting of two realities, earthly and heavenly, so also our bodies, receiving the Eucharist, are no longer corruptible, having the hope for the resurrection to eternity.[18]

In another context within this same work, however, Irenaeus uses the term to critique the heretical activities of Marcus, a Valentinian Gnostic, accusing him of 'pretending to eucharistize cups mixed with wine, and protracting to great length the word of invocation [ἐπίκλησις], makes them appear purple and reddish'.[19] This latter passage would seem to suggest that *epiklesis*, for Irenaeus, did not designate a specific invariable formula.[20] Furthermore, Robert Taft notes that the term can refer to the

---

17 Bradshaw, 'God, Christ, and the Holy Spirit', p. 61. Bradshaw notes a possible connection between Justin's theology on this point and this statement in 1 Tim. 4.4–5: 'For everything created by God is good, and nothing is to be rejected, provided it is received with thanksgiving; *for it is sanctified by God's word and by prayer*' (pp. 60–1, emphasis mine). The only explicit invocation of the Logos in a eucharistic prayer is found in the euchologion of Sarapion of Thmuis (see below); for other possible references to something like a Logos epiclesis in the theological writings of Clement of Alexandria (d. *c.*211) and Origen of Alexandria (d. *c.*254), see Maxwell E. Johnson, *The Prayers of Sarapion of Thmuis: A Literary, Liturgical, and Theological Analysis* (Rome: Pontifical Oriental Institute 1995), pp. 249–50.

18 Irenaeus, *Adv. Haer.* 4.18.5. ET from Alexander Roberts and James Donaldson (eds), *The Ante-Nicene Fathers: Translations of the Writings of the Fathers down to A.D. 325, Vol. 1: The Apostolic Fathers with Justin Martyr and Irenaeus* (Edinburgh and Grand Rapids, MI: T. & T. Clark/Eerdmans 1996, reprint of the 1926 edn), p. 486. A similar idea is found in 5.2.3: 'When, therefore, the mingled cup and the manufactured bread receives (*sic*) the Word of God … the Eucharist of the blood and the body of Christ is made …' (*ANF*, p. 528).

19 *Adv. Haer.* 1.13.2, see p. 334 in the above work. The translation in the text above is from Bradshaw, 'God, Christ, and the Holy Spirit', p. 60.

20 McKenna, *Eucharistic Epiclesis*, p. 48.

prayer over the eucharistic gifts in its *entirety* into the fourth century, making it difficult to determine whether the liturgical prayers with which Irenaeus was familiar might have included an explicit epiclesis of the Logos (or Spirit).[21]

The *Didascalia Apostolorum*, a third-century church order, gives the Holy Spirit a prominent role in the Church's ministry, including a part in the sanctification of the Eucharist. This text declares that 'the eucharist is accepted and sanctified through the Holy Spirit' (6.21) and 'sanctified by means of invocations' (6.22). These texts may be the forerunners of the theology of consecration articulated in later Syrian texts. Bradshaw proposes that language attributing sanctificatory power to the Spirit at this early stage may represent 'a regional variation of the invocation of the Logos found in other sources' such as Justin and Irenaeus; the pneumatic references alone do not prove that the eucharistic theology expressed in this text is at a significantly later stage of development.[22]

THE ORIGINS OF THE EPICLESIS: REASSESSING THE EVIDENCE

Until recently, most scholars presumed that a Spirit epiclesis would probably not have arisen prior to the heated pneumatological debates of the fourth century that were eventually 'resolved' at the Council of Constantinople in 381. The strongest evidence in support of this hypothesis is that orthodox defenders of the Spirit's divinity against the semi-Arians and Macedonians often discuss the action and formulae associated with the Spirit in baptism but are completely silent about the invocation of the Spirit in a eucharistic context.[23] Rather, especially in

---

21 Taft, 'From Logos to Spirit', p. 491.

22 Bradshaw, 'God, Christ, and the Holy Spirit', p. 62.

23 However, one could also argue in a similar vein that the lack of any appeal to a Logos epiclesis by proto-orthodox theologians during the time when the full divinity of the Son was questioned negates the idea that a Logos epiclesis could have existed in the early fourth century (or earlier). John McKenna, following E. G. Cuthbert F. Atchley, also suggests an alternative reason for silence about the Spirit's eucharistic role in the midst of the Pneumatomachian controversy: 'The main reason for the Cappadocians' failure to cite the Spirit epiclesis against the Pneumatomachians is to be found in the nature of the attack brought to bear against the divinity of the Holy Spirit. The Pneumatomachians . . . viewed the sending, the temporal mission of the Holy Spirit, as evidence of his inferiority. They also claimed the orthodox doctrine was not scriptural. To counter these claims, the Fathers would hardly have been well advised to appeal to an epiclesis which was not biblical and which spoke of the sending of the Holy Spirit. With the Matthean baptismal formula these problems did not present themselves. It was biblical and it put the Holy Spirit on equal footing with the Father and the Son.' McKenna, *Eucharistic Epiclesis*, p. 49; cf. E. G.

Egypt (the birthplace of the Arian controversy), the argument from silence together with reference to the Logos as the sanctifying agent of the Eucharist suggests that the widespread use of an explicit 'consecratory' Spirit epiclesis may not have predated the doctrinal crises. Furthermore, before the late fourth century, nowhere is the consecration of the eucharistic gifts credited to the Holy Spirit. This is seen for the first time in the late fourth (or early fifth) century in the *Mystagogical Catecheses* of Cyril (or John) of Jerusalem, which includes an explicit consecratory epiclesis.

Recent research by Gabriele Winkler has reopened the question about the origins of the epiclesis and the manner in which it might have been incorporated into eucharistic prayers before the developed anaphoras of the late fourth century, specifically in terms of reconsidering the significance of the Syrian apocryphal *Acts of the Apostles* as a source of liturgical evidence and development. Before considering Winkler's conclusions in detail, the larger scholarly paradigm into which these theories fit should be noted. Winkler follows the advice of Sebastian Brock in attending to the form of the verbs used in epicleses and in the divine person(s) addressed in order to trace a possible line of development among extant epicletic texts. From his initial investigation, Brock observed that

> the oriental eucharistic and baptismal epikleses divide up into two main types, those introduced by 'come' and those introduced by 'send.' The former is the only one to be found in the East Syrian epiklesis (of whatever kind), but it is not confined to them, since it is found in the Greek anaphora of Basil, and in several West Syrian anaphoras ... The latter, introduced by 'send,' is the norm of the Greek and West Syrian anaphoras as well as the West Syrian baptismal epiklesis, with the exception of the Maronite *ordo* ...[24]

Eucharistic epicleses contain several components that are also prominent in invocatory texts from other contexts, such as baptismal rites and

Cuthbert F. Atchley, *On the Epiclesis of the Eucharistic Liturgy and in the Consecration of the Font*, ACC 31 (London: Oxford University Press, H. Milford 1935), pp. 62–3 and 'The Epiclesis: A Criticism', *Theology* 29 (1934), pp. 33–4.
24 Sebastian P. Brock, 'The Epiklesis in the Antiochene Baptismal Ordines', *Symposium Syriacum* 1972 (Rome: Pontifical Oriental Institute 1974), pp. 213–14. For a prior study attending to the significance of verbal variations in early epicleses, see Palle Dinesen, 'Die Epiklese im Rahmen altkirchlicher Liturgien: Eine Studie über die eucharistische Epiklese', *ST* 16.1 (1962), pp. 42–107.

prayers for the blessing of objects and/or persons.[25] The main epicletic verb is typically some form of either 'come' or 'send', there is usually at least one other accompanying verb (and often several) further specifying the particular 'sanctifying action' requested through the epiclesis, and the invocation is typically directed towards one (or more) of the three members of the Trinity.[26] In his analysis of the verbs used in Antiochene baptismal *ordines*, Brock concludes that the imperative 'come' predates the petition that God 'send' the Holy Spirit upon the baptismal waters in the early Syrian sources that he examined. Furthermore, the most primitive form of the address ('come') was directed to Christ himself. At later stages of the invocation's evolution, Christ was asked more indirectly to bestow his Spirit upon the waters; the petitions asked Christ that he 'let his Spirit come' or that his Spirit 'may come'. Later still, the request that the Spirit 'may come' was directed not to Christ but to God (the Father). The imperative 'send', addressed to God, was a further development in this Syrian tradition, incorporated under the auspices of Greek influence in the fifth century.[27]

In a series of articles, Winkler has noted the connections between baptismal and eucharistic epicleses in the early Syrian tradition.[28] In the

---

25 On epicleses in Eastern texts with baptismal themes, see Mary K. Farag, 'A Shared Prayer over Water in the Eastern Christian Traditions' in Teresa Berger (ed.), *Liturgy in Migration: From the Upper Room to Cyberspace* (Collegeville, MN: Liturgical Press 2012), pp. 43–82 and Nicholas Denysenko, *The Blessing of Waters and Epiphany: The Eastern Liturgical Tradition* (Burlington, VT and Farnham: Ashgate 2012).

26 Brock, 'Invocations to/for the Holy Spirit', p. 382.

27 Brock, 'The Epiklesis in the Antiochene Baptismal Ordines', pp. 183–218, esp. pp. 213–14. In addition to the *Acts of Thomas* (discussed below), 'come' is used in the context of a eucharistic epiclesis in the Maronite *Sharar* (in an epiclesis that is addressed to Christ) and also in several East Syrian anaphoras where the address is directed towards the Father (e.g. the Anaphoras of Addai and Mari, Theodore, and Nestorius). Bryan Spinks also draws attention to a variant reading of the Lord's Prayer in Luke 11.2: 'Your Holy Spirit come (ἐλθάτω) and cleanse us.' He comments that, 'Here of course the petition is in the mouth of Christ to the Father, and its authenticity is extremely doubtful. But it might be possible to see in this the Epiklesis finding its way into the Lord's Prayer.' Bryan D. Spinks, 'The Consecratory Epiklesis in the Anaphora of St. James', *SL* 11.1 (1976), pp. 25–6, quote from p. 26. A number of attestations of this variant are listed in Taft, 'From Logos to Spirit', p. 495, along with the comment that 'the early date of this variant, and the theological context of that period, do not permit us to infer that the Holy Spirit means more here than the spirit of the Logos in an earlier, less determined sense'.

28 See Gabriele Winkler, 'Nochmals zu den Anfängen der Epiklese und des Sanctus im Eucharistischen Hochgebet', *Theologische Quartalschrift* 174.3 (1994), pp. 214–31; Gabriele Winkler, 'Weitere Beobachtungen zur frühen Epiklese (den Doxologien und dem Sanctus): Über die Bedeutung der Apokryphen für die Erforschung der Entwicklung der Riten', *OrChr* 80 (1996), pp. 177–200; Gabriele Winkler, 'Further Observations in Connection with the Early Form of the Epiklesis', *Le Sacrement de l'Initiation: Origines et*

latter category, she includes as evidence passages from the apocryphal *Acts of the Apostles*, particularly passages from the *Acts of Thomas* and the *Acts of John*.[29] While these passages were known to earlier generations of scholars, they were rarely taken seriously as possible witnesses to mainstream liturgical practice; their content at times appeared to reflect pagan 'magic' more than clear precursors of later practice which scholars would have expected to find in proto-orthodox texts.[30] The *Acts of Thomas* is the 'earliest extensive non-biblical Syriac text that survives', perhaps from East Syria and likely dating to the third century, although the current text appears to be an amalgamation of several developmental

---

Prospective (Antélias, Lebanon: Centre d'Études et de Recherches Pastorales 1996), pp. 66–80; and Gabriele Winkler, 'Zur Erforschung orientalischer Anaphoren in liturgievergleichender Sicht, I: Anmerkungen zur Oratio post Sanctus und Anamnese bis Epiklese', *OCP* 63.2 (1997), pp. 363–420. For a summary of Winkler's studies on the epiclesis in English, see Maxwell E. Johnson, 'The Origins of the Anaphoral Use of the Sanctus and Epiclesis Revisited: The Contribution of Gabriele Winkler and Its Implications' in Hans-Jürgen Feulner, Elena Velkovska and Robert F. Taft (eds), *Crossroad of Cultures: Studies in Liturgy and Patristics in Honor of Gabriele Winkler* (Rome: Pontifical Oriental Institute 2000), pp. 405–42.

29 Despite renewed attention to the importance of these texts, problems remain in terms of using them as liturgical sources. First, they represent the genre of 'living literature', which makes it hard to differentiate between what may be the 'original' text and what may have been added or changed by later redactors – a question which is further complicated by the existence of these texts in Syriac and Greek versions whose content sometimes differs significantly. Second, the narrative descriptions of supposedly 'apostolic' liturgical practices may have been coloured by the current practices known to contemporary editors of the text. Finally, even if the descriptions do provide a snapshot of actual liturgical practice at some point, the question remains open concerning whether these texts reflect widespread liturgical practices or the peculiar customs of groups at the margins of mainstream Christianity. See Paul F. Bradshaw, *The Search for the Origins of Christian Worship: Sources and Methods for the Study of Early Liturgy* (New York: Oxford University Press 2002), pp. 109–10.

30 See, e.g., Hans Lietzmann, *Mass and Lord's Supper: A Study in the History of the Liturgy* (ET of *Messe und Herrenmahl*), trans. Dorothea H. G. Reeve (Leiden: Brill 1953), p. 244. Concerning the reluctance to take these texts seriously, Bradshaw has written: 'There seems to be an illogical inconsistency here, fueled no doubt by a disinclination to admit into court any testimony that might point to a conclusion that the scholars a priori had decided was simply not true of what they thought of as mainstream Christianity' – a concern applicable to the eucharistic material even more so than to material related to initiation. See Bradshaw, 'God, Christ, and the Holy Spirit', p. 59. In addition to strings of invocations addressed to the Spirit, this work contains acclamations and petitions directed towards an array of elements, including 'waters from the living waters' (ch. 52), 'holy oil given to us for sanctification' (ch. 121) and 'bread of life' (ch. 133); Bradshaw, 'God, Christ, and the Holy Spirit', p. 63.

strata.[31] The source of the invocations is unknown, but a more recent study by Caroline Johnson highlights their correspondence with some aspects of magic spells of ancient Mediterranean culture, yet also their distinctiveness when compared to Jewish and pagan *prayers* from this same time period (which do not contain quite the same sort of invocations).[32]

Based on her own research, Winkler stresses the importance of several premises when tracing the developmental history of the eucharistic epiclesis. First, the vocabulary used in an epiclesis is presumed to provide clues about its native tradition (Greek or Syriac). Following Brock, she suggests that the verb 'send' characterizes the Greek tradition over and against the verb 'come', the latter being an indicator of what she considers the 'essentially older' Syrian tradition. Second, the root of the Syrian epiclesis, exemplified by those in the *Acts of Thomas*, is remarkably similar to the *maranatha* language of *Didache* 10 – with its request for the Lord to 'come' – and thus the Syrian epicleses reflect a very early layer of the Christian tradition. Third, the oldest form of the epicleses, attested from about the year 200 in the Syrian *Acts of Thomas*, was not an invocation of the *Logos* but rather a pure 'name' epiclesis. Although addressed to the Messiah, these early Syrian eucharistic epicleses oscillate between invoking the name of Jesus and that of the Spirit. Furthermore, as the petition is primarily a request for *presence* and communion with the Messiah and the Spirit (i.e. the Mother, the Spirit of Holiness), it should not be put in quite the same category as later communion epicleses, which are concerned with sharing in the blessed bread and wine as a means of encountering Christ's presence. Fourth, the later *Greek*

---

31 Brock, 'Invocations to/for the Holy Spirit', p. 379. The Greek text is reproduced in Richard Adelbert Lipsius and Maximilian Bonnet (eds), *Acta Apostolorum Apocrypha* (Hildesheim: G. Olms 1959), II.2, pp. 99–291 (= reprint of Leipzig: Hermann Mendelssohn 1903); for an ET see J. K. Elliott, *The Apocryphal New Testament: A Collection of Apocryphal Christian Literature in an English Translation* (Oxford and New York: Clarendon Press/Oxford University Press 1993), pp. 439–511. The Syriac text (accompanied by an ET) can be found in William Wright, *Apocryphal Acts of the Apostles* (Amsterdam: Philo Press 1968, reprint of 1871 London edn), I.171–333 (II.146–298). For a recent study of the eucharistic material, see Gerard Rouwhorst, 'La célébration de l'eucharistie selon les Actes de Thomas' in Herman A. J. Wegman and Charles Caspers (eds), *Omnes Circumadstantes: Contributions towards a History of the Role of the People in the Liturgy* (Kampen: J. H. Kok, 1990), pp. 51–77.
32 Caroline Johnson, 'Ritual Epiclesis in the Greek Acts of Thomas' in François Bovon, Ann Graham Brock and Christopher R. Matthews (eds), *Apocryphal Acts of the Apostles: Harvard Divinity School Studies* (Cambridge, MA: Harvard University Center for the Study of World Religions 1999), pp. 171–204.

epicleses bring this vacillation in address to further clarity by means of an explicit 'Spirit epiclesis' with an orientation towards communion (rather than consecration) – such as the epiclesis found in *Apostolic Tradition*. (The Spirit epiclesis containing the word 'send' likely betrays the dependence of *Apostolic Tradition* on the Greek rather than the Syriac milieu.) Fifth, it is not until the second half of the fourth century that an epiclesis with overt consecratory intent emerges (e.g. in *Mystagogical Catecheses* 5.7 from Jerusalem). Sixth, and finally, the connection of the epiclesis with the rites of Christian initiation must be taken seriously. At least in the Syrian context, Winkler is convinced that the original use of the epiclesis was in association with the prebaptismal anointing in that tradition (which acquired a pneumatic focus) and that its use in a eucharistic context is a secondary development.[33]

Winkler's first article revisiting the question of epicletic origins ('Nochmals zu den Anfängen der Epiklese und des Sanctus im Eucharistischen Hochgebet') problematizes the traditional classification of epicleses into the categories of 'Logos' or 'Spirit' and 'consecration' or 'communion'. These groupings, she argues, cannot adequately account for the evidence from the early Syrian tradition. Winkler proposes that the roots of the epiclesis may lie in a simple appeal to the Messiah or his Spirit to 'come' – with no explicit invocation on either the elements or the communicants (who could be viewed as the object of the invocation only by extension and not directly). Furthermore, while the early Syrian epicleses are not 'Spirit epicleses' of the sort that arise by the fourth century, calling them Logos epicleses makes little sense in the Syrian context. The Syrian term for 'word' (*melta*) that would be the equivalent of the Greek *Logos* is nowhere to be found in the *Acts*; the preferred term is rather the 'Messiah' (*Mᵉśiha*).[34] Even so, the texts from the apocryphal *Acts* do not clearly distinguish between the 'name of the Messiah' and his 'Spirit of holiness' (Syriac version) or the 'compassionate Mother' (Greek text).

According to Winkler, this oscillation of address can be observed in an epiclesis connected to a prebaptismal anointing in chapter 27 of the *Acts of Thomas*, and also in the eucharistic texts from chapters 50 and 133 (see Tables 1.1 and 1.2).

---

33 See Winkler, 'Nochmals zu den Anfängen', pp. 219–20. A similar list summarizing Winkler's theory of epicletic development, including qualifications based on further reflection and research, appears in Winkler, 'Further Observations', pp. 78–80. The movement from an initiatory to a eucharistic context is not surprising when the Eucharist is seen as an essential part of – and the ritual culmination of – the rites of initiation viewed as a unit; see Johnson, 'Origins of the Anaphoral Use of the Sanctus', p. 210.

34 Winkler, 'Nochmals zu den Anfängen', pp. 215–16.

Table 1.1: Eucharistic texts in *Acts of Thomas* 50

Syriac text[35]	*Greek text*[36]
Come, gift of the Exalted; come, perfect mercy;	Come, perfect compassion; Come, fellowship with the male;
come, holy Spirit; come, revealer of the mysteries of the Chosen among the Prophets; come, proclaimer by His Apostles of the combats of our victorious Athlete; come, treasure of majesty; come, beloved of the mercy of the Most High; come, (thou) silent (one), revealer of the mysteries of the Exalted; come, utterer of hidden things, and shewer of the works of our God;	Come, you who know the mysteries of the Chosen One; Come, you who have partaken in all the combats of the noble combatant; Come, rest, that reveals the great deeds of the whole greatness; Come, you who disclose secrets And make manifest the mysteries; Come, holy dove, Who bear the twin young; Come, secret mother;
come, giver of life in secret, and manifest in thy deeds; come, giver of joy and rest to all who cleave unto thee; come, power of the Father and wisdom of the Son, for Ye are one in all; come and communicate with us in this Eucharist which we celebrate, and in this offering which we offer, and in this commemoration which we make.	Come, you who are manifest in your deeds; Come, giver of joy And of rest to those who are united to you; Come and commune with us in this eucharist, Which we celebrate in your name, And in the agape In which we are united at your calling.

---

35 ET from Wright, *Apocryphal Acts of the Apostles*, p. 189.

36 ET from Elliott, *The Apocryphal New Testament*, p. 468. This invocation (addressed to Christ and without a direct invocation of the Spirit as 'secret mother' but retaining the reference to 'fellowship with the male') reappears as a eucharistic epiclesis in an Irish palimpsest sacramentary from the mid-seventh century. The Latin translation is clearly derived from the Greek of *Acts of Thomas* 50, but this version is not identical with the two surviving Latin versions of the Greek. The text of this epiclesis can be found in A. Dold and L. Eizenhofer OSB (eds), *Das irische Palimpsest Sakramentar im CLM 14429 der Staatsbibliothek München* (Texte und Arbeiten 53–4 (Beuron 1964)), p. 44 (as the *postpridie* prayer in this Gallican-style text for the feast of the Circumcision). It is discussed briefly in Brock, 'Invocations to/for the Holy Spirit', p. 380 and more extensively in Joseph H. Crehan, 'Eucharistic Epiklesis: New Evidence and a New Theory', *TS* 41.4 (1980), pp. 698–712.

Table 1.2: Eucharistic texts in *Acts of Thomas* 133

Syriac text[37]	*Greek text*[38]
'. . . We name the name of the Father over thee; We name the name of the Son over thee; We name the name of the Spirit over thee, the exalted name that is hidden from all.' And he [Judas Thomas] said: 'In thy name, Jesus, may the power of the blessing and the thanksgiving come and abide upon this bread, that all the souls, which take of it, may be renewed, and their sins may be forgiven them.'	'. . . we name over you the name of the mother, the hidden mystery of the hidden dominions and powers, we name over you the name of Jesus.' And he said, 'Let the power of blessing come [ἐλθάτω δύναμις εὐλογίας] and rest upon the bread, that all souls who partake of it be delivered from their sins.'

In addition, while these *Acts* were likely composed in Syriac, it seems to Winkler that the extant Greek texts offer a glimpse of the Syrian tradition at an earlier layer of development than what is apparent in the surviving Syriac texts themselves. Whereas the Greek text retains archaic phrases like 'compassionate Mother' (ch. 27) and communion or fellowship 'of

---

37 ET from Wright, *Apocryphal Acts of the Apostles*, p. 268.
38 ET from Elliott, *The Apocryphal New Testament*, p. 497. Frank Senn characterizes this eucharistic prayer as a whole as a blessing (in contrast to a thanksgiving) and suggests that both of these eucharistic passages in the *Acts of Thomas* 'clearly reflect early Christian usage', whether or not they were influenced by Gnostic ideas. Senn notes that invocations of a 'divine dyad', such as the combination Father–Mother, were prevalent in Gnostic groups. Frank C. Senn, *Christian Liturgy: Catholic and Evangelical* (Minneapolis: Fortress Press 1997), p. 84. However, if Winkler's interpretation of these texts is correct, phrases like 'fellowship with the male' and 'secret mother' (ch. 50) may not refer to separate masculine and feminine entities but to one reality (i.e. the Spirit) which is grammatically feminine in the Syriac language. Likewise, the assertion that these texts reflect 'the primitive Jewish-Christian understanding that consecration takes place by pronouncing the name of God over the person or object [such that] [t]he one named takes possession of the object and uses it according to his or her purposes' (Senn, *Christian Liturgy*, p. 84) may reflect the theological precision of a later era rather than the early third-century Syrian context. Analysing the textual and internal evidence for editorial activity, Susan Myers concludes, 'There is no compelling reason to date the work prior to the middle of the third century, and it may have been written in the second half of the century.' See Susan E. Myers, *Spirit Epicleses in the* Acts of Thomas, Wissenschaftliche Untersuchungen zum Neuen Testament 2. Reihe 281, ed. Jörg Frey *et al.* (Tübingen: Mohr Siebeck 2010), pp. 44–55, 57–107, 222; quoted text from p. 222.

the male' (ch. 27) or 'with the male' (ch. 50) to describe the Spirit, the Syriac text betrays evidence of later Trinitarian reworking and attribution of power to the *Father* rather than the *Mother*.[39] The use of the verb 'come' (and the address directly to Christ and/or his Spirit of holiness) also suggests to Winkler the primitive stage of these prayers. The Syrian *Acts of John* (from the mid-fourth century or perhaps earlier), in contrast, direct the address to the *Father* to let *his Spirit* of holiness come.[40]

Robert Taft had mentioned both of these texts in a prior article, 'From Logos to Spirit', suggesting that the invocation in chapter 50 (which he designated a Logos epiclesis) might be 'the earliest actual text of a eucharistic epicletic prayer' and also detecting parallels between *Acts of Thomas* 133 and the epiclesis of *Apostolic Tradition* 4.[41] Winkler challenges some of Taft's conclusions on philological grounds. For reasons discussed above, she would not classify the epiclesis in chapter 50 as a Logos epiclesis – but rather an invocation of the 'mother' (i.e. the Spirit) as reflected in the older Greek text. Also, the parallels between the epiclesis of chapter 133 and *Apostolic Tradition* are not as clear when one recognizes the differences in both the verb used ('let come' in the former, 'send' in the latter) and also the addressee (Jesus and/or the Spirit vs God the Father) coupled with the absence in the *Acts* of a direct invocation of either Christ or the Spirit on the eucharistic elements and/or communicants. What is invoked instead is the 'power of blessing', but *whose* power or blessing is not specified any more precisely.[42] The object of the epiclesis in *Apostolic Tradition* is not absolutely clear, but the request for the sending of the Spirit upon the gifts or oblation 'of the Holy Church' does have a greater degree of specificity than that of the *Acts of Thomas* 133.

Since the Greek version of the *Acts of Thomas* 133 preserves a more primitive pattern of epicletic invocation featuring oscillation in address between the 'name' of the 'Mother' (i.e. the Holy Spirit, the 'hidden Mother') and Jesus and is not particularly concerned about the further effects of this invocation in the immediate eucharistic context, Winkler contends that these texts reflect the anaphoral epiclesis at a very early

---

39 Winkler, 'Nochmals zu den Anfängen', p. 217.
40 Winkler, 'Nochmals zu den Anfängen', p. 218.
41 Taft, 'From Logos to Spirit', p. 491. Taft draws the comparison mainly on structural rather than philological grounds. Both *Acts of Thomas* 133 and *Apostolic Tradition* 4 seem, to Taft, to contain an invocation for the Spirit and a communion orientation, but they both lack the explicit request for the consecration of the eucharistic gifts that is commonly present in fourth-century anaphoras.
42 Winkler, 'Nochmals zu den Anfängen', pp. 217–19.

stage of development. This form, featuring the verb 'come', may provide the link between the *maranatha* invocation of *Didache* 10.6 and the more developed forms of the anaphoral epiclesis which are attested in the fourth century, such as the jussive 'may there come' witnessed in the East Syrian anaphoras (and also in certain West Syrian anaphoras, most notably the one attributed to Basil).[43] It is a request for presence rather than the consecration of the elements.[44]

Thus Winkler's initial study of the origins of the anaphoral epiclesis corroborates the conclusions of Brock's investigation of the epiclesis in Syrian baptismal texts. In each case, the earliest form of the epiclesis consisted of the imperative form 'come' – although Winkler would claim that the addressee may be either Christ or his Spirit of holiness. At a later stage of the tradition, epicleses arise requesting that Christ 'let' his Spirit come. Later still, God (the Father) became the addressee of the petition that the Spirit 'may come'. Eventually, direct requests to the Father to 'send' the Spirit arose out of Greek influence in the fourth to fifth century.

Winkler's later essays on this topic modify her initial conclusions somewhat, particularly in terms of the identity underlying the 'names' invoked in the epiclesis. Her methodology remains the same, but she considers a wider set of texts from the apocryphal *Acts* (especially *Acts of Thomas* 121 and 157 concerned with the blessing of oil used for the prebaptismal anointing and with the actual prebaptismal anointing) and also attends to the doxologies which occur in close conjunction with epicletic invocations in the apocryphal *Acts*. However, Winkler now contends that the address to the 'name' of the Messiah in chapter 27 and in the doxology of 133 does not, as she had earlier supposed, imply an oscillation of address to the Messiah and the Spirit, in that order. Rather, the 'name' of the Messiah, the Anointed One, is to be identified with the 'hidden power' that inhabits this name, a connection clearly seen in the epiclesis associated with a prebaptismal anointing in the Syriac *Acts*, 133.[45] Thus it is now clear to Winkler that appeal to the 'name' of the Messiah

---

43 Brock, 'Invocations to/for the Holy Spirit', p. 379.
44 Winkler, 'Nochmals zu den Anfängen', pp. 218–20.
45 Winkler, 'Further Observations', p. 69; cf. Winkler, 'Weitere Beobachtungen', pp. 182–4. The doxology in the Syriac reads:

> Glory to thee, (thou) beloved Fruit!
> Glory to thee, (thou) name of the Messiah!
> Glory to thee, (thou) hidden power that dwellest in the Messiah!

serves only as an introduction to the 'hidden power' behind this 'Name,' a clear insinuation to the Spirit who is the real addressee hidden in the 'Name' of the Messiah. The 'Name' of the Anointed serves as a vehicle to depict the action of the Spirit who is invoked by summoning down the 'Name' of the Anointed.[46]

Winkler still asserts that the earliest form of the eucharistic epiclesis is a 'name' epiclesis consisting of the 'mystery' of the name of the Messiah – but that the true addressee of the petition is, from start to finish, solely the Spirit, who is the hidden power behind this name.[47]

Winkler also reconsiders the earlier stratum preserved in the Greek version and claims that it is *only* the Holy Spirit, the 'hidden mother' (ch. 50), that is ultimately addressed in both eucharistic epicleses of the *Acts of Thomas*, a scenario which is clearer for chapter 50 than for 133. However, this is apparent from the eucharistic epiclesis of chapter 133 as well upon closer examination. The Syriac version conforms to a Trinitarian structure, suggesting later modification. The name of Jesus is present in the invocations of both the Greek and Syriac versions of the epiclesis – but in two *different* locations, a possible sign that the name of Jesus is a later interpolation in this context. The epiclesis of chapter 50 does not mention Jesus at all. Therefore, perhaps the name of the Messiah/Jesus was *not invoked at all* in the earliest stage of the epiclesis. Furthermore, when the eucharistic epiclesis of chapter 133 is compared to the invocation at the blessing of oil in chapter 157, there is significant overlap in vocabulary and syntax in the Greek version, with the Syriac text of 157 containing several unusual features. Winkler proposes that the second part of the eucharistic epiclesis in 133 may have taken over parts of the epiclesis native to an initiatory context (now found in 157).[48]

If the eucharistic epiclesis of chapter 133 is really a modified version of an epiclesis imported from the baptismal context, this may mean that the

---

ET from Wright, *Apocryphal Acts of the Apostles*, p. 267. Given that the meaning of the Greek texts in the last two exclamations is the same (although the first one differs, ascribing glory to 'you, love of mercy' – see Elliott, *The Apocryphal New Testament*, p. 497), it is curious that Winkler cites the Syriac instead of the Greek given her contention that the Greek text generally reflects the Syrian tradition at an earlier stage of development.

46 Winkler, 'Further Observations', p. 69.

47 Winkler, 'Further Observations', p. 71.

48 See Winkler, 'Further Observations', pp. 71–5. The epiclesis in ch. 157 (discussed further below) and also that of ch. 121 contain an additional verb, 'come *and abide*', and the epiclesis is 'may . . . come' rather than the imperative 'come'. Both of these features suggest to Winkler that these epicleses represent a further stage of development.

more original form of the Syrian baptismal epiclesis (attested, perhaps, in ch. 50) was a pure 'Spirit epiclesis' from the very beginning, in contrast to her earlier conclusions. An important cue, for Winkler, is that the invocation of the Messiah, the *Anointed One*, seems to arise first in a baptismal context in which this feature would be perfectly appropriate, given the importance of the pneumatic prebaptismal anointing in the earlier Syrian tradition.[49]

Winkler's case would be strengthened on this point if it could be demonstrated that the term 'Messiah' was used in the early Syrian tradition primarily in connection with initiation rather than as a more general designation for the person of Christ (or the power behind his name, which Winkler wishes to read as a designation for the Spirit) that could be equally appropriate in an initiatory or a eucharistic context. While it is clear to Winkler why 'this allusion to the Anointed, the Messiah, is missing in the epiklesis of the eucharist',[50] it would not seem to be outside the realm of possibility that an allusion to the Messiah could be equally plausible in the eucharistic context, especially at a later stage of development, as both of these rituals have a strong historical connection to the person of Christ.

It also would be helpful if the various layers of development in the apocryphal *Acts* could be isolated more precisely. The eucharistic invocation in chapter 133 is situated in the narrative context of a baptismal Eucharist where the preceding baptism featured a prebaptismal anointing of the head only. Winkler assigns this single prebaptismal anointing to the earliest stage of Syrian initiatory practice (in contrast to the later emergence of an anointing of both head and body found in chs 120–1 and 157).[51] This suggests that the invocation in chapter 133 may be early – if the whole initiatory event culminating in the celebration of the Eucharist belongs to a single traditional layer. However, the invocation which Winkler identifies as linguistically parallel to that of 133 occurs in the context of the blessing of prebaptismal oil in chapter 157 – in a baptism which features the anointing of both head and body,

---

49 Winkler, 'Further Observations', p. 69.
50 Winkler, 'Further Observations', p. 69.
51 Winkler, 'Further Observations', p. 71; cf. also Gabriele Winkler, *Das armenische Initiationsrituale: Entwicklungsgeschichtliche und liturgievergleichende Untersuchung der Quellen des 3. bis 10. Jahrhunderts* (Rome: Pontifical Oriental Institute 1982), pp. 136–46 on this point, as well as Gabriele Winkler, 'The Original Meaning of the Prebaptismal Anointing and Its Implications', *Worship* 52.1 (1978), pp. 24–45, which is reprinted in Maxwell E. Johnson (ed.), *Living Water, Sealing Spirit: Readings on Christian Initiation* (Collegeville, MN: Liturgical Press 1995).

suggesting a *later* stage of initiatory development than that apparent in chapter 133.[52] While Winkler may be right in positing the origins of the Syrian eucharistic epiclesis in an initiatory context (and its subsequent spread from Syria to other regions), this isolated example does not seem sufficient to clearly demonstrate that the direction of movement was from the context of prebaptismal anointing, with its occurrence in a eucharistic context being only secondary, as Winkler claims:

> There can be no doubt in my mind that the primary place of the presence of a fully fledged epiklesis is the anointing and that the inclusion of a true epiklesis at the eucharist reflects a secondary development. (I am not talking about the short and eschatological call of the Maranatha which is attested already at the inception of Christianity and probably belonged to the eucharistic meal but to a true and verbal invocation, the summoning down of the Spirit (of Christ) at the anointing which is probably older than its earliest witness in the Acts of Thomas around 200.)[53]

On the other hand, even if prayers for the consecration of oil are a late development in liturgical *texts*, this does not necessarily say anything conclusive about the order of the emergence of such invocations in actual *practice*. Winkler is correct to note that the calling down of the Spirit (of Christ) likely predates the earliest texts containing such an invocation. Nonetheless, dating these early texts (or at least establishing the most likely order of their emergence) would be crucial for resolving the question of the origin of the epiclesis in the Syrian milieu.

Winkler's hypothesis that the source of the epiclesis is to be sought in the rites of initiation relates to her theories about the appearance of the Sanctus in the Syrian tradition. The Syriac version of the *Acts of John*,

---

52 The text of this epiclesis is:

Yea, Lord, come, abide upon this oil ...
May Thy gift come ... and may it abide upon this oil,
over which we name Thy name.

ET of the Syriac from Wright, *Apocryphal Acts of the Apostles*, p. 323; the meaning of the Greek text is equivalent. According to Winkler, the shift in address (now to God the Father) plus the addition of yet another verb to the invocation ('come and rest *and abide*') may indicate still further development of the epiclesis, leading to 'considerable uncertainty who should be addressed with the invocation'. Winkler, 'Further Observations', p. 79; see also Winkler, 'Weitere Beobachtungen', pp. 196–8.

53 Winkler, 'Further Observations', p. 79; cf. Winkler, 'Weitere Beobachtungen', pp. 192ff.

which Winkler dates to the mid-fourth century, seems to exhibit an epiclesis at a later stage of development than those found in the *Acts of Thomas*.[54] The epiclesis is directed to the Father, asking that the Spirit of holiness 'may . . . come, and rest and abide upon the oil and upon the water'.[55] Moreover, the epiclesis is enmeshed in Trinitarian doxologies and also in the Sanctus (which is perhaps evident here for the first time in a Syriac text). Winkler suggests that the Syriac epiclesis began as extended invocations of the divine presence, then incorporated doxologies for 'the divine manifestations', doxologies which culminated in the cry of 'Holy, holy, holy' due to the glorious things the congregation witnessed (such as fire blazing over the oil following the epiclesis quoted above as the assembly gave glory to God in the words of the Sanctus). In the process, the extended epicleses of an earlier era were truncated, making way for the inclusion of more and more doxologies, this latter category eventually coming to include the Sanctus as well.[56]

Winkler admits that no particular conclusions can be drawn from this text to the use of the epiclesis and/or Sanctus in association with the eucharistic celebration that may have accompanied the initiatory ritual described in the *Acts of John*:

At the end of the narration about baptism we find only a short allusion to eucharist. Hence no details can be gleaned from it which form the epiklesis had and whether the Sanctus was already included in the eucharist and what shape it had. But it may be legitimate to conclude that the Sanctus was probably already part of the celebration of the eucharist.[57]

---

54 On the various recensions and dating of the apocryphal *Acts of John*, which combine to create considerable complexity concerning the associated textual tradition, see Winkler, 'Weitere Beobachtungen', pp. 192–3. Winkler remarks that the extant Syriac translation seems to be based on an unknown Greek precursor – as the Syriac translation does not correspond to any of the surviving Greek fragments. Furthermore, the Syriac translation seems to contain different theological and liturgical layers reflecting different stages of developmental evolution.

55 Wright, *Apocryphal Acts of the Apostles*, vol. 1, p. 58 (Syriac text), vol. 2, p. 53 (ET).

56 See Winkler, 'Further Observations', pp. 76–7. The *Acts of John* includes four occurrences of the Sanctus, which Winkler enumerates on p. 76. In one instance, Winkler thinks that repeated recitations of the Sanctus (plus a doxology) may have eclipsed an epicletic invocation at this juncture of the text. None of these occurrences of the Sanctus includes the Benedictus, which suggests to Winkler that the Benedictus was not attached to the earliest Syrian form of the Sanctus.

57 Winkler, 'Further Observations', p. 78.

While an account in a narrative style, as is found in the *Acts*, would not necessarily have been concerned to describe *all* parts of a ritual in detail, neither would it necessarily have been constrained to comment *only* on features which were relatively recent innovations in the tradition described. Thus an epiclesis and Sanctus *may* have been part of the eucharistic rites the author(s) of the *Acts of John* knew – or they may not have been present at all. No eucharistic epicleses are described in the text, and if the Sanctus appears to be a new element of initiatory practice around this time one need not presume that it would have been already well-established in eucharistic practice around this same time. Whatever the situation may have been in the mid-fourth century, by the time fully fledged epicleses appear in Syrian anaphoras by the late fourth and early fifth centuries, a close connection between the Sanctus and epiclesis is *not* a standard feature of Syrian texts. An intimate link between the Sanctus and epiclesis would seem to be a more logical explanation for the development of these features in the Alexandrian anaphoral tradition, characterized by the close connection between the conclusion of the Sanctus (without Benedictus) and the beginning of the epiclesis (full . . . fill).[58] (Even here, the epiclesis–Sanctus connection does not fit the pattern Winkler proposed, with extended invocations making way for doxologies that culminated in the Sanctus; rather, it is the Sanctus which *precedes* the epicletic invocation in Alexandrian anaphoras.) Thus this bond between the epiclesis and the Sanctus may be a more apt explanation for the emergence of these features in the fourth-century anaphoras of some regions than it is for others. Even if both components arose together, they do not seem to have invariably travelled as a unit (or been treated this way if once-united elements could eventually find their way into different sections of the prayers of various traditions), and the broken bond between these elements (if they were once linked) has left few textual traces in later sources.

Although Winkler notes that further research in this area remains to be done, she has highlighted an association between baptism and Eucharist that seems to be important for early Syrian liturgical texts and also focused renewed attention on the prebaptismal anointing in this tradition as a possible clue to the trajectory of later ritual development. Expanding upon the studies of Brock and Taft on the epiclesis and

---

58 Ironically, this may be one tradition for which the evidence of baptism and Eucharist always and necessarily occurring together is not as strong as it is in others. See Paul F. Bradshaw, 'Baptismal Practice in the Alexandrian Tradition: Eastern or Western?' in Johnson (ed.), *Living Water*, p. 99.

Spinks on the Sanctus, she has, as Maxwell Johnson notes, 'underscored an extremely important *sacramental* context out of which the development of specific anaphoral forms and use would appear to be quite plausible'.[59] If Winkler's conclusions are correct, the *Syrian Acts* may, as Taft had earlier supposed, preserve the earliest known text of a eucharistic epicletic prayer. Whereas Taft could assert that 'it is no longer possible to sustain the view that a Spirit epiclesis could not have existed before the second half of the fourth century',[60] Winkler's work provides more specific argumentation and evidence to back up this claim. Her research further reinforces the importance of attending to the verbs used in invocations (i.e. 'come' may represent an older layer of tradition than 'send') as well as the addressee (the 'name' of the Messiah, Logos, Spirit, etc.). Her careful comparative liturgical scholarship may necessitate a rethinking of the previously proposed paradigm of epicletic development 'from Logos to Spirit' to something like 'from the Coming of the "Name" of the Messiah or Spirit to the Sending of the Spirit'.[61] With these caveats in mind, attention will turn next to assessing the epicleses found in early Christian anaphoras.

---

59 Johnson, 'Origins of the Anaphoral Use of the Sanctus', p. 425, his emphasis.
60 Taft, 'From Logos to Spirit', p. 498.
61 Johnson, 'Origins of the Anaphoral Sanctus', p. 430.

Chapter 2

The epiclesis in early anaphoras

It seems that eucharistic praying likely evolved from a diverse collection of short, individual prayer units that, over time, expanded and multiplied before eventually being woven together into longer composite prayers comprising various distinct units.[1] The closest historical equivalent to the convergence in eucharistic prayer patterns in Western churches during the second half of the twentieth century may well be the multiplication of eucharistic prayers and the mutual exchange of prayer components across geographical and linguistic lines that occurred during the second half of the fourth century. 'New' elements such as the Sanctus, institution narrative and epiclesis were inserted into prayers which did not previously contain them. Sections of shorter, simpler anaphoras were recombined to form longer (and more theologically sophisticated) texts reflecting the doctrinal developments of the fourth century. Full prayers, such as the Anaphora of Basil, were apparently exported, imported and translated, yielding regional variations of 'common' texts. Early anaphoral diversity thus yielded to a variety of pressures favouring increasing standardization.[2] In terms of eucharistic praying, the practical result of liturgical convergence in general and the recent pneumatological controversies in particular was a proliferation of

---

1 See Paul F. Bradshaw, *Eucharistic Origins* (London: SPCK 2004), ch. 7, esp. pp. 121–3, and Enrico Mazza, *The Origins of the Eucharistic Prayer*, trans. Ronald E. Lane (Collegeville, MN: Liturgical Press 1995), pp. 59–60.

2 See Paul F. Bradshaw, 'The Homogenization of Christian Liturgy – Ancient and Modern: Presidential Address', *SL* 26.1 (1996), pp. 4–5. Other explorations of this fourth-century trend include John R. K. Fenwick, *Fourth-Century Anaphoral Construction Techniques* (Bramcote: Grove Books 1986); Bryan D. Spinks, *The Sanctus in the Eucharistic Prayer* (Cambridge and New York: Cambridge University Press 1991); and Robert F. Taft, 'The Interpolation of the Sanctus into the Anaphora: When and Where? A Review of the Dossier', *OCP* 57.2 (1991), pp. 281–308 (Part I) and 58.1 (1992): pp. 83–122 (Part II). For additional studies, see Bradshaw, 'Homogenization of Christian Liturgy', p. 5, n. 11.

anaphoral texts that featured more developed pneumatic language and, frequently, the incorporation of an explicit invocation of the Holy Spirit. It is at this stage that the comparative analysis of eucharistic epicleses becomes possible due to the multiplication of witnesses.

EPICLESES IN EARLY EAST SYRIAN ANAPHORAS

The East Syrian tradition will be considered first among anaphoral families because East Syrian prayers contain a large concentration of anaphoral epicleses featuring the invocation 'come'. If Brock and Winkler are correct about the significance of this point of vocabulary, these prayers may also provide insight into the epiclesis at an early stage of development. The epiclesis in these prayers typically appears just before the concluding doxology.[3]

The oldest extant East Syrian anaphora is that of Addai and Mari. The core of the oldest surviving manuscript, the *Mar Eša'ya* text (from the tenth or eleventh century), may preserve a fourth-century eucharistic prayer – although, especially if one abstains from the presupposition that a pneumatic epiclesis could not have existed before the fourth century, it contains nothing else that would prevent one from dating it to the third or even the second century.[4] This prayer lacks the institution narrative and locates the epiclesis in the penultimate position. The epiclesis will be considered here in conjunction with the Maronite *Sharar* (also known as the Third Anaphora of St Peter), with which it shares much text in common. *Sharar* may reflect the textual tradition at a later stage of development than Addai and Mari (as this prayer *does* contain an institution narrative) but it also may preserve some more ancient features

---

3 The usual structure of the East Syrian anaphora is: Dialogue, Praise and Thanksgiving, Pre-Sanctus, Sanctus, Post-Sanctus thanksgiving, Institution Narrative, Anamnesis, Intercessions, Epiclesis and Doxology – although Addai and Mari does not contain the institution narrative and some East Syrian anaphoras have a prayer of offering in place of the anamnesis. See Anton Hänggi, Irmgard Pahl *et al.*, *Prex Eucharistica* (Freiburg: Universitätsverlag 1998), p. 374 and John H. McKenna, *The Eucharistic Epiclesis: A Detailed History from the Patristic to the Modern Era* (Chicago: Hillenbrand 2009, 2nd edn), pp. 28–9.
4 See Bryan D. Spinks, 'The Epiclesis in the East Syrian Anaphoras', *Worship: Prayers from the East* (Washington, DC: Pastoral Press 1993), p. 89; and R. C. D. Jasper and G. J. Cuming (eds), *Prayers of the Eucharist: Early and Reformed* (New York: Pueblo 1987, 3rd edn, revised and enlarged), pp. 40–1. Scholars think that the nucleus of the prayer probably consisted of: '(a) praise to God as Creator and Redeemer; (b) thanksgiving for redemption; [and] (c) commemoration of Christ's death and resurrection' – a structure with significant parallels to Justin Martyr's description of the contents of the eucharistic prayer.

Table 2.1: East Syrian and Maronite epicleses

Addai and Mari	Sharar
May he come, O Lord, your Holy Spirit and rest upon this oblation of your servants, and bless and hallow it, that it may be to us, O Lord, for the pardon of debts and the forgiveness of sins, and a great hope of resurrection from the dead and a new life in the kingdom of heaven with all who have been pleasing before you.	And may he come, O Lord, your living and Holy Spirit, and dwell and rest upon this oblation of your servants. And may it be to those who partake for the pardon of debts and the forgiveness of sins and for a blessed resurrection from the dead and a new life in the kingdom of heaven for ever.

than the prayer attributed to the two saints who supposedly played an important role in evangelizing Edessa. The two prayers likely represent different derivations of a now-lost common ancestor.[5] (See the epicleses in Table 2.1.[6])

The addressee of the anaphora as a whole (and, by extension, the epiclesis) has been the subject of some debate. The post-Sanctus section of Addai and Mari and the remainder of the prayer following the Sanctus in *Sharar* are now addressed to Christ; if *Sharar* represents the more original form of the text, this means that the epiclesis of Addai and Mari might have been initially addressed to Christ as well.[7] According to Winkler's latest schema of epicletic development, either version would seem to represent a hybrid form. The verb form 'may come' reflects an intermediate stage of development in either case, while an address to the Father would be late. On the other hand, if Winkler is correct about the earliest Syrian epicleses being direct appeals to the *Spirit* to come (and not oscillation in address between the Messiah and the Spirit), there would seem to be little place in this paradigm for a direct epicletic appeal

---

5 Jasper and Cuming (eds), *Prayers*, p. 45.

6 ET is that of Spinks, 'Epiclesis in the East Syrian Anaphoras', pp. 90–1, based on the Urmiah text.

7 W. F. Macomber and Bryan D. Spinks argue that the address to the Son is earlier, but Anthony Gelston disagrees. See W. F. Macomber, 'The Oldest Known Text of the Anaphora of the Apostles Addai and Mari', *OCP* 32 (1966), pp. 335–71; Emmanuel J. Cutrone, 'Anaphora of the Apostles: Implications of the Mar Esa'ya Text', *TS* 34.4 (1973), pp. 624–42; Spinks, 'Epiclesis in the East Syrian Anaphoras', p. 91; and Anthony Gelston, *The Eucharistic Prayer of Addai and Mari* (Oxford and New York: Clarendon Press/Oxford University Press 1992).

to Christ – or at the very least it is not a possibility that Winkler considers in her latest studies.

According to the dominant textual tradition, 'dwell' is likely a later addition to the prayer with 'rest' being the more original verb specifying the Spirit's action after 'come' (although some manuscripts of Addai and Mari contain the term 'dwell' along with 'living' as a designation for the Spirit). The phrase 'bless and hallow' is not in *Sharar*, and it is likely a later interpolation in Addai and Mari via the epiclesis of the anaphora attributed to Nestorius.[8] Again, following Winkler, the addition of other verbs besides forms of 'come' and especially the concern for the Spirit's action of 'blessing' the gifts would represent later expansions of a primitive core.

Two additional eucharistic prayers from the East Syrian tradition contain epicleses which elaborate on that of Addai and Mari, particularly by developing the prayers for the fruits of communion much more extensively.[9] These prayers are attributed to Nestorius and to Theodore of Mopsuestia, and the origin and dating of both prayers are problematic.[10] The epiclesis in Nestorius is:

And may there come, my Lord, the grace of the Holy Spirit and may it [she] dwell and rest upon this oblation which we offer before you and may it [she] **bless and sanctify** it and *MAKE* this bread and this cup the Body and Blood of our Lord Jesus Christ, *changing* them and sanctifying [them] for us by the activity of the Holy Spirit, so that the

---

8 Spinks, 'Epiclesis in the East Syrian Anaphoras', p. 91; cf. Bernard Botte, 'L'épiclèse dans les liturgies syriennes orientales', *Sacris Erudiri* 6 (1954), pp. 48–72. The earliest form of the epiclesis may thus have resembled the following (as given in Spinks, 'Epiclesis in the East Syrian Anaphoras', p. 91): 'And may he come, O Lord, your Holy Spirit, and rest upon this oblation of your servants, that it may be to us for the pardon of debts and the forgiveness of sins, and for the resurrection from the dead, and for new life in the kingdom of heaven.' This arrangement resembles the anaphora from the *Apostolic Tradition* insofar as it requests the Spirit's coming upon the offering for the sake of the sanctification of the communicants (although *Apostolic Tradition* used the verb 'send') *without* requesting any change in the gifts. However, Addai and Mari's epiclesis is focused more strongly than *Apostolic Tradition*'s on the eschatological gifts which the communicants hope to receive as a result of their sharing in the eucharistic gifts. See Jasper and Cuming (eds), *Prayers*, pp. 40–1 and Spinks, 'Epiclesis in the East Syrian Anaphoras', p. 92.

9 Kevin Andrew Montgomery, 'When Sacraments Shall Cease: Toward a Pneumatological and Eschatological Approach to the Eucharist', MA thesis, Graduate Theological Union 2006, p. 19.

10 For details, see Bryan D. Spinks (ed.), *Mar Nestorius and Mar Theodore the Interpreter: The Forgotten Eucharistic Prayers of East Syria* (Cambridge: Grove Books 1999), esp. pp. 9–10, 19–22.

partaking of these glorious and holy mysteries may be to all those who receive them, eternal <u>life</u> and <u>resurrection from the dead</u> and the <u>pardon</u> of the body and soul. And for the light of knowledge and for <u>uncovered face</u> towards you: and for eternal salvation which you have promised us through our Lord Jesus Christ, so that we may be united together one with another in harmony to one bond of love and peace. And that we may be one Body and one Spirit, as we are called in one hope of our calling.[11]

The epiclesis of the anaphora attributed to Nestorius appears to draw from the epicleses of Addai and Mari and several Syro-Byzantine anaphoras. Spinks observes:

1. Nestorius has retained the initial petition of Addai and Mari, though requesting 'the grace' of the Holy Spirit, and the anaphora is unquestionably addressed to the Father. It has also qualified 'oblation' with 'which we offer before you.'
2. 'Bless and hallow and make' would seem to have been derived from Byzantine Basil ('bless and hallow') and St. James or Chrysostom ('make') . . .
3. The eschatological fruits of communion have been expanded from Addai and Mari, and the compiler has drawn on Scripture – 2 Corinthians 3:18, 2 Corinthians 4:6, Acts 15:25, Philippians 2:2, and Ephesians 4:4–6. However, these have been suggested by his probable sources. Twelve Apostles has 'health of soul and body' and 'enlightenment of mind' and makes reference to the 'life-giving mysteries.' Unity is the theme of Byzantine Basil, and St. James has 'eternal life' and 'sanctification of souls and bodies.'[12]

The epiclesis of Theodore is similar to that of Nestorius:

<u>And may there come</u> the grace of <u>the Holy Spirit</u> upon us and <u>upon this oblation and rest</u> and reside upon this bread and upon this cup. And may it [she] bless and hallow and seal them in the Name of the

---

11 ET from Spinks (ed.), *Mar Nestorius and Mar Theodore*, p. 33. Following Spinks' edition, material common to or resembling Addai and Mari is <u>underlined</u>, and material which may be drawn from the Greek versions of West Syrian anaphoras is italicized (*italics* = John Chrysostom, **bold italics** = **Basil**, ITALIC CAPITALS = JAMES). The word 'make' is common to both Chrysostom (CHR) and James (JAS).

12 See Spinks, 'Epiclesis in the East Syrian Anaphoras', p. 93 and *Mar Nestorius and Mar Theodore*, p. 18 for more detail.

Father and the Son and the Holy Spirit. And by the power of your Name may **this bread** become **the** holy **body of our Lord Jesus Christ**. And **this cup** the precious **blood** of our Lord Jesus Christ. And all who in true faith eat from this bread, and drink from this cup, may they be for them, my Lord, <u>for the pardon of debts and the forgiveness of sins, and a great hope of the resurrection of the dead,</u> and salvation of body and soul, <u>and new life in the kingdom of heaven</u> and glory for ever and ever. And make us all worthy by the grace of our Lord Jesus Christ that <u>with all those who have been</u> **well pleasing to your will** and have been guided by your commandments, we may rejoice in the kingdom of heaven, in the good things that are prepared and will not pass away.[13]

The text of this anaphora's epiclesis overlaps significantly with that of not only Addai and Mari but also Nestorius. However, both texts may have drawn upon Addai and Mari independently rather than the editor of Theodore borrowing directly from the words of Nestorius.[14] Furthermore, both may have taken over some ideas directly from the Catechetical Lectures of Theodore of Mopsuestia rather than through another intermediary text. The reference to 'the grace' of the Holy Spirit in both anaphoras and the request for the Spirit's coming not just upon the oblation but also upon the communicants are likely candidates in this regard.[15] The pneumatology of both of these East Syrian anaphoras

13 Spinks, *Mar Nestorius and Mar Theodore*, p. 37. As in Spinks, text shared by the anaphoras of Nestorius and Theodore is in **bold** and material common to or parallel with the text of Addai and Mari is <u>underlined</u>. For a critical edition of the text, see Jacob Vadakkel, *The East Syrian Anaphora of Mar Theodore of Mopsuestia: A Critical Edition, English Translation and Study* (Kottayam: Oriental Institute of Religious Studies India 1989), p. 282.

14 See Anthony Gelston, 'The Relationship of the Anaphoras of Theodore and Nestorius to that of Addai and Mari' in G. Karukaparampil (ed.), *Tuvaik: Studies in Honour of Rev. Jacob Vellian* (Kottayam: Mad'naha Theological Institute 1995), pp. 20–6. Gelston contends that this is especially likely for the epiclesis section of the prayers.

15 Spinks, 'Epiclesis in the East Syrian Anaphoras', p. 94 and *Mar Nestorius and Mar Theodore*, p. 26. In a lecture which mentions the epiclesis pronounced over the waters of baptism, Theodore of Mopsuestia notes that the *grace* of the Holy Spirit is invoked. In relation to the Eucharist, 'the priest offers . . . prayer and supplication to God that the Holy Spirit may descend, and that grace may come upon the bread and wine that are laid . . . the priest prays also that the grace of the Holy Spirit may come also on all those present'. However, Theodore does not quote the full text of the anaphora in his postbaptismal catecheses. See Alphonse Mingana, *Commentary of Theodore of Mopsuestia on the Lord's Prayer and on the Sacraments of Baptism and the Eucharist* (Cambridge: W. Heffer & Sons Ltd 1933), pp. 55 and 104 (for the baptismal and eucharistic material, respectively). Other possible sources for the anaphora of Theodore include Syriac James

probably corresponds more closely to that of Theodore of Mopsuestia than did the West Syrian anaphora upon which the authentic Theodore commented (in which the epiclesis is located between the anamnesis and intercessions).

> This fitted rather ill with [Theodore's] stress on intercessions being linked with the death of Christ, because the epiklesis had 'resurrected' the elements which had symbolized the passion. The anaphora of *Nestorius* (and ... *Theodore* also) gives much better liturgical expression to the theology of the Catechetical Lectures by placing the epiklesis (the 'resurrection') after the intercessions which have pleaded the passion.[16]

The fact that both of these anaphoras are clearly concerned about some transformation of the gifts in connection with the epiclesis and quite extensively occupied with reflection on the eschatological benefits of communion – combined with their allusion to (or perhaps direct dependence on) other texts not attested before the late fourth or early fifth century – suggests that these anaphoras are of a later date. Nonetheless, they may retain a more primitive form of epicletic address in their use of a form of the verb 'come' (rather than 'send'). This suggests that epicletic elements which are both older and newer may occur together in the same text, and thus the form of the verb must be considered in conjunction with other factors that could help to date an epicletic text more precisely.

EPICLESES IN EARLY WEST SYRIAN ANAPHORAS

By the time the developed anaphoras of the late fourth century appear, 'send' is the typical epicletic verb in most Greek and West Syrian anaphoras; however, the more primitive 'come' or 'let come' is found in

---

(or the Peshitta) for verb 'reside' (*gn* in Syriac), Nestorius or a Syro-Byzantine anaphora for 'bless and hallow', St James for 'holy' body and 'precious' blood, *Acts of Thomas* for the invocation of 'the Power of your Name' (with a loose parallel especially to *Acts* 27, 'Come, Power of grace'), and the East Syrian baptismal Ordo for the concept of seal. In addition to rearranging material from Addai and Mari (with some possible influence from Nestorius as well), the eschatological section may also contain allusions to the Anaphora of Basil (BAS), CHR and JAS, combined with some new material. Spinks concludes that, 'whatever [the redactor's] sources or inspiration, the material is woven to form a quite new and powerful epiklesis which is terminated by a brief doxology'. Spinks, *Mar Nestorius and Mar Theodore*, p. 26.

16 Spinks, *Mar Nestorius and Mar Theodore*, p. 16.

the Anaphora of Basil and in a handful of other West Syrian anaphoras. The developed form of the Antiochene anaphora contains a threefold prayer whose celebrant petitions God:

1. to send the Holy Spirit (on us and) on the offered gifts,
2. to make the bread and wine the body and blood of Christ by the power of the Holy Spirit,
3. so that they might be unto salvation for those who receive them in communion.[17]

These elements are present in various combinations and with varying degrees of emphasis in a number of Antiochene anaphoras from the late fourth and early fifth centuries. The epiclesis is almost always addressed to the Father, and the invocation most often commences with the verb 'send' (with the Spirit as the object of the sending); however, the second most common construction is introduced by 'may there come' with the Spirit as the subject of this coming.[18] In the Antiochene anaphoral structure, the epiclesis directly follows the anamnesis, thus forming a sort of 'bridge' between the oblation and communion.[19]

---

17 Robert F. Taft, 'From Logos to Spirit: On the Early History of the Epiclesis' in Andreas Heinz and Heinrich Rennings (eds), *Gratias Agamus: Studien zum eucharistischen Hochgebet: Für Balthasar Fischer* (Frieburg: Herder 1992), p. 490.

18 Other qualifying verbs, such as 'pour out', may be present, sometimes along with additional verbs describing the Spirit's activity in relation to the offerings (e.g. 'reside' and 'rest'). In some anaphoras the verbs 'come' and 'send' appear together. For a discussion of the variety of verbs used in West Syrian anaphoras, see Sebastian P. Brock, 'Towards a Typology of the Epicleses in the West Syrian Anaphoras' in Hans-Jürgen Feulner, Elena Velkovska and Robert F. Taft (eds), *Crossroad of Cultures: Studies in Liturgy and Patristics in Honor of Gabriele Winkler* (Rome: Pontifical Oriental Institute 2000), pp. 173–92, esp. pp. 177, 179–82. Brock's observations are based on a comparative study of 66 anaphoras which conform to the West Syrian pattern. He notes the extensive interrelationships among these anaphoras due to their tendency to incorporate material from older sources – and also the preservation of what appear to be quite ancient elements even in later anaphoras. As an example, he points to the anaphora of John Maro in which the epiclesis (and a section of the institution narrative) is addressed to Christ. See Brock, 'Towards a Typology', pp. 187–9. Brock also discusses five dominant patterns of verbal constructions and syntactical relationships in Syriac liturgical texts in Sebastian P. Brock, 'Invocations to/for the Holy Spirit in Syriac Liturgical Texts: Some Comparative Approaches' in Robert F. Taft and Gabriele Winkler (eds), *Comparative Liturgy Fifty Years after Anton Baumstark (1872–1948)* (Rome: Pontifical Oriental Institute 2001), pp. 382–6.

19 Taft, 'From Logos to Spirit', p. 490. The structure of the fully developed Antiochene anaphora is as follows: Sursum corda, Preface, Pre-Sanctus, Sanctus, Post-Sanctus, Institution Narrative, Anamnesis, Offering, Epiclesis, Intercessions, Doxology. See Jasper and Cuming (eds), *Prayers*, p. 6.

Anaphoras of this type, such as James, the Byzantine version of Basil, and John Chrysostom, appear to be more concerned with the consecration of the gifts (or, in William Crockett's words, the 'language of production and change') than the texts discussed previously (save for the anaphoras of Nestorius and Theodore, which may be partially dependent on the West Syrian anaphoras just mentioned). This may reflect a new orientation towards the application of philosophical language to eucharistic theology; on the other hand, it may represent a new manifestation of biblically based models of eschatological transformation.[20] Antiochene anaphoras also tend to enumerate the fruits of communion expected from sharing in the Eucharist through eating and drinking the sanctified gifts; the epiclesis is the part of the prayer in which these anaphoras 'traditionally express the "why" of the eucharist, the purpose for which the Church celebrates it and the benefits she hopes to receive from it'.[21]

Since the anaphoras of Basil, James and John Chrysostom have directly and indirectly influenced many other anaphoras (ancient, and, especially in the case of Basil, now modern as well), the epicleses of these three texts will now be considered in more detail.

Anaphora of Basil

If 'come' is a vestige of the earliest layer of the anaphoral epiclesis, the Anaphora of Basil (BAS) (the sole Greek anaphora to employ a form of the verb 'come' in connection with the request for the Holy Spirit) may provide a point of connection with an older layer of the

20 Crockett argues that, at least when the connection between the sanctification of the gifts and the community that will soon consume them for *their* sanctification is maintained (i.e. when the link between points (2) and (3) of Taft's characterization of the Antiochene epiclesis above is not sundered), 'the language of "making" and "change" suggests that the transformation of the gifts and the community are already by way of sacramental sign the anticipation of the transformation of all things that the New Testament speaks of in the language of resurrection and new creation'. William R. Crockett, *Eucharist: Symbol of Transformation* (New York: Pueblo 1989), p. 62. Crockett draws parallels between the theologies of Justin Martyr in his *First Apology* 66.2 and of Paul in Rom. 8 to argue that 'the language of the later epicleses in the eastern liturgies still reflect (*sic*) their eschatological roots' (see pp. 62–3, quote from p. 63).

21 Robert F. Taft, 'The Fruits of Communion in the Anaphora of St. John Chrysostom' in Ildebrando Scicolone (ed.), *Psallendum: Miscellanea di studi in onore del Prof. Jordi Pinell i Pons, O.S.B.* (Rome: Pontificio Ateneo S. Anselmo 1992), p. 285. For Taft, the 'why' of the Eucharist consists in praising and glorifying God by *eating and drinking* in remembrance of Christ (cf. 1 Cor. 11.26). Most early anaphoras (with the exception of Addai and Mari (which mentions it elsewhere in the prayer) and the *Testamentum Domini*) explicitly mention the congregation's partaking of the eucharistic gifts (see Taft, 'Fruits of Communion', pp. 285–6).

tradition of epicletic development.[22] In its various forms, the main verb associated with the epiclesis is 'come' rather than 'send'.[23] The Egyptian form (denoted E-BAS) is the earliest witness to this prayer, and the oldest known manuscript (in Sahidic Coptic, probably dating to the first half of the seventh century) may preserve a largely fourth-century (or perhaps earlier) anaphora.[24] The epiclesis of E-BAS simply asks God that the Spirit might come upon those gathered and on the gifts in order to 'sanctify' and 'make' them the holy of holies. The communion aspect of the epiclesis is developed more extensively (sanctification of soul and body, union in one body and one spirit, and a share with the saints).

The version of the anaphora with the most textual witnesses, Byzantine Basil (Byz-BAS), expands the epiclesis into a lengthy supplication, multiplying the words of consecration (bless, sanctify and make), and specifically requests that the bread be transformed into the precious body of 'our Lord and God and Saviour Jesus Christ', and the cup into the precious blood of 'our Lord and God and Saviour Jesus Christ'. The petition for the fruits of communion is also expanded considerably in comparison to E-BAS, expressing the hope that communion might lead to mercy and grace rather than judgement and condemnation. See Table 2.2 for the epicleses of these two forms.

Brock views the conjunction of 'bless and sanctify' in Byz-BAS as an indication of this text's connection with the Syriac world. This phrase is not present in the Sahidic Coptic version of E-BAS, but it does occur in the three major East Syrian Anaphoras (Addai and Mari, Nestorius, and Theodore), in the institution narratives of the Syriac Anaphora of James and the Anaphora of the Twelve Apostles (but *not* in Greek James or the

---

22 Brock notes that the phrase 'may there come' found its way into several Ethiopic anaphoras, quite possibly via Syriac influence. For a list, see Brock, 'Invocations to/for the Holy Spirit', p. 381, n. 14.

23 The textual tradition underlying the Anaphora of Basil is very complex; the anaphora survives in several languages and exists in Byzantine, Armenian, Syrian and Egyptian forms. For an overview, see D. Richard Stuckwisch, 'The Basilian Anaphoras' in Paul F. Bradshaw (ed.), *Essays on Early Eastern Eucharistic Prayers* (Collegeville, MN: Liturgical Press 1997), pp. 110–12; John R. K. Fenwick, *The Anaphoras of St. Basil and St. James: An Investigation into Their Common Origin* (Rome: Pontifical Oriental Institute 1992), pp. 49–57; and Anne Vorhes McGowan, 'The Basilian Anaphoras: Rethinking the Question' in Maxwell E. Johnson (ed.), *Issues in Eucharistic Praying in East and West: Essays in Liturgical and Theological Analysis* (Collegeville, MN: Liturgical Press 2010), pp. 221–8.

24 Jean Doresse and Emmanuel Lanne, *Un Témoin Archaïque de la Liturgie Copte de S. Basile* (Louvain: Publications Universitaires 1960), pp. 2, 4–5. This volume also contains a critical edition of the text.

Table 2.2: Epicleses of Egyptian and Byzantine Basil

E-BAS (from the Sahidic text)[25]	Byz-BAS[26]
And we, sinners and unworthy and wretched, pray you, our God, in adoration that in the good pleasure of your goodness your Holy Spirit may descend upon us and upon these gifts that have been set before you, and may sanctify them and make them holy of holies.	... we pray and beseech you, O holy of holies, in the good pleasure of your bounty, that your {all-}Holy spirit may come [ἐλθεῖν] upon us and upon these gifts set forth, and bless [εὐλογῆσαι] them and sanctify [ἁγιάσαι] and show [ἀναδεῖξαι] ... this bread [to be] the precious body of our Lord and God and Savior Jesus Christ. Amen. And this cup the precious blood of our Lord and God and Savior Jesus Christ, {Amen.} which is shed for the life of the world ... Amen.
Make us all worthy to partake of your holy things for sanctification of soul and body, that we may become one body and one spirit, and may have a portion with all the saints who have been pleasing to you from eternity.	Unite with one another all of us who partake of the one bread and the cup into fellowship with the one Holy Spirit; and make none of us to partake of the holy body and blood of your Christ for judgment or for condemnation, but that we may find mercy and grace with all the saints who have been well-pleasing to you ...

Greek Anaphora of John Chrysostom).[27] The idea of 'showing forth' conveyed by the verb ἀναδεῖξαι reflects a change from the earlier epicleses, which were concerned primarily with the eschatological presence of Christ and/or the Spirit experienced in the community's liturgical celebration, towards an 'epiphany' theology of consecration. Now the Spirit is invoked upon the gifts so that they might show forth

---

25 Jasper and Cuming (eds), *Prayers*, p. 71.
26 ET modified from that in Jasper and Cuming (eds), *Prayers*, pp. 119–20, which translates ἀναδεῖξαι (literally 'show [them] to be') as 'make'. Rubrics and phrases thought to be later additions have been omitted. Text commonly left out of later manuscripts is designated by curly brackets. The Greek text of the anaphora can be found in Hänggi, Pahl *et al.*, *Prex Eucharistica*, pp. 230–43.
27 See Brock, 'Invocations to/for the Holy Spirit', pp. 390–1. This phrase also occurs in the institution narrative of some other West Syrian anaphoras. Spinks proposes that these terms 'may have possibly been suggested by interpreting εὐλογήσας of the Gospel narratives of Matthew and Mark as applying to the elements'. Bryan D. Spinks, 'The Consecratory Epiklesis in the Anaphora of St. James', *SL* 11.1 (1976), p. 28.

the presence of Christ.[28] The epiclesis still retains an eschatological orientation, however, in its concern for unity and fellowship with the saints as fruits of communion. Taft identifies the concept of unity as 'the oldest and most basic fruit of eucharistic communion'.[29]

Anaphora of James

The Anaphora of James (JAS) survives in several different languages, with the two main versions being Syriac and Greek. While the Syriac in some places imports Greek terms, it also contains expansions, substitutions and the apparent retention of more primitive forms when compared to the extant Greek text. Regarding the epiclesis, the Greek version of James has a lengthier section requesting the sending of the Spirit upon the people and the gifts than does the Syriac version; in the second part of the epiclesis concerning the consecration of the bread and cup, the Syriac version is longer than the Greek.[30] According to Baumstark's 'laws' of liturgical development, it would seem that the Syriac version represents the earlier text for the first part of the epiclesis and the Greek the more primitive layer for the latter portion. The epiclesis in both versions is introduced by a petition for mercy, followed by the plea for the Father to send the Spirit. This petition is accompanied by a review of the Spirit's role in salvation history parallel to those for the Father and Son in the pre- and post-Sanctus sections, respectively.[31] The detailed attention to

---

28 See Albert Houssiau, 'The Alexandrine Anaphora of St. Basil' in Lancelot C. Sheppard (ed.), *The New Liturgy: A Comprehensive Introduction to the New Liturgy as a Whole and to Its New Calendar, Order of Mass, Eucharistic Prayers, the Roman Canon, Prefaces and the Sunday Lectionary* (London: Darton, Longman & Todd 1970), pp. 239–41; Crockett, *Eucharist*, p. 59; and Bradshaw, *Eucharistic Origins*, p. 156. According to Crockett, the designation of the gifts (just before the epiclesis) as 'likenesses' (ἀντίτυπα) of Christ's body and blood suggests a view 'of the relationship between symbol and reality characteristic of the patristic period' (p. 61).

29 Taft, 'Fruits of Communion', p. 296. See the same article for biblical references drawing out the ethical, communal and eschatological implications of this common theme in early (and modern) anaphoral epicleses.

30 Spinks, 'Consecratory Epiklesis', pp. 21–2. Spinks suggests that the Greek was likely translated into Syriac before the Council of Chalcedon in 451 (i.e. before the doctrinal split between East and West Syrian Christians).

31 For example, even in the shorter version in the Syriac, the Spirit is described as 'the Lord and giver of life, who shares the throne and the kingdom with you, God the Father and your Son, consubstantial and coeternal, who spoke in the law and the prophets and in your new covenant, who descended in the likeness of a dove upon our Lord Jesus Christ in the river Jordan, who descended upon your holy apostles in the likeness of fiery tongues'. Jasper and Cuming (eds), *Prayers*, p. 93. This encomium provides a succinct review of the pneumatology affirmed by the Council of Constantinople in 381. It stresses the divinity and distinct identity of the Spirit, suggesting a late fourth- or early fifth-century date for its

the Spirit's activity likely reflects the concerns of the late fourth century and is more expansive in the Greek version.[32] The anaphora described in *Mystagogical Catecheses* 5 has significant parallels with JAS and likely represents an earlier version of the Jerusalem anaphora; however, since the mystagogue could be paraphrasing sections of the anaphora rather than quoting a liturgical text, the full text of the anaphora underlying it cannot be discerned with certainty.[33] See Table 2.3 for the epicletic texts.[34]

---

composition. For a more extensive discussion of the theology of the epiclesis in JAS, see Baby Varghese, 'The Theological Significance of the Epiklesis in the Liturgy of Saint James' in István Perczel, Réka Forrai and György Geréby (eds), *Eucharist in Theology and Philosophy: Issues of Doctrinal History in East and West from the Patristic Age to the Reformation* (Leuven: Leuven University Press 2005), pp. 363–80 (and pp. 372–5 for more on the encomium of the Spirit).

32 Two characteristics of JAS in particular suggest to Crockett that this anaphora was forged in the crucible of theological controversy. The epiphany language of BAS has given way to production-oriented language concerning the gifts, and the prayer for the communicants (at least in the Greek version) is clearly concerned with the unity of the community as a defence against heresy while unity in God's kingdom has assumed a secondary role. Crockett, *Eucharist*, p. 61.

33 The structure of the anaphora known to the author of these lectures is also a matter of debate. The description of the anaphora does not mention the institution narrative; if the Jerusalem anaphora did not contain the narrative at the time of the text's composition, this would mean that the epiclesis may have directly followed the Sanctus, as in the Egyptian anaphoral tradition. Studies on this point include: Geoffrey J. Cuming, 'Egyptian Elements in the Jerusalem Liturgy', *JTS* 24 (1974), 117–24; Emmanuel J. Cutrone, 'Cyril's Mystagogical Catecheses and the Evolution of the Jerusalem Anaphora', *OCP* 44 (1978), pp. 52–64; Bryan D. Spinks, 'The Jerusalem Liturgy of the Catecheses Mystagogicae: Syrian or Egyptian?', *Studia Patristica* 2 (1989), pp. 391–6; John F. Baldovin, *Liturgy in Ancient Jerusalem* (Bramcote: Grove Books 1989); and Alexis James Doval, *Cyril of Jerusalem, Mystagogue: The Authorship of the Mystagogic Catecheses* (Washington, DC: Catholic University of America Press 2001).

34 ET of Syriac JAS from Spinks, 'Consecratory Epiklesis', pp. 29–31, based on the Syriac text in *Anaphorae Syriacae* II (2nd edn), ed. Odilo Heiming (Rome: Pontifical Oriental Institute, 1953), pp. 138ff. ET of the *Mystagogical Catecheses* from Jasper and Cuming (eds), *Prayers*, pp. 85–6, based on that of F. L. Cross, *St. Cyril of Jerusalem's Lectures on the Christian Sacraments: The Procatechesis and the Five Mystagogical Catecheses* (London: SPCK 1951). For a critical edition, see Cyril of Jerusalem, *Catéchèses Mystagogiques [par] Cyrille de Jérusalem*, ed. Auguste Piédagnel, trans. Pierre Paris (Paris: Cerf 1966). ET of Greek JAS largely from Jasper and Cuming (eds), *Prayers*, p. 93 – with addition concerning encomium of the Spirit from Spinks, 'Consecratory Epiklesis', p. 30; some of the rubrics have been omitted. The Greek text can also be found in Hänggi, Pahl *et al.*, *Prex Eucharistica*, p. 250. As in Spinks, phrases which are shared by Greek and Syriac James (and, where applicable, also by Cyril) are <u>underlined</u> (on the presumption that words common to both versions of JAS and to the *Mystagogical Catecheses* likely comprised part of the epiclesis known to the author of the *Catecheses*). Spinks discusses each of these sections of the epiclesis in greater detail (see pp. 31–5).

Table 2.3 Epicleses of the Anaphora of James and *Mystagogical Catecheses*

Syriac JAS	Mystagogical Catecheses	Greek JAS
Have mercy upon us, O God almighty Father	... we beseech God, lover of man,	Have mercy on us, Lord, God the Father, almighty; have mercy on us, God, our Savior. Have mercy on us, O God, according to your great mercy,
and send [sdr] *upon us and upon these oblations which we have placed* [*before*] *your Holy Spirit* [Encomium of the Spirit, shorter than Greek JAS]	to send forth [ἐξαποστεῖλαι] the Holy Spirit upon the (gifts) set before him	and send out [ἐξαπόστειλον] upon us and upon these holy gifts set before you your all-Holy Spirit [Encomium of the Spirit, longer than Syriac JAS] send down [καταπέμπω], Master, your all-Holy Spirit himself upon us and upon these holy gifts
so *that* overshadowing [*magen*]	that	set before you, that he may descend upon them, and by his holy and good and glorious coming [ἐπιφοιτῆσαν] may sanctify them,
She may make this bread the life-giving body, the redeeming body, the heavenly body, the body which frees our souls and bodies, *the body of* our Lord	he may make [ποιήσῃ] this bread the body of Christ,	and make [ποιήσῃ] this bread the holy body of Christ
and God and Saviour Jesus *Christ*, for the remission of sins and eternal life for those who receive.		

Syriac JAS	Mystagogical Catecheses	Greek JAS
Amen.		Amen.
And the mixture which is in this cup, She may make the blood of the New Testament, the redeeming blood, the life-giving blood, the heavenly blood, the blood which frees our souls and bodies, the blood of our Lord and God and Saviour Jesus Christ for the remission of sins and eternal life for those who receive.	and the wine the blood of Christ; for everything that the Holy Spirit has touched, has been sanctified and changed.	and this cup the precious blood of Christ.
Amen.		Amen.
		The bishop stands up and says privately:
		that they may become to all who partake of them for forgiveness of sins and for eternal life for sanctification of souls and bodies, for strengthening your holy, catholic, and apostolic Church ... rescuing it from every heresy, and from the stumbling blocks of those who work lawlessness ... until the consummation of the age.
		The clerics alone answer: Amen.

The text from *Mystagogical Catecheses*, in which the Spirit is invoked upon the gifts only (and not upon the people), may reflect an older form of the epiclesis in the Jerusalem tradition. The Greek version contains not one but *two* petitions for the sending of the Spirit, using different verbs (first ἐξαποστελλω – paralleled in Syriac JAS – and then καταπέμπω). Spinks postulates that ἐξαποστελλω was the earlier verb in the Jerusalem epiclesis, with καταπέμπω reflecting subsequent Antiochene influence on the text resulting in a fusion of epicletic forms.[35] While JAS shares with BAS the request for the Spirit's descent 'upon us and upon these gifts', the verb in JAS in any case is a form of 'send' rather than 'come' (as in BAS).[36]

The sanctification of the elements is described succinctly in the *Catecheses* and in Greek JAS whereas the Syriac text at this point is enriched with many adjectives to describe the body and blood. The origin of and rationale for this expansion is unclear. The added phrases resemble somewhat the long lists of epithets found in the Syrian *Acts of Thomas*, and there are parallels to such accretions in Greek and Syriac anaphoras.[37] The addition could also have theological motivations, perhaps to underscore the sacramental character of the blessed bread and wine.[38]

The terminology surrounding consecration in all three of these texts suggests a stage of theological development beyond that of the other anaphoras considered thus far. 'Make' is shared by the *Catecheses* and Greek JAS (which precedes this imperative with 'sanctify').[39] In the

---

35 See Spinks, 'Consecratory Epiklesis', pp. 33, 35–6. Spinks also discusses the question of what earlier forms of the Jerusalem epiclesis might have been and how forms of the verbs ἐξαποστελλω and καταπέμπω in *Egyptian* anaphoral texts may reflect the influence of the West Syrian anaphoral tradition (represented by Jerusalem and Antioch respectively) on Egyptian anaphoras between the fourth and seventh centuries. The second epiclesis in the Manchester Papyrus (a sixth-century manuscript which preserves fragments of an early Egyptian anaphora) bears striking resemblance to that of *Mystagogical Catacheses* 5.7, including a form of the verb ἐξαποστελλω. Spinks therefore wonders whether the Manchester Papyrus may contain 'a form of the Jerusalem Epiklesis more primitive than that of Greek and Syriac James' (p. 36).

36 On the relationship between these two anaphoras, see Fenwick, *Anaphoras of St. Basil and St. James*.

37 Spinks, 'Consecratory Epiklesis', p. 35. Another possibility is the modelling of this text after the baptismal epiclesis, possibly of the Byzantine rite, which similarly contains a string of descriptive phrases. The phrase 'for the remission of sins and eternal life' which concludes the parts of the epiclesis related to the bread and wine has parallels with the institution narrative of JAS.

38 Varghese, 'Theological Significance', p. 365.

39 This sort of 'conversionist' language used in relation to the gifts in connection with the epiclesis is attested for the first time in *Mystagogical Catecheses* 5.7. It appears also in the writings of other Greek Church Fathers from the fourth century and in a few anaphoras

Syriac text the Father is asked to send the Spirit, so that, 'overshadowing' (*magen*) the gifts, the Spirit might make the bread the body and the wine the blood of Christ – for the remission of sins and eternal life for those who receive then. Bryan Spinks hypothesizes that *magen* might be 'a technical Epikletic term' from the Syriac milieu, with the Greek parallel (ἐπιφοιτῆσαν) borrowed from elsewhere (as opposed to the Syriac adapting the Greek).[40] The Greek version concludes with a clerical prayer for the fruits of communion, stressing the immediate unity of the communicants as a defence against heresy with a slight nod towards eschatological unity.

Anaphora of St John Chrysostom

The Anaphora of John Chrysostom (CHR) adds little that is new regarding the content of the epiclesis; however, it does include a greater degree of precision about the transformation of the gifts that is requested. God is asked to send the Spirit upon the worshippers and the gifts to make the bread the precious body of Christ and the cup the precious blood of Christ, with the phrase 'changing it [μεταβαλών] by your Holy Spirit' added in each case to the words about the bread and cup. It is interesting to observe that, in this version, it is the Father who both sends the Spirit and makes the bread and wine into the body and blood through the Spirit. The epiclesis concludes with a petition for six fruits of communion – that the gifts might be for sobriety of soul, forgiveness of sins, communion in the Holy Spirit, fullness of the kingdom, and filial confidence before God, and not for judgement or condemnation. Taft sees this set of requests as evidence of 'the pristine core of the original communion epiclesis'.[41]

CHR shares a significant amount of text with the Syriac Anaphora of the Twelve Apostles (a prayer which also borrows text from JAS after the institution narrative). These two prayers may both be derivatives of an

---

which appear to date to this period. See R. J. Halliburton, 'The Patristic Theology of the Eucharist' in Cheslyn Jones, Geoffrey Wainwright, Edward Yarnold and Paul Bradshaw (eds), *The Study of Liturgy* (London and New York: SPCK/Oxford University Press 1992, revised edn), pp. 249–50.

40 Spinks, 'Consecratory Epiklesis', p. 34. *Magen* is from the Syriac root *gn*, which is used in the Peshitta to describe the Spirit's activity, most significantly for the overshadowing of the Spirit in connection with the Incarnation in Luke 1.35. Ἐπιφοιτῆσαν, in contrast, is not a biblical term.

41 Taft, 'Fruits of Communion', p. 279. Taft analyses each of the six fruits in detail on pp. 285–302.

older, unknown source.[42] Brock suggests that the text of the Syriac anaphora is likely closer to that of the lost precursor.[43] See Table 2.4 for the texts of the epicleses.[44]

The Anaphora of the Twelve Apostles appears to retain a more primitive 'epiphany' theology of consecration whereas, as noted above, CHR employs language of 'change' and a greater focus on the elements through the addition of the adjective 'precious' to describe Christ's body and blood. Twelve Apostles does not contain a request for the Spirit's sending upon the people. However, CHR (like BAS and JAS) invokes the descent of the Spirit on both the people and the gifts (in that order).

The communion portion of the epiclesis is more extensive in Twelve Apostles, but some of this (especially the emphasis on forgiveness of sins and the Last Judgement) may be due to influence directly from JAS or indirectly from the wider Syrian tradition. CHR's communion epiclesis contains several features which are not found in Twelve Apostles and which are likewise almost unique in the anaphoral tradition. 'Sobriety [or vigilance] of soul' as a fruit of communion is found only in CHR, in the Syriac Anaphora of Ignatius (which is dependent on CHR) and in the Egyptian Anaphora of St Mark. Unlike many other eucharistic epicleses, the theme of unity is implied but unstated. Finally, the prayer for boldness or 'filial confidence' (*parrhesia*) as a *result of* communion (rather than as an effect of baptism and thus a *prerequisite for* communion) is atypical. The origin of these unique features is unknown, but Taft contends that the possibility that they were part of the common Greek ancestor of CHR and Twelve Apostles cannot be ruled out merely because of their absence from the latter.[45]

---

42 For recent studies of the relationship of these prayers, see John R. K. Fenwick, '*The Missing Oblation': The Contents of the Early Antiochene Anaphora* (Bramcote: Grove Books 1989); Robert F. Taft, 'The Authenticity of the Chrysostom Anaphora Revisited: Determining the Authorship of Liturgical Texts by Computer', *OCP* 56.1 (1990), pp. 5–51; 'Some Structural Problems in the Syriac Anaphora of the Twelve Apostles', *Aram* 5 (1993), pp. 505–20; and 'St. John Chrysostom and the Byzantine Anaphora that Bears His Name' in Paul F. Bradshaw (ed.), *Essays on Early Eastern Eucharistic Prayers*, (Collegeville, MN: Liturgical Press 1997), pp. 195–226.

43 Based on syntax and terminology, there also may be some relationship between the epiclesis of CHR and Twelve Apostles and the epiclesis of the anaphora in *Apostolic Constitutions* 8. See Brock, 'Invocations to/for the Holy Spirit', pp. 386–8 for a more extensive discussion of the epicletic syntax in these prayers and its possible significance.

44 ET of Twelve Apostles from Jasper and Cuming (eds), *Prayers*, p. 127; late additions in angle brackets. ET of CHR from Jasper and Cuming (eds), *Prayers*, p. 133 with later additions in angle brackets and later omissions in square brackets; Greek text in Hänggi, Pahl *et al.*, *Prex Eucharistica*, p. 226.

45 Taft, 'Fruits of Communion', p. 302; on παρρησία, see pp. 299–300.

Table 2.4: Epicleses of the Anaphoras of the Twelve Apostles and Chrysostom

Twelve Apostles	*CHR*
We ask you therefore, almighty Lord and God of the holy powers, falling on our faces before you, that you send your Holy Spirit upon these offerings set before you, and show this bread to be the venerated body of our Lord Jesus Christ, and this cup the blood of our Lord Jesus Christ,	We offer you also this reasonable and bloodless service, and we pray and beseech and entreat you, send down [κατάπεμψον] your Holy Spirit on us and on these gifts set forth; and make this bread the precious body of your Christ, [changing it by your Holy Spirit,] Amen; and that which is in this cup the precious blood of your Christ, changing it by your Holy Spirit, Amen;
that they may be to all who partake of them for life and resurrection, for forgiveness of sins, and health of soul and body, and enlightenment of mind, and defence before the dread judgement-seat of your Christ; and let no one of your people perish, Lord, but make us all worthy that, serving without disturbance and ministering before you at all times of our life, we may enjoy your heavenly and immortal and life-giving mysteries, through your grace and mercy and love for man, now <and to the ages of ages> .	so that they may become to those who partake for vigilance of soul, for fellowship with the Holy Spirit, for the fullness of the kingdom <of heaven> , for boldness toward you, not for judgement or condemnation.

EPICLESES IN EARLY EGYPTIAN ANAPHORAS

Distinguishing features of prayers from the Alexandrian tradition include the situation of the intercessions in the first part of the prayer, preceding the Sanctus, and a tight connection between the Sanctus (lacking the Benedictus) and the epiclesis which immediately follows ('heaven and earth are full of your glory … fill, O God, this sacrifice also …').[46]

---

46 For a more thorough overview of the structure of these prayers, including a discussion of the possible theological rationale for including the intercessions towards the beginning of the anaphora, see Frank C. Senn, *Christian Liturgy: Catholic and Evangelical* (Minneapolis: Fortress Press 1997), pp. 134–5 and also Mazza, *Origins of the Eucharistic*

Sometimes called the '*pleni–vereplenum–imple* structure', it seems to be 'an indigenous characteristic of all extant full anaphoral texts of the Egyptian liturgical tradition'.[47]

The best-known anaphora in this family is the Anaphora of Mark (MARK). The fully developed form of the anaphora is only found in medieval manuscripts which do not predate the thirteenth century.[48] Earlier Greek witnesses to portions of the anaphora include Strasbourg Papyrus 254 (*c.*300–500), which contains part of the opening thanksgiving and the intercessions, concluding with a doxology in the place which the Sanctus would later occupy; this doxology might have concluded the prayer as a whole or just a section of it.[49] A wooden tablet from the eighth century now housed in the British Museum contains the Coptic text of the latter half of the anaphora, picking up at the conclusion of the Sanctus; its text is largely corroborated by a fragmentary Greek papyrus from the sixth century (now in the John Rylands Library, Manchester). The epiclesis following the Sanctus ('Fill this sacrifice with your blessing through your Holy Spirit') is not explicitly consecratory, but the second epiclesis (following the anamnesis and offering) clearly is.[50] The indistinct nature of the pre-institution

---

Prayer, pp. 177ff. The Alexandrine arrangement results in the following structure: Thanksgiving, Intercessions, Sanctus, Epiclesis, Institution Narrative, Anamnesis, Epiclesis, Doxology. Although the anaphora of Sarapion does not have a pneumatic epiclesis following the Sanctus, the 'full–fill' connection is still present, as God is asked at this point to, 'Fill also this sacrifice with your power and with your participation.' For text and translation, see Maxwell E. Johnson, *The Prayers of Sarapion of Thmuis: A Literary, Liturgical, and Theological Analysis* OrChrAn 249 (Rome: Pontifical Oriental Institute 1995), pp. 46–7.

47 Maxwell E. Johnson, 'The Origins of the Anaphoral Use of the Sanctus and Epiclesis Revisited: The Contribution of Gabriele Winkler and Its Implications' in Hans-Jürgen Feulner, Elena Velkovska and Robert F. Taft (eds), *Crossroad of Cultures: Studies in Liturgy and Patristics in Honor of Gabriele Winkler* (Rome: Pontifical Oriental Institute 2000), p. 410. Taft argues that this link makes the Sanctus a more integral part of the Egyptian anaphora than it is elsewhere ('Interpolation of the Sanctus, Part II', p. 118); perhaps the same could be said regarding the integrity of the epiclesis connected to the Sanctus in this location. There would seem to be a good argument in this case for the Sanctus and epiclesis either growing together in this tradition at a very early date or having been incorporated as a unit into Egyptian anaphoras.

48 Jasper and Cuming (eds), *Prayers*, pp. 57.

49 For an overview of this manuscript and associated scholarly debates about its content, see Bradshaw, *Eucharistic Origins*, pp. 131–3. The Greek text can be found in Hänggi, Pahl *et al.*, *Prex Eucharistica*, pp. 116ff.

50 See Jasper and Cuming (eds), *Prayers*, pp. 54–5; Greek text in Hänggi, Pahl *et al.*, *Prex Eucharistica*, pp. 120ff. A more detailed discussion of MARK and its precursors can be found in Geoffrey J. Cuming, *The Liturgy of St. Mark* (Rome: Pontifical Oriental Institute 1990).

epiclesis is preserved in Greek MARK but developed in an overtly consecratory direction in Coptic MARK.[51]

The epicleses of MARK and other early witnesses to the Egyptian tradition (the Barcelona Papyrus, the Louvain Coptic Papyrus and the Dêr Balyzeh Papyrus) will be discussed further in a later chapter in connection with what they may reveal about the so-called 'split epiclesis' in the Alexandrian liturgical tradition. For the moment, it should be noted that the verb used for 'send' in Greek MARK is ἐξαπόστειλον – as in Greek JAS. This may suggest that the text at this point has been influenced by the Jerusalem liturgy, whose characteristic epicletic verb seems to have been a form of ἐξαποστέλλω (as in both Greek JAS and *Mystagogical Catecheses* 5.7).[52]

Several aspects of the second epiclesis suggest a later date, including the extensive *Heilsgeschichte* of the Spirit that reflects the consensus opinion emerging from the Trinitarian controversies of the fourth century. So does the multiplication of verbs used to describe the Holy Spirit's action with regard to the gifts: *gignomai* (become), *hagiazo* (sanctify), *teleiow* (perfect/consecrate) and *poiew* (make), with the resultant juxtaposition of eucharistic theologies reflecting the interaction of different currents of thought and the shift towards a more articulated theology of consecration than is found in very early anaphoras. Nonetheless, the developed form of MARK also contains several features that may be vestiges of an earlier layer of tradition.

> The epiclesis begins with the phrase 'Look on us,' which immediately orients it toward the community. Moreover, the bread and wine are not described as objects, but as food and drink (loaves and cups), which reflects early tradition. The gifts are also specifically linked with the act of communion in the phrase 'that they may become to all of us who partake of them . . .'[53]

Another text from Egypt which is of particular interest for the question of epicletic origins is the anaphora found in a collection of prayers attributed to Sarapion of Thmuis (*c.*350), which contains the sole surviving incontrovertible example of a Logos epiclesis in a eucharistic

---

51 For the Greek text, see Hänggi, Pahl *et al.*, *Prex Eucharistica*, pp. 102ff.
52 Spinks, 'Consecratory Epiklesis', pp. 26–7. The Vatican and Messian manuscripts have variant readings (ἐπιδε, ἐφιδε) that may preserve an earlier form of the text.
53 Crockett, *Eucharist*, pp. 60–1.

prayer.[54] Like other Egyptian anaphoras, it contains an epiclesis following the Sanctus and a second invocation later in the prayer. Sarapion's second epiclesis occurs immediately after the institution narrative (which contains offering language interspersed among the two sections concerning the bread and cup and is not followed by a distinct anamnesis separating the narrative from the epiclesis). Neither of these invocations involves the Spirit, but the second mentions the Logos:

1 Fill also this sacrifice with your power [δυναμέως] and with your participation [μεταλήφεως].
2 God of truth, let your holy Word [λόγος] come [ἐπιδημησάτω] upon the bread in order that the bread may become body of the Word, and upon this cup in order that that cup may become blood of truth.[55]

Out of the four occurrences of 'holy Spirit' in this anaphora, two occur in a petition *preceding* the introduction to the Sanctus: 'Give us holy Spirit, in order that we may be able to proclaim and describe your inexpressible mysteries. Let the Lord Jesus speak in us and let holy Spirit also hymn you through us.'[56] Bryan Spinks has argued that the Sanctus–epiclesis

---

54 On the scholarly debates over the theological orthodoxy of Sarapion's epiclesis and the question of whether its text represents the reproduction of an archaic form (from the standpoint of the mid-fourth century) or a deliberate liturgical innovation (perhaps the work of a later author or editor with semi-Arian or Pneumatomachian tendencies) to downplay the role of the Spirit, see Johnson, *Prayers of Sarapion*, pp. 234–52. These ideas are reviewed and revisited in subsequent essays; cf. Maxwell E. Johnson, 'The Archaic Nature of the Sanctus, Institution Narrative, and Epiclesis of the Logos in the Anaphora Ascribed to Sarapion of Thmuis' in Paul F. Bradshaw (ed.), *Essays on Early Eastern Eucharistic Prayers* (Collegeville, MN: Liturgical Press 1997), pp. 73–107 and 'Origins of the Anaphoral Sanctus', pp. 418–20. Sarapion corresponded with Athanasius on the matter of the Spirit's divinity; see Athanasius, *Epistulae IV ad Serapionem Episcopum Thmuitanum* (*c*.359–60) in *PG* 26.529–676. Given this context, Senn supposes that, 'His concern about this [matter] undoubtedly led him to mention the Holy Spirit four times in this relatively brief anaphora. If there had existed a tradition of invoking the Holy Spirit on the gifts, Serapion would have been the last person to ignore it in favor of the invocation of the Logos.' Senn, *Christian Liturgy*, p. 136.
55 Greek text and ET of the anaphora can be found in Johnson, *Prayers of Sarapion*, pp. 46–51. The first epiclesis is inserted between the thanksgiving and offering sections of a prayer which resembles the content of the Strasbourg papyrus. Johnson, 'Archaic Nature of the Sanctus', p. 673. For this and for other reasons, Sarapion's prayer may be another precursor of the developed form of MARK. Johnson, 'Origins of the Anaphoral Use of the Sanctus', p. 413.
56 Johnson, *Prayers of Sarapion*, p. 47. On this passage, Johnson remarks: 'although ὑμνησάτω is a singular third-person imperative and calls for a singular subject, the sense of this phrase seems to be "let the Lord Jesus and holy Spirit speak in us and hymn you through us"'. Cf. the ET from Jasper and Cuming (eds), *Prayers*, p. 76. Although the

unit was in place prior to the emergence of Sarapion's anaphora and that its use in the Egyptian tradition was not directly related to the use of the Sanctus in Antiochene anaphoras.[57] More recently, he proposed a parallel between Jewish and Gnostic invocations in Nag Hammadi texts and the Egyptian Greek magic tradition and the post-Sanctus epiclesis of Sarapion, which invokes God's power and participation after reciting the divine name in the Sanctus.[58] This suggestion has interesting parallels with Winkler's hypothesis concerning the development of the Sanctus and epiclesis as a unit in the Antiochene tradition based on evidence from the apocryphal *Acts* (although her proposal is that invocations *culminate* in doxologies and eventually the Sanctus, rather than invocations flowing from the Sanctus as in Sarapion).[59]

Maxwell Johnson suggests in passing that the close connection between the Logos and Spirit in Athanasius' theology might illumine the theological meaning of the post-Sanctus epiclesis in Sarapion. Athanasius noted that the Spirit sanctifies human persons, is the 'power' (δύναμις) that animates the Son, and is 'participated in' (*metaschomen*) by the Christian community. According to Johnson, this might 'render intelligible Sarapion's request for the filling of the sacrifice with God's

---

resemblance may be coincidental, this passage may have some connection, at least conceptually, to the following passage from the *Mystagogical Catecheses* which the mystagogue uses as a transition between discussion of the Sanctus and epiclesis: 'Then, having sanctified ourselves with these spiritual hymns, we beseech God, the lover of man, to send forth the Holy Spirit upon the gifts . . .' (ET from Jasper and Cuming (eds), *Prayers*, p. 85). If the 'hymning' in both cases is a reference to the Sanctus, this unit in Sarapion (but not in the *Mystagogical Catecheses*) corresponds in its general outline to the pattern which Winkler has recently proposed for the emergence of the epiclesis – an invocation of the Spirit enmeshed in a doxology which culminates in the Sanctus.

57 Bryan D. Spinks, 'A Complete Anaphora? A Note on Strasbourg Gr. 254', *Heythrop Journal* 25 (1984), p. 52. Earlier, Anton Baumstark had argued that the more original location of the anaphoral Logos epiclesis in the Egyptian tradition was in this post-Sanctus location (rather than after the institution narrative), with the result being a single contiguous prayer for the sanctification of the Eucharist. In MARK, the post-Sanctus invocation for the Logos has been reworked into a Spirit epiclesis; in Sarapion, another type of invocation altogether now appears at this juncture. See A. Baumstark, 'Die Anaphora von Thmuis und ihre Überarbeitung durch den h.l. Serapion', *Römische Quartalschrift* 18 (1904), pp. 134–5 and Johnson, *Prayers of Sarapion*, p. 688. It is interesting to note that this arrangement (i.e. a post-Sanctus Logos epiclesis) would have placed an epiclesis that could have been interpreted as 'consecratory' *before* the institution narrative – a view that would likely have proved popular in Western circles during the first half of the twentieth century.

58 Spinks, *Sanctus in the Eucharistic Prayer*, pp. 90–3.

59 See above, p. 47.

δυναμέως and μεταλήψεως in the first petition as an implicit petition for the Holy Spirit'.[60]

Mary K. Farag has recently challenged such readings of δύναμις in liturgical texts based on a close reading of the role of δύναμις in the theological writings of Athanasius, claiming that:

As the texts stand, they make no unequivocal statement as to the underlying referent, if any, to the 'power' they request, and, thus, an interpretive move must be made: an act of exegesis. Up to the present, the unanimous interpretive move of scholars has been to understand 'power' as Holy Spirit without any grounds to undergird such exegesis. Athanasius' use of 'power,' however, provides clear grounds for making an alternative interpretive move: understanding 'power' as the Son.[61]

Therefore, texts such as the Sanctus epiclesis in Sarapion's anaphora are not implicit references to the Spirit, but underscore the crucial role of the

---

60 Johnson, 'Archaic Nature of the Sanctus', p. 687; cf. Athanasius, *Orationes contra Arianos* I–II (pp. 339–40). (See Johnson, pp. 686–7 for a list of passages in Athanasius which appear to connect Logos and Spirit.) In a later article, Johnson wonders whether this could be, along the lines of Winkler's understanding of the power behind the 'Name' in early Syrian invocations, 'an implicit invocation of the Spirit as the "hidden power" Herself?' Johnson, 'Origins of the Anaphoral Use of the Sanctus', p. 440.
61 Mary K. Farag, 'Δύναμις Epicleses: An Athanasian Perspective', *SL* 39.1 (2009), p. 75. In addition to the post-Sanctus epiclesis in Sarapion's anaphora, Farag also challenges Winkler's assumption that the 'hidden power' underlying the 'name of the Messiah' is the Spirit, based on the same reasoning. (For more on the concept of 'hidden power', see Jarl Fossum, 'Jewish-Christian Christology and Jewish Mysticism', *VC* 37.3 (1983), pp. 260–87.) Drawing on the work of Michel René Barnes (*The Power of God: Δύναμις in Gregory of Nyssa's Trinitarian Theology* (Washington, DC: Catholic University of America Press 2001)), Farag argues that 'Power' without further qualification is a unique designation for the Son that underscores Christ's divinity and co-equality with God; furthermore, Athanasius is careful not to conflate the titles of the Son and Spirit in his Trinitarian analogies. Therefore, 'Athanasius' use of δύναμις with respect to the Spirit is . . . twofold. On the one hand, "the power of the Spirit" works within creation to draw it to the Son and the Father via divinization and participation. On the other hand, "the Spirit of Power" is a title by which the Spirit may be called, since the Son is Power and the Spirit is in the Son. Note that such a twofold distinction is merely a matter of contextual use . . . [W]hile it does not contradict the later clear insistence of Gregory of Nyssa, Gregory of Nazianzus, and Basil of Caesarea that "the power of the Spirit is included in the power of the Father and Son," [quoting Barnes, *Power of God*, p. 298] it also does not assume such a concept. That is to say, whereas the Cappadocians' theologies of the Holy Spirit imply that the Holy Spirit, too, is the Power of God in the same sense that Christ is the Power of God, Athanasius' theology simply does not arrive at such an inference.' Farag, 'Δύναμις Epicleses', pp. 67–72, quote from p. 72.

concept of 'Christ the Power of God' (cf. 1 Cor. 1.24) in the theological controversies of the fourth century.[62] If Farag is correct that the invocation of power in this epiclesis should be read as an invocation for the Son, this would lead to the interesting possibility that the Sanctus epiclesis in Sarapion would then resemble the *maranatha* invocation of 1 Corinthians and the *Didache* – insofar as it could then be read as a plea for Christ's presence in the midst of the worshipping community.

However, much would seem to hinge on whether Athanasius' theology on this point is conservative or innovative. Liturgical texts (and apparently Sarapion's anaphora in particular) tend to be conservative. Even though Sarapion and Athanasius were contemporaries, Sarapion was likely editing a received text rather than articulating current theological trends (or, depending on the age of the text he received, even concepts emerging from the doctrinal controversies of the first half of the fourth century). If there was a tradition going back further than this, in some places, of referring to the power of the Spirit – that is, if such an idea might predate the Trinitarian debates of the fourth century – the Athanasian perspective need not, necessarily, decide the question of how Sarapion's Sanctus epiclesis should be interpreted. Finally, even if the Athanasian reading holds sway for *Egyptian* sources, the question remains of how universally applicable this interpretation would have been in the mid-fourth century – especially if Syrian epicleses might have influenced Egyptian epicleses (rather than vice versa).

In his studies of Sarapion's euchologion, Maxwell Johnson argues for the traditional dating of these prayers to the mid-fourth century (or perhaps even earlier). The Logos epiclesis may be a relatively late addition to an earlier anaphoral core, but it nonetheless appears to conserve potentially early prayer patterns and theological concepts.[63] Although there are no early liturgical texts that corroborate the existence of a

---

62 Farag, 'Δύναμις Epicleses', p. 79. The only known eucharistic prayers that include a δύναμις epiclesis are the Sanctus epiclesis of Sarapion and the partial prayer preserved in the British Museum tablet (in the second epiclesis). If other Egyptian anaphoras took Sarapion's as a starting point, they apparently did not incorporate the idea of δύναμις into their epicleses. While δύναμις is not widely attested outside the Egyptian anaphoral tradition, Farag draws attention to two Syrian epicleses (those of Twelve Apostles and the Anaphora of Theodore) that *mention* power and are thus potentially related, perhaps, she proposes, through 'subtle' Egyptian influence. See Farag, 'Δύναμις Epicleses', pp. 72ff. Beyond suggesting some possible Egyptian influence, Farag does not make a case for why an Athanasian or *Alexandrian* perspective would necessarily provide the interpretative key to *Syrian* texts emerging from a milieu where focus on the Spirit's activity from an early time period seems more prevalent than for the Egyptian tradition.
63 Johnson, 'Archaic Nature of the Sanctus', pp. 701–2.

eucharistic Logos epiclesis in Egypt around this time, there is no evidence either that attests that a pneumatic epiclesis was already established in Egyptian anaphoras prior to the mid-fourth century. There are, however, some suggestions that the Logos could be understood as enacting the Incarnation and as the 'content' of the Eucharist. Therefore,

> What Sarapion expresses in a liturgical form is consistent with an archaic christological understanding, a theology of the λόγος as old as Justin Martyr and still operative to some extent in Athanasius. This, of course, does not prove the existence of a λόγος epiclesis prior to Sarapion's anaphora. But, given the content and theology of his sanctus unit, the possible archaic shape of the eucharist reflected in his bi-partite institution narrative, and the possible parallels to the development of the baptismal epicleses in the Syriac tradition, the most logical conclusion is that the epiclesis of the λόγος also represents the preservation, or at least the remnant, of an earlier euchological form. That all of this would change in the light of both further anaphoral development and greater attention to the role of the Holy Spirit in relation to the incarnation and the eucharist, is exactly what one would expect to happen in the later Egyptian tradition.[64]

The first definite reference to a eucharistic invocation of the *Spirit* in the Egyptian tradition comes from Peter II (373–80), Athanasius' immediate successor as bishop of Alexandria. If the textual reference from the mid-fifth century accurately reflects the fourth-century context in which it supposedly originated, a pneumatic epiclesis may have been a recent introduction to the Egyptian tradition at that time. Furthermore, even after an invocation of the Holy Spirit was certainly incorporated into the Alexandrian anaphora, theologians such as Cyril of Alexandria (d. 444)

---

64 Johnson, *Prayers of Sarapion*, p. 253. Athanasius of Alexandria's (295–373) theology of the Eucharist, as presented by Eutychius (patriarch of Constantinople 552–65 and 577–82), *may* suggest that a Logos epiclesis was a part of the anaphora he knew; alternatively, he could be making a theological point which did not have explicit liturgical articulation. Athanasius supposedly said: 'as soon as the great prayers and holy supplications have been sent up, the Logos comes down upon the bread and the chalice, and it becomes his body' (*PG* 86.2.2401 AB). See Johnson, *Prayers of Sarapion*, pp. 241–2. Other possible references to an early epiclesis of the Logos are discussed in Johnson, *Prayers of Sarapion*, pp. 247–51 and Taft, 'From Logos to Spirit', pp. 491, 494–6. The ET of the 'Athanasius' text quoted above is from Taft, p. 495. In that same place, Taft observes that 'it is to the Logos that the earlier texts usually assign the role of sanctifier in the eucharist'.

can still conceive of the Logos as the primary actor and 'power' (δύναμις) behind eucharistic consecration.[65]

Johnson also argues for an early date for the epiclesis on comparative liturgical grounds, working with Brock's suggestion that the verb 'come' reflects an earlier layer of the Syrian tradition than 'send'. Johnson notes that neither the post-Sanctus nor the post-narrative invocation in Sarapion's anaphora employs the verb 'send' and that the Logos epiclesis uses a form of 'come' (ἐπιδημησάτω). Noting that parallels exist between Egyptian and Syrian rites of initiation, Johnson wonders whether something similar might have occurred in the case of the Eucharist as well. Thus Sarapion's Logos epiclesis in the anaphora 'may well represent an early stage in the development of the Egyptian epiclesis, a stage which preserves both an archaic verb form and an archaic theology of the role of the λόγος in the sacramental rites of the Church'.[66]

Meanwhile, Gabriele Winkler has challenged translations of the verb in Sarapion's Logos epiclesis on the ground that the Latin translation (*adveniat*) in *Prex Eucharistica* and English translations which render the verb with some form of 'come' create the illusion of a Syrian parallel where none exists. The verb ἐπιδημέω has a complex range of meanings – 'coming' in the sense of coming home, coming by or coming to rest in.[67] Given her conviction that the Syrian form of the epiclesis, exemplified first by the invocations in the *Acts of Thomas*, is earlier and that the emergence of an overtly consecratory epiclesis before the end of the fourth century is unlikely, Winkler implicitly discounts the possibility that Sarapion's anaphora could be an important source for deciphering the origins of the eucharistic epiclesis.[68] Even before Winkler's reassessment of the early evidence Spinks hypothesized that the term ἐπιδημέω which characterizes the Egyptian tradition 'may represent a stage of development beyond that of "Come" and may in fact preserve in one word the ideas found in the East Syrian Anaphoras – come, rest, and dwell'.[69]

---

65 See Johnson, *Prayers of Sarapion*, pp. 242–6.
66 Johnson, *Prayers of Sarapion*, pp. 251–2, quote from p. 252.
67 Spinks lists an even broader range of meanings: 'come home, go home, go to dwell permanently, come to reside in, come upon, visit, dwell'. Spinks, 'Consecratory Epiklesis', p. 26.
68 See Gabriele Winkler, 'Nochmals zu den Anfängen der Epiklese und des Sanctus im Eucharistischen Hochgebet', *Theologische Quartalschrift* 174.3 (1994), pp. 218–20 and Johnson, 'Origins of the Anaphoral Use of the Sanctus', pp. 429–30. Winkler may be especially inclined to dismiss Sarapion's testimony to a *Logos* epiclesis because it does not fit easily into her paradigm of epicletic development, which argues that the Syrian epiclesis was an invocation addressed to the Spirit from the very beginning.
69 Spinks, 'Consecratory Epiklesis', p. 26.

Johnson concedes that a translation which conveys the sense of the Logos coming to reside or dwell in the gifts might better reflect the evidence and that the consecratory aim which seems to underlie Sarapion's Logos epiclesis is likely a secondary development. However, he claims that this does not negate the possibility that there could be *some* connection between this text and the early Syrian tradition.[70] First, even if early Syrian eucharistic epicleses constituted direct appeal to the Holy Spirit to 'come', 'this does not rule out the antiquity of invoking the Logos elsewhere, especially within the early *Greek* liturgical tradition'.[71] Second, while neither the post-Sanctus nor the post-narrative epicleses of Sarapion contain the exact equivalent of the Syriac imperative form, 'come', it is also true that neither of them uses the verb 'send' which became characteristic of the later Alexandrian tradition exemplified by MARK. Furthermore, the second epiclesis occupies the position in the anaphora where the consecratory pneumatic epiclesis will eventually reside in the developed forms of Antiochene anaphoras. Third, among the baptismal texts in Sarapion's euchologion is an epiclesis of the Logos that features a form of the verb κατέρχομαι, which is clearly derived from ἔρχομαι – a possible parallel to the transitional stage in the Syrian tradition where the direct imperative 'come' yielded to 'let come' or 'may come' before 'send' was introduced via later Greek influence.[72] Last, the verb associated with Sarapion's Logos epiclesis, ἐπιδημέω, *does* occur as part of the invocation of prebaptismal oil in the Greek *Acts of Thomas* 157.

Therefore, according to Johnson, it is possible 'that in spite of the absence of the Logos in the early Syrian liturgical sources, it is Sarapion's epiclesis of the Logos that has preserved some remnant of that early tradition in Egypt, albeit within a world of thought so conceptually and theologically distinct'.[73] Some connection between early Egyptian and Syrian sources could help to explain one point that Winkler's theory by

---

70 For what follows, see Johnson, *Prayers of Sarapion*, pp. 438–40.
71 Johnson, 'Origins of the Anaphoral Use of the Sanctus', p. 438, his emphasis.
72 In fact, ἔρχομαι appears often in Greek translations of Syrian sources. However, Brock has written on this point: 'The presence of καταπχέσθω in a baptismal invocation (to the Logos) in Serapion's Euchologion might at first be thought to provide an Egyptian witness to the use of "come" rather than "send"; the compound element κατ-, however, indicates that this is not the case, and in fact the use of "come down" rather than "come" rather strongly disassociates this invocation from usage in the Syrian/Syriac area, since "come down" is rare, occurring in a single late Syriac eucharistic epiclesis and only occasionally elsewhere.' Brock, 'Invocations to/for the Holy Spirit', p. 381.
73 Johnson, 'Origins of the Anaphoral Use of the Sanctus', p. 440.

itself cannot. If Winkler wants to maintain a close connection between the Sanctus and the epiclesis in the evolution of the anaphoral epiclesis, Egypt would seem to be one region where this tradition remained very much intact, suggesting either that this came about independently of developments elsewhere or that it was the result of very early influence *from* elsewhere – perhaps Syria.

THE EPICLESES OF *APOSTOLIC TRADITION* AND RELATED TEXTS

Once almost unanimously attributed to Hippolytus of Rome and assigned a date in the early third century, recent scholarship has reopened the question of *Apostolic Tradition*'s authorship and provenance. None of the surviving texts appear to predate the last few decades of the fourth century. It is quite likely that its contents, in whole and in part, represent a composite text drawing upon material from different time periods and traditions.[74] This appears to be true of the model eucharistic prayer provided for the occasion of an episcopal ordination in *Apostolic Tradition* 4 as well as of its epiclesis. The oldest (Latin) version of the text contains this epiclesis following the institution narrative, anamnesis and oblation:

> And we ask that you would send [*mittas*] your Holy Spirit in the oblation of [your] holy church, [that] gathering [them] into one you will give to all who partake of the holy things [to partake] in the fullness of the Holy Spirit, for the strengthening of faith in truth, that we may praise and glorify you through your Child Jesus Christ . . .[75]

Enrico Mazza has suggested that the second part of the epiclesis, oriented towards the unity of the communicants and their sharing in the Spirit, is older than the first part which requests the sending of the Spirit upon the church's oblation (a sending whose direct expected effects are not

---

74 See Paul F. Bradshaw, *The Search for the Origins of Christian Worship: Sources and Methods for the Study of Early Liturgy* (New York: Oxford University Press), pp. 81–3 and Paul F. Bradshaw, Maxwell E. Johnson and L. Edward Phillips, *The Apostolic Tradition: A Commentary* (Minneapolis: Fortress Press 2002).

75 ET from Bradshaw, Johnson and Phillips, *Apostolic Tradition*, p. 40. The Latin text reads: 'Et petimus, ut mittas spiritam tuum sanctam in oblationem sanctae ecclesiae; in unum congregans des omnibus qui percipient sanctis in repletionem spiritus sancti ad confirmationem fidei in veritate, ut te laudemus et glorificemus per puerum tuum Iesum Christum . . .' Text from Erik Tidner (ed.), *Didascaliae Apostolorum Canonum Ecclesiasticorum Traditionis Apostolicae Versiones Latinae*, Texte und Untersuchungen zur Geschichte der altchristlichen Literatur 75 (Berlin: Akademie-Verlag 1963), pp. 125–6.

expressed).[76] The concern for the Spirit's presence in the gifts may have migrated into the older core of the anaphora along with the anamnesis and oblation portions; the first and the second parts of the epiclesis are rather inelegantly joined, suggesting a possible textual seam at this point.[77] In Taft's opinion, it is at least possible that 'a rudimentary Spirit communion epiclesis' such as the one found in this text *could have* existed prior to the latter half of the fourth century – although perhaps it was not precise enough to serve as an adequate apology for the role of the Spirit in the Eucharist in the theological debates of the fourth century, or perhaps the text had not achieved wide circulation by this point[78] – leaving aside the question of whether it was ever actually used in this form in liturgical celebrations. Recently, Matthieu Smyth suggested that *Apostolic Tradition* contains, at least in nascent form, most of the hallmarks of what will become the West Syrian anaphora pattern. Although the pneumatic epiclesis does ask the Father to 'send' the Spirit, it is otherwise relatively underdeveloped theologically.[79]

If the Greek form of the Spirit epiclesis with a definite orientation towards communion is first seen in *Apostolic Tradition* 4, the studies of Winkler and Brock could further illuminate the role of the epiclesis in this text. The fact that God is asked to 'send' the Holy Spirit could lead one to suspect that the epiclesis is a fourth-century interpolation. An early date for this section of the text is problematic not because it contains a pneumatic epiclesis but because the form of the address (i.e.

---

76 Even so, 'oblation' here probably refers to the wider context of the eucharistic celebration in its entirety as an 'offering', a communion-sacrifice of praise, rather than a specific focus on the elements. This could help interpret the linkage in this text between the invocation on the offering and the prayer for communicants. See Crockett, *Eucharist*, p. 58 and McKenna, *Eucharistic Epiclesis*, pp. 8–9.

77 See Mazza, *Origins of the Eucharistic Prayer*, pp. 169–74.

78 Taft, 'From Logos to Spirit', p. 498. Some prior arguments that the epiclesis in *Apostolic Tradition* was a late interpolation were based on circular logic: 'if such an epiclesis could not have existed before midfourth century, and if Apostolic Tradition is an early third-century text (ca. 215), then, ineluctably, its Spirit epiclesis must be a later interpolation' (p. 497). The existence of just *one* such text of an early date that did contain a Spirit epiclesis would render this sort of claim moot. Some sources prior to the fourth century, such as the *Didascalia Apostolorum* from the early third century, do seem to reflect on the role of the Holy Spirit in the Church's ministry, including the Eucharist (see 4.21–22).

79 Matthieu Smyth, 'The Anaphora of the So-Called "Apostolic Tradition" and the Roman Eucharistic Prayer' in Maxwell E. Johnson (ed.), *Issues in Eucharistic Praying in East and West: Essays in Liturgical and Theological Analysis* (Collegeville, MN: Liturgical Press 2010), pp. 94–5. Smyth places the final redaction of the anaphora during the first half of the fourth century.

directed to God the Father using the verb 'send') seems to be of a relatively late date in the development of Greek eucharistic theology.[80]

While *Apostolic Tradition* may have exercised more direct influence on liturgical practice in the twentieth century than it ever did prior to this, it did leave its mark on several other church orders from the fourth and fifth centuries. Book 8 of the *Apostolic Constitutions* (a composite work produced in Syria *c*.375–80) draws upon the *Apostolic Tradition* and material from elsewhere, greatly adapting what it borrowed from its sources.[81] The epiclesis of the lengthy anaphora in Book 8 shares with the epiclesis of *Apostolic Tradition* the request for the sending of the Spirit, although the immediate object of the Spirit's sending seems to be more narrowly understood as the eucharistic gifts. The epiclesis is also more clearly consecratory in intent. Like *Apostolic Tradition*, the prayer for the communicants is that those who partake of the gifts be filled with the Holy Spirit and strengthened in faith. The epiclesis is otherwise greatly expanded:

> And we beseech you that you would look graciously upon these gifts set here before you – though you, O God, lack nothing – and approve of them for the honour of your Christ, and send [καταπέμψης] your Holy Spirit upon this sacrifice [θυσίαν], the witness of the sufferings of the Lord Jesus, that he may make [ἀποφήνη] this bread the body of your Christ and this cup the blood of your Christ, so that those who partake may become pious with confidence, gain forgiveness of their sins, be rescued from the Devil and his erring, be filled with the Holy Spirit, become worthy of your Christ and obtain eternal life, after being reconciled with you, eternal Lord.[82]

The description of the Holy Spirit as the 'witness' of Christ's sufferings seems to be based on 1 Peter 5.1, and the purpose of the Spirit's sending

---

80 Johnson, 'Origins of the Anaphoral Use of the Sanctus', p. 434. Since *Apostolic Tradition* has been preserved in languages other than Greek, it is unclear what the Greek equivalent of *mittas* in the Latin text might have been; καταπέμψης has been proposed – which is the verb used in the related document *Apostolic Constitutions* – as has ἀποστείλης, which is not attested in this group of texts. Spinks suggests that a form of καταπέμπω, as in *Apostolic Constitutions*, could be an epicletic verb from the Antiochene milieu. See Spinks, 'Consecratory Epiklesis', pp. 32–3.

81 For an overview of this church order, see Bradshaw, *Search for the Origins*, pp. 84–6.

82 ET from Bridget Nichols and Alistair MacGregor, *The Eucharistic Epiclesis*, Ushaw Library Publications 4 (Durham: Ushaw College Library 2001), p. 1; Greek text in Hänggi, Pahl *et al.*, *Prex Eucharistica*, p. 92.

is to manifest or show (*apophene*) the gifts as Christ's body and blood.[83] The mention of the devil is highly unusual, perhaps unique, among epicletic texts.[84]

The *Testamentum Domini*, a church order now surviving only in Syriac and probably dating to the early fifth (or perhaps late fourth) century, includes much of the content of *Apostolic Tradition* but expands its text with the insertion of a considerable amount of additional material. The redactor(s) did not, however, add the Sanctus to *Apostolic Tradition*, although some intercessions have been added between the epiclesis and concluding doxology. The text includes a form of the epiclesis that seems to be a paraphrase of *Apostolic Tradition*'s, sidestepping the sort of grammatical difficulties attested in the Latin version of that text.[85] The text of the main epicletic section now reads:

> We offer to you this act of thanksgiving, eternal Trinity, Lord Jesus Christ, Lord Father, from whom all creation and all nature trembles as it flees into itself. Lord, send your Holy Spirit upon this drink and upon this your holy food. Grant that it may not be for us condemnation nor ignomy nor destruction, but for the healing and strength of our spirit.[86]

The opening invocation to the Trinity is unusual, as is the inverted arrangement of the elements – first 'drink', then 'food'. Nichols and MacGregor note that the address to the 'eternal Trinity' is followed by the explicit naming of only two of the three divine persons, which suggests to them 'that the doctrine of the Trinity which underpins this epiclesis had not been fully worked out at the time of its composition'.[87] Beyond the identification of the elements as food and drink, there is no mention of the communicants sharing in them, although the concept of the gifts being 'for us' highlights the expected fruits of communion.

---

83 Senn, *Christian Liturgy*, p. 123.
84 Nichols and MacGregor, *Eucharistic Epiclesis*, p. 1.
85 Jasper and Cuming (eds), *Prayers*, p. 138. For an overview of the *Testamentum Domini* as a whole, see Bradshaw, *Search for the Origins*, pp. 86–7. For debates on whether the epiclesis was an original component of the *Testamentum Domini* (a line of reasoning sometimes used to cast doubt on the existence of an epiclesis in *Apostolic Tradition*), see Louis Bouyer, *Eucharist: Theology and Spirituality of the Eucharistic Prayer*, trans. C. U. Quinn from the 2nd French edition (1968) (Notre Dame, IN: University of Notre Dame Press 1968), pp. 170–7.
86 ET from Nichols and MacGregor, *Eucharistic Epiclesis*, p. 1.
87 Nichols and MacGregor, *Eucharistic Epiclesis*, p. 2.

After a series of intercessions comes a passage resembling the latter section of the epiclesis of *Apostolic Tradition*, which leads into the prayer's concluding doxology:

> ... but grant that all who partake and receive of your holy things may be united to you so that they may be filled with the Holy Spirit for the strengthening of faith in truth; that they may always lift up a doxology to you and your beloved Son Jesus Christ, through whom be glory and might to you with your holy Spirit to the ages of ages. Amen.[88]

If both of these sections are taken together, 'the epiclesis asks that God unite those partaking to himself so that they may be filled with the Holy Spirit for the confirmation of their faith in truth so that, in turn, they may glorify the Trinity'.[89] This doxology would then form a fitting inclusio to the opening address of the epiclesis to the Trinity.

EARLY EASTERN EPICLESES: VARIANT FORMS AND THEIR GEOGRAPHICAL AND TEMPORAL DISTRIBUTION

The above discussion corroborates Brock's conclusion (based on his examination of a number of West Syrian anaphoras) that the eucharistic epiclesis is 'a very complex organism whose syntactical structure can vary a great deal from one anaphora to another'.[90] However, the question remains open as to whether this variation depends most on time, on geography, or on a combination of both factors.[91] Table 2.5 presents the primary verb associated with the eucharistic invocation of the Holy Spirit in the anaphoras discussed in this chapter – with additional verbs related directly to the immediate effect of the Spirit's coming or sending as such (rather than in relation to the gifts or the people specifically) noted where applicable. While the dating and provenance of some of the texts discussed is uncertain (and thus their relative arrangement below should

---

88 Jasper and Cuming (eds), *Prayers*, p. 141.
89 McKenna, *Eucharistic Epiclesis*, p. 11.
90 Brock, 'Invocations to/for the Holy Spirit', p. 382.
91 Spinks has suggested that 'the terminology found in most Greek and West Syrian anaphoras may represent not so much a geographical variant as yet a further stage of development'. Spinks, 'Consecratory Epiklesis', p. 27. Brock, on the other hand, considers geography a more important factor while also noting the importance of time. He thinks that the verb 'come' in BAS 'indicates that we are not dealing with a difference in usage that is based on language (i.e. "send" representing Greek, and "come" Syriac usage); rather, it is a matter of geography and (to some extent) of time'. Brock, 'Invocations to/for the Holy Spirit', p. 381.

Table 2.5: Verbs associated with the invocation of the Holy Spirit in early anaphoras

	East Syria	West Syria	Egypt	Unknown/ Disputed
Third century	*Acts of Thomas* 50 (Greek) ελθὲ *Acts of Thomas* 133 (Greek) ἐλθάτω			
Early fourth century (*c*.300–50)	(?) Addai and Mari 'may ... come' (*veniat*)	E-BAS (Sahidic) 'descend'		
Mid-fourth century (*c*.350–75)		Byz-BAS ἐλθεῖν	Sarapion 1 πλήρωσον 2 ἐπιδημησάτω (?) Barcelona Papyrus 1 'send' 2 —	*Apostolic Tradition mittas*
Late fourth century (*c*.375–400)		JAS (Syriac) 'send' (*sdr*) JAS (Greek) ἐξαπόστειλον καταπέμπω *Twelve Apostles* 'send' (*sdr*) CHR κατάπεμψον *Apostolic Constitutions* καταπέμψῃς		
Fifth century	(?) Anaphora of Nestorius 'may ... come', 'dwell', 'rest' (*veniat, quiescat*)	*Testamentum Domini* 'send'		

East Syria	West Syria	Egypt	Unknown/ Disputed
(?) Anaphora of Theodore 'may ... come', and 'rest' and 'reside' (*veniat, illabitur, inhabitat*)		MARK (Greek) 1 πλήρωσον 2 ἐξαπόστειλον (variants: ἐπιδε, ἐφιδε) Dêr Balyzeh 1 πλήρωσον 2 (? text of this section lacking)	

not be taken as absolute), this chart does provide a glimpse of the intricacies involved in unravelling the origins of the epiclesis and the possible relationships among various forms of the epiclesis that emerge in different regions and time periods. The dating of prayers preceded by question marks is not established very precisely and thus their placement within this table should be considered approximate.

Based on this, a few general conclusions can be made that may serve to nuance the studies of Brock and Winkler about the development of the epiclesis according to the pattern of 'come', 'let come' and 'send'. First, it should be noted that the overall pattern, developed in particular to explain the connections among Syriac texts, seems to hold true (as a general rule, at least) when other traditions such as Egypt are considered as well. However, the *only* witness to the imperative form, 'come', as an invocation of the Spirit in an unequivocally *eucharistic* text is to be found in the apocryphal *Acts of Thomas*. Otherwise, a mixture of invocations containing variations on the idea of 'let come' or 'come down' or 'come and rest' and perhaps even 'send' as well seem to crop up during the mid-fourth century with no clear indication of the literary relationship among or precise ordering of these forms.

Second, it is *only* in Syrian sources that all three stages – come, let come, and send – occur, and only if the evidence from East and West Syria is considered together. The East Syrian tradition has 'come' and 'may come' but does not seem to acquire 'send' before the sixth century (by which time the epiclesis is widely attested elsewhere). 'Send' in the later Syrian tradition may be due to Greek influence from Antioch (καταπέμπω) or Jerusalem (ἐξαποστελλω).[92] However, Syriac JAS in this section and Twelve Apostles (thought to preserve older forms of the

---

92 See Spinks on the Anaphora of James above, p. 65.

pertinent part of the epiclesis than Greek JAS or CHR) both have *sdr*, and it is at least theoretically possible that 'send' was a native Syriac idea that was rendered differently into Greek in different regions. The Egyptian tradition has no early witness to 'come', and, depending on the date of the Barcelona Papyrus, a variation of 'let come' and 'send' may emerge in Egypt around the same time (especially if the variant readings of MARK might preserve a layer of the text that could be dated roughly to this time period as well).

Two further points are worth mentioning here. The first is the question of the significance of language for tracing the historical development of a liturgical unit. Tracing the occurrence of similar words among languages and across geographical regions can give the impression that one can correlate the use of words in one language to their meaning in other languages. While this may be helpful to a point, it is also a method that has its limitations. Winkler's philological method (and, by extension, Brock's as well) may not bear the weight which Winkler wishes to ascribe to it. Spinks has noted that the meanings of words like 'come' and 'send' can vary with context and that this meaning is far less fixed than static dictionary definitions might indicate. Furthermore, many of the sources which Winkler examines are difficult to date with precision. Therefore, while Winkler's studies surface intriguing literary comparisons between texts, the absence of certainty regarding the dates of these texts may mitigate the significance of these comparisons as far as *historical* liturgical development is concerned. Finally, the philological method is of limited use for addressing questions about the very human process of liturgical transmission and adaptation and the theological motives which might have accompanied it.[93]

Furthermore, an underlying assumption of this paradigm of epicletic development is that the eucharistic epiclesis had a point of origin from which it was subsequently dispersed to other regions via its incorporation into liturgical texts. Paul Bradshaw and Bryan Spinks both point out that Winkler's proposals about the development of the epiclesis and the Sanctus represent only one possible interpretation of the evidence. For example, Bradshaw notes that there may not have been a single 'original form' of the epiclesis – rather, 'a much wider primitive diversity of

---

93 See Bryan D. Spinks' review of Gabriele Winkler, *Das Sanctus: Über den Ursprung und die Anfänge des Sanctus und sein Fortwicken*, *JTS* 55.1 (2004), pp. 365–8.

imperative epicleses may only gradually have narrowed down to those found in later liturgical texts'.[94]

The following chapter briefly reviews some questions concerning the early development of the epiclesis that preoccupied scholars and reformers in the first decades of the twentieth century. Such issues as whether the epiclesis was a universal feature of early eucharistic prayers and whether it was necessary to articulate the Spirit's activity in a eucharistic prayer shaped the thinking of those who would be involved in liturgical revision efforts in the latter part of the twentieth century. In contrast to the conclusions of this chapter, earlier research into the eucharistic epiclesis gave more weight to a single line of development in eucharistic praying, which made the widespread *lack* of acknowledgement of the Spirit's role in Western eucharistic prayers seem increasingly problematic to some scholars and liturgists.

---

94 A wider epicletic diversity is evident even in the *Acts of Thomas*, where invocations are addressed not only to the Spirit and Christ but also to 'waters from the living waters' (ch. 52) and to oil (ch. 121). See Bradshaw, *Eucharistic Origins*, p. 128.

Chapter 3

(Re)constructing the early epiclesis: recovery and revision in the twentieth century

The so-called 'epiclesis question', which received much attention in twentieth-century scholarship on eucharistic praying, is certainly not a new question. Theological reflection about the role of the epiclesis in the eucharistic prayer reaches back at least as far as the late fourth century.[1] Similarly, the 'answers' which emerged over the past few decades in the form of revised Western eucharistic prayers are not completely original either; rather, they represent a creative recombination and rearrangement of treasures old *and* new, typically drawing upon the insights and liturgical genius of many traditions and sometimes of multiple historical eras as well. To better appreciate the full context of these revised rites, it is helpful to glance at the historical reconstruction which ultimately contributed to their development.

The remoter origins of the resurgence of interest in the epiclesis in the early decades of the twentieth century can likewise be sought in renewed attention to early sources, especially early Eastern sources, on the part of Western liturgical scholars. Once the epiclesis question emerged with renewed vigour after 1900, many studies involved a parallel search for the meaning and origin of the epiclesis. These two issues are closely related, since perception about what an epiclesis *is* and *does* impacts perceptions about what does and does not serve as an unqualified example of an

---

1 Several examples can be found in catechetical or mystagogical lectures and in homilies dating to the late fourth and early fifth centuries. Pertinent texts include: Cyril (or John) of Jerusalem, *Mystagogical Catecheses* I.7.5; III.3.5; V.4–9; Ambrose of Milan, *De sacramentis* 4; John Chrysostom, *De proditione Judae* 1, 2 and *In Joannem* 45.2; and Theodore of Mopsuestia, *Catecheses* 15, 16.

epiclesis when searching for its origins in the sources preserved from the first few centuries of Christianity's existence.

In the late nineteenth century, the discovery or 'rediscovery' of a number of liturgical texts fuelled renewed interest in the study of ancient liturgical forms, including the epiclesis.[2] This scholarship even resulted in some monographs devoted solely to the epiclesis.[3] Before the first few decades of the twentieth century, however, much of the work on the epiclesis was scattered and fragmented, consisting of journal articles that were not always widely accessible, and residing in appendices and notes connected to books whose primary focus lay elsewhere. In this latter context, discussion of the eucharistic epiclesis often arose within the broader category of eucharistic consecration. For example, the epiclesis was considered in *Consecration of the Eucharist* by Henry Riley Gummey (1908) and in articles such as W. C. Bishop's 'Primitive Form of Consecration in the Holy Eucharist' (1908) and Edmund Bishop's 'Moment of Consecration' – an appendix to Dom Connolly's *Liturgical Homilies of Narsai* (1909).[4] Encyclopedia entries such as Sévérien Salaville's 'Épiclèse eucharistique' in the *Dictionnaire de Théologie Catholique* (1913) and Fernand Cabrol's entry 'Épiclèse' in the *Dictionnaire d'Archéologie Chrétienne et de Liturgie* (1922) summarize the research undertaken during this era.[5]

---

2 Among these, the most influential by far was the 'Egyptian Church Order', later designated as the 'Apostolic Tradition' and attributed to Hippolytus of Rome in the early third century.

3 These monographs included Ludwig Augustin Hoppe, *Die Epiklesis der griechischen und orientalischen Liturgieen und der römische Consekrationskanon* (Schaffhausen: F. Hurter 1864); J. Marković, *Über die Eucharistie mit besonderer Rücksicht der Epiklese* (Agram, 1874; 2nd edn 1894); Rudolph Buchwald, *Die Epiklese in der römischen Messe* (Vienna: Verlag der Leo-Gesellschaft 1907); Francisque Varaine, *L'Épiclèse eucharistique* (Lyon, 1910); and Joseph Höller, *Die Epiklese der griechisch-orientalischen Liturgien: Ein Beitrag zur Lösung der Epiklesisfrage* (Vienna: Mayer 1912).

4 See Henry Riley Gummey, *The Consecration of the Eucharist: A Study of the Prayer of Consecration in the Communion Office from the Point of View of the Alterations and Amendments Established Therein by the Revisers of 1789* (Philadelphia and London: H. F. Anners Press/De la More Press 1908); W. C. Bishop, 'The Primitive Form of Consecration of the Holy Eucharist', *Church Quarterly Review* 66 (1908), pp. 385–404; and Edmund Bishop, 'The Moment of Consecration' in R. H. Connolly (ed.), *The Liturgical Homilies of Narsai* (Cambridge: Cambridge University Press 1909).

5 Sévérien Salaville, 'Épiclèse eucharistique' in A. Vacant, E. Mangenot and E. Amann (eds), *Dictionnaire de Théologie Catholique*, vol. 5.1 (Paris: Letouzey et Ané 1913), cols 194–300; and Fernand Cabrol, 'Épiclèse' in F. Cabrol, H. Leclercq and H. Marrou (eds), *Dictionnaire d'Archéologie Chrétienne et de Liturgie*, vol. 5.1 (Paris: Letouzey et Ané 1922), cols 142–84.

DEFINING TERMS

Historical scholarship at the turn of the twentieth century surfaced a number of questions surrounding the epiclesis. One set of debates centred on the perceived understanding of the purpose of the epiclesis in ancient texts and the terminology which should consequently be applied for such appeals for the presence and power of the Holy Spirit. Should the early epicleses be understood as pure invocations? Did the request for the Spirit entail (either explicitly or implicitly) a petition that the Holy Spirit then *do* something on behalf of the assembled community and/or specific persons or elements designated for holy use? Are the categories of 'invocation' and 'petition' mutually exclusive?[6] While some of these debates over terminology were coloured by the desire to defend the theological path adopted by the churches to which the authors of these articles belonged, another underlying assumption was that the eucharistic epiclesis had just one single origin and meaning.[7]

Given that the traditional Western theology of consecration had focused on Christ's words of institution as the consecratory 'moment' par excellence in the prayer, the idea that the epiclesis did or could play a complementary or even secondary role in eucharistic consecration could have been perceived as a threat to this long-standing tradition (for Roman Catholics, Lutherans and some Anglicans especially). On the other hand, the idea that the epiclesis could have had biblical origins (or at least a biblical precursor) could have made it more acceptable in some other circles (as long as its consecratory dimension – which did not have

---

6 A heated debate over epicletic terminology raged in print from 1917 to 1924 between J. W. Tyrer and R. H. Connolly, noted Anglican and Roman Catholic liturgical scholars, respectively. The former argued that the term ἐπίκλεσις designated a petition; the latter interpreted ἐπίκλεσις primarily along the lines of invocation. The debate between these scholars, and the contributions of others which nuanced and extended it, are summarized in John H. McKenna, *The Eucharistic Epiclesis: A Detailed History from the Patristic to the Modern Era* (Chicago: Hillenbrand 2009, 2nd edn), pp. 94–105.

7 While not responding directly to the Tyrer–Connolly debate, F. Cabrol offered an alternative definition of epiclesis that alleviated the pressure to find the single 'original' meaning of the epiclesis. Cabrol differentiated between two types of epicleses – an epiclesis in the narrow sense and an epiclesis in the general sense. The narrow or strict sense of a consecratory *epiclesis* involves the invocation of the Holy Spirit upon the elements, and some sort of transformation of the elements in the direction of Christ's body and blood is anticipated as a result. This sort of epiclesis is not a universal feature of either early or modern eucharistic prayers. On the other hand, what Cabrol calls a general epiclesis is nearly universal, understood as a sort of 'allusion to the sanctifying work of the Holy Spirit in the Eucharist, which we find in one form or another in almost all the liturgies'. A. E. Burn, 'Invocation in the Holy Eucharist', *Theology* 9 (1924), p. 317, referring to Cabrol's definition of epiclesis; cf. Cabrol, 'Épiclèse', pp. 143–4.

an explicit biblical precedent in relation to the Eucharist – was not overemphasized). For example, it may have proved appealing to Western theologians who were looking for a model for eucharistic prayers that was faithful to ancient tradition but *not* dependent on *Roman* tradition.

By the late 1950s and 1960s, several descriptions of the epiclesis emerge which are either more general than some earlier definitions (and thus capable of encompassing a broad range of epicletic styles found in early texts) or more specific (informed by the fully fledged epicleses found in anaphoras dating from the late fourth century onwards). Some characterizations of the epiclesis emerge which are quite general indeed; for example, the Reformed theologian J. J. von Allmen, writing in *Essai sur le Repas du Seigneur* in 1966, claims that the epiclesis is 'the prayer which asks the Holy Spirit to intervene so that the Lord's Supper might really become what Jesus Christ intended it to be when he instituted it'.[8] A description such as this does not impose either limitations or expectations on the precise content of the epiclesis or stress one aspect of the epiclesis (e.g. 'consecration' or 'communion') at the expense of the others.[9] Strictly speaking, it might not even require that the Holy Spirit be asked in an explicit way to intervene in the eucharistic action. However, in its attempt to be inclusive of a wide range of epicletic possibilities, it does not necessarily do justice to the scope of the more fully developed epicleses which appear in some early anaphoras by the late fourth and early fifth centuries.

Other definitions of the epiclesis do try to take early liturgical evidence into account and, in the process, arrive at characterizations with a higher degree of specificity. G. C. Smit, for example, presents the eucharistic epiclesis as

> that invocation for the eucharistic anaphora or canon, which – through the intervention of the Word and of the Holy Spirit or not – expressly appeals for: 1) the transformation of the gifts presented on the altar into the Body and Blood of Christ; 2) a salutary action of the gifts (considered as already consecrated) upon those who partake of them – i.e., a worthy and fruitful Communion; 3) the sanctification of the gifts (always regarded as consecrated) as salutary instruments –

---

8 Jean-Jacques von Allmen, *Essai sur le Repas du Seigneur* (Neuchâtel: Delachaux et Niestlé 1966), p. 22 (ET: Jean-Jacques von Allmen, *The Lord's Supper* (Richmond, VA: John Knox Press 1969)), as quoted in McKenna, *Eucharistic Epiclesis*, p. 101.
9 McKenna, *Eucharistic Epiclesis*, p. 101.

consequently, an objective sanctification of the gifts in order to constitute the 'sacramentum.'[10]

Thus, for Smit, the epiclesis is a prayer for some form of transformation and/or sanctification of the gifts – but the role of the intervening agent (e.g. Word or Holy Spirit) might not be explicitly consecratory in this context in light of (2) and (3). By extension, the epiclesis also involves some effect on the communicants who share in these gifts – although the role of the Holy Spirit (or Word) need not be articulated and this figure need not even be named at any point in the prayer. This raises the possibility of detecting an epiclesis in texts which do not mention the Spirit – as J. W. Tyrer's definition of the epiclesis had intimated several decades before.

Other definitions enumerate some of the benefits that may result from the epiclesis as articulated in some of the developed anaphoras from the late fourth and early fifth centuries. These sorts of definitions give a better sense of the specific content of the more elaborate epicleses, but may be less apt at capturing other epicletic texts which do not describe the theological intent of the epiclesis with this level of detail – such as the eucharistic epicleses in the *Acts of Thomas*, for example, which simply invite the Spirit to come – or for epicleses like those in the anaphora of Sarapion that invoke the Logos instead of the Spirit for similar purposes. For example, H. C. Schmidt-Lauber designates the epiclesis as:

> the prayer for the coming of the Holy Spirit upon those celebrating (1) and upon the gifts of bread and wine (2) so that they fulfill the function which Christ instituted for them by becoming, in the course of the Eucharist, Christ's body and blood (3) and so that through them the faithful may be given a fuller participation in the 'whole Christ' and in his work (4) so that the faithful in turn, might reveal themselves as the one Body of Christ (5) and might not partake of this food unworthily.[11]

---

10 G. C. Smit, 'Épiclèse et théologie des sacrements', *Mélanges de Science Religieuse* 15 (1958), p. 95, as quoted in McKenna, *Eucharistic Epiclesis*, p. 104. For Smit, as McKenna describes, '"Sacramentum" is here understood in the sense of an *objective* instrument suited for, adapted to, subjective reception. It does not include, as does the usual use of the word "sacrament," the subjective element, i.e. the attitude of those partaking.' (McKenna, p. 101; see Smit, p. 95, n. 3).

11 Hans Schmidt-Lauber, *Die Eucharistie als Entfaltung der Verba Testamenti* (Kassel: Stauda 1957), pp. 155–6, as quoted in McKenna, *Eucharistic Epiclesis*, p. 103.

This epiclesis highlights the intrinsic connection between the two traditional functions of the epiclesis as 'consecration' and communion'. In a similar vein, Palle Dinesen writes:

> The epiclesis is an appeal to God (1) for his intervention through the Holy Spirit (2) in regard to the elements of the Thanksgiving, the bread and wine (3) that they manifest [*offenbaren*] (5) the body and blood of Christ (4) and in regard to those partaking in the Lord's Supper (6) that they might be one (7) and attain (among other things) (10) forgiveness of sins (8) and eternal life (9).[12]

Some definitions which have been supplied for the epiclesis, intentionally or not, give the impression that the consecratory dimension is primary and the communion aspect secondary, likely because many debates over the epiclesis in recent centuries have been concerned with the relationship of the epiclesis to the words of institution in terms of making the eucharistic gifts what Christ might have intended them to be. For example, the Lutheran theologian Peter Brunner, after discussing the epiclesis as an invocation for both the transformation of the gifts and a fruitful reception of communion, goes on to limit the practical scope of his consideration of the epiclesis to an 'appeal for consecration' – as its communion aspect raises no theological controversy.[13]

SEARCHING FOR ORIGINS[14]

It is quite possible that the issue of epicletic terminology sparked a more heated debate (in scholarly circles, at least) in the early twentieth century than at any previous time.[15] The dating of the epiclesis is also connected to a much earlier controversy, since the emergence of the early epiclesis in

---

12 Palle Dinesen, 'Die Epiklese im Rahmen altkirchlicher Liturgien: Eine Studie über die eucharistische Epiklese', *ST* 16.1 (1962), p. 72, as quoted in McKenna, *Eucharistic Epiclesis*, p. 103.

13 Peter Brunner, 'Zur Lehre vom Gottesdienst der im Namen Jesu versammelten Gemeinde', *Leiturgia* 1 (1954), pp. 84–364 (ET Peter Brunner, *Worship in the Name of Jesus*, trans. M. H. Bertram (St Louis: Concordia 1968).

14 The discussion in this section owes much to McKenna, *Eucharistic Epiclesis*, pp. 106–21.

15 One potential exception would be the debate stirred up over the epiclesis and the moment of consecration surrounding the Council of Florence (1439) and its aftermath. However, for the most part, the East and West had recourse to entrenched theological positions on the role of the Holy Spirit in the Eucharist rather than innovative theological reflection to respond to this problem. The positions of both East and West were biased by polemics and entangled in political concerns, making it difficult to reconcile their variant

relation to the Pneumatomachian controversy of the latter half of the fourth century becomes significant. If there are no pneumatic epicleses in any eucharistic prayers which can be dated with confidence before *c.*360, the debate over the Spirit during the middle and later decades of the fourth century could have supplied sufficient justification for the new addition of such prayers to Christian anaphoras and/or the widespread adoption of previously isolated local customs of acknowledging the Spirit's role in the eucharistic action.

If, on the contrary, a pneumatic eucharistic epiclesis was more widespread before *c.*360 and not confined to only one region of then-emerging Christendom, its origin must be traced to another cause (or to different causes in different places), and, so the reasoning went, there was no firm reason why such an epiclesis could not have been in use much, much earlier (even, some authors argued, into the second century).[16] The most popular view was that doctrinal development regarding the role of the Holy Spirit in general contributed to greater precision regarding the action of the Spirit in the Eucharist, especially in the East, where the pneumatological debates of the fourth century were fiercest.[17]

Even in the absence of such doctrinal developments, some theories posited a progressive elaboration of the epiclesis from an origin in the tradition of blessing objects for quotidian and especially for sacramental use to a conviction that such a blessing was particularly necessary in the case of the Eucharist. For example, J. Brinktrine proposes three stages in the development of the eucharistic epiclesis. The first stage consisted of 'sanctifying' the eucharistic bread and wine before sharing in them in communion, in a parallel manner to the way in which other materials (e.g. cheese, olives, water, oil) were blessed before being used by Christians, whether in an explicitly sacramental context or otherwise. These simple blessing prayers evolved into a second stage – prayers which requested the blessing, sanctification and/or descent of the Holy Spirit upon sacramental elements, sometimes for the sake of their transform-

---

theological outlooks on the place of pneumatology in relation to eucharistic consecration. For more on this discussion and its consequences, see McKenna, *Eucharistic Epiclesis*, pp. 78ff.

16 J. W. Tyrer, *The Eucharistic Epiclesis* (London and New York: Longmans, Green 1917), p. 28.

17 See, e.g., Walter Howard Frere, *The Primitive Consecration Prayer: A Lecture Given at the Annual Meeting of the [Alcuin] Club, June 7, 1922* (London and Milwaukee: Mowbray/Morehouse 1922), pp. 19–22 and Walter Howard Frere, *The Anaphora, or Great Eucharistic Prayer: An Eirenical Study in Liturgical History* (London and New York: SPCK/Macmillan 1938).

ation, and for God's acceptance of the gifts brought to the altar. Eventually, when this sort of prayer was perceived as *necessary* for the Eucharist, the prayers of the final stage appealed to God, through the Spirit, to 'realize' Christ's eucharistic presence for the gathered community. In sum, an epiclesis of 'sanctification' developed into an epiclesis of 'consecration'.[18]

Other theories granted this general trajectory of development while contending that the original epiclesis was oriented less towards the hallowing of the eucharistic elements as such and more towards filling them with (pneumatic) power for the sake of the communicants who would consume them. According to this line of reasoning, sanctification was originally for the sake of communion, with consecration being a secondary and later development – and possibly one at odds with the original intent of the epiclesis.[19] Alternative theories agree that a consecratory epiclesis could have developed from an earlier epiclesis of sanctification but that the forerunner already contained some, albeit unarticulated, conviction of the Holy Spirit's transforming, consecratory action relative to the eucharistic bread and wine. From this perspective, therefore, the tendency towards greater emphasis on consecration could be viewed as one of continuity rather than disjunction with earlier stages of development. Historical and doctrinal conditions may have combined to favour greater specificity with regard to the epicletic petition than was previously perceived as necessary. John McKenna suggests that the 'absence of any outcry against the explicit mention of a transformation in later epicleses' seems to lend support to theories which see the epicleses of the late fourth and early fifth centuries as standing in continuity with earlier tradition insofar as they may make explicit what was only implicit at an earlier stage.[20]

A final theory concerning the origins of the epiclesis which had emerged by the mid-twentieth century detected a connection between the epiclesis

---

18 Johannes Brinktrine, 'Zur Entstehung der morgenländischen Epiklese', *Zeitschrift für Katholische Theologie* 42 (1918), pp. 301–26, 483–518, as summarized in McKenna, *Eucharistic Epiclesis*, pp. 110–11.

19 Examples of this nuancing of the development from eucharistic sanctification to consecration can be found in Cyril Charles Richardson, 'The Origin of the Epiclesis', *AThR* 28.3 (1946), pp. 148–53 and Anton Baumstark, 'Zu den Problemen der Epiklese und des römischen Messkanons', *Theologische Revue* 15 (1916), p. 341. Reginald Woolley suggested that the later trajectory of the development of the epiclesis as outlined here was 'fundamentally different' from its earlier origins. See Reginald Maxwell Woolley, *The Liturgy of the Primitive Church* (Cambridge: Cambridge University Press, 1910), pp. 93–120, esp. pp. 111, 117–18.

20 McKenna, *Eucharistic Epiclesis*, p. 114.

and Jewish prayer forms. In *Eucharistie* (1966), Louis Bouyer identifies the seed of Christian models of eucharistic praying in the Jewish meal *berakoth*. A prayer for the unity of the community, based on the third Jewish meal *berakah*, lent itself quite naturally to Trinitarian elaboration as the community prayed that God (the Father) might be glorified through the Son – with *mention* of the Holy Spirit as the 'seal of unity' and 'Spirit of glory' rounding out the prayer. By the late fourth century, when it became imperative to emphasize the equal divinity of the Spirit and assign the Spirit definite functions with respect to the Christian community, this *mention* of the Spirit grew into an *invocation* of the Holy Spirit to realize the fruits of the Eucharist in the lives of the communicants.

Around the same time, a prayer for the acceptance of the sacrifice (which Bouyer considered to be of ultimate Jewish origin as well) evolved into a request for 'consecration' of the elements that was combined with the epiclesis. From then on, the epiclesis assumed three related purposes as a prayer for (1) the acceptance of the eucharistic sacrifice-memorial, (2) the consecration of the gifts, (3) 'and finally (which alone is original), that this descent of the Spirit, uniting us all in the body of Christ which is the Church, permit us all in this unity to glorify the Father eternally'.[21]

Bouyer was not alone in looking for the origin of the epiclesis in Jewish prayer forms. Gregory Dix in *The Shape of the Liturgy* (1945) and Louis Ligier in 'De la cène de Jésus à l'anaphore de l'Église' (1966) had previously or concurrently developed comparable hypotheses.[22] Similarly, others had likewise speculated that an initial eschatologically oriented appeal for the unity of the community could have been the starting point in a line of development that culminated in the epicleses of the late fourth century and thereafter with their dual focus on consecration and communion.[23]

These historical reconstructions of the origins of the epiclesis are often interesting; however, like many aspects of the study of early liturgy, they are difficult to prove (or disprove) definitively. Furthermore, many aspects of them are not mutually exclusive and it would be possible to piece together alternative reconstructions which combine various aspects

---

21 See Louis Bouyer, *Eucharist: Theology and Spirituality of the Eucharistic Prayer*, trans. C. U. Quinn from the 2nd French edition (1968) (Notre Dame, IN: University of Notre Dame Press 1968), esp. pp. 183–4, 310–13; quote from p. 313.

22 See Gregory Dix, *The Shape of the Liturgy*, with additional notes by Paul V. Marshall (New York: Seabury Press 1982, reprint of 2nd (1945) edn), pp. 182–4 and Louis Ligier, 'De la cène de Jésus à l'anaphore de l'Église', *La Maison-Dieu* 87 (1966), pp. 36, 42–6.

23 Such scholars include Ligier, Cabrol, Paul Cagin, J. Souben, Henry Chadwick, Connolly and L. Labauche. See citations in McKenna, *Eucharistic Epiclesis*, p. 119, n. 52.

of these theories. The interest in presenting them here is to indicate the sorts of scholarly ideas about how the epiclesis arose which were available to liturgical reformers of the late twentieth century who sought to construct epicleses of their own in traditions where none had existed before or to modify existing ones based in part on the insights of contemporary scholarship regarding the early intention (or range of intentionality) underlying the epicleses surviving in texts from the early Church.

AN EPICLESIS IN THE ROMAN CANON?

While some scholars were debating authorial intent behind occurrences of ἐπίκλεσις and related terms when they occurred in eucharistic contexts, other scholars, particularly Roman Catholic ones, were debating whether the Roman Canon had – or once had – any epicletic elements. In the early twentieth century, many were convinced that the eucharistic liturgy preserved in Book 8 of the *Apostolic Constitutions*, which contained a clear invocation of the Holy Spirit, 'even if not genuinely apostolic, still represented universal Christian practice in the second and third centuries'.[24] The Roman Canon contained no clear equivalent for this pneumatic section of an 'apostolic' prayer – an apparent deficiency which became increasingly problematic. Attempts to pinpoint an epiclesis in the Roman Canon persisted even as it became progressively clearer that invoking the Holy Spirit in a eucharistic context was neither extremely early nor ubiquitous in surviving eucharistic prayers from the first few centuries.

Scholarly opinions on the matter involved identifying the epicletic element(s) of the Roman Canon and debating whether or not the Roman Canon ever included an explicit epiclesis of the Holy Spirit. The presence or absence of an epiclesis in the Roman Canon bears theological significance, since, if it was determined that the Roman Canon in its modern form functioned as a genuine eucharistic prayer with no epiclesis at all, it would have been difficult for Catholic scholars to argue that an explicit pneumatic epiclesis was a 'necessary' component of a eucharistic prayer, strictly speaking. If, however, it were determined that the Roman Canon contained an implicit epiclesis, this scenario raised a different set of questions about how eucharistic consecration ought to be understood in general, and, more particularly, how the efficacy of the words of

---

24 Paul F. Bradshaw, 'The Rediscovery of the Holy Spirit in Modern Eucharistic Theology and Practice' in Teresa Berger and Bryan D. Spinks (eds), *The Spirit in Worship – Worship in the Spirit* (Collegeville, MN: Liturgical Press 2009), p. 81.

institution was related to the eucharistic epiclesis (whether the Holy Spirit was mentioned specifically in the epiclesis or not).[25]

Since the Roman Canon does not mention the Spirit outside the final doxology, a *pneumatic* epiclesis in the Roman Canon was ruled out. Some scholars located the Roman Canon's epiclesis in the *Supra Quae* and/or *Supplices Te*, since they resided in the corresponding structural location of most Eastern epicleses and echoed their content, being, according to Louis Duchesne, 'a prayer to God for his intervention in the mystery'.[26] Others detected the epiclesis in the *Hanc igitur* and/or *Quam oblationem* segment(s) preceding the words of institution. Joseph Jungmann, for example, contended that the early tradition of the patriarchates of Alexandria and Rome 'involved an invocation of divine power *before* the words of institution'.[27] Edmund Bishop proposed that the Roman Canon *did* have an epiclesis, albeit an insufficient and poorly located one. The phrase '*Quam oblationem* ...' could be read as an invocation or petition over the bread and wine – although not one which called for the Holy Spirit's involvement.[28] Nichols concludes, 'It is thus possible to see a case being defended for an epicletic intention which is always part of a eucharistic prayer, even where there is no explicit invocation of the Holy Spirit.'[29]

Bishop's 'definition' of an epiclesis was closely tied to the issue of eucharistic consecration. Bishop did *not* detect an epicletic dimension in the *Supplices* section. Rather, he identified the *Supplices* as a prayer for the communicants – in distinction to the (developed) Eastern epicleses which clearly requested consecration of the eucharistic elements.[30] John McKenna has highlighted Edmund Bishop's comments on the epiclesis in the Roman Canon as a good example of how one's conception or

---

25 Bridget Nichols and Alistair MacGregor, *The Eucharistic Epiclesis*, Ushaw Library Publications 4 (Durham: Ushaw College Library 2001), p. vii.

26 Louis Duchesne, *Les Origines du Culte Chrétien* (Paris: Thorin 1899), p. 173; ET from Louis Duchesne, *Christian Worship: Its Origin and Evolution: A Study of the Latin Liturgy up to the Time of Charlemagne*, trans. M. L. McClure (London: SPCK 1956, 5th edn), p. 181. See also Maurice de la Taille, *Mysterium Fidei* (Paris: Beauchesne 1931, 3rd edn), p. 276. References from Bradshaw, 'Rediscovery', p. 83.

27 Josef A. Jungmann, *The Mass of the Roman Rite*, trans. Francis A. Brunner (New York: Benziger 1951), vol. 2, p. 193. Italics in the original.

28 Bishop, 'Moment of Consecration', p. 136. Many decades later, W. Jardine Grisbrooke came to similar conclusions, arguing that, far from being lacking in the Roman Canon, the epiclesis is quite full. See W. Jardine Grisbrooke, 'Anaphora' in J. G. Davies (ed.), *A New Dictionary of Liturgy and Worship* (London: SCM Press 1986), p. 19.

29 Nichols and MacGregor, *Eucharistic Epiclesis*, p. ix.

30 Bishop, 'Moment of Consecration', pp. 131–6.

expectations for an epiclesis colour one's identification of epicleses or potential epicleses in liturgical texts:

> Here, for instance, if one considers the epiclesis proper as only looking to the consecration and not to the reception of Communion the case for *Quam oblationem* as an epiclesis becomes stronger and that for the *Supplices* weaker. If the stress were on the epiclesis being an appeal for worthy Communion, then the strength of the case for the *Supplices* becomes stronger and that for the *Quam oblationem* weaker. If, moreover, one considers the mention of the Holy Spirit as necessary for an epiclesis then the case for either of these being an epiclesis proper vanishes.[31]

Several scholars suggested that the Roman Canon must have contained an explicit pneumatic epiclesis which was excised at some later point, perhaps to minimize theological controversy surrounding the institution narrative. Adrian Fortescue claimed that invocation of the Spirit was removed, 'apparently deliberately, because of the growing Western insistence on the words of institution as the Consecration form'.[32] Rudolph Buchwald (*Die Epiklese in der römischen Messe*) and W. C. Bishop, 'The Primitive Form of Consecration in the Holy Eucharist', affirmed variations of this point of view.[33]

Others challenged the view that the Roman Canon once had an epiclesis that was subsequently 'lost' either inadvertently or intentionally. Edmund Bishop found no convincing evidence of an overtly consecratory epiclesis in the West before the late fourth century.[34] Joseph

---

31 McKenna, *Eucharistic Epiclesis*, p. 100.
32 Adrian Fortescue, *The Mass: A Study of the Roman Liturgy* (London and New York: Longmans, Green and Co. 1917), pp. 402–7. The notion that growing Eastern and Western theological divergence might have led to a situation which remained contentious in the twentieth century may have arisen more from the modern context than from ancient disputes. As Paul Bradshaw has noted, 'Roman Catholic attitudes toward the role of the Holy Spirit in relation to the eucharist were generally distorted for much of the twentieth century as a result of polemics with the Eastern Orthodox Church. As the latter tended to assert that consecration was brought about by the invocation of the Spirit alone, the Roman Catholic response was to insist that on the contrary it was effected by recitation of the dominical words alone – a doctrine that had been specifically reaffirmed by Pius X in 1910.' (*Acta Apostolica Sedis* 3 (1911), pp. 118ff.) Bradshaw, 'Rediscovery', p. 80.
33 See Buchwald, *Die Epiklese* and Bishop, 'Primitive Form', pp. 385–404; citations from Bradshaw, 'Rediscovery', p. 81, n. 7.
34 Bishop, 'Moment of Consecration', pp. 123–63. See also W. C. Bishop, 'Liturgical Comments and Memoranda II', *JTS* 10 (1909), pp. 592–603.

Jungmann argued for the fully fledged epiclesis as a tradition of the East, while Rome traced its invocation to a different but equally venerable and antique tradition. Rather than searching for a 'lost' epiclesis in the Roman rite, it should be granted that the epiclesis 'represents the fourth century custom of only one of the three great patriarchates, namely, that of Antioch, while in the other two, Alexandria and Rome, the traditional practice, going back at least to the same early period, involved an invocation of the divine power *before* the words of institution'.[35] Therefore, an invocation that did not refer to the Spirit was, at the very least, an equally legitimate and ancient practice of eucharistic praying. Furthermore, the same could be said of positioning such an invocation before the institution narrative instead of afterwards; the former preference was not limited to Rome but found elsewhere (i.e. the see of Alexandria) as well. Eventually, agreement converged around the position that the epicletic elements of the Roman Canon were to be found in both the *Supplices Te* and the *Quam oblationem* sections; these two portions of the prayer combined formed the Western counterpart to the Eastern epiclesis. However, the Western option resulted in a 'split epiclesis' with a consecratory aspect in the invocation over the bread and wine before the institution narrative and a communion dimension in the petition following the narrative.[36]

Edmund Bishop further argued against the epiclesis as an *early* and universal feature of eucharistic prayers, concluding that 'the idea of a single primitive rite from which the extant liturgies all derive' – if not in traceable textual lineage at least through the handing on of memory and oral tradition – was highly questionable.[37] There did not seem to be one early form of eucharistic consecration, there was no clear evidence of an epiclesis of the Holy Spirit before the mid-fourth century, and the fourth-century debates over the Spirit's divinity did not make recourse to the role of the Spirit in a eucharistic context, even when discussions of the Spirit's role in liturgical practice came up in other contexts such as baptism and doxologies.[38] For Bishop, a key question was whether the epiclesis was a development – or innovation – which originated in the East and was subsequently adopted in some parts of the West, or whether

35 Jungmann, *Mass of the Roman Rite*, vol. 2, p. 193.
36 See, e.g., Bouyer, *Eucharist*, pp. 144–6 and Bradshaw, 'Rediscovery', p. 84.
37 Bishop, 'Moment of Consecration', p. 146.
38 George Every, 'Edmund Bishop and the Epiclesis' in A. H. Armstrong and E. J. B. Fry (eds), *Re-discovering Eastern Christendom: Essays in Commemoration of Dom Bede Winslow* (London: Darton, Longman & Todd 1963), p. 85.

the epicletic aspects in certain Gallican and Mozarabic rites were independent developments.[39] If the theory of Eastern influence on these Western rites is suspended, it is possible to view the Gallican and Mozarabic epicleses as less developed (and thus possibly earlier) than some Eastern epicleses.[40]

Bishop did recognize the connection of pneumatic metaphors such as 'drinking the Spirit' (cf. 1 Cor. 12.13) with a eucharistic context in Syria,[41] but initially thought that their spread beyond Syria must have happened relatively late – at least until a similar idea (i.e. sharing in the fullness of the Spirit) turned up in a prayer attributed to Hippolytus of Rome in the early third century. A few years before Bishop died (in 1917), the connection of 'The Egyptian Church Order' with the lost *Apostolic Tradition* of Hippolytus from the early third century (and its status as the document from which Book 8 of *Apostolic Constitutions* was ultimately derived) seemed to affirm Bishop's position that there was no

39 The issue of the epiclesis in non-Roman Western rites, especially the Gallican and Mozarabic liturgies, is incredibly complex and deserves a detailed study of its own; this issue will not be treated in detail here since the epicleses of these rites seem to have had little direct influence on the epicleses of later Western eucharistic prayers. Beyond the fixed text of the Sursum corda, Sanctus, institution narrative and doxology, the eucharistic prayers of these rites are characterized by a collection of variable segments arranged within a set pattern. The *post-secreta* (or *post-mysterium*) following the institution narrative (i.e. *secreta*) in the Gallican rites sometimes contains an epiclesis, and an epiclesis is likewise found occasionally in the equivalent *post-pridie* section of the Mozarabic rite. See R. C. D. Jasper and G. J. Cuming (eds), *Prayers of the Eucharist: Early and Reformed* (Collegeville, MN: Liturgical Press 1990, 3rd edn, revised and enlarged), pp. 147, 151. These rites are discussed more extensively in W. C. Bishop, 'The Mass in Spain' in C. L. Feltoe (ed.), *The Mozarabic and Ambrosian Rites: Four Essays in Comparative Liturgiology* (Oxford: Mowbray, for the Alcuin Club 1924), pp. 18–54 and John Mason Neale and G. H. Forbes, *The Ancient Liturgies of the Gallican Church; Now First Collected with an Introductory Dissertation, Notes, and Various Readings Together with Parallel Passages from the Roman Ambrosian, and Mozarabic Rites* (reprint: New York: AMS Press 1970; original: London: n. pub. 1855); citations from Kevin Andrew Montgomery, 'When Sacraments Shall Cease: Toward a Pneumatological and Eschatological Approach to the Eucharist', MA thesis, Graduate Theological Union 2006, pp. 27–8, n. 75. On the question of the epiclesis in these rites, see the references in the notes of McKenna, *Eucharistic Epiclesis*, pp. 35ff.
40 George Every provides several examples of the 'primitive' character of some of these prayers; see Every, 'Edmund Bishop', p. 82. McKenna includes five epicletic excerpts which either parallel or directly or indirectly support other theories on the origin and development of the epiclesis, observing that, 'Even this small sample should, however, give one an inkling of the variety and at times the state of confusion often found in the *Post Secreta* and *Post Pridie* of these liturgies. It should also make one circumspect in regard to historical or theological theories that appeal to these prayers as their main support.' See McKenna, *Eucharistic Epiclesis*, pp. 36–8 for examples and p. 39 for the quoted text.
41 Bishop, 'Moment of Consecration', pp. 147–9.

single eucharistic rite from which all others had evolved and also supported his contention that there was no single universally understood form of eucharistic consecration in the early Church. Although the eucharistic prayer in *Apostolic Tradition* does contain a request after the institution narrative that God send the Spirit on 'the oblation of your Church', this need not be read as an explicitly consecratory petition (as the text does not specify that the sending of the Spirit is for the purpose of the change or transformation of the gifts into Christ's body and blood). But did the presence of a pneumatic epiclesis in this text, consecratory or not, mean that the epiclesis could have emerged before the fourth century?

Combined with the position taken by some scholars that this section of *Apostolic Tradition* was a later interpolation to the prayer (and thus not a reliable witness to early third-century Roman practice), the need to justify the lack of an epiclesis in the Roman Canon was alleviated somewhat. Nonetheless, 'the theory that a major dislocation of the Canon had taken place after Hippolytus' day lived on for several decades'.[42] Even if a eucharistic invocation of the Holy Spirit was only early but not primitive, subsequent theological development in the Roman Catholic Church demanded that scholars from this tradition safeguard the status of the Roman Canon as a representative in its own right of a venerable ancient tradition of prayer.

THE EPICLESIS AND EARLY TWENTIETH-CENTURY ANGLICAN LITURGICAL REVISION

If some Roman Catholic scholars were on the defensive during the early decades of the twentieth century with regard to the place of the epiclesis in eucharistic praying, some scholars and ecclesiastical officials in the Church of England were actively campaigning meanwhile for the inclusion of an epiclesis in their rites. It is much easier to trace the fate of the epiclesis in the Anglican Liturgical Tradition, whose early origins included an (albeit short-lived) eucharistic epiclesis. The First Book of Common Prayer of Edward VI (1549) had included an epiclesis before the institution narrative – 'with thy Holy Spirit and word vouchsafe to bless and sanctify these thy gifts and creatures of bread and wine' – which was absent from the Second Book of Common Prayer issued in

---

42 Bradshaw, 'Rediscovery', p. 82. As an example, Bradshaw directs attention to references in Bouyer's *Eucharist*, pp. 187–8, with Bouyer's contestation of this view on pp. 188–91.

1552.[43] A fully developed, explicitly pneumatic epiclesis would not find an official place again in the Church of England's liturgies until the Series 3 eucharistic prayers took effect in 1973. However, the epiclesis had generated heated discussion some decades before. Although this debate culminated in a proposed epiclesis in the 1928 Book of Common Prayer (a book which failed to gain the support of Parliament), the aftermath of these discussions created repercussions that saw epicleses introduced in other parts of the Anglican Communion.

Tensions over liturgical matters in the late nineteenth and early twentieth centuries eventually prompted this statement from the Royal Commission on Ecclesiastical Discipline in 1906:

> The law of public worship in the Church of England is too narrow for the religious life of the present generation. It needlessly condemns much which a great section of Church people, including many of her most devoted members, value; and modern thought and feelings are characterised by a care for ceremonial, a sense of dignity in worship, *and an appreciation of the continuity of the Church*, which were not similarly felt at the time when the law took its present shape.[44]

Although this report purportedly dealt with concerns related to discipline of the clergy, liturgical topics were a major point of discussion in it as well. Bridget Nichols credits its publication with 'creat[ing] a climate in which liturgical questions relevant to its finding on the state of worship in the Church of England could be pursued'.[45] And the epiclesis was one topic which was pursued; a proposed eucharistic prayer with an epiclesis

---

43 Cranmer's 1549 epiclesis, although absent from subsequent English revisions, did re-emerge in Scotland in 1637. In 1755, this epiclesis was relocated to the 'Eastern' position after the institution narrative, due in part to conclusions drawn from the study of early liturgies among the English Non-Jurors. (See W. Jardine Grisbrooke, *Anglican Liturgies of the Seventeenth and Eighteenth Centuries* (London: SPCK 1958).) This epiclesis eventually found its way into the American Book of Common Prayer (1789).

44 Report of the Royal Commission on Ecclesiastical Discipline, 1906, §400, as quoted in Nichols and MacGregor, *Eucharistic Epiclesis*, p. x; emphasis added. The full text of this report is available online through Project Canterbury at: <http://anglicanhistory.org/pwra/>.

45 Nichols and MacGregor, *Eucharistic Epiclesis*, p. x. Nichols notes that attempting to address issues of clergy and ritual discipline as one item proved problematic, and directs readers to Bishop George Bell's biography of Archbishop Randall Davidson for a good overview of the issues involved. See George Kennedy Allen Bell, *Randall Davidson, Archbishop of Canterbury* (London and New York: Oxford University Press 1952), vol. 2, pp. 1357–8.

resembling that of the 1549 BCP and the Scottish (1637) and American (1789) counterparts was voted down in the Convocation of Canterbury in 1911 – but not by a huge margin.[46]

During the next several years, an epiclesis was among the Prayer Book revisions discussed in a number of published works.[47] Among them was the anonymous *A Prayer Book Revised* (1913), which presented a eucharistic prayer with the epiclesis from the 1637 (Scottish) Book of Common Prayer. In the Preface Charles Gore, Bishop of Oxford, designated the epiclesis as 'so important a feature of all the early Liturgies and still of the Eastern Liturgies to-day'.[48] *A Revised Liturgy* (1914) by Canon B. W. Randolph included a similar variation based on the 1637 Scottish epiclesis. In this book, Randolph stated that 'the absence of any *Epiklesis* or Invocation of the Holy Spirit has been felt by all liturgical students to be a blot in our Service'.[49] The Anglican priest R. J. Edmund Boggis also published a book of proposed revisions in 1914, in which he claimed that

> so important was the invocation of the Spirit in all ancient liturgies (as it is also in those of the eastern rites now) that this, rather than the recitation of the words of Institution, was regarded as the essential part of the Consecration . . . and it is a matter of first importance that its use should be at least permitted to English Churchmen.[50]

When official revision of the Prayer Book was considered beginning in 1914,[51] some scholars wanted to reintroduce an epiclesis into the Prayer of Consecration (although there was considerable debate over the best

46 See Donald Gray, *The 1927–28 Prayer Book Crisis, Vol. 2: The Cul-de-sac of the 'Deposited Book' . . . Until Further Order Be Taken* (Norwich: SCM-Canterbury Press 2006), p. 19.

47 I owe the collection of references which follows to Bradshaw, 'Rediscovery', pp. 84–6.

48 Charles Gore, *A Prayer-Book Revised: Being the Services of the Book of Common Prayer, with Sundry Alterations and Additions Offered to the Reader* (London and Milwaukee: Mowbray/Young Churchman 1913), p. xii. Percy Dearmer was eventually revealed as the 'anonymous' author behind the body of the work. See Donald Gray, *The 1927–28 Prayer Book Crisis, Vol. 1: Ritual, Royal Commissions, and Reply to the Royal Letters of Business* (Norwich: SCM-Canterbury Press 2005).

49 Church of England, *A Revised Liturgy: Being the Order of the Administration of the Lord's Supper According to the Use of the Church of England: With Divers Enrichments and Alterations* (London and Milwaukee: Mowbray/Young Churchman 1914), p. 4.

50 Robert James Edmund Boggis, *Revision of the Book of Common Prayer from the Point of View of a Parish Priest* (Canterbury: Cross & Jackman 1914), p. 78.

51 For an overview of the process leading to the proposed 1928 Book of Common Prayer, see Bell, *Randall Davidson*, vol. 2, ch. 82 ('The Prayer Book').

way to accomplish this), while others preferred to leave the prayer as it was, at least for the time being. Among those of the latter opinion was Walter Frere, who cautioned that, until the theological differences concerning eucharistic consecration between the 'Latin West' and the 'more primitive East' were closer to a resolution, 'it would be inopportune to take any steps towards the reinsertion of the Invocation of the Holy Spirit . . . When our own mind is clearer, we may be able to go forward; but not until then'[52] – although he himself looked forward to a time when restoration of the epiclesis in the Church of England might be feasible. Recognizing the importance of *both* the institution narrative *and* the epiclesis would allow the Church of England to serve in this instance, as in many others, as a mediator between the either–or stances towards eucharistic consecration that had historically been adopted by Roman and Eastern churches.[53]

F. E. Brightman, the compiler of *The English Rite*, advocated for an epiclesis in the position it had occupied in the 1549 Prayer Book or else no epiclesis at all.[54] Others wanted to follow the tradition of the Church of Scotland as well as the practice of the Eastern Churches in locating an epiclesis in the 'Eastern' position, following the words of institution. In 1918, an alternative prayer with this arrangement (along with three additional changes to the sequence of the Prayer of Consecration) was proposed. Walter Frere was instrumental in advocating for this arrangement.[55] While other proposed changes to the BCP were eventually approved, this alternative prayer was not.

Several years later, desire for an alternative canon surfaced again, and support for this project had grown. Those who desired to include an epiclesis in an alternative prayer (essentially a revised version of the prayer from 1918–19) claimed that adding one would '[guard] against a tendency to lay all the weight of consecration on the actual words of institution'.[56] An alternative prayer, with an epiclesis, was approved in 1926 and survived subsequent stages of revision to be included in the last

---

52 Walter Howard Frere, *Some Principles of Liturgical Reform: A Contribution towards the Revision of the Book of Common Prayer* (London: John Murray 1911), pp. 188–9.

53 Frere, *Some Principles*, pp. 188–9.

54 F. E. Brightman, *The English Rite, Being a Synopsis of the Sources and Revisions of the Book of Common Prayer, with an Introduction and an Appendix* (London: Rivingtons 1915). See also F. E. Brightman, 'Correspondence: Eucharistic Invocation', *Theology* 9.49 (1924), pp. 33–40.

55 Bradshaw, 'Rediscovery', p. 85.

56 Bell, *Randall Davidson*, vol. 2, p. 1331, as quoted in Nichols and MacGregor, *Eucharistic Epiclesis*, p. xi.

round of proposals presented to Parliament in 1927, although it did encounter criticism from some quarters as 'too Eastern'.[57] While some challenged the need to include such an invocation in the Church of England's repertoire of eucharistic prayer at all, others were more disturbed by its location in the prayer. Darwell Stone and F. E. Brightman, among others, contended that a post-narrative epiclesis would 'undermin[e] the Western Catholic belief in the consecratory power of the dominical words in the narrative'.[58] Walter Frere sought to soothe tensions by advocating the provision of an option to place the epiclesis before the institution narrative, but this proposal failed to win widespread support.[59]

The 1928 Prayer Book revision process also sought to textualize a long-standing turn to history, particularly the history of the early Church, which had influenced some circles of Anglican liturgists for over 200 years. '1928, whatever other defects it may have, is affirmedly in the pseudo-fourth century tradition of eucharistic prayer, which had held sway among Anglican liturgists ever since the non-jurors in the eighteenth century.'[60] Even though the 1928 Canon was not influenced directly by the *Apostolic Tradition*, it had been raised as a potential source of inspiration for a reformed eucharistic rite during the process, especially by Frere, who had been drawing the attention of liturgical scholars to the importance of this text for some years previously.

The proposed revisions were critiqued quite extensively. For example, A. G. Hebert remarked that the

> 1927–1928 Canon seems to be based, not on an understanding of the meaning of the eucharistic action, but on a liturgiological theory that the proper mode of consecration is by the invocation of the Holy Spirit. Because of this lack of understanding it fails to achieve that

---

57 Nichols and MacGregor, *Eucharistic Epiclesis*, p. xi.
58 Bradshaw, 'Rediscovery', p. 86.
59 Gray, *1927–28 Prayer Book Crisis*, vol. 2, pp. 19–20.
60 Grisbrooke, *Anglican Liturgies*, p. 379, quoted in Kenneth W. Stevenson, *Gregory Dix – Twenty-Five Years On* (Bramcote: Grove Books 1977), p. 10. For further details about the Non-Jurors and other previous movements inspired, at least in part, by impulses towards patristic recovery in Anglican circles, see David J. Kennedy, *Eucharistic Sacramentality in an Ecumenical Context: The Anglican Epiclesis* (Aldershot and Burlington, VT: Ashgate 2008) and Bryan D. Spinks, *Sacraments, Ceremonies and the Stuart Divines: Sacramental Theology and Liturgy in England and Scotland, 1603–1662* (Aldershot and Burlington, VT: Ashgate 2002). See also Grisbrooke, *Anglican Liturgies*.

'inevitability' which is the mark of rightness in liturgical as in other art; and the ordinary person feels that it is somehow wrong.[61]

A. E. Burn too advocated that satisfaction with the eucharistic doctrine of the Western church would best be expressed by *not* incorporating an epiclesis into the Anglican Eucharist. He invokes the words of Bishop John Wordsworth: 'Beautiful as the Oriental Invocation is, we cannot think it indispensible.'[62] Expressing a position similar to Cabrol (who argued that most liturgies had a sort of 'general epiclesis' even if they did not have a consecratory epiclesis in the strict sense), Robinson identifies an epicletic moment in the current Anglican rite, as a defence against those 'who plead that dishonour is done to the Third Person of the Blessed Trinity by the refusal to make express mention of His action in our solemn worship'. Such individuals should 'be reminded that at the very outset of our Office of Holy Communion we have a Collect in which we pray in the most impressive terms for "the inspiration" of the Holy Spirit, that we may worthily magnify God's Holy Name'.[63] Robinson also argued against the introduction of an Eastern-style epiclesis as a possible ecumenical move that could backfire; the East and the West had long held fundamentally different ideas of consecration, a difference that changing the words of the prayers alone would not and could not resolve.[64]

The proposed Prayer Book revisions were ultimately defeated in Parliament, in part due to lack of consensus over adaptations like the epiclesis among both Anglo-Catholic and Evangelical groups, although, as Bradshaw notes, the underlying reasons for the opposition differed: 'while Anglo-Catholics did not want anything that challenged the role of the institution narrative, Evangelicals did not want anything that implied a change in the bread and wine'.[65]

Although the proposed revisions of 1927–8 did not have an immediate impact in England, they did have repercussions on liturgical reform elsewhere in the Anglican Communion. In 1929, South Africa incorporated a eucharistic epiclesis along the lines of what had been proposed in England a few years earlier. In the coming years Ceylon (in

61 A. G. Hebert, 'Anaphora and Epiclesis', *Theology* 37 (1938), p. 94.

62 Burn, 'Invocation', p. 321, quoting from John Wordsworth, *The Holy Communion* (Oxford: Parker 1891), p. 145.

63 J. Armitage Robinson, 'Invocation in the Holy Eucharist', *Theology* 8 (1924), pp. 94–5.

64 Robinson, 'Invocation', p. 100.

65 Bradshaw, 'Rediscovery', p. 86.

1933) and India (in 1960) did the same. Revisions in Japan in 1953 introduced a petition similar to that of the 1549 Book of Common Prayer *before* the institution narrative. In 1959, Canada and the West Indies introduced a pneumatic dimension to their eucharistic prayers (while stopping short of incorporating a fully fledged pneumatic epiclesis) through the addition of 'by the power of the Holy Spirit' to the petition for communicants near the end of the Prayer of Consecration.[66]

The epiclesis question emerged with renewed vigour around the turn of the twentieth century after a period of relative dormancy. It was situated within a series of larger movements which reawakened interest in studying the liturgy, particularly its historical roots. At least indirectly, this renewed interest in historical liturgical scholarship made more extensive research into the epicleses of a broad range of periods and places possible. In turn, research on the epiclesis which was carried out in this atmosphere of rediscovery and renewal (and, increasingly, desire for some ritual reform) comprised an essential foundation upon which the revised eucharistic rites of the latter half of the twentieth century were constructed.

While many of the discussions described in this chapter were conducted with a scholarly audience in mind, some of the insights from historical liturgical scholarship were distilled and repackaged for popular consumption. For example, as time went on, research into the origins of the Roman rite became accessible to an educated and liturgically informed public through works such as Theodor Klauser's *Abendländische Liturgiegeschichte* (first published in 1944)[67] and Joseph Jungmann's *Missarum Solemnia* (1949).[68] Significantly, these works did not treat their subject matter with a detached curiosity but went further to suggest how liturgies which had developed and changed in the past might continue to evolve in the future. Therefore, 'one result of this research was that what had hitherto been a movement urging renewal was beginning to be a movement which hinted at the desirability of some reform'.[69]

The scholars who conducted this research could not help but be influenced by the climate of their churches (many of which were

---

66 See Bradshaw, 'Rediscovery', p. 86.
67 ET: *The Western Liturgy and Its History* (London: Mowbray 1952).
68 ET: *The Mass of the Roman Rite*.
69 John R. K. Fenwick and Bryan D. Spinks, *Worship in Transition: The Liturgical Movement in the Twentieth Century* (New York: Continuum 1995), p. 31.

impacted by the liturgical movement – or movements – and increasing ecumenical awareness) and the climate of the age. While the immediate underlying motivations may have varied somewhat, common social and pastoral problems in Europe (and, eventually, also in North America) affected the established churches in similar ways, and thus it is not surprising that their scholar-members, some of whom were also deeply involved in the various 'liturgical movements' of the twentieth century, would turn their thoughts to how liturgical scholarship on matters such as the epiclesis might inform current discussion of pastoral liturgical reforms. While research on historical origins continued, some of its emphasis shifted from a primary focus on recovering and analysing ancient texts to a concern for deploying the insights gained from such study towards present and/or future reform of the rites of various ecclesial traditions. This shift in focus can be detected in titles such as Cipriano Vagaggini's *The Canon of the Mass and Liturgical Reform*.[70]

By the 1950s, a solid foundation had been laid through the study of ancient liturgies, and contemplating reform became somewhat more feasible than it had been even a few decades earlier. 'Good ancient models had been identified, principles were emerging, and the deficiencies of current forms increasingly recognized'[71] – including the lack of a pneumatic epiclesis in the eucharistic prayers of Western churches. However, despite growing agreement among liturgical scholars both within and across denominational lines about the desirability of some reform and even the outline of the 'shape' such reform might take, most churches were still some years away from meaningful pastoral application of the scholarly and pastoral insights of the liturgical movement – both because these insights had not penetrated deeply to the people in the pews in many cases and because many churches did not have official structures in place with the authority to initiate and execute large-scale reforms.

Scholarship conducted from an ecumenical perspective (either consciously or unconsciously) created a common basis for beginning to translate biblical claims and historical developments into liturgical texts and pastoral practices which met the needs of contemporary worshipping

---

70 Cipriano Vagaggini, *The Canon of the Mass and Liturgical Reform*, ed. and trans. Peter Coughlan (Staten Island, NY: Alba House 1967). Vagaggini's work serves as one example of an instance in which the work of a scholar had clear and documentable impact on the actual course of liturgical reform. This work will be discussed more extensively in Chapter 5.

71 Fenwick and Spinks, *Worship in Transition*, p. 53.

communities across denominational divides. The polemical tone of much scholarship from the first half of the twentieth century had diminished considerably.

> While some research is clearly intended to show the rightness of a particular Church's stance, most of it, especially as the century has progressed, is 'pure' in the sense that the results are presented for the different Churches to assess and assimilate. Frequently the results challenge all traditions equally.[72]

Many churches responded to this 'challenge' through study, communal dialogue, and prayer that led to changes in eucharistic praying as well as revisions to other liturgical rites. 'In many of the Western Churches we find a similar pattern to that in the Roman Catholic Church – a period of rediscovery, research, and renewal, and then, particularly in the 1960s and beyond, a deluge of new liturgical rites.'[73] This 'deluge' of new rites, with a particular eye to the epiclesis, will be the focus of the following chapters.

---

72 Fenwick and Spinks, *Worship in Transition*, p. 4.
73 Fenwick and Spinks, *Worship in Transition*, p. 37.

Part II

Modern epicleses

Chapter 4

The influence of 'early' liturgical evidence on contemporary Western reforms

The widespread 'recovery' of the epiclesis in contemporary Western eucharistic praying can be attributed to the combined influence of a number of factors, especially the confluence of liturgical, ecumenical and pastoral concerns. First, historical liturgical scholarship of the sort described in the previous chapter played an important role during the first half of the twentieth century, even before a more general resurgence of interest in Trinitarian theology in general and pneumatology in particular took hold in the latter half of the century. John R. K. Fenwick and Bryan D. Spinks credit the liturgical movement's interest in 'renewal and rediscovery' at a pastoral level for influencing the trajectory of historical liturgical scholarship. While scholars of previous generations had long been interested in investigating the origins of liturgical rites, they typically refrained from using this knowledge to critique contemporary liturgical practice. However, as the influence of the liturgical movement grew in the early twentieth century, scholarly investigations increasingly challenged present ritual forms.[1] Studies of early eucharistic prayers for example, such as the *Apostolic Tradition* (then thought to be a composition by Hippolytus of Rome from the early third century), led scholars to question why later Roman prayers had no comparable invocation of the Holy Spirit. Paul Bradshaw has suggested that historical research contributed to the perception 'that some reference to the work of the Spirit had been a standard feature of early eucharistic

---

1 John R. K. Fenwick and Bryan D. Spinks, *Worship in Transition: The Liturgical Movement in the Twentieth Century* (New York: Continuum 1995), p. 30.

prayers, and so needed to be replicated in modern revisions that were attempting to get back to the historical roots of Christian liturgy'.[2]

Second, the work of liturgical revision in the latter half of the twentieth century was, in many ways, an ecumenical project. Those involved in the work of liturgical revision from the perspective of their own ecclesial traditions were informed by the same scholarly insights into the Church's early liturgical rites and were frequently aware of the reforms implemented or proposed by other churches.[3] Ecumenical dialogue helped to create a sense of agreement about many features of eucharistic praying, including the elements which typically comprised a eucharistic prayer. Mutual ecumenical awareness (and in some cases direct ecumenical collaboration) contributed to eucharistic prayers whose format and even language sounded quite similar across denominational boundaries.[4] The adoption of the epiclesis by some Western churches led other denominations exploring or undergoing reform to at least consider incorporating this feature into some of their eucharistic prayers. Furthermore, the success of the ecumenical movement helped to create an environment of liturgical reform in which 'no church can any longer do something without affecting another church'.[5]

Third, the pastoral context of the Western churches in the midst of an increasingly secular society led churches undertaking liturgical reform in the closing decades of the twentieth century to seek a balance between contemporary relevance and fidelity to Christian tradition. The eucharistic epiclesis was a clear candidate for inclusion on both of

---

2 Paul F. Bradshaw, 'The Rediscovery of the Holy Spirit in Modern Eucharistic Theology and Practice' in Teresa Berger and Bryan D. Spinks (eds), *The Spirit in Worship – Worship in the Spirit* (Collegeville, MN: Liturgical Press 2009), p. 91.

3 This was especially true in the English-speaking world, where liturgical and textual reform 'had a multinational dimension which also fostered cooperation'. Eugene L. Brand, 'An Ecumenical Enterprise' in Ralph R. Van Loon (ed.), *Encountering God: The Legacy of Lutheran Book of Worship for the 21st Century* (Minneapolis: Kirk House 1998), p. 12.

4 One example of such ecumenical collaboration is 'A Common Eucharistic Prayer', based on the Egyptian version of the Anaphora of St Basil. This prayer in modern English was composed by an ecumenical committee which included representatives from the Roman Catholic, Episcopalian, Lutheran, Presbyterian and Methodist traditions. See Leonel L. Mitchell, 'The Alexandrian Anaphora of St Basil of Caesarea: Ancient Source of "A Common Eucharistic Prayer"', *AThR* 58.2 (1976), p. 194. A version of 'A Common Eucharistic Prayer' is included in the official liturgical books of the Episcopal Church's *Book of Common Prayer* (Prayer D) and the Presbyterian Church (USA)'s *Book of Common Worship* (as Prayer F).

5 James F. Puglisi, 'Introduction' in James F. Puglisi (ed.), *Liturgical Renewal as a Way to Christian Unity* (Collegeville, MN: Liturgical Press 2005), p. vii.

these grounds. Even if calling down the Holy Spirit in the eucharistic context was not a biblical or apostolic practice, it was attested in the first few centuries of the Church's common heritage. A clearly articulated eucharistic pneumatology, achieved in part through the epiclesis, also aligned nicely with concerns for openness to the movements of the Spirit in the wider world and for inclusiveness on the part of ecclesial communities that characterized much of the Western church in the last few decades of the twentieth century. Ruth Meyers notes that '[s]ocial and cultural upheaval was accompanied by a rejection of much of the tradition, or at least radical questioning of its significance for contemporary people', yet liturgical reformers nonetheless desired to keep Christian liturgy grounded in the tradition from which it arose.[6] A compromise between tradition and innovation is evident in certain emphases of recent liturgical texts, particularly a modern self-awareness about the function of symbols in the life of Christian communities, an attempt to incorporate liturgical language that resonates with the concerns and values of contemporary people into official denominational texts, the invitation for all members of the body of Christ to take a 'full, conscious, and active part in liturgical celebrations' (cf. *Sacrosanctum Concilium* 14), and a renewed emphasis on both action and sacraments.[7]

The stress on action and participation contributed in part to the implementation of weekly eucharistic celebrations in many traditions that had not previously known this practice. Meyers points out that 'while this fulfils a goal of the Reformation and is often described as a recovery of the practice of the early Church, it also reflects the contemporary emphasis on involvement in worship'.[8] For churches accustomed to a preaching or prayer service as the typical content of Sunday worship, the regular repetition of the sacrament had the capacity

---

6 See Ruth Meyers, 'Liturgy and Society: Cultural Influences on Contemporary Liturgical Revision' in Paul Bradshaw and Bryan D. Spinks (eds), *Liturgy in Dialogue: Essays in Memory of Ronald Jasper* (Collegeville, MN: Liturgical Press 1994), pp. 164–5, 170–1, quote from p. 164. As an example of the continued concern with Christian tradition in this age of experimentation, Meyers cites the work of the sociologist Robert Bellah. Bellah contended that the combination of traditional eucharistic liturgy with aspects drawn from contemporary culture situated particular religious rituals within the Christian tradition while simultaneously making the Eucharist a 'present reality' for the celebrating community. Since traditional religious symbols served to challenge as well as affirm elements of contemporary culture, such services did not uncritically endorse the culture of the 1960s and 1970s. See Robert N. Bellah, *Beyond Belief: Essays on Religion in a Post-Traditional World* (New York: Harper & Row 1976), pp. 212–15.
7 See Meyers, 'Liturgy and Society', pp. 174–6.
8 Meyers, 'Liturgy and Society', p. 175.

to 'speak' to and engage modern congregations in a different way. Massey Shepherd speculated that 'the sacramental actions, because they are symbolic forms of immediate, existential experience, are preferred to the steady round of the undramatic Daily Offices'.[9]

The epiclesis question also touched upon the situation of the Church and the churches in the midst of a rapidly changing world. Christianity could no longer claim to be *the* dominant cultural influence in the Western world; meanwhile, Christianity was flourishing and growing more inculturated in parts of Asia, Africa and Latin America as the Church was becoming more and more a *world* Church. The optimism of the age (especially the 1960s and 1970s) and ecumenical hopes focused on shared elements of the common Christian tradition rather than points which had proved problematic – if not polemical – in the past nourished the pastoral vision that prayer in common might contribute to fuller and more visible unity among the Christian churches.[10] This visible unity, in turn, might help the churches be a more powerful witness which could evangelize the surrounding culture (in which the churches increasingly found themselves to be a minority voice). For Vischer the epiclesis as a sign of unity and renewal needed to be viewed in the context of the Spirit's work in the Church and in the world – work which was always consonant with the will of Christ.

> This sign retains its proper meaning . . . only if it is viewed in the context of the Spirit's work, i.e. when it becomes clear that the continuity [of the church] lies in the promise itself and not in the sign, and that the church experiences it only when she ever and ever again places herself under the promise.[11]

ECUMENICAL CONSENSUS IN EUCHARISTIC PRAYING

As a result of the combined influence of and cooperation between the liturgical and ecumenical movements and the application of the principles of both to pastoral issues, the latter half of the twentieth century witnessed a remarkable degree of ecumenical liturgical 'convergence' or 'consensus' as the fruit of this process. One of the areas of

9 Massey Shepherd, 'The Dimension of Liturgical Change', *AThR* 51.4 (1969), pp. 254–5, as quoted in Meyers, 'Liturgy and Society', p. 175.
10 For an example of this attitude see Lukas Vischer, 'The Epiclesis: Sign of Unity and Renewal', *SL* 6.1 (1969), pp. 30–9.
11 Vischer, 'Epiclesis', p. 38.

emerging agreement has concerned the 'shape'[12] or 'ordo' of the eucharistic celebration as a whole and the eucharistic prayer in particular.

Several statements produced in the latter half of the twentieth century have provided guidelines regarding both the structure and content of the Eucharist. Many of these suggestions provided explicit or at least implicit support for the inclusion of an epiclesis – or, at the very least, a consciousness of the Spirit's action in the eucharistic encounter on the part of the celebrant and congregation. The 1963 World Council of Churches (WCC) Montreal Conference provided a list of elements which are generally found in 'Orders of Holy Communion' consisting of a celebration of both word and sacrament. With respect to the latter, the 'shape' of the eucharistic portion of the service follows Gregory Dix's fourfold model of taking, blessing, breaking and giving.[13] The Holy Spirit is mentioned in the 'blessing' section, which features these elements: 'Blessing God for creation and redemption and invoking the Holy Spirit, or referring in some other way to the Holy Spirit, reciting the Words of Institution, whether before or after the prayer of thanksgiving, [and] saying the Lord's Prayer'.[14] The consensus structure presented by the Joint Liturgical Group of Great Britain in *Initiation and Eucharist* (1972) has many features in common with this outline.[15] *Baptism, Eucharist and Ministry* lists numerous components of the eucharistic liturgy (while recognizing variations in both order and relative importance in the process of historical development in different churches), including

> the invocation of the Holy Spirit (*epiklesis*) on the community, and the elements of bread and wine (either before the words of institution or after the memorial, or both; or some other reference to the Holy Spirit which adequately expresses the 'epikletic' character of the eucharist).[16]

---

12 The fourfold 'shape' of the eucharistic action based on the synoptic Last Supper accounts in which Jesus took bread, blessed it, broke it and shared it with his disciples was popularized in the twentieth century by Gregory Dix, especially in his *The Shape of the Liturgy* (Westminster, MD and London: Dacre Press 1945).

13 See Dix, *Shape of the Liturgy*, esp. ch. 5, 'The Classical Shape'. For a critique of Dix's fourfold characterization of the eucharistic celebration, see Bryan D. Spinks, 'Mis-shapen: Gregory Dix and the Four-Action Shape of the Liturgy', *LQ* 4.2 (1990), pp. 161–77.

14 In *SL* 2 (1963), p. 248; cited in Fenwick and Spinks, *Worship in Transition*, p. 115.

15 Fenwick and Spinks, *Worship in Transition*, p. 116.

16 World Council of Churches, *Baptism, Eucharist and Ministry*, Faith and Order Paper 111 (Geneva: WCC 1982), pp. 15–16 (Eucharist section, III.27). The text is available online: <http://www.oikoumene.org/en/resources/documents/wcc-commissions/faith-and-order-commission/i-unity-the-church-and-its-mission/baptism-eucharist-and-ministry-faith-and-order-paper-no-111-the-lima-text.html>.

Gradually, an ecumenical consensus emerged that eucharistic prayers should 'express the meaning of the celebration', that 'eucharistic meanings are multiple' (and thus different themes might come to the forefront according to the predilections of various time periods and geographic regions), and that there is no single ideal form for the eucharistic prayer (although some components are shared by most eucharistic prayers).[17] While not all traditions arrange the elements of their prayers in the same way or adopt the same pattern in all their prayers, the existence of such frameworks as starting points or guidelines in the composition of new eucharistic prayer texts or the revision of older prayers does provide certain advantages. For example, Gordon Lathrop insists that:

> The use of an *ordo* combines both conservation and critique: conservation in the passing on of the great shape of the Mass, for example; critique in using that shape to welcome deeper participation in new cultural contexts, and critique in the sense that such a shared *ordo* is not a matter of ceremonial compulsion.[18]

In addition to trends which have contributed to a similar 'shape' underlying most of the eucharistic prayers in the churches which rely on official liturgical texts, there has also been a movement towards multiple options for the eucharistic prayer within a particular ecclesial tradition. This tendency is especially significant given that, until quite recently, each tradition generally relied on a single eucharistic prayer at any one time. As Frank Senn recalls,

> Christians in Western Churches may have become so accustomed to having a selection of eucharistic prayers from which the presiding minister chooses one for a particular celebration that it may have all but passed out of memory that this was not always the case.[19]

---

17 Frank C. Senn, 'Introduction' in Frank C. Senn (ed.), *New Eucharistic Prayers: An Ecumenical Study of Their Development and Structure* (Mahwah, NJ: Paulist Press 1987), p. 3.

18 Gordon W. Lathrop, 'Conservation and Critique: Principles in Lutheran Liturgical Renewal as Proposals toward the Unity of the Churches' in James F. Puglisi (ed.), *Liturgical Renewal as a Way to Christian Unity* (Collegeville, MN: Liturgical Press 2005), p. 100.

19 Senn, 'Introduction', p. 1.

Although some Eastern Christian traditions had long been accustomed to a collection of eucharistic prayers – typically one or a handful for regular use and a larger repertoire drawn upon for special feasts or seasons throughout the year, it seems to have been the liturgical reforms of the Roman Catholic Church after the Second Vatican Council that led the way for the wider introduction of this practice in Western churches. Adrien Nocent identifies the introduction of several new eucharistic prayers during the course of the liturgical reforms following the Second Vatican Council as the 'single boldest reform' of the Roman rite.[20] It was this move that, at least in part, inspired other churches to broaden their eucharistic *theology* through providing a more expansive eucharistic *euchology*.[21] Although a diverse collection of prayers and prayer patterns survives from the early Church, the Roman Canon[22] became *the* dominant eucharistic prayer in the Western church for nearly a millennium – at least from the early Middle Ages until the Reformations of the sixteenth century. This Canon would retain its role as the Roman Catholic Church's one and only eucharistic prayer for another several hundred years, from the sixteenth century until nearly the end of the twentieth, with the promulgation of the reforms initiated by the Second Vatican Council.

The Reformation brought sweeping change to the realm of eucharistic praying, but what remained unchanged was the general 'rule' that each tradition was limited to one eucharistic text at a time. Furthermore, while the Reformation orders parted ways with the Roman Canon in a number of significant respects, this did not necessarily translate into greater diversity in the overall pattern or structure of eucharistic prayers. As Senn has noted,

> The Reformation of the sixteenth century produced a proliferation of liturgical orders, each with its own eucharistic or communion texts . . . Yet a patient analysis of the multitude of Reformation church orders reveals a remarkable uniformity within the variety of liturgical orders.[23]

---

20 Adrien Nocent, *A Rereading of the Renewed Liturgy*, trans. Mary M. Misrahi (Collegeville, MN: Liturgical Press 1994), p. 25.
21 A related issue was that, with the introduction of more regular eucharistic celebrations to Western churches that had been accustomed to celebrating the Eucharist only quarterly, more variety was perceived as desirable.
22 The earliest witness to a prayer very similar to the Roman Canon can be found in Ambrose of Milan's *De Sacramentis* (IV.5.21–6.27).
23 Senn, 'Introduction', p. 1.

Especially among the Lutheran and Reformed traditions, the 'recovery' of a full eucharistic prayer occurred in stages rather than a single leap – and again liturgical scholarship, particularly the recovery and reassessment resulting from historical study of the sources of early Christian worship, played a role in this recovery.[24] The place of the words of institution vis-à-vis the eucharistic prayer was a major issue for both of these churches, reaching not only back to the Reformation origins of these traditions but even further back to the patristic sources which inspired their liturgies.

> For Lutherans the Verba functioned as an act of consecration by proclamation of the Word (a view which could appeal to Sts. Ambrose of Milan and Augustine of Hippo). For the Reformed the Verba served as a scriptural warrant for the celebration; but following Calvin Reformed liturgies were able to give a greater role to the Holy Spirit in the form of the epiclesis (a view which could appeal to Sts. Cyril of Jerusalem and Theodore of Mopsuestia).[25]

Both of these churches made tentative steps towards full eucharistic prayers by sidestepping (for the time being) the words of institution. Initially, prayers were crafted which incorporated many elements of traditional eucharistic prayers (such as praise, anamnesis and epiclesis) but left the words of institution outside the confines of this prayer.[26] Eventually, the words of institution came to be regularly included within the eucharistic prayer (Lutheran)[27] or at least as an option within the prayer (Reformed).[28] The Anglican churches (and to some extent the

---

24 Senn, 'Introduction', p. 3.
25 Senn, 'Introduction', p. 3.
26 Senn, 'Introduction', pp. 3–4.
27 The first Lutheran prayer to include the words of institution may have been one composed by Paul Z. Strodach which was included, in somewhat modified form, in the *Book of Worship* of the Lutheran Churches in India (1936). Strodach's prayer served as a model for the eucharistic prayer written by Luther D. Reed which appeared in the *Service Book and Hymnal* of the Lutheran Church in America (1958). Senn, 'Introduction', p. 4.
28 The Reformed tradition was more hesitant to include the Verba within a eucharistic prayer proper. *The Service for the Lord's Day* (1984) of the Presbyterian Church (USA) and the Cumberland Presbyterian Church presents the words of institution as an optional element of the eucharistic prayer. (They may also be said later, immediately preceding the breaking of the bread.) See Senn, 'Introduction', p. 4. The current official texts, found in the *Book of Common Worship* (1993), likewise present several options for the placement of the words of institution in most of these prayers – either before the Great Thanksgiving as a warrant for the celebration, within the eucharistic prayer itself, or at the fraction.

Methodist and Episcopal traditions as well) implemented reforms which moved their prayers towards the ecumenical consensus 'shape' of the eucharistic prayer by fundamentally 'reshaping' their existing material in response to pan-Anglican and ecumenical discussion and historical scholarship.[29]

Regardless of the process by which older prayers were adapted and new ones created, the prayers which resulted have much in common with each other, both within and across denominational boundaries. The fact that in many cases the reform process was carried out as an ecumenical project either explicitly (through collaboration on common texts) or implicitly (through an awareness of the reforms recently completed or currently in progress in other churches) likely contributed to this situation. The similarity is often so striking that, in some respects, as Senn notes, 'to have read one new rite is to have read them all. There is indeed a remarkable consensus.' However, Senn continues, 'It is useful . . . to look behind this consensus.'[30] Upon closer examination, the current 'consensus' on the role of the epiclesis in the eucharistic prayer is not as consistent as it might appear at first glance. Even within prayers modelled upon the same ancient texts (such as *Apostolic Tradition* 4 or the Egyptian Anaphora of Basil), the epicletic language of the 'common' prayers which have resulted sometimes 'sounds' in different theological tones.

While both ancient and modern eucharistic epicleses share some elements in common yet are characterized by tremendous diversity, closer examination suggests that the unity and diversity apparent in modern Western eucharistic epicleses may be of a different sort from that which is represented in early anaphoras. Although the location and language of the epicleses incorporated into Western eucharistic prayers during the last half century have varied, many of these pneumatic invocations were influenced at some stage of their development by early models (and often early *Eastern* models) of eucharistic praying. The emergence of new sources (e.g. the *Didache* and the *Apostolic Tradition*) and the greater accessibility of (critical) editions of ancient texts made it much more possible than it had been in the sixteenth century to reform Christian worship in light of the perceived practices of the early Church, the epiclesis among them. Contemporary scholarship on ancient liturgical texts in general and the epiclesis in particular during the past few decades, however, has since challenged some of the interpretations which grounded the formulations of the epicleses in contemporary

---

29 Fenwick and Spinks, *Worship in Transition*, pp. 116–18.
30 Fenwick and Spinks, *Worship in Transition*, p. 116.

Western eucharistic prayers. Recent scholarship has even called into question, to some degree, the function which the framers of these 'new' texts intended for the epicleses they contain. Three cases concerning the modern use of ancient epicleses will be considered here as examples of this phenomenon: (1) the status of the 'split epiclesis' in the early Alexandrian tradition of eucharistic praying, (2) the dominance of the West Syrian or Antiochene 'shape' of eucharistic praying that served to introduce a Trinitarian pattern of prayer to Western churches (and often an epiclesis following the anamnesis), and (3) some noteworthy differences between ancient and modern 'diversity' with regard to epicletic prayer patterns.

THE SPLIT EPICLESIS: RECONSIDERING THE ALEXANDRIAN SYNTHESIS

Several modern anaphoras feature a 'split epiclesis', typically consisting of a supplication for the Spirit's presence (and possible cooperation in the work of sanctifying the eucharistic bread and wine) preceding the institution narrative and a further petition, often oriented towards the Spirit's role of realizing the fruits of communion in those who partake of the eucharistic bread and wine, after the anamnesis.[31] The principal employment of this structure is found in Roman Catholic eucharistic prayers composed since the conclusion of the Second Vatican Council; all but one of these prayers locate an explicit pneumatic consecratory epiclesis in a location equivalent to the Roman Canon's *Quam oblationem*.[32] The heritage of the Alexandrian tradition is often cited as precedent for this development. For example, Cipriano Vagaggini, an individual intimately involved with composing the new prayers which appeared in the 1969 editio typica of the *Roman Missal*,[33] commented

---

31 This arrangement is also sometimes referred to as a 'double epiclesis', emphasizing the fact that prayers of this type feature two distinct petitions for the Spirit's presence and activity in the eucharistic context. The term 'split epiclesis', on the other hand, draws attention to the perception that the consecratory and communion aspects of the epiclesis are really two dimensions of a single reality, whether the invocations for consecration and communion are conjoined or separated in the prayer. Prime examples of 'split epicleses' include the prayers of the Roman Catholic Church (in addition to the Roman Canon) and Eucharistic Prayers A and B of the Church of England's *Common Worship*.
32 The sole exception is Eucharistic Prayer for Masses with Children III. While the content of the epiclesis preceding the institution narrative otherwise resembles that of the other Roman prayers, the Holy Spirit is not mentioned.
33 For the role of Vagaggini in the reform of the Roman eucharistic prayers, see Annibale Bugnini, *The Reform of the Liturgy, 1948–1975* (Collegeville, MN: Liturgical Press 1990), pp. 228–9.

upon the structural parallels between early Egyptian prayers and the Roman Canon:

> Dêr Balizeh and the Louvain fragment separate the two ideas contained in an epiclesis, and put the prayer for consecration before the institution, and the prayer for a fruitful communion after the anamnesis, as is the practice of the Roman canon (*Quam oblationem; Supplices . . . ut quotquot*).[34]

Although a number of Egyptian anaphoras do contain epicletic petitions both before and after the institution narrative, a close examination of the early Egyptian evidence raises the question of whether the Alexandrian pattern can really serve to justify the modern epicleses which claim it as inspiration. The primary problem here for the theory – based on historical evidence – is that early Egyptian texts do not contain *both* (1) a preliminary pneumatic epiclesis before the institution narrative oriented towards consecration of the gifts *and* (2) a subsequent invocation of the Spirit whose emphasis is communion.[35] While the Dêr Balyzeh Papyrus (*c.*500–700) does frame the connection between the Sanctus and the institution narrative as a consecratory epiclesis, nothing is known about the content of a 'second' epiclesis in this document – or even if there was a second epiclesis at all.[36] The testimony of the Louvain Coptic Papyrus (*c.*600), which contains a portion of an anaphora extending from the conclusion of the Sanctus through the institution narrative, likewise is not complete enough to

---

34 Cipriano Vagaggini, *The Canon of the Mass and Liturgical Reform*, ed. and trans. Peter Coughlan (Staten Island, NY: Alba House 1967), p. 69.

35 Some of the issues discussed below were previously raised by Aidan Kavanagh, in 'Thoughts on the New Eucharistic Prayers', *Worship* 43.1 (1969), pp. 5–6, 9–12 and by Thomas Julian Talley in 'The Literary Structure of the Eucharistic Prayer', *Worship* 58.5 (1984), pp. 416–17.

36 The post-Sanctus section of the Dêr Balyzeh fragment (*c.* sixth–seventh centuries) reads: 'Both fill us with the glory which comes from you, and deign to send your Holy Spirit upon these creatures, and make the bread the body of our Lord and Saviour Jesus Christ, and the cup the blood of the new covenant of our same Lord and God and Saviour Jesus Christ . . .' There is a second mention of the Holy Spirit after the institution narrative which may have comprised part of an epiclesis, but the fragmentary nature of the manuscript evidence permits little clarity regarding either the content or function of this part of the prayer: ' . . . and give to us your servants in the power of the Holy Spirit for the strengthening and increase of faith in the hope of eternal life to come'. ET from Bridget Nichols and Alistair MacGregor, *The Eucharistic Epiclesis*, Ushaw Library Publications 4 (Durham: Ushaw College Library 2001), pp. 4–5.

testify to a consecratory epiclesis preceding the institution narrative *and* a communion epiclesis following it.[37]

In a recent article, Michael Zheltov has drawn renewed attention to a fourth-century papyrus containing a complete anaphora and thanksgiving prayer which is an earlier Greek version of the prayer of the Louvain papyrus. While this 'Barcelona Papyrus' does definitely contain a consecratory epiclesis preceding the institution narrative, once again, the evidence for an explicitly pneumatic communion epiclesis following the narrative is lacking. The epiclesis prior to the institution narrative reads:

> Through Him [Jesus Christ] we offer You these Your creations, the bread and the cup: we ask and beseech You to send onto them Your Holy and Comforter Spirit from Heaven, to represent them materially and to make the bread the Body of Christ and the cup the Blood of Christ, of the New Covenant . . .[38]

After the anamnesis, there is a prayer for worthy communion that mentions 'communion of the Holy Spirit' as one of the benefits of communion, but the epicletic petition itself is *not* framed as an invocation of the Spirit:

> Even so, we pray to You, Master, that in blessing You will bless and in sanctifying sanctify . . . for all communicating from them for undivided faith, for communication of incorruption, for communion of the Holy Spirit, for perfection of belief and truth, for fulfillment of all Your will.[39]

Among the 'peculiarities' Zheltov detects in this anaphora, two relate specifically to the epiclesis. The characteristic Egyptian link between the Sanctus ('full are heaven and earth . . .') and the first epiclesis ('fill . . .') is disrupted by a christological post-Sanctus section (a feature commonly found in Antiochene anaphoras), and the second epiclesis requests the

---

37 The text of the post-Sanctus epiclesis is: 'We pray and beseech you to send out over them [this bread and this cup] your Holy Spirit, the Paraclete, from heaven . . . to make (?) the bread the body of Christ and the cup the blood of Christ of the new covenant.' ET from R. C. D. Jasper and G. J. Cuming (eds), *Prayers of the Eucharist: Early and Reformed* (Collegeville, MN: Liturgical Press 1990, 3rd edn, revised and enlarged), p. 81.

38 Michael Zheltov, 'The Anaphora and the Thanksgiving Prayer from the Barcelona Papyrus: An Underestimated Testimony to the Anaphoral History in the Fourth Century', *VC* 62.5 (2008), p. 490.

39 Zheltov, 'Anaphora and Thanksgiving Prayer', p. 491.

sanctification of the communicants but not the gifts.[40] Furthermore, the petition of the first epiclesis is not 'fill' at all but rather 'send' – a construction of the epiclesis not certainly attested in Egypt – or anywhere else – before the second half of the fourth century.[41] Drawing attention to this and other features of this anaphora whose Egyptian provenance is doubtful, Paul Bradshaw concludes that, together, 'these differences suggest that the original nucleus of the prayer either was not composed in Egypt or alternatively represents a variant tradition there that was probably subject to some significant influence from elsewhere'.[42]

Other Egyptian anaphoras do not lend much more support to a primitive Egyptian pattern resembling that of the split epiclesis found in current Western eucharistic prayers. Twentieth-century scholars viewed the anaphora of Sarapion as something of an anomaly[43] and did not draw upon it specifically as a model for contemporary prayers. Nonetheless, considering the epicleses of this prayer does contribute to a portrayal of the Egyptian epicleses that is much more complex than a classification of

---

40 Zheltov, 'Anaphora and Thanksgiving Prayer', p. 494. Zheltov suggests the need, based on this anaphoral witness, to distinguish between *two* types of the Egyptian anaphora based on the content of the section between the Sanctus and the institution narrative: (1) Sanctus → epiclesis → institution narrative (represented, e.g., by the Anaphora of Mark) and (2) Sanctus → post-Sanctus → epiclesis → institution narrative (as in the prayer of the Barcelona Papyrus).

41 On the significance of the verbs used in the epiclesis, see Sebastian P. Brock, 'The Epiklesis in the Antiochene Baptismal Ordines', *Symposium Syriacum 1972*, OrChrAn 197 (Rome: Pontifical Oriental Institute 1974), pp. 183–218; 'Towards a Typology of the Epiclesis in the West Syrian Anaphoras' in H.-J. Feulner, E. Velkovska and R. F. Taft (eds), *Crossroad of Cultures: Studies in Liturgy and Patristics in Honor of Gabriele Winkler* (Rome: Pontifical Oriental Institute 2000), pp. 173–92; and 'Invocations to/for the Holy Spirit in Syriac Liturgical Texts: Some Comparative Approaches' in R. F. Taft and G. Winkler (eds), *Comparative Liturgy Fifty Years after Anton Baumstark (1872–1948)* (Rome: Pontifical Oriental Institute 2001), pp. 377–406. Gabriele Winkler has developed Brock's insights in a series of articles: 'Nochmals zu den Anfängen der Epiklese und des Sanctus im Eucharistischen Hochgebet', *Theologische Quartalschrift* 174.3 (1994), pp. 214–31; 'Further Observations in Connection with the Early Form of the Epiklesis', *Le Sacrement de l'Initiation: Origines et Prospective*, Patrimoine Syriaque Actes du colloque III (Antélias, Lebanon: Centre d'Études et de Recherches Pastorales 1996), pp. 66–80; and 'Weitere Beobachtungen zur frühen Epiklese (den Doxologien und dem Sanctus): Über die Bedeutung der Apokryphen für die Erforschung der Entwicklung der Riten', *OrChr* 80 (1996), pp. 177–200.

42 Paul F. Bradshaw, 'The Barcelona Papyrus and the Development of Early Eucharistic Prayers' in Maxwell E. Johnson (ed.), *Issues in Eucharistic Praying in East and West: Essays in Liturgical and Theological Analysis* (Collegeville, MN: Liturgical Press 2011), p. 132.

43 Vagaggini deemed it 'not in the least typical' (see Vagaggini, *Canon of the Mass*, p. 67) although Louis Bouyer supplies a more circumspect discussion in *Eucharist: Theology and Spirituality of the Eucharistic Prayer*, trans. C. U. Quinn from the 2nd French edition (Notre Dame, IN: University of Notre Dame Press 1968), pp. 203ff.

epicleses into the categories of 'consecration' or 'communion' can easily accommodate. In Sarapion's anaphora, there is a request in the post-Sanctus section that the Father 'Fill also this sacrifice with your power and with your participation';[44] however, besides lacking specifically pneumatic content, this request need not be read as implying 'consecration' in the sense of transforming the gifts of bread and wine. The case for this interpretation is strengthened by the presence of an invocation of the *Logos* for the consecration of the bread and cup *after* the institution narrative: 'God of truth, let your holy Word come [ἐπιδημησάτω] upon this bread in order that the bread may become body of the Word, and upon this cup in order that the cup may become blood of truth.'[45] In fact, the only possible explicit invocation of the Spirit in this anaphora immediately *precedes* the Sanctus. Its content resembles neither 'consecration' nor 'communion' intentions but serves instead as a petition for the realization of the Trinitarian mystery in the midst of the gathered assembly: 'Give us holy Spirit, in order that we may be able to proclaim and describe your inexpressible mysteries. Let the Lord Jesus speak in us and let holy Spirit also hymn you through us.'[46]

Although the more developed forms of the Alexandrian anaphora (e.g. the Coptic and Greek recensions of the Anaphora of Mark) display some parallels to the modern 'split epiclesis' pattern, even this evidence is not as conclusive as has sometimes been supposed. While the epiclesis preceding the institution narrative may or may not be consecratory,[47] the

---

44 ET from Maxwell E. Johnson, *The Prayers of Sarapion of Thmuis: A Literary, Liturgical, and Theological Analysis*, OrChrAn 249 (Rome: Pontifical Oriental Institute 1995), p. 47.

45 Johnson, *Prayers of Sarapion*, p. 49. For a discussion of the translation of the verb, see Maxwell E. Johnson, 'The Origins of the Anaphoral Use of the Sanctus and Epiclesis Revisited: The Contribution of Gabriele Winkler and Its Implications' in Feulner, Velkovska and Taft (eds), *Crossroad of Cultures*, pp. 437ff.

46 Johnson, *Prayers of Sarapion*, p. 47. On this point, Johnson observes that 'Sarapion's anaphora does not say that the Son and Holy Spirit are praised by the sanctus of both the seraphim and the community. What it does say is that the Son and Holy Spirit themselves are to "speak in" the community and "hymn" *God* through the sanctus' (p. 213); emphasis his.

47 Even in the thirteenth-century manuscript tradition, the pre-institution epiclesis petition of Greek MARK, which reads, 'Make this sacrifice also full of your blessing through the coming of your Holy Spirit', need not be read as explicitly consecratory in intent. As Nichols and MacGregor note, much depends on whether 'sacrifice' here is to be read as a specific reference to the eucharistic elements or more generally as referring to a sacrifice of praise and thanksgiving; see Nichols and MacGregor, *Eucharistic Epiclesis*, p. 8. Geoffrey Cuming deems this epiclesis 'so vague'; see Geoffrey J. Cuming, 'The Anaphora of St. Mark: A Study in Development', *Le Muséon* 95 (1982), p. 125. The petition of the Coptic version is more explicitly consecratory with its specification of the eucharistic

second epiclesis located after the narrative clearly contains both consecratory and communion dimensions:

> For we pray and beseech you, generous lover of the human race, that you would send from your holy height, from your prepared dwelling-place, from your embrace that cannot be circumscribed, the Paraclete himself, the Holy Spirit of truth, the life-giving Lord, who has spoken in the law and through the prophets and apostles; who is ... consubstantial with you, proceeding from you, sitting with you on the throne of your kingdom and with your only-begotten Son, our Lord and God and Saviour Jesus Christ. Look upon us and send upon these loaves and cups your Holy Spirit to sanctify and consecrate them, as Almighty God, *(aloud)* and make the bread the body and the cup the blood of the new covenant of our Lord and God and Saviour and supreme King, Jesus Christ, that they may become to all of us who partake of them for faith, for sobriety, for healing, for temperance, for sanctification, for renewal of soul, body, and spirit, for fellowship in the blessedness of eternal life and immortality, for the glorification of your most holy name, and for the remission of sins; so that in this as in all things your most holy, precious, and glorious name may be glorified, praised and sanctified with Jesus Christ and the Holy Spirit.[48]

Thus the neat distinction placing consecration before the institution narrative and concerns for communion afterwards is simply not to be found in the textual record of early (or even relatively late) Alexandrian anaphoras.

Finally, the question must be raised as to whether the epiclesis structure in some of these prayers is ultimately 'Egyptian' at all. Several scholars have suggested that the second epiclesis may be a West Syrian interpolation since its location corresponds to that of the sole epiclesis in the Antiochene form.[49] More recently, the claim has been made that West Syrian influence might have shaped the 'Alexandrian' anaphora from the Sanctus to the final doxology. The most primitive form of the

---

elements as the objects of blessing and sanctification: '... and in blessing bless, and in sanctifying sanctify, these your precious gifts which have been set before your face, this bread and this cup'. ET from Nichols and MacGregor, *Eucharistic Epiclesis*, p. 7.

48 ET from Nichols and MacGregor, *Eucharistic Epiclesis*, pp. 7–8.

49 Hans Lietzmann, for example, called this epiclesis a 'Fremdkorper' within the prayer. See his *Mass and Lord's Supper: A Study in the History of the Liturgy*, trans. Dorothea H. G. Reeve (Leiden: Brill 1979), p. 63.

Alexandrian eucharistic prayer would then have been similar to that which survives in the Strasbourg Papyrus 254 (*c*.300–500), a likely predecessor of the developed form of MARK. Both of these anaphoras begin by praising God who created all things in Christ and continue with an offering of 'sacrifice' (whose most likely connotations are that of a sacrifice of praise and thanksgiving) and intercessions. Then the two forms diverge. Whereas the 'developed' form of MARK introduces the Sanctus at this point, the Strasbourg Papyrus continues with a doxology which may represent the conclusion of the prayer, making the earliest Egyptian core a simple structure of praise, offering and intercession.[50]

An extensive role for Syrian traditions in this prayer, especially as far as the epiclesis is concerned, could lend support to Gabriele Winkler's recent theories about the geographic origin of the epiclesis in Syria. A perennial problem in the Alexandrian anaphoral tradition has been explaining the presence of the *two* epicletic units in the prayer. While West Syrian origin has been logical for the latter, Winkler's theory of the Sanctus and epiclesis originating (and perhaps initially circulating) as an integral unit[51] may lend credence to the idea that the earlier section could possibly have its origins in Syria as well. Although the first epiclesis in the developed Alexandrian anaphoras has been difficult to dismiss as a late interpolation given its intimate link with the Sanctus,[52] this does not rule out the possibility that it could have been one component of a relatively *early* interpolation of the Sanctus–epiclesis unit into a structure which

---

50 See Talley, 'Literary Structure', p. 416. The status of the Strasbourg Papyrus as a complete anaphora in itself was suggested by Edward J. Kilmartin, 'Sacrificium Laudis: Content and Function of Early Eucharistic Prayers', *TS* 35.2 (1974), pp. 268–87 and developed further in Cuming, 'Anaphora of St. Mark'. Zheltov has recently criticized this view, contending that, 'as a liturgical text, the prayer from the Strasbourg papyrus should have been mirroring the current Egyptian liturgical practice, which by the time of creation of this papyrus already knew the anaphoral Sanctus, epiclesis, etc. . . . the discovery of the Barcelona papyrus leaves the hypothesis of the Strasbourg papyrus' integrity unfounded . . . [and] it leaves the different variants of the "4th-century interpolations" theory without any actual documentary proof' (Zheltov, 'Anaphora and Thanksgiving Prayer', p. 502). Much would seem to depend on the relative dating of the Strasbourg and Barcelona papyri. Zheltov suggests that the contents of the Barcelona papyrus predate those of the Strasbourg papyrus – as the text of the Barcelona papyrus 'is not younger than the mid-4th century and may go back to the 3rd' (p. 502). However, the first half of the fourth century falls within the 200-year span to which the Strasbourg Papyrus is commonly dated as well. If the two texts are roughly contemporaneous, it becomes more difficult to dismiss the seemingly 'primitive' pattern of the Strasbourg Papyrus as an anachronism.
51 See, e.g., Winkler, 'Further Observations', pp. 79–80.
52 This connection has been dubbed the '*pleni–vereplenum–imple*' construction, with the 'full is heaven and earth of your glory' of the Egyptian Sanctus (which lacks the Benedictus) providing a logical transition to the following epicletic petition, 'Fill . . .'

previously lacked both these components. Given Winkler's contention that both the Sanctus and epiclesis arose in Syria and that, by the middle of the fourth century, 'the initial epiklesis is steadily making room for doxologies, eventually including the Sanctus as well',[53] it is curious that a close literary or structural link between the Sanctus and epiclesis is *not* a characteristic of later Syrian prayers. Rather, in the developed Antiochene or West Syrian pattern, following the Sanctus (with Benedictus), the post-Sanctus section focuses on thanksgiving to God the Father for redemption in Christ (culminating in the institution narrative) with a Spirit epiclesis following in the third part of the prayer, providing a tidy Trinitarian framework for the whole. Winkler has argued that the situation of epicleses within a Trinitarian framework was a later reworking of a more original petition addressed to the Spirit.[54]

Regardless of the ultimate origin of the Sanctus and epiclesis, if the Sanctus and epiclesis ever *did* travel together and if Winkler's theory about an original layer of pneumatic eucharistic epicleses being subsequently reworked to accommodate their placement in a broader Trinitarian context is correct, the Anaphora of Mark could provide an example of a case where this unit had not yet been worked into an explicitly Trinitarian framework. This possibility in itself might suggest the relatively early origin of the first epiclesis in Egyptian texts. This could explain why the first epiclesis seems much more integral to the anaphora than the second epiclesis following the anamnesis – which could more logically be a later interpolation under West Syrian influence.

From this brief survey, it seems that the Alexandrian anaphoral tradition tended to keep consecration and communion dimensions of the epiclesis together after the anamnesis, whatever the epicletic content preceding the narrative. In contrast, modern Western eucharistic prayers containing a 'split epiclesis' overtly separate the consecration and communion dimensions of the anaphora by relegating these aspects of the Spirit's work to different sections of the anaphora. Insofar as these newer epicleses are inconsistent, in this way, with their supposed predecessors in the Alexandrian anaphora tradition, the modern split epicleses raise theological issues which the older Egyptian epicleses do not. Some have argued that a split epiclesis obscures the inherent unity of the Spirit's activity in the eucharistic context, namely, that the Spirit is invoked on the eucharistic gifts *so that* all who share in them may in turn

---

53 Winkler, 'Further Observations', p. 79.
54 See Winkler, 'Further Observations', p. 79 and also Winkler, 'Weitere Beobachtungen', pp. 192ff.

be brought together in unity in the one body of Christ.[55] Another way to put this is that the connection between the pneumaticized body of Christ consumed in the eucharistic species and the pneumaticized body of Christ which the Church is called to be is downplayed. Furthermore, as Aidan Kavanagh noted, locating a pneumatic epiclesis immediately before the institution narrative has inevitable and undesirable consequences insofar as it

> not only welds both sections into a unity that is longer and more strongly consecratory than before: it also interrupts the flow of sequence in narrating the divine mercies for which eucharistic prayer is made and sets the institution narrative off from this cursus.[56]

Therefore, the phenomenon of the 'split epiclesis' is one which might fruitfully be revisited in future reforms of eucharistic praying. In addition to the 'Alexandrian' split epiclesis, however, Western churches picked up other prayer patterns from the practice of ancient churches, including a preference for the West Syrian or Antiochene 'shape' of the eucharistic prayer.

RESHAPING EASTERN PRAYERS: ANCIENT WEST SYRIAN INFLUENCE ON MODERN WESTERN CHRISTIANITY

Ecumenical consensus increasingly affirms the role of the Spirit in the eucharistic action as a whole and more cautiously assigns some effect to the invocation of the Spirit in eucharistic prayers. A good example can be found in the agreed ecumenical statement, *Baptism, Eucharist and Ministry* (1982) produced by the Faith and Order Commission of the World Council of Churches.[57] The commentary associated with a subsection of the document entitled 'The Eucharist as Invocation of the Spirit' assigns an important role to the eucharistic epiclesis in connection

---

55 See, e.g., John H. McKenna, 'Eucharistic Epiclesis: Myopia or Microcosm?', *TS* 36.2 (1975), p. 283 and Bradshaw, 'Rediscovery', p. 88.
56 Kavanagh, 'Thoughts', p. 9. For similar critiques see John H. McKenna, *The Eucharistic Epiclesis: A Detailed History from the Patristic to the Modern Era* (Chicago: Hillenbrand 2009, 2nd edn), p. 227 and Frank C. Senn, 'Toward a Different Anaphoral Structure', *Worship* 58.4 (1984), esp. p. 358.
57 *Baptism, Eucharist and Ministry*, Faith and Order Paper no. 111. See esp. nos 14–18 in the 'Eucharist' section.

with the words of institution and the promise of Christ's presence realized in the liturgical context, claiming that a renewed appreciation of the epiclesis in light of the eucharistic encounter as a whole might even help to resolve present theological difficulties:

> In the early liturgies the whole 'prayer action' was thought of as bringing about the reality promised by Christ. The invocation of the Spirit was made both on the community and on the elements of bread and wine. Recovery of such an understanding may help us overcome our difficulties concerning a special moment of consecration.[58]

While the latter statement may indeed be true, the implied link between the words of institution and the epiclesis may have set up a temporal expectation for these elements within the anaphora that leads to West Syrian structure being somewhat selectively employed to serve the ends of Western theology, with its traditional emphasis on the consecratory efficacy of the words of Christ. The tension between these two approaches is similarly expressed in this comment from Philip Pfatteicher:

> The whole Eucharist has an epicletic character because it all depends on the work of the Holy Spirit. In the liturgy the presence of the risen and reigning Lord – Christ filled with the Spirit – is actualized. Specifically at this point in the prayer the epiclesis asks God's response to the church's obedience to the command of Christ to 'Do this in *anamnesis* of me.'[59]

This lends support to Bryan Spinks' claim that the West Syrian pattern of eucharistic praying has been touted 'not only [as] the perfect and only paradigm for authentic eucharistic prayer', but also as a form which 'can be traced back directly to the Jewish euchology used by Jesus at the Last Supper, and implied by him in the words "Do this in remembrance of me"'.[60] Many of the 'new' Western eucharistic prayers did in fact

---

58 *Baptism, Eucharist and Ministry*, 'Eucharist', no. 14.
59 Philip H. Pfatteicher, *Commentary on the Lutheran Book of Worship: Lutheran Liturgy in Its Ecumenical Context* (Minneapolis: Augsburg Fortress, 1990), p. 167. Pfatteicher is commenting here specifically on the epicleses of the *Lutheran Book of Worship* (1978), which are found in the standard 'West Syrian' post-anamnesis location.
60 Bryan D. Spinks, 'Berakah, Anaphoral Theory and Luther', *LQ* 3.3 (1989), pp. 267–8.

adopt what has come to be known as an 'Antiochene' or 'West Syrian' structure, which traditionally contains the following elements:[61]

1 Sursum corda	7 Anamnesis
2 Preface	8 Offering
3 Pre-Sanctus	9 Epiclesis
4 Sanctus	10 Intercessions
5 Post-Sanctus	11 Doxology
6 Institution Narrative	

Although it does not seem that the contemporary prayers, for the most part, were deliberately patterned after this structure per se,[62] Frank Senn has provided several plausible reasons why this format might have proved quite attractive to those involved in the reform of eucharistic prayers in the late twentieth century.[63] First, this structure had the benefits both of antiquity and orthodoxy, 'represent[ing] a post-Nicene synthesis of archaic form and developed Trinitarian theology'. Second, 'Wittingly or unwittingly, the West Syrian anaphoras follow a tripartite scheme similar to the Jewish *birkat ha-mazon*.' Although Senn does not make this connection explicit, it should be noted that many of the new eucharistic prayers were written in an era when the theory that Christian eucharistic prayers developed from Jewish table prayers such as the *birkat ha-mazon* had wide currency.[64] It was thought that this Jewish prayer (with its tripartite structure featuring praise of God for creation, thanksgiving in memory of God's saving acts, and petition for God's fulfilment of promises made to the people of Israel) was adapted and reworked into a

---

61 As outlined by Jasper and Cuming in the Introduction to *Prayers of the Eucharist*, p. 6. Ancient anaphoras which fit this pattern, thought to have emerged by the late fourth century, include the Anaphoras of St Basil, St James and St John Chrysostom as well as the *Apostolic Constitutions*.

62 Fenwick and Spinks remark that 'no really sound argument has been advanced as to why West Syrian fifth-century forms should be the basis for twentieth-century prayers'. Fenwick and Spinks, *Worship in Transition*, p. 131.

63 The following ideas are presented in Senn, 'Toward a Different Anaphoral Structure', p. 347.

64 Discussion of possible Jewish precedents for the use of epicleses in Christian anaphoras can be found in, e.g., Louis Ligier, 'De la cène de Jésus à l'anaphore de l'Église', *La Maison-Dieu* 87 (1966), pp. 7–49; Bouyer, *Eucharist*, pp. 106ff.; and William R. Crockett, *Eucharist: Symbol of Transformation* (New York: Pueblo 1989), pp. 54–63. For a more recent assessment of Jewish influences on early Christian worship, see Paul F. Bradshaw, *The Search for the Origins of Christian Worship: Sources and Methods for the Study of Early Liturgy* (New York: Oxford University Press 2002), pp. 23ff.

threefold Christian prayer of praise, remembrance and supplication, with the works of the Father, Son and Spirit as the dominant focus, respectively, of each section of the prayer.

Third, the West Syrian anaphoral form held narrative appeal for reformers and congregations of the late twentieth century faced with the challenge of fitting the story of salvation history into the form of a prayer. Elsewhere, Senn has suggested that the Antiochene form of eucharistic praying also provided the necessary flexibility to accommodate a compromise between traditional prayer forms and the requirements of contemporary vernacular liturgical language. Given this context, Senn suggests that the inclination towards the West Syrian structure 'was because its narrative style allowed for including issues from contemporary life within the scope of salvation history, or for retelling the biblical story in such a way as to address it to the concerns of contemporary life'.[65] Finally, this structure made it easy to introduce congregational acclamations within the prayer – acclamations which were consistent with the reformers' desire to promote the active participation of the whole community in the Eucharist. Despite the general preference for the West Syrian anaphoral pattern, there is significant diversity among current Western eucharistic prayers – although the influence of contemporary theological concerns renders this diversity of a different sort from that which is characteristically found in early eucharistic prayers. Even the correspondence of two prayers based on the same ancient text cannot be presumed.

'COMMON' PRAYERS? ANCIENT AND MODERN EPICLETIC DIVERSITY

Regardless of the process by which older prayers were adapted and new ones created, the prayers which resulted have much in common with each other both within and across denominational boundaries. Upon closer examination, however, the current euchological 'consensus' on the role of the epiclesis in the eucharistic prayer is not as consistent as it might initially appear. Even among contemporary prayers modelled upon the *same* ancient text, the epicletic language of the 'common' prayers which have resulted sometimes 'sounds' quite different theologically. Diversity is also to be found in the somewhat selective

---

65 Senn, 'Introduction', p. 5.

incorporation of ancient themes and language into modern prayers. Examples of each of these cases will be considered here.[66]

Example one: *Apostolic Tradition* and its contemporary incarnations

Although drawing on ancient texts was a common project in the recent decades of liturgical reform, two early prayers in particular served as models for many modern compositions: *Apostolic Tradition* 4 and the Egyptian version of the Anaphora of Basil have both entered the repertoire of eucharistic praying in a number of Western churches. The modifications made were typically more drastic than translating these texts into modern vernacular languages, and in many cases the prayers were 'adapted' so extensively that they might be almost unrecognizable to the communities that originally produced and prayed them. While elements of these eucharistic prayers are now held in 'common' across modern traditions, the means of modification were not as common – and the inconsistencies suggest other theological motives at work. A comparison of the epiclesis of *Apostolic Tradition* 4 with some modern renditions of this text is revealing.

The epiclesis in chapter 4 of the *Apostolic Tradition* reads:

And we ask that you would send your Holy Spirit in the oblation of [your] holy church, [that] gathering [them] into one you will give to all who partake of the holy things [to partake] in the fullness of the Holy Spirit, for the strengthening of faith in truth, that we may praise and glorify you through your Child Jesus Christ . . .[67]

---

66 Adrien Nocent has suggested at least two forces operative behind the Western reworking of what were largely Eastern eucharistic prayers. First, there was a 'desire for similarity in the wording of the various Eucharistic prayers'. In some cases (especially Roman Catholic), the text of the original may have been altered beyond the requirements of a simple translation out of a desire to harmonize the wording of certain parts of the prayer among all the eucharistic prayers in a particular tradition's repertoire. This explains, for example, the changes the Roman Catholic Church introduced to the doxology of *Apostolic Tradition*. Second, modifications were made out of 'fear of being outside the orthodoxy of the faith'. This can be seen in the introduction of an epiclesis *before* the institution narrative in Roman Catholic Eucharistic Prayer II, producing a 'split epiclesis'. See Nocent, *A Rereading*, pp. 46–7.

67 Paul F. Bradshaw, Maxwell E. Johnson and L. Edward Phillips, *The Apostolic Tradition: A Commentary* (Minneapolis, Fortress Press 2002), p. 40. The Latin text reads: 'Et petimus, ut mittas spiritam tuum sanctam in oblationem sanctae ecclesiae; in unum congregans des omnibus qui percipient sanctis in repletionem spiritus sancti ad confirmationem fidei in veritate, ut te laudemus et glorificemus per puerum tuum

Although there has been scholarly debate over whether this petition requests any specific transformation of the eucharistic gifts (with recent consensus favouring the opinion that it does not),[68] it is clear that its author sought to make a connection between the community's celebration of the Eucharist, the unity of this community and the strengthening of the community's faith.

While still recognizable as deriving from *Apostolic Tradition*, contemporary Western prayers which use this ancient prayer as a model mould the epiclesis in certain ways which reflect theological concerns of their own times and traditions. Contemporary prayers derived from the *Apostolic Tradition* include Roman Catholic Eucharistic Prayer II, Eucharistic Prayer IV in *Lutheran Book of Worship* (= Great Thanksgiving XI in *Evangelical Lutheran Worship*), Great Thanksgiving G in the Presbyterian *Book of Common Worship*, and Eucharistic Prayer B in the Church of England's *Common Worship* (see Table 4.1).

In Roman Catholic Eucharistic Prayer II, the integral connection between Eucharist, unity and the faith of the community is disrupted by the introduction of a consecratory epiclesis before the institution narrative (designated I in the chart above) which does explicitly request a transformation of the gifts and subsequent modification of the communion aspect of the epiclesis after the institution narrative (II). In this section, *Apostolic Tradition*'s concern for unity is maintained; the petition for the strengthening of the community's faith in truth is not. *Common Worship*, Eucharistic Prayer B, follows a similar pattern, with mention of the Holy Spirit's action on the gifts before the institution narrative and mention of the Spirit's action in relation to the people afterwards. The reference to strengthening in faith has likewise disappeared, and the sense of unity conveyed here ('in your kingdom') could be heard in an eschatological rather than in an immediate sense. *Lutheran Book of Worship* and the Presbyterian *Book of Common Worship* both follow the structure of the ancient prayer with regard to the epiclesis, leaving it intact after the

---

Iesum Christum ...' Text from Erik Tidner (ed.), *Didascaliae Apostolorum Canonum Ecclesiasticorum Traditionis Apostolicae Versiones Latinae* (Berlin: Akademie-Verlag 1963), pp. 125–6.

68 See, e.g., Frank C. Senn, *Christian Liturgy: Catholic and Evangelical* (Minneapolis: Fortress Press 1997), p. 79: '[T]here is no suggestion that consecration is associated with either the institution narrative or the epiclesis. Rather, the communicants receive the fruits of Holy Communion through the operation of the Holy Spirit: unity with God, being filled with the Spirit of Christ, and being confirmed in true faith.'

Table 4.1: Contemporary prayers derived from the *Apostolic Tradition*

Roman Missal Eucharistic Prayer II[69]	Lutheran Book of Worship Eucharistic Prayer IV[70]	Book of Common Worship (Presbyterian) Great Thanksgiving G[71]	Common Worship (Church of England) Eucharistic Prayer B[72]
(I): Make holy, therefore, these gifts, we pray, by sending down your Spirit upon them like the dewfall, so that they may become for us the Body and (+) Blood of our Lord, Jesus Christ. (II): Humbly we pray that, partaking of the Body and Blood of Christ, we may be gathered into one by the Holy Spirit.	And we ask you: Send your Spirit upon these gifts of your Church; gather into one all who share this bread and wine; fill us with your Holy Spirit to establish our faith in truth that we may praise and glorify you through your Son Jesus Christ.	We ask you to send your Holy Spirit upon the offering of the holy church. Gather into one all who share these holy mysteries, filling them with the Holy Spirit and confirming their faith in the truth, that together we may praise you and give you glory, through your Servant, Jesus Christ.	(I): Lord, you are holy indeed, the source of all holiness; grant that by the power of your Holy Spirit, and according to your holy will, these gifts of bread and wine may be to us the body and blood of our Lord Jesus Christ; (II): Send the Holy Spirit on your people and gather into one in your kingdom all who share this one bread and one cup, so that we, in the company of [N. and] all the saints, may praise and glorify you for ever, through Jesus Christ our Lord . . .

69 *The Roman Missal: Study Edition* (Collegeville, MN: Liturgical Press 2012), nos 101, 105. ET © ICEL, 2010.

70 Inter-Lutheran Commission on Worship, *Lutheran Book of Worship* (Minneapolis: Augsburg 1978, Minister's Desk edn), p. 298.

71 The Theology and Worship Ministry Unit for the Presbyterian Church (USA) and the Cumberland Presbyterian Church, *The Book of Common Worship* (Louisville, KY: Westminster John Knox Press 1993), p. 151.

72 The Church of England, 'Eucharistic Prayers for Use in Order One', <http://www.cofe.anglican.org/worship/liturgy/commonworship/texts/hc/prayerb.html>.

anamnesis.[73] Both translations retain the original's connections between the eucharistic context, the unity of the community and the nourishment of the community's faith. Presbyterian Great Thanksgiving G is the only prayer which renders *oblationem* in English as 'offering'. The other churches opted to translate the object of the invocation as 'gifts', although the Lutheran translators in particular might have been especially concerned with avoiding the connotations of 'offering' the eucharistic gifts in this instance. The Presbyterian version retains the more primitive language of Christ as servant/child (*puerum* in Latin or *pais* in Greek) of God in the transition to the concluding doxology.

Example two: the Anaphora of Basil

The Alexandrine or 'Egyptian' form of the Anaphora of Basil has also gained renewed currency through its use in contemporary prayers. Prayers inspired by or adapted from this anaphora can be found as Eucharistic Prayer IV in the *Missal of Paul VI*, as Prayer D in the Episcopal Church's *Book of Common Prayer*, as Great Thanksgiving F in the Presbyterian Church's *Book of Common Worship* and as Prayer F in the Church of England's *Common Worship*. As was the case with the *Apostolic Tradition*, this ancient text also underwent some modification in various traditions before being inserted into the contemporary repertoire of eucharistic praying.

The epiclesis of Egyptian Basil reads:

> We therefore . . . have set forth before you your own from your own gifts, this bread and this cup. And we, sinners and unworthy and wretched, pray you, our God, in adoration that in the good pleasure of your goodness your Holy Spirit may descend upon us and upon these gifts that have been set before you, and may sanctify them and make them holy of holies. Make us all worthy to partake of your holy things for sanctification of soul and body, that we may become one body and one spirit, and may have a portion with all the saints who have been pleasing to you from eternity.[74]

Table 4.2 compares the epiclesis in several contemporary renditions of the Anaphora of Basil.

---

73 Frank Senn notes that it is *only* in the *Lutheran Book of Worship*, Minister's Edition, that *Apostolic Tradition* is used according to the pattern preserved in ancient texts (i.e. without the addition of the Sanctus or other acclamations). *With One Voice* (Minneapolis: Augsburg Fortress 1995) changed the earlier precedent of the 1978 book by framing *Apostolic Tradition* as a post-Sanctus prayer. See Senn, *Christian Liturgy*, p. 79, n. 72.
74 ET from Jasper and Cuming (eds), *Prayers*, p. 71.

Table 4.2: The epiclesis in several contemporary renditions of the Anaphora of Basil

Roman Missal *(1970)* Eucharistic Prayer IV *(Translation: ICEL, 2010)*[75]	*'A Common Eucharistic Prayer' (1975)*[76] = Book of Common Prayer *(Episcopal Church in the USA, 1979),* Eucharistic Prayer D = Book of Common Worship *(Presbyterian Church USA, 1992)* Great Thanksgiving F	Common Worship *(Church of England, 2000)* Eucharistic Prayer F[77]
(I): Therefore, O Lord, we pray: may this same Holy Spirit graciously sanctify these offerings, that they may become the Body and Blood of our Lord Jesus Christ for the celebration of this great mystery, which he himself left us as an eternal covenant. (II): Look, O Lord, upon the Sacrifice which you yourself have provided for your Church, and grant in your loving kindness to all who partake of this one Bread and one Chalice that, gathered into one body by the Holy Spirit, they may truly become a living sacrifice in Christ to the praise of your glory.	Lord, we pray that in your goodness and mercy your Holy Spirit may descend upon us, and upon these gifts, sanctifying them and showing them to be holy gifts for your holy people, the bread of life and the cup of salvation, the body and blood of your Son Jesus Christ. Grant that all who share this bread and cup may become one body and one spirit, a living sacrifice in Christ, to the praise of your name.	As we recall the one, perfect sacrifice of our redemption, Father, by your Holy Spirit let these gifts of your creation be to us the body and blood of our Lord Jesus Christ; form us into the likeness of Christ and make us a perfect offering in your sight. Amen. Come, Holy Spirit.

---

75 *Roman Missal,* nos 118, 122.

76 *Book of Common Prayer,* p. 375; *Book of Common Worship,* p. 148. The only difference between the two texts is the capitalization of the words 'body', 'blood' and 'name' in the former but not the latter.

77 The Church of England, 'Eucharistic Prayers for Use in Order One', <http://www. churchofengland.org/prayer-worship/worship/texts/principal-services/holy-communion/ epsforonefront/prayerf.aspx>.

Although there were initial discussions in committee following the Second Vatican Council to use this prayer of St Basil as it was, it proved an insurmountable difficulty for theologians of the Roman rite to include an invocation of the Spirit for the consecration of the elements *after* the words of Christ had already been spoken in the institution narrative. The Roman Catholic tradition opted, as with all eucharistic prayers composed since the Council, to split the epiclesis of this ancient prayer, reworking it into a consecratory petition before the institution narrative and a communion petition after the anamnesis. In English translation, much of the original prayer is unrecognizable due to extensive reworking of the text.

The text of the epiclesis in the Episcopal Church's Prayer D and in Presbyterian Great Thanksgiving F is identical, as both of these texts are based on 'A Common Eucharistic Prayer', which was the result of an ecumenical project.[78] The majority of the text represents a different English translation of the Latin text of Roman Catholic Eucharistic Prayer IV, with the most significant changes in the anamnesis and epiclesis section. The group deleted the preliminary epiclesis found in the Catholic prayer and reintroduced a shortened form of the epiclesis of Egyptian Basil in its traditional location after the anamnesis, also restoring the accompanying offering of the bread and wine at this point in the prayer.[79] This translation follows the pattern of the ancient prayer

---

78 'A Common Eucharistic Prayer', © 1975 by Marion J. Hatchett for The Committee for a Common Eucharistic Prayer. For more details on this prayer, see Mitchell, 'Alexandrian Anaphora', pp. 194–206 and Marion J. Hatchett, *Commentary on the American Prayer Book* (New York: Seabury Press 1980), pp. 377–8. In hopes that the prayer might be prayed by members of a variety of Christian traditions with different expectations about the standard contents of a eucharistic prayer, options in the text included conforming the text of the institution narrative to match that of the church in which it was prayed and omitting the intercessions. Hatchett commented: 'The text of the prayer up to the institution narrative is a translation of the Latin original of the Roman sacramentary. The institution narrative [in the Episcopal *Book of Common Prayer*] is that of Prayers A and B [in the *BCP*]. The anamnesis, oblation, and epiclesis are basically those of the earliest known manuscript of the prayer, with the addition of the phrase, "the bread of life and the cup of salvation, the Body and Blood of your Son Jesus Christ," from later manuscripts. The petition for the communicants is based on the Roman sacramentary Latin version; the petition for the church is from the earliest manuscript, and the bracketed intercessions are based on those of the Roman sacramentary. The final petition, that we may find our inheritance with the saints, contains phrases from the early manuscripts and from the old Roman prayer. The concluding expression of praise and the doxology are from the Latin version of the Roman sacramentary' (p. 377).
79 Harry Boone Porter, 'Episcopal Anaphoral Prayers', in Senn (ed.), *New Eucharistic Prayers*, p. 70.

quite closely. The Church of England's rendering of Egyptian Basil also follows the general themes of the original, with the addition of a concluding acclamation, 'Amen. Come, Holy Spirit.' However, the sense of unity through sharing in communion as well as the eschatological orientation of the original text seems to have been 'lost' (or at least diminished) in translation.

What all these variations suggest is that Western churches are open to using eucharistic prayers inspired by Eastern anaphoras, but they are not always content with the theology these prayers convey. In the case of the Anaphora of Basil and its epiclesis, a liturgical unit was imported from the East, but some of its features, particularly the location of the epiclesis within the prayer and some of its language, were changed to make the prayer resonate better with the expectations of Western eucharistic theology.

Example three: modern rereading of ancient intent?

Furthermore, while the current diversity in the wording of the epiclesis among various traditions has a long history, Paul Bradshaw has remarked that

> at least some of this diversity seems to stem from a theological uncertainty as to what it is precisely that the Holy Spirit is expected to do in relation to the Eucharist or alternatively from a fear of saying something that might imply a belief that the framers [of the prayers] did not wish to articulate.[80]

As John McKenna has similarly noted, a survey of modern expressions of the epiclesis 'is revealing liturgically, theologically, and ecumenically'.[81]

While not wishing to take early eucharistic prayers as an 'inflexible norm', McKenna has highlighted several ways in which the emphases in these texts can serve as a standard against which modern prayers could be compared. In early Christian prayers which feature the fully developed form of the eucharistic epiclesis, most expect some sort of change of the bread and wine, if not into, at least 'in the direction of', Christ's body and

---

80 Bradshaw, 'Rediscovery', p. 96.
81 John H. McKenna, 'Eucharistic Prayer: Epiclesis' in A. Heinz and H. Rennings (eds), *Gratias Agamus: Studien zum eucharistischen Hochgebet: Für Balthasar Fischer* (Freiburg: Herder 1992), p. 288.

blood.[82] The eschatological aspect of the Eucharist is often highlighted in ancient prayers, alongside a diverse collection of additional graces flowing forth as fruits of communion. Last, some mention of sharing in the eucharistic gifts is almost invariably present.[83]

While an exhaustive survey is not possible here, it can be observed that the four aspects just mentioned – change in/of bread and wine, eschatology, fruits of communion, and sharing in the eucharistic gifts – are not *consistently* found together in the epicleses of contemporary prayers (see Table 4.3).

While one would not expect any single prayer to touch upon all of these elements thoroughly, the complete absence of certain of these dimensions from *all* of a tradition's prayers could be telling theologically. Hence the lacunae in the chart below are the most interesting. For instance, Lutheran prayers do not directly attribute any change in the gifts to the power of the Spirit. McKenna wonders, 'Is its absence due to an emphasis on the institution narrative as "consecratory" or a desire to avoid the implications of certain terms, e.g. "make them be for us the body and blood of Christ", "may they be for us...", "...that they become...", "...to change..." – or both?'[84] While 'be' (the typical verb in the Episcopal Eucharistic Prayers and the Methodist Great Thanksgivings) conveys the idea of change less forcefully than 'become' (the typical request in the Roman Catholic prayers) there is still suggested the idea of some difference, perceptible at least by faith, between the eucharistic elements in connection with the prayer for the coming of the Spirit upon them. The Presbyterian Great Thanksgivings' characteristic request that the Spirit come upon the people and gifts so that the gifts (or the meal) 'may be a communion' in or of Christ's body and blood may or may not imply consecration of the gifts.

In terms of eschatology, at least some of the epicleses of most traditions considered here do look with hope towards the kingdom

82 Of course, language that requests some sort of conversion or change of the elements need not, at this early stage, imply anything approaching a change of 'substance' similar to the concerns that would arise in later Western theology. The question could be posed whether the change in view here is one of substance or rather one of use (a question raised by G. W. H. Lampe in R. E. Clements *et al.*, *Eucharistic Theology Then and Now* (London: SPCK 1968), p. 51. For a fuller discussion of this issue see Donald Macleod, 'Calvin into Hippolytus?' in Bryan D. Spinks and Iain R. Torrance (eds), *To Glorify God: Essays on Modern Reformed Liturgy* (Grand Rapids, MI: Eerdmans 1999), pp. 266–7.
83 McKenna, 'Eucharistic Prayer: Epiclesis', p. 288. For a presentation of these elements in early eucharistic texts, see 'Table 1.1: The Epiclesis in Ancient Anaphoras' in McKenna, *Eucharistic Epiclesis*, pp. 40–1.
84 McKenna, 'Eucharistic Prayer: Epiclesis', p. 289.

Table 4.3: Four aspects of the epiclesis in contemporary prayers

Tradition (text)	Change in bread/ wine -> Christ's body/ blood?	Eschatological references?	Fruits of communion?	Sharing in gifts?
Roman Catholic (*Roman Missal*)	Yes ('may become')	No	Yes	Yes
Evangelical Lutheran Church in America (ELCA) & Evangelical Lutheran Church in Canada (ELCIC) (*Lutheran Book of Worship, Evangelical Lutheran Worship*)	No (Some prayers in *ELW* ask God to send the Spirit to 'bless' the gifts and/or the meal, but no change of the bread and wine is mentioned specifically.)	Yes (in some)	Yes	Yes (in most)
Episcopal Church in the United States of America (*Book of Common Prayer*)	Yes (expression varies) in all but Rite I, Prayer I	*Rite I: No Rite II: Yes (in some)	*Rite I: No Rite II: Yes (in all but Prayer C, which has a pre-institution epiclesis only)	Yes (in some)
United Methodist Church (*United Methodist Book of Worship*)	Yes ('be for us') in all but IV	Yes (in most)	Yes	Yes (in some)
Presbyterian Church (USA) (*Book of Common Worship*)	Yes (?) ('may be a/the communion of') in most	Yes (in some)	Yes (in most)	Yes (in most)
Church of England (*Common Worship*)	Yes ('be to [or for] us') in most	Yes (in some)	Yes (in most)	Yes (in most)

* Note: The Prayers of Rite I in the Episcopal *Book of Common Prayer* are not 'new' compositions per se, but rather are framed in traditional Prayer Book idiom.

For purposes of the table above, the designation 'some' indicates that a particular feature is not absent from a particular tradition's prayers but is present in less than half of the eucharistic prayers in this church's official worship book(s). 'Most' means that a feature is present in the majority (i.e. more than half) of a tradition's prayers (but not in all of them).

Christ proclaimed or hint at the relation between the sacrament shared by the community in the present in memorial of Christ's past sacrifice as an anticipation of future sharing in the messianic banquet. Other traditions have fairly little eschatology in their epicleses or none at all. The only definite hint of final fulfilment in the Roman Catholic Prayers is the epiclesis of the four Eucharistic Prayers for Various Needs: 'Through the power of your Spirit of love include us now *and for ever* among the members of your Son, whose body and blood we share' – a rather meagre reference indeed.[85]

The preceding survey highlighted some tensions between current scholarship on the dynamics of early eucharistic epicleses and contemporary Western adaptations of early eucharistic prayers and their epicleses. The interplay of language, euchological structure and theology – with different denominations emphasizing particular themes – will be observed again throughout the next several chapters which explore how several Western churches incorporated epicleses into their eucharistic prayers. In many instances, theological motivations (stated or implied) will be seen to have shaped the final form of the epicletic prayers and contributed to the distinctive theological emphases which characterize the epicleses of Roman Catholic, Anglican and Protestant churches.

---

85 In this tradition and others, eschatology does figure prominently in the intercessions which follow the post-anamnesis epiclesis and thus is not absent from the eucharistic prayer as a whole.

Chapter 5

The eucharistic epiclesis in recent Roman Catholic liturgical reforms

Although some of the other denominations considered in this study were actively engaged in the reform of eucharistic prayer texts prior to the Second Vatican Council (1962–5), the appearance of the Constitution on the Sacred Liturgy (*Sacrosanctum Concilium*) in December 1963 initiated a process of reform in the Roman Catholic Church that would subsequently influence the eucharistic prayers of other churches – both in terms of process of development and also in terms of the structure (and occasionally content) of some prayers in other Western traditions. Although Roman Catholic scholars had contributed their insights about the historical formation of the Roman Canon and other ancient anaphoras during the previous decades, discussion of specific reforms based on these conclusions had been rather limited.[1]

Sacrosanctum Concilium (*SC*) provided some general guidelines for liturgical revision, but the concrete application of its directives to specific rites or components of rites (such as the eucharistic prayer in general and the epiclesis in particular) required extensive discussion and negotiation. Several of the aspects of *SC* cited by Cipriano Vagaggini as 'principles of liturgical reform'[2] could be interpreted as promoting 'new' texts rooted in 'old' traditions, and the subsequent history of the progress of Roman Catholic reforms suggests that they were in fact treated in this manner.[3]

---

1 Frederick R. McManus, 'Preface' in Cipriano Vagaggini, *The Canon of the Mass and Liturgical Reform*, ed. and trans. Peter Coughlan (Staten Island, NY: Alba House 1967), p. 9.
2 See Vagaggini, *Canon of the Mass*, pp. 18–19 on 'principles of liturgical reform' and the Roman Canon.
3 See, e.g., the first heading and subheading in the chapter on eucharistic prayers in Annibale Bugnini, *The Reform of the Liturgy, 1948–1975* (Collegeville, MN: Liturgical Press 1990), p. 448: 'I. NEW EUCHARISTIC PRAYERS; 1. *Return to Authentic Tradition*'.

For example, *SC* 23 specifies that:

In order that sound tradition be retained, and yet the way remain open to legitimate progress, a *careful investigation – theological, historical, and pastoral* – should always, first of all, be made into each section of the liturgy which is to be revised. Furthermore, the *general laws governing the structure and meaning of the liturgy* must be taken into account, as well as the experience derived from recent liturgical reforms and from the concessions granted in various places. Finally, there must be no innovations unless the good of the church genuinely and certainly requires them, and care must be taken that any new forms adopted *should in some way grow organically from forms already existing.*[4]

With regard to the epiclesis, recent research had demonstrated that models for the epiclesis *did* indeed exist. Even if an explicitly pneumatic eucharistic epiclesis was not native to the Roman tradition, the recognition by many scholars of epicletic components within the Roman Canon could provide at least the basis for argument that an explicit pneumatic epiclesis could be perceived as an organic development from a form already extant within the tradition.

Similarly, *SC* 50 directs that:

The rite of the Mass is to be revised in such a way that the *intrinsic nature and purpose of its several parts, as well as the connection between them, may be more clearly shown*, and that devout and active participation by the faithful may be more easily achieved. To this end, the rites are to be simplified, due care being taken to preserve their substance. Duplications made with the passage of time are to be omitted, as are less useful additions. *Other parts which were lost through the vicissitudes of history are to be restored according to the ancient tradition of the holy Fathers, as may seem appropriate or necessary.*[5]

The lack of an explicit pneumatic epiclesis in the Roman Canon, in the

---

4 The Constitution on the Sacred Liturgy, *Sacrosanctum Concilium*, 4 December 1963 in Austin Flannery (ed.), *Vatican Council II: The Basic Sixteen Documents: Constitutions, Decrees, Declarations: A Completely Revised Translation in Inclusive Language* (Northport, NY: Costello 1996); emphasis as added by Vagaggini. Unless otherwise stated, subsequent quotations of *SC* will be taken from this edition. Commenting upon *SC* 23, Vagaggini adds, 'However, once such benefit is indeed proven, we should not shirk the task of creating afresh if necessary.' Vagaggini, *Canon of the Mass*, p. 19.

5 Emphasis as in Vagaggini, *Canon of the Mass*, p. 19. However, as the Council of Trent had likewise advocated restoration of the *Roman Missal* 'to the pristine norm of the Holy Fathers' (Pius V, *Quo primum*, 14 July 1570, as quoted in Frederick R. McManus, 'Back

view of some scholars at this time, may have represented an instance in which a once-universal feature of early anaphoras had subsequently been 'lost' due to just the sort of historical accident envisioned by *SC* 50.

In terms of the specific case of the epiclesis, however, the text of *Sacrosanctum Concilium* provided no advice; in fact, this Constitution devotes relatively little attention to the Holy Spirit at all. Among its five references to the Holy Spirit, the single one in the immediate context of worship speaks to the role of the Spirit in the midst of the community's eucharistic celebration (without, however, suggesting or implying that the Spirit's role needed more explicit articulation in the rite itself). In celebrating the Eucharist, the Church remembers 'the victory and triumph' of Christ's death while 'at the same time "giving thanks to God for his inexpressible gift" (2 Cor 9:15) in Christ Jesus, "in praise of his glory" (Eph 1:12) through the power of the Holy Spirit' (*SC* 6).[6]

REFORMING THE ROMAN PRAYERS: THE WORK OF *COETUS* X AND THE DEVELOPMENT OF EUCHARISTIC PRAYERS I–IV

It was left to the Consilium for the Implementation of the Constitution on the Sacred Liturgy and its subsidiary study groups or *coetus* to give practical structure to the *SC*'s suggestions. *Coetus* X was charged with addressing the Ordinary of the Mass; consequently the work of reforming or otherwise adapting the Roman Canon fell under its jurisdiction. Eventually 19 consultors, including many liturgical scholars, comprised its membership.[7] After several years of work, this group proposed three 'new' eucharistic prayers for the Roman rite along with slight revisions to the Roman Canon.[8]

---

to the Future: The Early Christian Roots of Liturgical Renewal', *Worship* 72.5 (1998), p. 390), perhaps too much should not be read into *SC* 50 as an innovative aspect of the Council in response to the recent trend of patristic *ressourcement*.

6 For a critique of the minimal mention of the Holy Spirit in *Sacrosanctum Concilium* see, among others, Vilmos Vajta, 'Renewal of Worship: De Sacra Liturgia' in George A. Lindbeck (ed.), *Dialogue on the Way: Protestants Report from Rome on the Vatican Council* (Minneapolis: Augsburg 1965), p. 107. However, as Teresa Berger has recently emphasized, lack of explicit mention of the Holy Spirit does not necessarily indicate a chronic 'inattentiveness' to the Spirit's presence and activity in the Roman Catholic tradition. See Teresa Berger, '*Veni Creator Spiritus*: The Elusive Real Presence of the Spirit in the Catholic Tradition' in Teresa Berger and Bryan D. Spinks (eds), *The Spirit in Worship – Worship in the Spirit* (Collegeville, MN: Liturgical Press 2009), pp. 141–54.

7 For a list, see Bugnini, *Reform of the Liturgy*, p. 450, n. 4.

8 Annibale Bugnini's chapter, 'The Eucharistic Prayers' (in Bugnini, *Reform of the Liturgy*, pp. 448–87), is a valuable source that provides not only an overview of the process but also an insider's insight into the development of these Roman Catholic eucharistic prayers. The discussion which follows here relies primarily on this source.

Perhaps no single individual was more influential in the work of Vatican-II era Roman Catholic revision of eucharistic prayers than the Italian liturgical scholar Cipriano Vagaggini OSB.[9] His initial preparatory work on eucharistic prayers for *Coetus* X of the Consilium, later published in 1966 as *Il Canone della Messa e la riforma liturgica: problemi e progetti* (ET: *The Canon of the Mass and Liturgical Reform*, 1967),[10] laid the foundations for the work of developing or adapting suitable prayers for the Roman rite. Significantly for the purposes of this study, Vagaggini was under the impression that the Roman rite had once contained an epiclesis that was subsequently lost or removed due to the vicissitudes of history.[11] When reviewing the merits and defects of the Roman Canon, he ranks 'the lack of a theology of the part played by the Holy Spirit in the Eucharist' among the prime defects.[12]

---

9 For the role of Vagaggini, see Bugnini, *Reform of the Liturgy*, p. 450.

10 Cipriano Vagaggini, *Il Canone della Messa e la riforma liturgica: problemi e progetti*, Quaderni de revista litúrgica 4 (Turin: Leumann 1966); ET Vagaggini, *Canon of the Mass*.

11 Cipriano Vagaggini, *Theological Dimensions of the Liturgy: A General Treatise on the Theology of the Liturgy* (Collegeville, MN: Liturgical Press 1976), pp. 228–9. Today, it seems more prudent to conclude that 'the Roman Canon lacks an *epiclesis* because it was redacted, in large part, prior to the pneumatological controversies of the late fourth century'. Nicholas V. Russo, 'The Validity of the Anaphora of *Addai and Mari*: Critique of the Critiques' in Maxwell E. Johnson (ed.), *Issues in Eucharistic Praying in East and West: Essays in Liturgical and Theological Analysis* (Collegeville, MN: Liturgical Press 2011), p. 61.

12 Vagaggini, *Canon of the Mass*, pp. 100–1. A significant number of the ten items Vagaggini lists as 'defects' of the Roman Canon have something to do, either directly or indirectly, with the Holy Spirit. In addition to points five ('the number and disorder of epicletic-type prayers in the canon') and six ('the lack of a theology of the part played by the Holy Spirit in the Eucharist'), the epiclesis is also implicated in point two ('the lack of a logical connection of ideas') – insofar as the connection between the epiclesis and the intercessions is not nearly as clear in the Roman Canon as in Eastern anaphoras, distorting the implications inherent in this connection. Alan F. Detscher, summarizing Vagaggini on this matter, wrote: 'the Church is nourished and united by the body and blood of Christ and thus it can pray for itself (clergy and laity), recall those who have died in the faith (the saints), and can intercede on behalf of those who have died. These relationships are not easily seen in the Roman canon because of the split intercessions.' Alan F. Detscher, 'The Eucharistic Prayers of the Roman Catholic Church' in Frank C. Senn (ed.) *New Eucharistic Prayers: An Ecumenical Study of Their Development and Structure* (Mahwah, NJ: Paulist Press 1987), p. 26. Other points which may be at least tangentially related to the epiclesis include points eight (on the *Supplices*), and ten ('the lack of an overall presentation of the history of salvation'). Compared to, for example, the Antiochene anaphoras with their characteristic Trinitarian structure (praise of God the Father as God and as Creator in the preface; thanksgiving to God for Christ's role in salvation history offered through the post-Sanctus, institution narrative and anamnesis; and invocation of the Spirit with a view towards the future effects of this Eucharist in the life of the Church and the communicants through the epiclesis and intercessions), the Roman Canon, with

Instead of overhauling the Roman Canon in a way that would amount to restructuring the prayer (and thus minimizing the merits it did possess),[13] Vagaggini suggested leaving the Roman Canon largely intact as it was and compensating for the 'defects' by complementing the canon with other prayers which were stronger in areas in which the Roman Canon might be perceived to be weaker.[14] He suggested a eucharistic prayer that could accommodate the rich tradition of the Roman Canon's prefaces and also another anaphora featuring a fixed preface – which could therefore present a more comprehensive portrayal of the grand sweep of salvation history – which would take up the words of the Roman Canon after the institution narrative.[15] The set of four eucharistic prayers promulgated in 1968 for use in the Roman rite followed the general framework of Vagaggini's schematic for reform if not its specific details (such as incorporating parts of the Roman Canon into other prayers).[16] The reform process produced a slightly modified version of the canon (Eucharistic Prayer I), and then not just one but

limited reference to God's saving activity in the world beyond the prefaces which accompany it, would appear defective when judged according to this standard. Vagaggini, *Canon of the Mass*, pp. 93ff.

13 Among the 'merits' of the Roman Canon, Vagaggini included the 'antiquity of the text and its traditional character and use in the West', 'the variable prefaces of the Roman church', 'theology of offering the gifts', and 'stylistic merits' according to classical Latin liturgical style.

14 In *Canon of the Mass*, Vagaggini critiqued proposals for reform of the Roman Canon set forth by Hans Küng and Karl Amon. (See Hans Küng, 'Das Eucharistiegebet: Konzil und Erneuerung der römischen Liturgie', *Wort und Wahrheit* 18 (1963), pp. 102–7; Küng's proposed revised text of the Roman Canon is found on pp. 103–4, which is presented in English in Vagaggini, *Canon of the Mass*, pp. 76–9. For Amon's schema, see Karl Amon, 'Gratias Agere: Zur Reform des Messcanons', *Liturgisches Jahrbuch* 15 (1965), pp. 79–98; the text of Amon's 'corrected' Roman Canon is on pp. 95–8, with an ET in Vagaggini, *Canon of the Mass*, pp. 79ff.) The more radical proposal of Amon, which includes dropping the epicletic element before the institution narrative and substituting a christologically oriented post-Sanctus comes in for especially harsh criticism by Vagaggini. Amon, Vagaggini decides, has rewritten rather than revised the prayer; instead of adding to the clarity of the Canon, the resultant prayer does not end up with a cohesive grounding in salvation history, and the consecratory epiclesis (which, in his opinion, is a standard feature of eucharistic prayers) has been eliminated entirely. Thus Amon's proposal, according to Vagaggini, has at least three strikes against it from the outset.

15 See Vagaggini, *Canon of the Mass*, p. 123.

16 See Vagaggini, *Canon of the Mass*, pp. 124ff. Annibale Bugnini states: 'Father Vagaggini's work and its accompanying documentation in [*Canon of the Mass*] ... was the basis for the new Eucharistic Prayers of the Missal. The variants it shows in comparison with the definitive text in the Missal were the fruit of the discussion and cultural contributions of the *periti* and the Fathers of the Consilium.' Bugnini, *Reform of the Liturgy*, p. 450, n. 4.

three more anaphoras featuring a combination of fixed and variable prefaces. The additional anaphoras featured a eucharistic prayer modelled after *Apostolic Tradition* 4, which was accompanied by its own preface but could also be used with variable prefaces (Eucharistic Prayer II), a 'new' anaphora for use with proper prefaces which bears some resemblance to Vagaggini's proposed additional anaphora (Eucharistic Prayer III), and an anaphora loosely patterned after the Alexandrine anaphora of Basil that featured a fixed preface with a thorough Trinitarian grounding in salvation history (Eucharistic Prayer IV).[17]

Annibale Bugnini credits historical research with opening the way forward that was eventually adopted by the study group assigned to revise or develop eucharistic prayer texts. 'Once euchological pluralism and rubrical flexibility had been rediscovered after centuries of fixism, it was unthinkable that a monolithic approach to the Eucharistic Prayer should long endure.'[18] For both historical and literary reasons, the possibility of providing multiple options for the eucharistic prayer and alternative structure(s) to that of the Roman Canon seemed beneficial avenues for exploration. The ultimate decision to pursue this strategy would prove influential not only within the Roman Catholic tradition but also for other Western churches which subsequently provided more

---

17 The desire for a brief, concise anaphora was met through a prayer based on the anaphora of *Apostolic Tradition* 4, then thought to be one of the oldest known eucharistic prayers in existence – and attributed to Hippolytus of Rome. Eucharistic Prayer III was intended to be flexible enough for use with a variety of prefaces already part of the Roman tradition as well as potential new ones. It fitted the need for 'an anaphora of medium length and clear structure, in which the transitions from part to part would leap directly to the eye'. Bugnini, *Reform of the Liturgy*, p. 452. While clear transitions were a stated goal underlying the work of *Coetus* X, the desire for an anaphora whose transitions 'would leap directly to the eye' seems like an odd designation for anaphoras, given that they are typically *heard*, but not *read*, by the majority of the congregation. Finally, there was the aim of balancing out the approach of attention to particular feasts and seasons provided through the prefaces with an anaphora that would encapsulate the *entire* history of salvation more along the lines of the Eastern anaphoras. To avoid potential repetition, a fixed preface was decided upon in this case, with the part of the anaphora between the Sanctus and the first epiclesis providing an opportunity to celebrate the salvific economy from the creation of man and woman to the gift of the Spirit at Pentecost, providing a natural transition to the epiclesis which followed immediately thereafter. Such a pattern was adopted in Eucharistic Prayer IV. (See Bugnini, *Reform of the Liturgy*, pp. 452–3.) On the whole, this prayer is patterned most deliberately on the Antiochene anaphoral tradition, although the other new prayers have much in common with the Antiochene tradition as well.
18 Bugnini, *Reform of the Liturgy*, p. 448.

than one version of the eucharistic prayer in their official liturgical books.[19]

Once established, *Coetus* X began its work by soliciting the opinions and proposals of experts, bringing the fruit of twentieth-century liturgical scholarship to bear on suggestions for reform. (Vagaggini's research from the summer of 1966, later published as *The Canon of the Mass and Liturgical Reform*, represented one such scholarly contribution.[20]) In addition, the group sought to address two outstanding issues related to the way in which to proceed. Pope Paul VI had implied that ancient anaphoras might serve as either models for or even the actual texts of contemporary eucharistic prayers when he suggested that 'anaphoras for use at particular specified times are to be composed or looked for'.[21] The anaphora then attributed to Hippolytus (i.e. *Apostolic Tradition* 4) as well as the Egyptian form of the Anaphora of Basil immediately stood out as candidates in this regard as it was thought that these prayers might meld well with other aspects of the Latin liturgy.[22] While it is unlikely that these two prayers were singled out *because* they contained an explicit pneumatic epiclesis, it may have proved significant for the future course of Roman reforms regarding the epiclesis that this element was part of the structural framework of both of these prayers.

The Pope had also intimated that entirely new prayers might be written, which led to other sorts of questions about what characteristics or elements might make a eucharistic prayer particularly suitable for the

---

19 Historical research of the past century or so had demonstrated that variability rather than uniformity seemed to be the early 'rule' of eucharistic praying. This variability persisted in the East insofar as no tradition prayed a single anaphora throughout the course of the year – and some traditions had many more than a handful in their repertoire. E.g. the West Syrian rite has 80 anaphoras and the Ethiopian rite 14. Western traditions of eucharistic praying and even the Roman rite had once known more variation than was present in the 1960s. The Mozarabic and Gallican rites had many changeable structural elements, and the Ambrosian rite and even the Roman Canon knew some variability through the presence of many prefaces. The Roman Missal in use from 1570 to 1968 contained a mere 14 prefaces, but earlier texts such as the 'Leonine' and Gelasian sacramentaries knew considerably more than this, containing 267 and 184 prefaces respectively. Both the Ambrosian and Roman rites introduced some additional variety through variable options within the Canon for certain occasions.

20 Bugnini, *Reform of the Liturgy*, p. 450.

21 Pope Paul VI's response to an update (20 June 1966) presented to him by Cardinal Giacomo Lercaro on the Consilium's efforts to revise the rites of the Mass, as quoted in Bugnini, *Reform of the Liturgy*, p. 450. Bugnini contends that with this statement the Pope was giving his blessing to the search for suitable anaphoras within 'the traditional treasury of prayers' (p. 450).

22 Bugnini, *Reform of the Liturgy*, p. 451.

Roman rite. Bugnini outlines eight such criteria for eucharistic prayers.[23] Some of the characteristics that were adopted have implications for the placement of the epiclesis and the style in which it appears – some of the very elements which have been critiqued in these prayers. The first criterion was concerned with a 'common structure' underlying the prayers. Since one of the criticisms of the Canon made by people like Vagaggini was that its structure was not very clear, it was felt that anaphoras should have a common structure with only minimal accommodations allowed for the unique character of individual anaphoras or anaphoral families. Several schemas were developed, and one was ultimately selected as a model for all new compositions.

The second criterion Bugnini mentions is 'the principle of variety'. Any new anaphoras were to be detectably different from each other as well as from the Roman Canon.[24] While this criterion might have been met for the anaphoras as a whole, the epicleses do not express a high degree of variety, perhaps in part because of the strictures of structure (cf. the first criterion) that have limited the role epicleses are allowed to play in the prayer. In other words, the desire for variety within the bounds of a common anaphoral structure potentially limits the theological range a particular epiclesis may have, given that the epiclesis must always be located in the same part of the prayer.

In Bugnini's opinion, the new anaphoras are a felicitous meeting of 'tradition and novelty' (criterion eight). He writes, 'In the new anaphoras, more than elsewhere, care has been taken to be true to article 23 of the Constitution on the Liturgy, which urges that "sound tradition" and "legitimate progress" be combined.'[25] Tradition was to be found in the structure, concepts and images (the framework being a blend of the Roman structure and Antiochene location of intercessions while many concepts and images were derived from biblical and patristic sources, including early liturgical texts). The contemporary or new was achieved 'by simply emphasizing, among the biblical and traditional elements, those which are most responsive to the concerns of today's men and women and which they can most easily understand'.[26]

Bugnini does not specifically cite the epiclesis among either the traditional or new elements of eucharistic prayers; however, it would seem that a case could be made for placing it in either or both of these

---

23 See Bugnini, *Reform of the Liturgy*, pp. 451–6.
24 Bugnini, *Reform of the Liturgy*, p. 452.
25 Bugnini, *Reform of the Liturgy*, p. 455.
26 Bugnini, *Reform of the Liturgy*, p. 456.

categories. While perhaps not a traditional feature of *Roman* eucharistic praying, a pneumatic epiclesis was well-established in other early traditions of eucharistic praying. Furthermore, revived interest in the Holy Spirit in the latter half of the twentieth century could have made the epiclesis a 'new' element of eucharistic prayers achieved through selective emphasis of strands present in earlier tradition. However, given what was done to traditional elements such as the epiclesis in order to be able to incorporate them into new prayers of a tradition to which they perhaps were not native at all, the question could be raised as to what tradition they are made to serve – an ancient one or a more medieval–scholastic one which privileged certain views about eucharistic consecration. At the same time, however, those undertaking liturgical reform took positive steps to incorporate a stronger pneumatology into Roman Catholic eucharistic prayers, despite the constraints imposed by previous tradition which inevitably affected the theology of the epicleses to some degree.

The presentation of the new prayers to the episcopal conferences by Cardinal Benno Gut, the president of the Consilium, hailed the publication of the three new prayers for use in the Roman rite as 'a new canticle placed on the lips of the praying Church by the Holy Spirit'.[27] The Apostolic Constitution *Missale Romanum* (3 April 1969) outlined the more significant modifications to the Order of Mass. Critique prompted further revisions to both the Order of Mass and the General Instruction of the Roman Missal, both of which were promulgated along with a letter from the Congregation for Divine Worship on 26 March 1970. The 1970 edition also included an introduction that 'attempted to provide the historical context for the changes to calm the fears of traditionalists, who judged that the new Mass was calculated to undermine the traditional theology of the eucharist'.[28]

The three new eucharistic prayers crafted by the working group of the Consilium share a similar structure, in large part resembling the West Syrian or Antiochene pattern of eucharistic praying with the notable anomaly of an epicletic component oriented towards the consecration of

27 Cardinal Benno Gut, in the letter *La publication* concerning the new eucharistic prayers, dated 2 June 1968. See Thomas C. O'Brien, *Documents on the Liturgy, 1963–1979: Conciliar, Papal, and Curial Texts*, trans. Thomas C. O'Brien (Collegeville, MN: Liturgical Press 1982), p. 243, nos 1942–4 for an ET of this letter; quoted here from Bugnini, *Reform of the Liturgy*, p. 484.

28 Mary Alice Piil, 'The Local Church as the Subject of the Action of the Eucharist' in Peter C. Finn and James M. Schellman (eds), *Shaping English Liturgy: Studies in Honor of Archbishop Denis Hurley* (Washington, DC: Pastoral Press 1990), p. 185.

the gifts located immediately before the institution narrative. The result is that these prayers have a 'split' or 'double' epiclesis, with a consecratory petition before the institution narrative and an element of communion thereafter. Most of the prayers composed subsequently (e.g. the Prayers for Reconciliation and for Masses with Children) have adopted this outline as well. The Antiochene structure as reflected in these Roman prayers can be summarized as follows:

Preface (variable or fixed)[29]

Sanctus

Post-Sanctus

Epiclesis I (oriented towards consecration of the bread and wine)

Institution Narrative

Memorial Acclamation

Anamnesis/Oblation

Epiclesis II (oriented towards the sanctification of the community)

Commemoration of the Saints and Intercessions (some prayers invert the order of these elements)

Doxology

Bugnini's outline of the structure (which aligns with that of the General Instruction of the Roman Missal of 1970) lists only a *single* 'consecratory epiclesis' before the institution narrative with no mention of the second epicletic component which arises later in the prayer in conjunction with a section designated 'prayer for acceptance of the offering and for a fruitful communion'.[30] While not necessarily implying that the epiclesis in the Roman Catholic tradition is solely or even primarily oriented towards the consecration of the gifts in a limited sense, this tension between the prayer structure outlined in the General Instruction of the

---

29 The preface is variable in Eucharistic Prayers II (which does also have its own proper preface) and III (which must be used with a variable preface since it has none of its own) but fixed in IV.

30 Bugnini, *Reform of the Liturgy*, p. 451. Elsewhere, in connection with a discussion of the epiclesis of the Alexandrine Anaphora of Basil, Bugnini does demonstrate an awareness that consecratory and communion dimensions are normally found together, designating the epiclesis of Egyptian Basil as an 'epiclesis in its oldest form, in which the Holy Spirit is invoked in order that the gifts may be consecrated and the offerers may be sanctified and led, as a single body with the single spirit, to the full enjoyment of God's kingdom and the glorification of the entire Trinity'. (Bugnini, *Reform of the Liturgy*, p. 459.)

Roman Missal and the actual content of the prayers does hint at some uncertainty or ambivalence within the current Roman tradition regarding the function of the epiclesis in the eucharistic prayer.[31]

Bugnini notes that

> the specifically Roman character of the structure of the new prayers is sufficiently preserved by having a single (consecratory) epiclesis before the account of institution; of all the characteristics of the Roman tradition that might be mentioned, this is the most typical (in the Roman Canon, the *Quam oblationem*).[32]

It is curious that Bugnini identifies a *single* epiclesis as a *typical* feature of the Roman Canon. Given that only a few years earlier scholars were debating whether the Canon had any epiclesis at all – one, or two or more – one wonders whether this may be a bit of revisionist history being wielded to justify what the reformers had decided to do. At any rate, it does not seem that the epiclesis had been stressed prior to this as a 'typical' feature of the Canon. It implies that the Roman Canon had a long-standing respect for the role of the epiclesis (and the Holy Spirit in general) in its eucharistic prayers when the prior textual evidence, at least, belies the force of such claims.

The epiclesis texts of the four eucharistic prayers found in the 1970 *Roman Missal* will now be considered in greater detail.

THE EPICLESES OF ROMAN CATHOLIC EUCHARISTIC PRAYERS I–IV

Eucharistic Prayer I

Since the Holy Spirit is not mentioned at all, the 'epiclesis' of Eucharistic Prayer I is not like those of the other 'new' Roman Catholic eucharistic prayers. As with the prayer as a whole, the wording of the epicletic elements amounts to a slightly adapted version of the traditional Roman Canon. The epicletic elements are phrased in terms of 'prayers for acceptance' rather than fully fledged pneumatic epicleses. Table 5.1 presents the first of these, located before the institution narrative.[33]

---

31 On more recent tensions that have emerged in this regard, see Patrick Regan, 'Quenching the Spirit: The Epiclesis in Recent Roman Documents', *Worship* 79.5 (2005), pp. 386–404.

32 Bugnini, *Reform of the Liturgy*, pp. 451, 452.

33 The rubrics direct the priest to pray this prayer 'holding his hands extended over the offerings' (*tenens manus expansas super oblata*). At its conclusion, the priest 'joins his hands' (*iungit manus*).

Table 5.1: First 'prayer of acceptance' of Roman Catholic Eucharistic Prayer I

Missale Romanum, *editio typica* (1970), *editio typica tertia* (2002)[34]	International Commission on English in the Liturgy (ICEL)(2010)[35]
Quam oblationem tu, Deus, in omnibus, quaesumus, benedictam, adscriptam, ratam, rationabilem, acceptabilemque facere digneris: ut nobis Corpus et Sanguis fiat dilectissimi Filii tui, Domini nostri Iesu Christi.	Be pleased, O God, we pray, to bless, acknowledge, and approve this offering in every respect; make it spiritual and acceptable, so that it may become for us the Body and Blood of your most beloved Son, our Lord Jesus Christ.

As McKenna notes, 'This does contain a typical epiclesis element, viz., a prayer that the offering become for us Christ's body and blood. The appeal to bless, approve, make acceptable is also similar to appeals found in other fully developed epicleses.'[36] Nonetheless, the consecratory emphasis of other epicleses is lacking in the Roman Canon, even if an implicit reference to the Spirit is inferred behind the power of blessing invoked upon the gifts. Enrico Mazza stresses that this prayer does not contain a *direct* request for the transformation of the eucharistic bread and wine into Christ's body and blood as the newer eucharistic prayers do.

> Rather, what is directly and formally requested is that the offering may be blessed, accepted (rather than 'consecrated': *adscriptam*, not *consecratam*), approved, made reasonable and acceptable. It is by hearing and granting it that the Father transforms the offerings into the body and blood of his Son.[37]

Even the request that the offerings become the body and blood of Christ here may represent a later stage in the theological development of the

---

34 Ordo Missae cum populo 88, in Roman Catholic Church, *Missale Romanum: Ex Decreto Sacrosancti Oecumenici Concilii Vaticani II Instauratum: Auctoritate Pauli PP. VI Promulgatum: Ioannis Pauli PP. II Cura Recognitum* (Civitate Vaticana: Typis Vaticanis 2002).

35 *The Roman Missal: Study Edition* (Collegeville, MN: Liturgical Press 2012), no. 88. ET © ICEL, 2010.

36 John H. McKenna, 'Epiclesis Revisited', in Senn (ed.), *New Eucharistic Prayers*, p. 178.

37 Enrico Mazza, *The Eucharistic Prayers of the Roman Rite*, trans. Matthew J. O'Connell (New York: Pueblo 1986), p. 71.

Table 5.2: Second 'prayer of acceptance' of Roman Catholic Eucharistic Prayer I

Missale Romanum, *editio typica* (1970), *editio typica tertia* (2002)	ICEL (2010)[38]
Supplices te rogamus, omnipotens Deus: iube haec perferri per manus sancti Angeli tui in sublime altare tuum, in conspectu divinae maiestatis tuae; ut quotquot ex hac altaris participatione sacrosanctum Filii tui Corpus et Sanguinem sumpserimus, omni benedictione caelesti et gratia repleamur.	In humble prayer we ask you, almighty God: command that these gifts be borne by the hands of your holy Angel to your altar on high in the sight of your divine majesty, so that all of us who through this participation at the altar receive the most holy Body and Blood of your Son may be filled with every grace and heavenly blessing.

Roman Canon. In contrast to the known precursors of the Roman Canon (i.e. Ambrose's *Quam oblationem* and the *post pridie* prayer of the Mozarabic liturgy), in which 'the Father was asked to bless, ratify, and accept because the bread and wine *are* the sacrament of the Lord's body and blood', the text of the Roman Canon requests that God 'bless, ratify, and accept *in order that the bread and wine may become* the sacrament of Christ's body and blood'.[39] In a changed context in which the bread and wine prior to the institution narrative are no longer clearly conceived as the *figura* (to use Ambrose's term) or the *imago et similitudo* (in the language of the Mozarabic liturgy) of the body and blood of Christ, the petition may have been reoriented in a more explicitly consecratory direction.[40]

The second 'prayer for acceptance' in the Roman Canon is located after the institution narrative (see Table 5.2).

McKenna recognizes a rather singular dynamic in the imagery of this prayer when compared to that of most other eucharistic prayers. 'Instead of involving a descent it calls for an ascent to the heavenly altar at the hand of God's angel. The benefits for those receiving are sweeping – every grace and blessing.'[41] The *Supplices* section reflects attentiveness to

---

38 *Roman Missal*, no. 94.
39 Mazza, *Eucharistic Prayers*, p. 71, emphasis added.
40 Mazza notes that some contemporary vernacular translations, such as the Italian, make this connection even more overtly than the Latin text of the Canon itself does, rendering the *Quam oblationem* in a style similar to that of the first epiclesis of the eucharistic prayers approved since 1969. See Mazza, *Eucharistic Prayers*, pp. 71–2.
41 McKenna, 'Epiclesis Revisited', p. 178.

the concept of an ongoing heavenly liturgy (and thus incorporates an eschatological consciousness into the Canon). Mazza proposes that:

> The purpose of the angelic intervention is to give our celebration the fruitfulness described in 1 Corinthians 10:18: Those who eat of the victims become participants in the altar. We participate in the heavenly altar because we eat the body and blood of the Son of God. But that participation would not be possible if the angel or angels had not carried the victim from our altar to the heavenly altar.[42]

Eucharistic Prayer II

The texts for the epiclesis are to be found in the post-Sanctus section (comprising the majority of the text in the very brief transition section between the Sanctus and the institution narrative) and in a very brief section between the anamnesis/offering and the intercessions (see Table 5.3).[43]

Table 5.3: Epicletic texts of Roman Catholic Eucharistic Prayer II

Missale Romanum, *editio typica* (1970), *editio typica tertia* (2002)[44]	ICEL (2010)[45]
Haec ergo dona, quaesumus, Spiritus tui rore sanctifica, ut nobis Corpus et (+) Sanguis fiant Domini nostri Iesu Christi.	101. Make holy, therefore, these gifts, we pray, by sending down your Spirit upon them like the dewfall, so that they may become for us the Body (+) and Blood of our Lord, Jesus Christ.
Et supplices deprecamur ut Corporis et Sanguinis Christi participes a Spiritu Sancto congregemur in unum.	105. Humbly we pray that, partaking of the Body and Blood of Christ, we may be gathered into one by the Holy Spirit.

---

42 Mazza, *Eucharistic Prayers*, pp. 82–3.
43 The rubrics for the first epiclesis direct the priest to join his hands and extend them over the offerings, joining them again and making the sign of the cross once over both bread and cup at the words 'so that they may become for us the Body (+) and Blood of our Lord ...' ('Iungit manus, easque expansas super oblata tenens, dicit ... iungit manus et signat semel super panem et calicem simul, dicens ... Iungit manus.' At the second epiclesis, the priest prays 'with hands extended' ('Deinde sacerdos, extensis manibus, dicit ...'). The rubrics for Eucharistic Prayers III and IV are virtually identical.
44 See *Missale Romanum* (2002), nos 101, 105.
45 *Roman Missal*, nos 101, 105.

While Eucharistic Prayer II is an adaptation of the single, post-anamnesis epiclesis in *Apostolic Tradition* 4, its theology is more consistent with scholastic and subsequent Roman Catholic theology than with the sensibilities of the early Church. Consistent with the desire for a unified structure of the new Roman Catholic eucharistic prayers loosely patterned after that of the Roman Canon, the 'consecratory' and 'communion' dimensions of the epiclesis are relegated to different sections of the prayer, resulting in a split epiclesis.[46]

Compared to *Apostolic Tradition*, the first epiclesis in Eucharistic Prayer II asks more forcefully than the original that the gifts 'may become for us' (*ut nobis ... fiant*) Christ's body and blood. In contrast, it is unlikely that *Apostolic Tradition*'s epiclesis – which implores God to 'send your Holy Spirit in the oblation of [your] holy church, [that] gathering [them] into one you will give to all who partake of the holy things [to partake] in the fullness of the Holy Spirit, for the strengthening of faith in truth' – was directly concerned with consecration of the gifts at all.[47]

The Spirit does not act directly as the agent of sanctification for the gifts; rather, the petition is addressed to the Father, who is asked to sanctify the gifts through *Spiritus Sancti rore* (literally, the 'dew of the Holy Spirit'); the English translations follow the Latin of *Apostolic Tradition* in rendering this as a petition that God 'send' (*mittas*) the Spirit. As Mazza notes, the transition to the first epiclesis (*ergo* – 'therefore') 'leads to a petition that God would act in accordance with his nature and sanctify the gifts set before him'.[48] Furthermore, for those steeped in the biblical and patristic tradition in which the giving of the Spirit is associated with God's definitive intervention in the last days, the outpouring of the Spirit upon the gifts requested in this epiclesis hints that the gifts (and those who will share in them) are now participants in the eschatological age, which impinges upon the community's eucharistic celebration here and now. The image of 'dew', present in the Latin and the 2010 English translation, carries connotations of the effect of God's word raining down from heaven (cf. Isa. 55.10–11 and Hos. 14.5). 'This efficacious dew which the Father sends during the celebration of the eucharistic prayer is the Holy Spirit. It penetrates the sacred gifts and transforms them into the sacrament of the Lord's body

---

46 For an overview of the structural changes made to the text of *Apostolic Tradition* in crafting Roman Catholic Eucharistic Prayer II, see Mazza, *Eucharistic Prayers*, pp. 92–100.
47 For the Latin text and ET of the epiclesis of *Apostolic Tradition*, see above, p. 78.
48 Mazza, *Eucharistic Prayers*, p. 109.

and blood.'[49] This connection between the Holy Spirit and dew is not found in *Apostolic Tradition*; the source is the post-Sanctus for the Easter Vigil in the *Missale Gothicum*.[50]

The second epicletic component of Eucharistic Prayer II abbreviates the text of *Apostolic Tradition*, emphasizing the theme of unity[51] without mentioning the 'strengthening of faith in truth' that seems to be integrally connected to the community's celebration of the Eucharist and the resultant unity in the text which served as its model. In Eucharistic Prayer II, the Holy Spirit is credited as the agent of the community's unity realized in the eucharistic encounter (making a connection that was implicit in *Apostolic Tradition* more explicit); however, the broader dimensions of sharing in the 'fullness of the Holy Spirit' – with all that this might entail for the life of the church which celebrates the Eucharist – are not to be found in the modern Roman version.[52] The connection between *Apostolic Tradition*'s 'holy things' (*sanctis*) and the 'body and blood of Christ' mentioned in Eucharistic Prayer II similarly makes what was a rather vague reference in the model text much more specific, consistent with a trajectory of development through which 1 Corinthians 10.16 shaped the text of *Apostolic Tradition* as early as the version of it found in *Apostolic Constitutions* 8.[53] Thus it seems that the epiclesis of *Apostolic Tradition* 4 was deemed unsuitable for direct appropriation into a Roman Catholic prayer in which clarity of expression within the prayer and parallel structure in relation to other prayers in use in the tradition were important concerns. This adaptation of *Apostolic Tradition* opted to highlight two key components of its epiclesis – namely the unity of the communicants and the Spirit as the source of this unity – and recast them

---

49 Mazza, *Eucharistic Prayers*, p. 110.

50 Mazza, *Eucharistic Prayers*, p. 315, n. 87. The text of the *Missale Gothicum* reads here: 'We ask you to bless this sacrifice with your blessing and to pour over it the dew of your Spirit (*et Spiritus Sancti tui rore perfundas*)'; see L. K. Mohlberg (ed.), *Missale Gothicum* (Rome, 1961), p. 69, no. 271 (as given in Mazza). See Mazza, *Eucharistic Prayers*, p. 315, n. 87 for other associations between the Holy Spirit and dew in Mozarabic texts.

51 McKenna, 'Epiclesis Revisited', p. 179.

52 Mazza views this change not as an impoverishment but as an emphasis on a tradition more primitive even than *Apostolic Tradition*. The exclusive focus on unity is characteristic of early prayers like *Didache* 10 whose sole request is the eschatological unity of the community as a sign of its participation in the messianic age. According to Mazza, in Eucharistic Prayer II, 'the theme of unity has been isolated to highlight a basic truth about the Eucharist, namely, that it is the sacrament of unity. Unity is prayed for; if it does not become a reality, then the sacrament and the sacramental action of the Spirit will have been frustrated.' Mazza, *Eucharistic Prayers*, p. 120.

53 Mazza, *Eucharistic Prayers*, p. 119.

Table 5.4: First epiclesis of Roman Catholic Eucharistic Prayer III

Missale Romanum, *editio typica* (1970), *editio typica tertia (2002)*	*ICEL (2010)*[54]
Supplices ergo te, Domine, deprecamur, ut haec munera, quae tibi sacranda detulimus, eodem Spiritu sanctificare digneris, ut Corpus et + Sanguis fiant Filii tui Domini nostri Iesu Christi, cuius mandato haec mysteria celebramus.	109. Therefore, O Lord, we humbly implore you: by the same Spirit graciously make holy these gifts we have brought to you for consecration, that they may become the Body and (+) Blood of your Son our Lord Jesus Christ, at whose command we celebrate these mysteries.

within a style and structure more consistent with the other 'new' Roman Catholic eucharistic prayers.[55]

Eucharistic Prayer III

The first epiclesis of Eucharistic Prayer III concludes the post-Sanctus section, which is slightly more extensive than that of Eucharistic Prayer II – and which *does* mention the Spirit as a source of life and holiness active in the economy of salvation through God's Son, 'Jesus Christ our Lord, by the working of the Holy Spirit'. Appearing shortly thereafter, the first epiclesis continues this theme and provides a clear transition to the institution narrative which immediately follows (see Table 5.4).

The Latin text, phrasing the opening petition as 'we implore' or 'we entreat' (*deprecamur*), may be deliberately patterned after the Roman Canon's *Quam oblationem*, as the 2010 English translation makes clearer than the 1973 (and 1985) ICEL translations. The Latin (and all three English translations) request that God sanctify the eucharistic gifts through the Spirit; in doing so, the basic dynamic underlying the Roman Canon's *Quam oblationem* is given a more pneumatic orientation.[56] The 2010 English translation aligns more closely with that of the Latin in rendering the verb of offering in the perfect tense ('we have brought',

---

54 *Roman Missal*, no. 109.

55 See Mazza, *Eucharistic Prayers*, p. 99.

56 Some other vernacular translations, such as the Italian (at least as of 1986), reworked this petition into a request for the coming of the Spirit. Thus the 'Latin takes the theme in the *Quam oblationem* and relates it to the Spirit, whereas the Italian constructs an epiclesis based on the coming of the Spirit'. Mazza, *Eucharistic Prayers*, p. 129.

Table 5.5: Second epiclesis of Roman Catholic Eucharistic Prayer III

Missale Romanum, *editio typica* (1970), *editio typica tertia* (2002)	ICEL (2010)[57]
… concede, ut qui Corpore et Sanguine Filii tui reficimur, Spiritu eius Sancto repleti, unum corpus et unus spiritus inveniamur in Christo.	113. … grant that we, who are nourished by the Body and Blood of your Son and filled with his Holy Spirit, may become one body, one spirit in Christ.

corresponding to the Latin *detulimus*) rather than the present tense ('bring') of the 1973 and 1985 ICEL translations.

> The Latin verb is in the perfect tense and, therefore, indicates an action that has taken place … the Latin *detulimus* must, therefore, refer to bringing the gifts to the altar, an action that has indeed taken place.[58]

The second epiclesis, conjoined to a brief post-anamnesis prayer for God's acceptance of the Church's offering, again emphasizes the theme of unity (like the second epiclesis of Eucharistic Prayer II) but also draws attention to the act of sharing in and being nourished by Christ's body and blood (see Table 5.5).

Despite the many similarities, the epiclesis of Eucharistic Prayer III does emphasize more strongly than the epiclesis of Eucharistic Prayer II that one 'fruit' of communion is itself the indwelling of the Spirit, without whose presence the desired unity could not be realized. In so doing, this second epiclesis cements the link between consecration and communion to an extent which some of the other Roman prayers do not. In the words of Detscher,

> The Spirit who transforms the gifts also transforms those who receive the gifts. The Spirit who causes the bread to be the body of Christ also causes those who receive the sacramental body of the Lord to be the body of Christ, the Church.[59]

---

57 *Roman Missal*, no. 113.
58 Mazza, *Eucharistic Prayers*, p. 129. Mazza advises that, 'We must not confuse the act of offering, which follows the anamnesis, with the preparation of the gifts, during which the gifts are carried to the altar' (p. 129).
59 Detscher, 'Eucharistic Prayers', p. 35.

Hence the role of the Holy Spirit in the *entire* eucharistic celebration emerges more clearly here, especially when the first and second epicleses of Eucharistic Prayer III are joined side by side.

Mazza draws attention to the connection between eucharistic eating and drinking, communion with Christ, the indwelling of the Holy Spirit, and Christian discipleship as a true initiation into the life of the risen Christ, whose death and resurrection (particularly in Johannine theology) made the sending of the Spirit possible:

> The verb 'feed upon,' 'be nourished' (*reficimur*) signifies both the physical activity of eating and drinking and the personal activity of the disciples who live and are nourished by something that is part of the master's own life. Communion is an action of the whole person, and it is 'following' . . . To feed upon or be nourished means to attain to *metanoia*. Otherwise there would be no 'communion' but only a swallowing.[60]

In this way, sharing in Christ (and in Christ's body and blood) entails sharing in Christ's Spirit – and, by extension, the unity which is to characterize his followers (see, e.g., John 17.20–23; Acts 4.32). The desire expressed in this anaphora that these Spirit-filled followers might become 'one body, [and] one spirit in Christ' is taken over from the Anaphora of Basil, which incorporates the Pauline notion of unity among those who share in 'one bread' (1 Cor. 10.17) with the pneumatological implications of unity through 'one body and one Spirit' derived from Ephesians 4.4.

> The epiclesis thus ends in contemplation of the unity among those who are 'in Christ.' This unity is, as it were, a pathway built by the Spirit who is given to us in his fullness. He is the reality by which we are nourished when we feed upon the body and blood of Christ, since 'the Lord is the Spirit' (2 Cor 3:17).[61]

Eucharistic Prayer IV

Based on the shorter Egyptian form of the Anaphora of Basil, Roman Catholic Eucharistic Prayer IV splits the single, post-anamnesis epiclesis of Basil into pre-institution and post-anamnesis petitions for consecration of the gifts and the fruits of communion, respectively. The post-

---

60 Mazza, *Eucharistic Prayers*, p. 141.
61 Mazza, *Eucharistic Prayers*, p. 142.

Table 5.6: First epiclesis of Roman Catholic Eucharistic Prayer IV

Missale Romanum, *editio typica* (1970)	ICEL (2010)[62]
Quaesumus igitur, Domine, ut idem Spiritus Sanctus haec munera sanctificare dignetur, ut Corpus et + Sanguis fiant Domini nostri Iesu Christi ad hoc magnum mysterium celebrandum,* quod ipse nobis reliquit in foedus aeternum. *Editio typica tertia (2002) reads **celebríndum** here.	118. Therefore, O Lord, we pray: may this same Holy Spirit graciously sanctify these offerings, that they may become the Body (+) and Blood of our Lord Jesus Christ for the celebration of this great mystery, which he himself left us as an eternal covenant.

Sanctus epiclesis flows logically from the mention of the Pentecost experience of Christ sending the Spirit upon his followers and leads into the institution narrative (see Table 5.6).

Because of the logical connection established by the recounting of salvation history, this epiclesis seems less like an intrusion into the flow of the prayer than some of the other Roman epicleses do. Nonetheless, the broader Trinitarian movement of Basil as a whole (focusing on the Father, then the Son, and finally on the Spirit in the final sections of the prayer) is still interrupted by the inclusion of an explicit pneumatic epiclesis at this point of the prayer. Once again, the request is that God (the Father) sanctify the gifts through the Holy Spirit so that they might become Christ's body and blood – in this way overtly associating the Spirit with a change in the gifts to a degree that the Roman Canon does not. Mazza notes that this prayer

> uses the traditional liturgical term *sanctificare* instead of the technical theological term *consecrare* . . . Retention of the word 'sanctify' helps to highlight the close continuity between the action of the Holy Spirit on the bread and wine and on [the Spirit's] action on the faithful in eucharistic communion.[63]

The language used clearly envisions some transformation of the gifts but leaves the theological question of *how* this change happens open.[64]

---

62 *Roman Missal*, no. 118.
63 Mazza, *Eucharistic Prayers*, p. 331, n. 118.
64 Mazza, *Eucharistic Prayers*, p. 173. Mazza deems this 'noncommittal approach . . . normative for liturgical texts' (p. 173).

Table 5.7: Second epiclesis of Roman Catholic Eucharistic Prayer IV

Missale Romanum, *editio typica* (1970), *editio typica tertia* (2002)	ICEL (2010)[65]
Respice, Domine, in Hostiam, quam Ecclesiae tuae ipse parasti, et concede benignus omnibus qui ex hoc uno pane participabunt et calice, ut, in unum corpus a Sancto Spiritu congregati, in Christo hostia viva perficiantur, ad laudem gloriae tuae.	122. . . . grant in your loving kindness to all who partake of this one Bread and one Chalice that, gathered into one body by the Holy Spirit, they may truly become a living sacrifice in Christ to the praise of your glory.

The second epiclesis connects God's acceptance of the sacrifice and its impact on the communicants (see Table 5.7).

Just as the Holy Spirit is earlier asked to transform the bread and wine into Christ's body and blood, the second epiclesis requests the 'transformation' of the communicants into the body of Christ that they might become a living sacrifice. Oddly, for the Roman Catholic tradition at least, the second epiclesis names the now-consecrated 'gifts' as 'Bread' and 'Chalice' rather than body and blood.[66] Perhaps, as Mazza suggests, this is because it is the bread and cup that serve at this point in the eucharistic celebration as the tangible reminders of the fruits of communion expected through the Spirit's activity in connection with Christ's eucharistic body and blood:

> The epiclesis of Anaphora IV does not explicitly ask for the descent of the Holy Spirit; rather it supposes that this has already occurred, and thus reinforces the connection between the anamnesis and epiclesis. This approach to the epiclesis strongly emphasizes the identity between the fruit of the Spirit's action and the fruit of the body and blood of the Lord as made sacramentally visible in the one bread and the one cup.[67]

Detscher draws attention to the close connection between the oblation and the epiclesis highlighted in this prayer, which emphasizes that

---

65 *Roman Missal*, no. 122.
66 McKenna, 'Epiclesis Revisited', pp. 179–80.
67 Mazza, *Eucharistic Prayers*, p. 182.

the sacrifice is offered only through the power of the Holy Spirit who transforms the bread and cup which we offer, and transforms us who receive the body and blood of Christ, that we may offer ourselves as a living sacrifice. The anaphora thus echo (*sic*) the teaching of Saint Paul in Corinthians and Romans.[68]

Unity again emerges as a central theme among the fruits of communion; the Holy Spirit is envisioned as gathering the communicants into 'one body'. In light of the first part of Eucharistic Prayer IV, which presents Christ as the revelation of God in salvation history, such unity is associated with the hope of salvation and redemption for all who share in the Eucharist as the memorial of Christ's death and resurrection – consistent with Johannine theology. Furthermore, the conclusion of this epiclesis, oriented towards worship ('the praise of your glory') likely contains echoes of Pauline theology with its cultic references conceiving of life in Christ *as* worship. 'The epiclesis ends with a vision of Christian life that is put not in ethical but in cultic terms: Christ's life in us as a prolongation and fruit of the eucharistic memorial.'[69]

THE EPICLESES OF OTHER ROMAN CATHOLIC EUCHARISTIC PRAYERS

In addition to the four numbered prayers found in the *Roman Missal*, there are several other additional prayers in use in Roman Catholic circles – three for Masses with Children,[70] two for Masses of Reconciliation,[71] and one for Masses for Various Needs and Occasions.[72] The epicletic portions of the children's prayers are given in Table 5.8.

The epicleses of all three of these prayers are split and succinct. Perhaps what is most immediately striking about these children's prayers is the presence of the word 'change' in the first epiclesis of Children II and III. This strong statement of real presence, however, is unique to the

---

68 Detscher, 'Eucharistic Prayers', p. 41.
69 Mazza, *Eucharistic Prayers*, pp. 182–6 (esp. pp. 185–6), quote from p. 186.
70 On the background and compositional history of these prayers, see Reiner Kaczynski, 'Direktorium und Hochgebetstexte für Messfeiern mit Kindern', *Liturgisches Jahrbuch* 29 (1979), pp. 157–75; Bugnini, *Reform of the Liturgy*, pp. 477–82; Mazza, *Eucharistic Prayers*, pp. 238–40; and John Barry Ryan, 'Eucharistic Prayers for Masses with Children' in Senn (ed.), *New Eucharistic Prayers*, pp. 53–62.
71 See Detscher, 'Eucharistic Prayers', p. 47 and Mazza, *Eucharistic Prayers*, p. 191.
72 For more on the origins of this prayer, see Bugnini, *Reform of the Liturgy*, p. 477 and Mazza, *Eucharistic Prayers*, p. 216.

Table 5.8: Eplicletic portions of prayers for Masses with Children

	Latin (1974)[73]	*ICEL (1975)*
Eucharistic Prayer for Masses with Children I	1. Pater sancte, grátias tibi réferre voléntes, panem et vinum attúlimus; fac ut virtúte Spíritus Sancti Corpus fiant et Sanguis Iesu Christi, (+) dilectíssimi Fílii tui. Sic tibi offérre potérimus, quod tuo múnere nobis praebétur.	1. We bring you bread and wine and ask you to send your Holy Spirit to make these gifts the body (+) and blood of Jesus your Son. Then we can offer to you what you have given to us.
	2. Pater, qui nos tantópere díligis, ad hanc tuam sine nos mensam accédere et mitte nobis Spíritum Sanctum ut, Fílii tui Corpus et Sánguinem sumámus, et simus cor unum et ánima una.	2. Father, because you love us, you invite us to come to your table. Fill us with the joy of the Holy Spirit as we receive the body and blood of your Son.
Eucharistic Prayer for Masses with Children II	1. Te Deum, Patrem nostrum, rogámus mitte Spíritum tuum, ut haec dona panis et vini Corpus et (+) Sanguis fiant Iesu Christi, Dómini nostri.	1. God our Father, we now ask you to send your Holy Spirit to change these gifts of bread and wine into the body (+) and blood of Jesus Christ, our Lord.
	2. Exáudi nos, Dómine Deus, et dona Spíritum tui amóris cunctis, qui de hoc partícipant convívio, ut in Ecclésia magis magísque sint unum, cum Papa nostro N., et Epíscopo nostro N., ceterísque Epíscopis	2. Lord, our God, listen to our prayer. Send the Holy Spirit to all of us who share in this meal. May this Spirit bring us closer together in the family of the Church, with N., our Pope, N., our bishop, all other

73 Although the Latin text of these prayers is not intended for liturgical use, they are included as Appendix VI (Preces Eucharisticae pro Missis cum Pueris) in the third typical edition of the Missal; see Roman Catholic Church, *Missale Romanum*, pp. 1271ff. ET from appendix VI of the *Roman Missal*, revised according to the second typical edition of the *Missale Romanum* (1975), 1 March 1985, for use in the dioceses of the United States of America.

	Latin (1974)	ICEL (1975)
	et ómnibus, qui plebi tuae mínistrant.	bishops, and all who serve your people.
Eucharistic Prayer for Masses with Children III	1. Pater óptime, haec dona panis et vini per virtútem Sancti Spíritus sanctificáre dignéris, ut nobis fiant Corpus et (+) Sanguis Fílii tui Iesu Christi.	1. Father, we ask you to bless these gifts of bread and wine and make them holy. Change them for us into the body (+) and blood of Jesus Christ, your Son.
	2. Pater sancte, qui nos vocásti, ut de hac mensa in laetítia Corpus Christi sumerémus, tríbue, quáesumus, ut huius cibi virtúte roboráti, tibi magis magísque placeámus, et per communiónem Spíritus Sancti unum corpus in caritáte fiámus.	2. Father in heaven, you have called us to receive the body and blood of Christ at this table and to be filled with the joy of the Holy Spirit. Through this sacred meal give us strength to please you more and more.

English-language translation of these prayers. The 1968 prayers, as well as the Latin, French and German versions of the children's prayers, all have something along the lines of 'that they [the gifts] may become (for us) the body and blood of Jesus ...'. As Ryan notes, the term 'change' 'seems ... to be a word more at home in talking about the eucharist than within the prayer itself'.[74] Perhaps this reflects the intention behind the prayers as liturgical catechesis in themselves and a starting point for more formal catechesis on the Eucharist. All three of the epicleses are addressed to God (the Father) and make a direct request that God would act to accomplish the desired change in the gifts, through sending the Spirit in I and II and through blessing and sanctifying the gifts in I – although without direct mention of the Spirit. For practical purposes then, Children I in Latin and Children III in Latin and English have a single epiclesis in terms of their explicit pneumatological content. Mazza remarks that the 'elimination of the "first" epiclesis solves in a felicitous way the problem of having a single anaphora with two epicleses (one of which is there for reasons which appeal solely to theologians)'.[75]

74 Ryan, 'Eucharistic Prayers for Masses with Children', p. 59.
75 Mazza, *Eucharistic Prayers*, p. 240.

The post-institution epiclesis differs a bit from the new adult prayers approved in 1968. 'First, unlike the 1968 prayers, which purposely stress the unity of the Church in Christ, none of these prayers do so, although II does allude to the concept of unity as it moves from the epiclesis into the intercessions.'[76] The theme of unity is generally carried elsewhere in the prayer, either in the intercessions – or, in the case of Children I, communion with the Pope, the local bishop, Mary and the saints is transferred to the preface as the transition into the Sanctus.[77] Mazza speculates that this de-emphasis of unity in the children's prayers may be because this abstract idea is hard for children to grasp whereas relational concepts like love resonate better with their experience.[78]

If the words chosen in the first epiclesis highlight the sacrificial aspect of the Eucharist as transubstantiation and real presence, the words chosen in the second epiclesis – 'table' in Children I and III and 'meal' in II – consistently emphasize that this presence is to be consumed in communion.[79] Perhaps this was also to highlight connections between this eucharistic meal and other meals familiar to children in their family and communal setting.

The most unusual of this group is the epiclesis in Children III:

> The desired effect in the first part is similar to the others (bless, make holy, change) but there is no mention of the Spirit. In the second part the request is to fill those partaking with the joy of the Holy Spirit and strengthen them to please God.[80]

Thus the joy of the Spirit is presented as one of the fruits of communion without the Spirit being implicated in an integral way with the ongoing eucharistic action itself.

The texts of the epicleses for Masses of Reconciliation are given in Table 5.9.

---

76 Ryan, 'Eucharistic Prayers for Masses with Children', p. 60.
77 Ryan, 'Eucharistic Prayers for Masses with Children', p. 58. Ryan remarks that these elements thus become 'an expression of a communion of praise throughout the world as well as a vertical movement of praise from earth to that of the saints, with Mary and the apostles and the angels in heaven. Thus, this part of the preface is also an introduction to the Sanctus' (p. 58).
78 Mazza, *Eucharistic Prayers*, p. 247.
79 Ryan, 'Eucharistic Prayers for Masses with Children', p. 60. Regarding the words 'table' and 'meal', Ryan comments that, 'In each of the prayers, there is the same suppleness of language that is found in the institution narrative as well as throughout the prayers.'
80 McKenna, 'Epiclesis Revisited', p. 181.

Table 5.9: Epicleses for Masses of Reconciliation

	Latin (1974)[81]	ICEL (2010)
Eucharistic Prayer for Masses of Reconciliation I	1. Réspice, quáesumus, múnera pópuli tui et super ea Spíritus tui virtútem effúnde ut Corpus et (+) Sanguis fiant dilécti Fílii tui, Iesu Christi, in quo et nos fílii tui sumus.	1. Look, we pray, upon your people's offering and pour out on them the power of your Spirit, that they may become the Body and (+) Blood of your beloved Son, Jesus Christ, in whom we, too, are your sons and daughters.
	2. Réspice, benígnus, clementíssime Pater, quos tibi coniúngis Fílii tui sacrifício, ac praesta ut, Spíritus Sancti virtúte, ex hoc uno pane et cálice partícipes, in unum corpus congregéntur in Christo, a quo omnis auferátur divísio.	2. Look kindly, most compassionate Father, on those you unite to yourself by the Sacrifice of your Son, and grant that, by the power of the Holy Spirit, as they partake of this one Bread and one Chalice, they may be gathered into one Body in Christ, who heals every division.[82]
Eucharistic Prayer for Masses of Reconciliation II	1. ... te deprecámur: Spíritus tui effusióne haec dona santífica, ut fiant Corpus et (+) Sanguis Fílii tui, cuius mandátam implémus haec celebrántes mystéria.	1. And now, celebrating the reconciliation Christ has brought us, we entreat you: sanctify these gifts by the outpouring of your Spirit that they may become the Body and Blood of your Son, whose command we fulfill when we celebrate these mysteries.
	2. Pater sancte, súpplices deprecámur, ut nos quoque accéptos hábeas cum Fílio tuo et in hoc salutári convívio eiúsdem Spíritum nobis praestáre dignéris, qui ómnia áuferat quae nos ínvicem aliénant.	2. Holy Father, we humbly beseech you to accept us also, together with your Son, and in this saving banquet graciously to endow us with his very Spirit, who takes away everything that estranges us from one another.[83]

---

81 The text of the Eucharistic Prayers for Masses of Reconciliation can be found in Roman Catholic Church, *Missale Romanum ... Cura Recognitum*, pp. 675ff.
82 *Roman Missal*, pp. 761, 763 (in Appendix to the Order of Mass).
83 *Roman Missal*, pp. 768–9, 770 (in Appendix to the Order of Mass).

The preface of Reconciliation I introduces 'a trinitarian theme: through Christ and in the power of the Holy Spirit we are forgiven and reconciled with our loving Father'.[84] The first epiclesis intrudes rather abruptly into the post-Sanctus section; there is little inherent link between the epiclesis and what comes immediately before it, and, in fact, after the epiclesis the post-Sanctus section continues the theme of Christ establishing a new covenant from the preface. The epiclesis implores God to 'look' (*respicere*) on the assembled people and to 'pour out' (*effunde*) the power (*virtutem*) of the Holy Spirit – so that the bread and wine might become the 'Body and Blood of your Beloved Son, Jesus Christ', providing a transition to *further* reflection on Christ's activity for the sake of human salvation. The extension of the christological section after the first epiclesis is highly unusual for a Roman prayer.[85]

If the intrusive nature of the first epiclesis in this prayer is a negative aspect, a positive move is its awareness of the inherent connection between the consecration and communion dimensions of the epiclesis – i.e. that the consecration of the gifts is for the sake of their transformative effects on the assembled congregation.[86] Furthermore, in the context of this prayer's theme of reconciliation, it highlights the relational nature of the Eucharist (in terms of drawing the communicants into a more intimate union both with God and with one another) and perhaps even the potential of the eucharistic action itself to reunify and heal such relationships broken by sin.

The second epiclesis connects 'the sacrificial Victim who reconciles to [God] the human race' mentioned in the anamnesis to Christ's sacrifice on the cross made present now in the eucharistic encounter which reconciles Christians to God, to one another and to all members of the human family. The initial verb of the second epiclesis, 'look' (*respice*), echoes the first epiclesis of this prayer and also the beginning of the second epiclesis of Eucharistic Prayer IV. The emphasis on unity, as a fruit of the Spirit, among the communicants as one body – and even the language itself – closely resembles that of Eucharistic Prayer IV here as well. The resultant unity is then related to the prayer's theme of reconciliation; it is hoped that the communicants will become 'one Body in Christ, who heals every division'. Although this expression 'is admittedly inadequate for expressing the biblical concept of unity ... [t]he "truth" of the prayer has been given precedence over the wealth of

---

84 Detscher, 'Eucharistic Prayers', p. 43.
85 Mazza, *Eucharistic Prayers*, p. 200.
86 Detscher, 'Eucharistic Prayers', p. 43.

theology that might have been included in dealing with the theme of unity'.[87]

As in the first epiclesis, the power (*virtus*) of the Holy Spirit is likewise implicated in the action of this second epiclesis; however, similar references to power are lacking entirely in Reconciliation II.[88] There is seemingly a connection, however, between the union with God achieved through eucharistic communion and the extension of its benefits, through the Spirit's power, to the rest of the human family. *Testamentum Domini* alters a phrase from *Apostolic Tradition* ('*in unum congregans*') to relate it more clearly to union with God – 'that all may be united to you' ('*ut tibi uniantur omnes*'), and Mazza proposes that such references may be lurking behind this contemporary prayer for reconciliation.[89]

Taken together, the two parts of the epiclesis emphasize important truths.

> The sending forth of the Spirit's power is to lead to the gifts becoming 'for us' the body and blood of Christ. The sharing of the one sacrifice of Christ is to lead to unity, i.e., healing of all division.[90]

And the Holy Spirit is to be the agent of this unity. In terms of the fruits of communion, unity is the dominant benefit emphasized (i.e. one undivided body). Perhaps because of the extensive attention to the Spirit elsewhere in the prayer, especially in the preface, the epiclesis of Reconciliation II is comparatively brief in both consecration and communion dimensions.[91] McKenna dubs this 'the most concise of all epicleses' and observes that

> [t]his is the only time in a Roman Catholic prayer that there is no mention of Christ's body and blood. There is simply an appeal to sanctify the gifts and to fill those sharing the meal with the Holy Spirit so that divisions disappear.[92]

87 Mazza, *Eucharistic Prayers*, pp. 203–4.
88 Thus 'we must therefore conclude that the "power" of the Spirit does not have any special connection with the mystery of reconciliation'. Mazza, *Eucharistic Prayers*, p. 200.
89 Mazza, *Eucharistic Prayers*, p. 203.
90 McKenna, 'Epiclesis Revisited', p. 181.
91 Detscher, 'Eucharistic Prayers', pp. 45–6.
92 McKenna, 'Epiclesis Revisited', pp. 181, 182. What McKenna says is true of the English translation of the prayer; however, Christ's body and blood *are* mentioned in the Latin text.

Table 5.10: The fixed epiclesis of the Eucharistic Prayer for Various Needs

Latin (1991)	ICEL (2010)[93]
Rogámus ergo te, Pater clementíssime, ut Spíritum Sanctum tuum emíttas, qui haec dona panis et vini sanctíficet, ut nobis Corpus et (+) Sánguis fiant Dómini nostri Iesu Christi.	Therefore, Father most merciful, we ask that you send forth your Holy Spirit to sanctify these gifts of bread and wine, that they may become for us the Body and (+) Blood of our Lord Jesus Christ.
In oblatiónem Ecclésiae tuae, in qua paschále Christi sacrifícium nobis tráditum exhibémus, réspice propítius, et concede, ut virtúte Spíritus caritátis tuae, inter Fílii tui membra, cuius Córpori communicámus et Sánguini, nunc et in diem aeternitátis numerémur.	Look with favor on the oblation of your Church, in which we show forth the paschal Sacrifice of Christ that has been handed on to us, and grant that, by the power of the Spirit of your love, we may be counted now and until the day of eternity among the members of your Son, in whose Body and Blood we have communion.

After the mention of the Spirit in the preface, the first aspect of the epiclesis emerges as a brief transition between mention of Christ's reconciling work in the post-Sanctus and the institution narrative. The phrase, 'And now, celebrating the reconciliation Christ has brought us', introduces the epiclesis using words reminiscent of a phrase in the intercessions of Eucharistic Prayer III ('this sacrifice by which we are reconciled').[94] As in Reconciliation I, the primary activity of the Spirit in the second epiclesis is unity, insofar as the Spirit 'takes away everything that estranges us from one another'.

The Eucharistic Prayer for Various Needs (conceived as one prayer with four thematic variations in the preface and intercessions) represents a unique arrangement for a Roman Catholic eucharistic prayer (see Table 5.10 for the fixed epiclesis text).

The epiclesis itself is relatively straightforward. The first epiclesis requests the sending of the Spirit so that the hallowed gifts might become, for the community, Christ's body and blood. Like some of the other Roman Catholic eucharistic prayers (e.g. Eucharistic Prayer IV and Reconciliation I), the second epiclesis is introduced with a request that

---

93 *Roman Missal*, pp. 777, 778 (in Appendix to the Order of Mass).
94 Mazza, *Eucharistic Prayers*, p. 209. The 2010 ET reads 'this Sacrifice of our reconciliation' here.

God 'look' favourably on the Church's offering (and, by implication, on the assembled congregation). The sacrifice is identified as a *paschal* sacrifice, which ties in well with the Emmaus theme introduced by the words of the post-Sanctus directly preceding the first epiclesis in the second variation of the prayer: 'as once for the disciples, so now for us, [Christ] opens the Scriptures and breaks the bread'.[95] The theme of unity among the communicants is highlighted indirectly in the second epiclesis through the themes of love, inclusion and membership. The desire that this unity become a reality 'now and until the day of eternity' hints at an eschatological orientation of the epiclesis – an element that is not at all typical of Roman Catholic epicleses. However, aside from the references that place this epiclesis in the immediate context of the eucharistic sacrifice, its inherent connection with the Eucharist is somewhat tenuous. As Adrien Nocent has observed, an epiclesis referring to the 'Spirit of [God's] love' 'has nothing to do with the Eucharist and can be used anywhere, at any time. It seems strange that this particular form was adopted.'[96]

THE EPICLESES OF ROMAN CATHOLIC EUCHARISTIC PRAYERS: ANALYSIS AND CRITIQUE

The new Roman Catholic eucharistic prayers do succeed in presenting a more conscious awareness of the role of the Holy Spirit in the celebration of the Eucharist than was explicitly present in the Roman Canon. The Spirit is involved in changing the bread and wine (brought forth by the congregation and offered to God on their behalf by the presiding priest) into the body and blood of Christ. The Spirit is also, ultimately, the agent which indwells and 'sanctifies' those who receive this body and blood, uniting them into Christ's body and mediating the other fruits of communion for Christian living. They imply that the community gathered by the Spirit is the primary subject of the eucharistic action.[97]

Some praised the inclusion of an epiclesis in the new Roman prayers as an opportunity for ecumenical engagement between the West and the East and even for its potential to heal some long-standing divisions among the Western churches. Louis Bouyer claimed that, 'undoubtedly, this will contribute toward a rapprochement with the East as well as toward the reunion of the Christian West'. Even if the texts of the new

---

95 *Roman Missal*, p. 782 (in Appendix to the Order of Mass).
96 Adrien Nocent, *A Rereading of the Renewed Liturgy*, trans. Mary M. Misrahi (Collegeville, MN: Liturgical Press 1994), p. 32.
97 Piil, 'The Local Church', pp. 182–3.

prayers still drew attention to the words of institution as privileged or important for consecration, the wider context opened up both a place for a broader Trinitarian appreciation and greater respect for the eucharistic prayer in its entirety. Bouyer remarks that eucharistic consecration 'becomes effective in each celebration within the prayer of the Church in which she uses these words herself in order to invoke their accomplishment from the Father through the sole power of his Spirit'. Bouyer does not find the split epiclesis a negative component but rather 'a recognition of the underlying harmony' of historic Eastern and Western emphases in eucharistic praying.[98] J. D. Crichton highlighted the second component of the epiclesis as a connection between the church's *lex orandi* and its *lex agendi*: the communion component of the epiclesis underscored the reality that

> the church is the Spirit-filled body of Christ; in that body the Holy Spirit is regarded as the animating principle and it is to him that the fruitfulness of Christ's saving work in the hearts of Christians is attributed. Now that people can *hear* the invocation they become more aware of the work of the Spirit in their midst and the eucharist becomes a more adequate sign of the church.[99]

Others, however, were much more circumspect or even critical about the epicleses in the new Roman prayers, either on principle or in terms of the specific ways in which the epiclesis was deployed in them. The status of the 'split' or 'double' epiclesis has been repeatedly singled out for criticism in the current Roman Catholic prayers. Some have argued that a split epiclesis compromises the unity of the Spirit's work by creating an unnatural division between the Spirit's role in sanctifying the gifts and the purpose of this sanctification. The Spirit is invoked upon the community's gifts of bread and wine *so that* those who share in them may be more fully what they already are: the body of Christ. Therefore, the 'consecration' and 'communion' aspects of the epiclesis are not distinct prayers but two dimensions of a single request for communion in Christ and in the Spirit – and this theological unity is more readily apparent

---

98 See Louis Bouyer, *Eucharist: Theology and Spirituality of the Eucharistic Prayer* (Notre Dame 1968), pp. 460–1, as quoted in Paul F. Bradshaw, 'The Rediscovery of the Holy Spirit in Modern Eucharistic Theology and Practice' in Teresa Berger and Bryan D. Spinks (eds), *The Spirit in Worship – Worship in the Spirit* (Collegeville, MN: Liturgical Press 2009), p. 88.
99 J. D. Crichton, *Christian Celebration: The Mass* (London: G. Chapman 1971), pp. 92–3; italics in the original (quoted in Bradshaw, 'Rediscovery', p. 88).

when these two dimensions of the epiclesis remain together. According to Adrien Nocent, a split epiclesis does not present a convincing theological argument for 'why we participate in the bread and wine which the Holy Spirit has transformed, [namely] that we are transformed and reunited in one body'.[100] Aidan Kavanagh questioned whether it was appropriate to locate a pneumatic epiclesis immediately before the institution narrative as this action had inevitable and undesirable consequences; it

> not only welds both sections into a unity that is longer and more strongly consecratory than before: it also interrupts the flow of sequence in narrating the divine mercies for which eucharistic prayer is made and sets the institution narrative off from this cursus.[101]

If theology is not conveyed adequately by text, this is further compounded by the way the text is celebrated in many parishes. Kevin Seasoltz notes that most of the faithful experience the eucharistic prayer, most of the time, as primarily a doctrinal statement intoned by the presider. Consequently, 'most worshipers have scarcely begun to internalize the meanings that are proclaimed in the prayer ... reform efforts have generally failed to engage communities in the eucharistic prayer to the extent that they should be engaged'.[102]

On the positive side, the addition of an epiclesis to Roman Catholic eucharistic prayers is a welcome addition theologically, liturgically and ecumenically. The somewhat marginalized status of the epiclesis may have arisen from a desire not to detract from the role of Christ in the Eucharist, which was historically the dominant emphasis in the West. Commenting on this tendency more generally, the Lutheran Frank Senn calls this 'the Western church's emphasis on the power of the word to bear Christ's presence', a trend he detects as early as Ambrose and Augustine and continuing through Thomas Aquinas and Martin Luther.[103]

---

100 Nocent, *A Rereading*, p. 252.
101 Aidan Kavanagh, 'Thoughts on the New Eucharistic Prayers', *Worship* 43.1 (1969), pp. 2–12; quote above from p. 9. For similar critiques from another Roman Catholic and a Lutheran, respectively, see John H. McKenna, *The Eucharistic Epiclesis: A Detailed History from the Patristic to the Modern Era* (Chicago: Hillenbrand 2009, 2nd edn), pp. 226–7 and Frank C. Senn, 'Toward a Different Anaphoral Structure', *Worship* 58.4 (1984), esp. p. 358.
102 Seasoltz, 'Non-Verbal Symbols and the Eucharistic Prayer' in Senn (ed.), *New Eucharistic Prayers*, p. 230.
103 Senn, 'Toward a Different Anaphoral Structure', p. 348.

It would be problematic in this tradition for the church to petition the Holy Spirit to do what the authoritative and creative words of Christ do with regard to the gifts, notwithstanding a generally appreciative regard for the role of the Holy Spirit in the Eastern eucharist on the part of Western theologians since the sixteenth century.[104]

Put negatively, it may reflect a hesitancy to associate anything that might seem like 'consecratory' power to the Holy Spirit, particularly after the words of Christ in the institution narrative have been pronounced. In John McKenna's assessment, 'Most probably this is a vestige of the older (but *not* ancient) "moment of consecration" problem and the fear that mentioning a change in the gifts *after* the institution narrative would somehow rob the latter of its consecratory power.'[105] While this has been a particular issue for Roman Catholic theology, other Western traditions have also had to grapple with this 'moment of consecration' problem to some extent as well.

It seems that 'traditional' precedent (i.e. appealing to the Alexandrine anaphoral family as inspiration for the split epiclesis) has been used to support more recent theological developments which the Roman Catholic Church desired to uphold in its current euchological repertoire. In addition to overlooking the more prevalent pattern of ancient epicleses (which, in their developed form, held consecratory and communion dimensions together), the split epiclesis has other limitations. In some of the prayers, it interrupts the flow of salvation history from Father to Son to Spirit – the last of these fitting more naturally with the concerns of the church and communicants mentioned after recalling the Son's institution of the Eucharist. Instead of balancing the role of Son and Spirit in the institution narrative, the location of the pre-institution epiclesis has the effect of actually heightening it, drawing even more attention by both word and gesture to something resembling a 'magic moment' focused on the action of the priest *in persona Christi* to the detriment of the role of the praying, believing assembly (which is nonetheless unable to accomplish Christ's presence and can only pray, in hope, for its revelation within and among the members of the community).[106] Senn adds,

---

104 Senn, 'Toward a Different Anaphoral Structure', pp. 348–9.
105 McKenna, 'Epiclesis Revisited', p. 183.
106 McKenna, 'Epiclesis Revisited', p. 183.

It has been held that the *ingenium Romanum* calls for a double epiclesis ... [but t]his approach can only reinforce a 'magical' notion of the *Verba Christi* and hinder the perception that the eucharistic prayer is an economic whole.[107]

If the first component of the epiclesis risks receiving too much attention, the second epiclesis risks being subsumed into the intercessions that typically follow it. McKenna draws attention to one example in an unofficial text,[108] but some of the official texts have similar problems. The most obvious example is Children II, in which the epiclesis blurs into the intercessions: 'Send the Holy Spirit to all of us who share in this meal. May the Spirit bring us closer together in the family of the Church, with N., our Pope ...'

These prayers *do* highlight effectively Roman Catholic belief that the Eucharist involves a transformation of the gifts of bread and wine into Christ's body and blood. In terms of fruits of communion, unity is amply highlighted, being stressed in the epicleses of seven of the ten prayers examined above and, for all practical purposes, as the *sole* additional benefit requested in Eucharistic Prayers II, III, Children II, and Reconciliation I and II.

If new Roman Catholic eucharistic prayers are composed in the future, experimenting with a wider variety of prayer structures, particularly those which could draw more attention to the Spirit's role in the Eucharist without detracting from the larger dynamics of the prayer, might be a fruitful avenue for exploration. 'While traditional elements of a particular genre of prayer should be contained in the newly composed prayers, they need not in every instance follow exactly the structure of the prayers now in the *Sacramentary* or other ritual books.' Furthermore, 'all of the elements of a eucharistic prayer developed in the General Instruction of the Roman Missal need to be present in any new composition yet there may be an original way to reorder certain elements for more effective proclamation'.[109] Might there be a way to introduce

---

107 Senn, 'Toward a Different Anaphoral Structure', p. 350.
108 The example he cites is from *An Original Eucharistic Prayer: Text 1* (Washington, DC: ICEL, 1984), p. 11, 13–14. An early draft of the second epiclesis asked: 'May the Spirit of holiness move among us always inspiring our vision and guiding our hearts in union with N., our pope, N., our bishop, and all who preach the gospel of peace to the poor.'
109 Both of the above quotes are from Kathleen Hughes, 'Original Texts: Beginnings, Present Projects, and Guidelines' in Finn and Schellman (eds), *Shaping English Liturgy*, p. 243.

variability – as is currently the case for embolisms within, for example, eucharistic prayers in the context of marriage and funerals – to highlight the role of the Spirit and thus bind an anaphora with a fairly fixed text (outside of the preface) to the season or event being celebrated when this might be particularly appropriate? (Pentecost, Christmas and the Baptism of the Lord would be obvious examples, but the Easter season and other occasions could provide possibilities as well.) Since the Roman Catholic eucharistic prayers were composed, such a strategy has been tried with success in other traditions (such as the United Methodist Church – whose epicleses feature seasonal variations which elaborate upon a basic framework).

Whatever might happen to Roman Catholic eucharistic prayers in the future, the trajectory established by Roman Catholic reforms of the eucharistic prayer in general and the epiclesis in particular in the late 1960s and early 1970s provided a model for other Western churches to reform their existing prayers (or craft new prayers). Just as the Roman Catholic Church looked to its own tradition for guidance in incorporating an explicit pneumatic epiclesis into its new eucharistic prayers, so other Western churches mined the available resources of their own traditions as well as considering options that had been tried by other churches. The 'recovery' of the epiclesis in a selection of Anglican and Protestant traditions will be the focus of the next two chapters.

Chapter 6

The epiclesis in contemporary Anglican eucharistic prayers

Many other Western churches also engaged in sweeping reforms of their liturgical practice during the closing decades of the twentieth century either concurrent with or subsequent to the reforms that took place in the Roman Catholic Church. The reforms were informed by an ongoing 'exchange' of ideas among traditions (Roman Catholic, Anglican and Protestant, Eastern and Western, and ancient and modern). The result was a general convergence in worship patterns which extended to eucharistic prayers and, to some extent, the treatment of the eucharistic epiclesis within these eucharistic prayers. 'Indeed', James F. White has written, 'new service books from Roman Catholic, Methodist, Lutheran, Reformed, and Anglican traditions seem to be similar recensions of a single text.'[1]

While intentional ecumenical dialogue, consultation and even collaboration explains some of the similarities, another factor was that many of these churches were looking to the liturgies of the early Church for inspiration as they sought to 'recover' their common Christian heritage. This return to the original streams of early Christian tradition held particular appeal for Anglican and Protestant reformers of the twentieth century. As J. Dudley Weaver explains, the 'rediscovery' of ancient liturgical texts such as the *Didache* and the *Apostolic Tradition* 'provided the resources for doing precisely what the sixteenth-century reformers sought to do – reform the church's worship in light of the biblical witness *and* the practice of the ancient church'.[2]

---

1 James F. White, *Protestant Worship: Traditions in Transition* (Louisville, KY: Westminster John Knox Press 1989), p. 34.
2 J. Dudley Weaver Jr, *Presbyterian Worship: A Guide for Clergy* (Louisville, KY: Geneva Press 2002), p. 28.

In several traditions where this was not the case before, Word *and* Sacrament has been recovered as the presumed pattern of Sunday worship at least in theory (if not always in actual practice). This has resulted in increased attention to the texts used to celebrate the Eucharist in traditions where such celebration may have been infrequent in the middle of the last century. At least in terms of official liturgical texts, notes United Methodist liturgical scholar Karen Westerfield Tucker, the Lord's Supper in Protestant churches 'is no longer to be regarded as an intrusion into the typical service. Rather, a service without the eucharist is an abbreviation, a truncation, a part of the whole; it is the exception and not the rule.'[3]

Insight into the process of revision of the Sunday service and the eucharistic prayer in a particular church provides important context for understanding the theological and practical decisions which were made in the tradition with regard to the number, variety, shape and theology of official eucharistic prayers represented within a tradition and the location and content of the epicleses they contain.[4] These issues, however, can be treated only briefly here. The primary focus of this chapter will be the epicleses in several official liturgical books representative of the Anglican tradition – *The Book of Common Prayer* of the Episcopal Church in the United States of America (1979), *The United Methodist Book of Worship* (1992), and *Common Worship* from the Church of England (2000).

EPISCOPAL PRAYERS: BACKGROUND, EPICLETIC TEXTS AND ANALYSIS

The American Prayer Book, accepted in 1979 after over a decade of study, preparation and trial use, was the most thorough revision of the Book of Common Prayer undertaken in the English-speaking world up to that time.[5] When the General Convention of the Episcopal Church met in 1964, the Standing Liturgical Commission was given the

---

3 Karen B. Westerfield Tucker, 'The Eucharist in the *Book of Common Worship (1993)*', *PSB* 16.2 (1995), pp. 139–40.
4 Another related issue is the status of liturgical texts in these traditions. Are they required, authorized, commended, or simply set forth as good models which may be used as they stand, adapted as needed to fit a particular congregation, or used as inspiration for new (and perhaps extemporaneous) compositions by the presider at the eucharistic celebration? The answers given to such questions vary in different denominations.
5 Harry Boone Porter, 'Episcopal Anaphoral Prayers' in Frank C. Senn (ed.), *New Eucharistic Prayers: An Ecumenical Study of Their Development and Structure* (Mahwah, NJ: Paulist Press 1987), p. 63. For more on the process of revision that led to these prayers, see esp. Marion J. Hatchett, *Commentary on the American Prayer Book* (New York: Seabury Press 1980); H. B. Evans, *Prayer Book Renewal: Worship and the New Book of*

assignment of presenting plans for liturgical revision at the next convention (in 1967).[6] At least some of the impetus for reform at this time can likely be traced to discussions by bishops from the worldwide Anglican Communion gathered at the 1958 Lambeth Conference concerning aspects which might profitably be attended to in subsequent revisions of Anglican eucharistic rites. The Subcommittee on the Book of Common Prayer determined that the structure and theology enshrined in the 1662 Book of Common Prayer could no longer serve as the single standard for the entire Anglican communion. Furthermore, the Lambeth Conference signalled greater openness towards 'realist' approaches to eucharistic theology, particularly concerning sacrifice, consecration and the epiclesis.[7]

When the Standing Liturgical Commission began to consider revision of the Prayer Book in the early 1960s, recommitting to making the Holy Eucharist the norm of public corporate worship across the board in the Episcopal Church on Sundays and other important occasions within the life of the church was a priority for the revisers.[8] Drafts of the various sections of the proposed Prayer Book appeared between 1966 and 1975, with the Eucharist being among the first services to receive detailed attention. The immediate process of revision of the eucharistic liturgy that culminated with the texts of the 1979 *Book of Common Prayer* can be dated to 1967 when *The Liturgy of the Lord's Supper* (1966), one in a series of Prayer Book Studies produced by the Standing Liturgical Commission, was authorized for trial use by the General Convention.[9] For the most part, the prayers in *The Liturgy of the Lord's Supper* comprised a revision of those of the 1928 Prayer Book in the direction of modern English.

The epiclesis of the 1966 prayer reads:

> We pray thee, Gracious Father, of thine almighty power, to bless and sanctify us and these holy Mysteries with thy Life-giving Word and

Common Prayer (New York: Seabury Press 1978); Porter, 'Episcopal Anaphoral Prayers', pp. 63–73; and David J. Kennedy, *Eucharistic Sacramentality in an Ecumenical Context: The Anglican Epiclesis* (Aldershot and Burlington, VT: Ashgate 2008), pp. 169–82.

6 Hatchett, *Commentary*, p. 12.

7 *Lambeth Conference Report, 1958*, Report of the Subcommittee on the Book of Common Prayer, 2.81–2.85.

8 Porter, 'Episcopal Anaphoral Prayers', p. 64; cf. Harry Boone Porter, 'An American Assembly of Anaphoral Prayers' in *Sacrifice of Praise* (Rome: CLV – Edizioni Liturgiche 1981), pp. 182–3.

9 Harry Boone Porter and Associated Parishes, *The Holy Eucharist: Rite Two: A Commentary* (Alexandria, VA: Associated Parishes 1976), p. 2.

Holy Spirit. Fill with thy grace all who partake of the Body and Blood of our Lord Jesus Christ. Make us one Body, that he may dwell in us and we in him. And grant that with boldness we may confess thy Name in constancy of faith, and at the last Day enter with all thy saints into the joy of thine eternal kingdom.[10]

Concerning this text, David J. Kennedy observes that,

> with the exception of statements about unity and eschatology in the *epiclesis* inspired by Harry Boone Porter, the prayer of consecration still reads as a revision of a Cranmerian text rather than as a text arising from a return to first principles.[11]

Based on feedback received about language, subsequent revisions of the eucharistic rites (1970–6) appeared in two different styles – Rite One in traditional sixteenth-century Prayer Book English and Rite Two in more contemporary English – as well as a supplemental Order intended for less formal celebrations.[12] Beginning with *The Holy Eucharist* (Prayer Book Studies 21, 1970), multiple options for the eucharistic prayer were provided, all conforming to a similar structure. The epiclesis, however, was an element of the Episcopal eucharistic prayers that did *not* undergo significant evolution during the course of these successive revisions. Despite the effect of feedback from trial use on other parts of the prayer (such as the institution narrative), the epicleses persist almost unchanged from *The Holy Eucharist* (Prayer Book Studies 21, 1970) to *Services for Trial Use* (1971) to *Authorized Services* (1973) and finally to the *Draft Proposed Book of Common Prayer* (1976), which, with some minor

---

10 The Standing Liturgical Commission of the Protestant Episcopal Church in the United States of America, *The Liturgy of the Lord's Supper: A Revision of Prayer Book Studies IV* (New York: Church Pension Fund 1966), pp. 15–16.

11 Kennedy, *Eucharistic Sacramentality*, p. 170. Kennedy remarks further that, 'The text is of note because the invocation of the Spirit is not directly related to the elements "becoming" the Body and Blood of Christ. The full-stop between "Spirit" and "Fill" makes an implicit rather than an explicit link' (p. 170). Harry Boone Porter himself noted that this epiclesis text was 'vague, probably to allow theological elbow room to those who saw as consecratory the Words of Institution'; see Porter, 'Meaning and Theology in Eucharistic Prayers A and B', *The Anglican* 24 (1995), p. 7; I owe this reference to Kennedy's book.

12 Massey Hamilton Shepherd, 'The Patristic Heritage of the American Book of Common Prayer of 1979', *The Historical Magazine of the Protestant Episcopal Church* 53 (1984), pp. 222, 232. For a more detailed overview of the process of revision oriented towards the production of the Draft Proposed Book in 1976, see [The Standing Liturgical Commission], *Authorized Services, 1973* (New York: Church Hymnal Corporation 1973, Pew edn), pp. x–xii.

modifications introduced at the General Convention of 1976, was overwhelmingly approved on this occasion (now as the *Proposed Book*) and again in 1979.[13] The *Proposed Book* became the new standard *Book of Common Prayer* in the United States 'according to the use of the Episcopal Church'.[14]

EPISCOPAL EPICLESES IN THE *BOOK OF COMMON PRAYER* (1979)

The American *Book of Common Prayer* presents six full eucharistic prayers 'for use as the Great Thanksgiving in the Holy Eucharist' as well as outlines for the structure of two more (in 'An Order for Celebrating the Holy Eucharist').[15] The 1979 *BCP* introduces more diversity to the Episcopal repertoire of eucharistic praying. The prayers rely on elements characteristic of the Anglican heritage of the American Episcopal Church while also incorporating traditional features often found in eucharistic prayers more generally but not well represented in the standard American prayer, 'including fuller or more precise forms of the anamnesis and epiclesis'.[16] The newer additions provide variety in terms of literary forms and emphases, which may 'be used according to local preference, or in keeping with the intentions of particular seasons or occasions'.[17] Rite One features the standard American Episcopal eucharistic prayer in traditional and contemporary language, and Rite Two introduces four 'new' prayers in modern English. Despite the proliferation of options, there is extensive textual similarity, including the way the Holy Spirit is portrayed in these prayers.

In terms of the theology of consecration connected to the Spirit, Porter comments that:

---

13 Shepherd, 'Patristic Heritage', p. 232.

14 For an explanation of the designation 'use' in this context, see the preface of the *BCP* (pp. 9–11).

15 The designation of each of these prayers as a 'Eucharistic Prayer' is an innovation for the tradition. Hatchett notes that, 'The first Prayer Books gave no title to the eucharistic prayer (though a rubric in the 1549 form for the Communion of the Sick referred to it as "the Canon"), but the Scottish Book of 1637 included a title "Prayer of Consecration" in the rubric which, unfortunately, came after the Sanctus rather than before the Sursum corda. The 1662 revision picked this up and American books perpetuated it. The present revision has dropped both the division and the title, restoring the most ancient title for the prayer, "The Great Thanksgiving"', and has placed this title 'as in the ancient liturgies . . . at the beginning of the prayer, which once again is a unit from the Sursum corda through the people's Amen'. Hatchett, *Commentary*, p. 361.

16 Hatchett, *Commentary*, p. 360.

17 Porter, 'Episcopal Anaphoral Prayers', p. 72.

It is assumed that the Holy Spirit hallows the elements themselves, and also enables the worshipers to receive them to their salvation. At the same time, this takes place in the context of thanksgiving. The operative verb, 'sanctify,' which appears in most of these prayers, may be understood in this context.

Porter explains that what it means for God to 'sanctify' bread and wine so that it might 'be' for the people Christ's body and blood is situated within a broader array of imagery than such terminology tended to entail in older Anglican prayer books. While the latter tended to focus more narrowly on Christ's Passion in the eucharistic context and hence the reception of the flesh and blood of Christ who sacrificed his life for humanity, both the newer prayers themselves and also the range of prefaces which may accompany them envision that the Passion is *one* way among many to view the mystery of the Eucharist. The prayers situate the Eucharist within the entire framework of salvation history and emphasize that the body of Christ received in communion is that of Jesus in the full scope of the paschal mystery. The eucharistic bread and cup are also connected to all the members of Christ who have gone before and shared in this meal, introducing the notion of the communion of saints to the wider reach of the eucharistic action.[18] Some of this imagery is also incorporated into the epicletic texts of the prayers.

The typical structure of the prayers is as follows – although not all of the prayers place these elements in this exact order:

Thanksgiving (consisting of preface and Sanctus)
Institution Narrative
Anamnesis
Epiclesis
[Prayer of Acceptance and/or Intercessions]
Doxology and Amen

All eight of the complete or skeletal prayers feature these elements,[19] and six of them do so in this precise order, influenced by the Antiochene

---

18 Porter, 'Episcopal Anaphoral Prayers', pp. 72–3; extract above from p. 72; cf. Porter, 'An American Assembly', p. 196.

19 In addition to the eucharistic prayers discussed above, the American Prayer Book also includes an 'Order for Celebrating', which provides a skeletal outline which liturgy planners can enflesh with specific components when planning special eucharistic services. Forms 1 and 2 include some components which parallel those of the eucharistic prayers in the BCP. Form 1 includes a brief epiclesis preceding the institution narrative and Form 2 contains an epiclesis following the anamnesis. See Episcopal Church, *The Book of Common*

anaphoral pattern and the structure of the Scottish Book of Common Prayer that had long influenced the American Book. The traditional American prayer, featured in every edition of the American Prayer Book since 1789 and preserved in the 1979 *Book of Common Prayer* as Eucharistic Prayer I, has this form, and the other five 'new' eucharistic prayers included in this book follow suit, with the exception of Eucharistic Prayer C which reverts to the pattern of the 1549 Book of Common Prayer with its pre-institution epiclesis. According to Charles R. Price, since the services of the Episcopal Book do not presume a 'moment of consecration', the location of the epiclesis within a eucharistic prayer does not carry theological significance in this regard.[20] If the predominant Antiochene shape reflects Eastern influence, most of the prayers (including I and II, A and B, and Forms I and II) incorporate the *Western* tradition of providing for (or at least permitting, in the case of the outline prayers of Forms I and II) the use of a variable proper preface highlighting themes of the liturgical year or the occasion of the current eucharistic celebration.

The structure and content of the epicleses of Prayer C and of Form 1 in 'An Order for Celebrating the Holy Eucharist' resemble that of the split epiclesis of the new Roman Eucharistic Prayers insofar as the Holy Spirit is invoked on the bread and wine between the Sanctus and the institution narrative and there is a further petition for the fruits of communion after the anamnesis; they differ from most of the Roman Prayers insofar as the Spirit is not mentioned explicitly in the latter location. All the prayers contained in Rites One and Two request the intervention of the Holy Spirit at some point, and there is considerable consistency among the epiclesis in all these prayers.[21] The specific

---

Prayer and Administration of the Sacraments and Other Rites and Ceremonies of the Church: Together with the Psalter or Psalms of David: According to the Use of the Episcopal Church (New York: Church Hymnal Corporation 1979, Pew edn), pp. 402–5. Subsequent references to pages in the *Book of Common Prayer* will be given in parentheses in the body of the text where appropriate.

20 Charles P. Price, *Introducing the Draft Proposed Book* (New York: Church Hymnal Corporation 1976), p. 84. Leonel Mitchell similarly remarked that these prayers do not view consecration as a 'moment'. Leonel L. Mitchell, *Praying Shapes Believing: A Theological Commentary on* The Book of Common Prayer (Harrisburg, PA: Morehouse 1991), p. 171. These references are from Kennedy, *Eucharistic Sacramentality*, p. 178, n. 29.

21 On its history in the Episcopal tradition, see Hatchett, *Commentary*, pp. 370–1: 'The American Book of 1789 inserted an abbreviated form [of the epiclesis] from the Wee Bookies which preceded the 1764 printing, a form which omitted "that they may be unto us the body and blood of thy most dearly beloved Son." "Word" was capitalized in the first Standard Book (1793), thereby appearing to refer to the incarnate Word rather than to

content and range of the epicleses in these prayers will now be considered in more detail.

THE EPICLESES OF THE HOLY EUCHARIST: RITE ONE

The section of the liturgy between the offertory and the fraction (followed by the distribution of Holy Communion) is labelled 'The Great Thanksgiving', patterned after the fourfold shape of Gregory Dix. Eucharistic Prayer I has been imported unchanged from the 1928 Book (which in turn essentially comprised the prayer first given in the American Book of 1789 with only a few minor changes in the intervening editions);[22] however, the surrounding content is quite different.[23] Eucharistic Prayer I (see *BCP*, pp. 333–6) is preserved intact from the 1928 American Book.[24] There is a new rubric, however, added just before the words of institution, which is repeated in each of the other prayers as well:[25]

At the following words concerning the bread, the Celebrant is to hold

---

our Lord's promise in the institution as the lower case "word" had done. Only Sarapion's prayer includes an epiclesis of the incarnate Word, and it had not been discovered in 1793. The form adopted in 1789, with the capitalization of 1793, is the one included in Prayer I of Rite One in this Book. In Prayer II the result clause is changed from that which is capable of a receptionist interpretation to conform with that of the 1549 Book and the Scottish Wee Bookies which preceded 1764. In the prayers in Rite Two there are variations upon this: "to be for your people" (A); "that they may be the Sacrament of" (B); "to be" (C); and "showing them to be" (D). Prayer A, B, and D have also recovered the epiclesis on the people. The Eastern position for the epiclesis, adopted in the Scottish Wee Bookie of 1755, is maintained in all prayers except C, where it occupies the position of the preliminary epiclesis in the Coptic prayers and those of the Roman Church.'
22 See Paul Victor Marshall (ed.), *Prayer Book Parallels: The Public Services of the Church Arranged for Comparative Study* (New York: Church Hymnal Corporation 1989).
23 Porter, 'Episcopal Anaphoral Prayers', p. 65. Primarily, the connection between the eucharistic prayer and salvation history is enhanced by the provision of 22 proper prefaces which connect feasts, seasons and occasions within the life of God's people (e.g. Baptism, Marriage) to the wider sweep of salvation history. These prefaces place the eucharistic prayer in its entirety, as well as specific components within it, such as the epiclesis, in a broader context; however, these references can also be easy to miss.
24 R. H. Miller, *Study Guide for the Holy Eucharist (Proposed Book of Common Prayer)* (Wilton, CT: Morehouse-Barlow 1977), p. 24.
25 Porter observes that, 'This rubric is deliberately permissive. Imposition of the hand or a modest elevation are equally legitimate and cease to have polemical connotations.' Porter, 'An American Assembly', p. 185. The 1549 BCP included similar rubrics which were removed in 1552 and then reinserted in 1662 alongside a new directive stipulating that the minister was to break the bread while reciting 'he brake it' during the institution narrative. This last direction is not included in the 1979 BCP as the fraction has been relocated to its traditional context after the conclusion of the prayer proper and before the distribution of communion. Hatchett, *Commentary*, p. 364.

it, or lay a hand upon it; and at the words concerning the cup, to hold or place a hand upon the cup and any other vessel containing wine to be consecrated. (*BCP*, p. 334)

In contrast, no manual acts are specified to accompany the epiclesis in this or any of the other prayers in the 1979 *Book of Common Prayer*.

The epiclesis of Eucharistic Prayer I is located in the traditional West Syrian, post-anamnesis location, reproducing most (but not all) of the text which appeared in Cranmer's first edition of the BCP from 1549 and the first editions of the American Prayer Book as well, mediated through the Scottish 'Wee Bookies' of the mid-eighteenth century:

> And we most humbly beseech thee, O merciful Father, to hear us; and, of thy almighty goodness, vouchsafe to bless and sanctify, with thy Word and Holy Spirit, these thy gifts and creatures of bread and wine; that we, receiving them according to thy Son our Savior Jesus Christ's holy institution, in remembrance of his death and passion, may be partakers of his most blessed Body and Blood. (*BCP*, p. 335)

This prayer asks God (the Father) to 'bless and sanctify' God's gifts, which are identified here (after the institution narrative) as 'bread and wine' (rather than with terminology such as 'Christ's body and blood' that might indicate that the status of the bread and wine has changed as a result of the preceding words spoken over them). The omission from this prayer of a phrase found in the epiclesis of the 1549 BCP – 'that they may be unto us the body and blood of thy most dearly beloved Son' – further suggests hesitance about attributing a sense of consecration or even change in the elements resulting from the epiclesis.

Given that this prayer has been maintained intact from previous Episcopal Books, it may suggest as much or more about earlier Episcopal eucharistic pneumatology as it does about its contemporary incarnations. 'By retaining the first Standard Book's (1793) capitalization of "Word" the prayer seems to refer to the incarnate Word and not, as Cranmer had intended, to the institution narrative.'[26] The sanctification of the gifts is requested *so that* the communicants might share in Christ's body and blood, but the Spirit's presence is not invoked on the people directly. The eschatological implications of this reception are not in view in this epiclesis.[27]

---

26 John H. McKenna, 'The Epiclesis Revisited' in Frank C. Senn (ed.), *New Eucharisstic Prayers: An Ecumenical Study of Their Development and Structure* (Mahwah, NJ: Paulist Press, 1987), p. 170; cf. Hatchett, *Commentary*, pp. 369–71.
27 See McKenna, 'Epiclesis Revisited', p. 170.

The Alternative Form of the Great Thanksgiving: Eucharistic Prayer II (pp. 340–3) is very similar to Prayer I and likewise stands in the tradition of Cranmerian eucharistic theology.[28] Overall, Prayer II constitutes a reworking and abbreviation of Prayer I.[29] Cranmer's original result clause concerning the invocation – i.e. 'that [the gifts] may be unto us the Body and Blood of thy dearly beloved Son Jesus Christ' (which appeared in the 1549 BCP and in Scottish liturgies prior to 1765) – has been restored in place of the petition for worthy reception which Eucharistic Prayer I inherits from the 1552 BCP.[30] The content of the prayer is quite similar to that of Eucharistic Prayers A and B of Rite Two, despite the differences in language. The epiclesis of this prayer, located after the narrative and anamnesis, reads:

> And we most humbly beseech thee, O merciful Father, to hear us, and, with thy Word and Holy Spirit, to bless and sanctify these gifts of bread and wine, that they may be unto us the Body and Blood of thy dearly-beloved Son Jesus Christ.   (*BCP*, p. 342)

The language of Eucharistic Prayer II either directly reproduces or closely parallels the intention behind that of Eucharistic Prayer I. As with the first prayer, the epiclesis of the second eucharistic prayer is likewise addressed to God the Father (a feature which is consistent throughout all the eucharistic prayers of the *Book of Common Prayer*, despite some variation in the language of the address). The request that God the Father 'bless and sanctify' the gifts 'with thy Word and Holy Spirit' is likewise identical.[31] Compared to Prayer I, the epiclesis of Prayer II requests a transformation of the gifts in more objective terms – 'that they may be unto us the Body and Blood . . .' (as compared to the request in Prayer I that those who receive the gifts 'may be partakers of his most blessed

---

28 This prayer evolved from a draft by the Very Rev. Dr Robert H. Greenfield; the original 'Greenfield canon' had a slightly different epiclesis derived from the 1928 prayer. See Kennedy, *Eucharistic Sacramentality*, p. 174.

29 See Hatchett, *Commentary*, pp. 373–4 for an overview of other minor differences between Eucharistic Prayers I and II. Hatchett notes (on p. 374) that, 'Some of these changes were proposed as early as *Prayer Book Studies* (1953), and many were included in *The Liturgy of the Lord's Supper* (1967).' Eucharistic Prayer II also contains some additions relative to Eucharistic Prayer I. These often introduce theological enrichments which provide further context for the sacrament of the Eucharist, including a reference to Creation and the Incarnation in the post-Sanctus and mention of Christ's second coming in the anamnesis.

30 Hatchett, *Commentary*, pp. 373–4.

31 McKenna, 'Epiclesis Revisited', p. 170.

Body and Blood').[32] In this way, the prayer draws more attention to the gifts themselves.

While there is no epiclesis upon the people directly, the structure of this epiclesis does parallel the pattern of many ancient prayers insofar as there is a request for the Spirit's presence to bless the gifts and make them holy *so that* they might be Christ's body and blood for those who receive them in communion. 'One might simply note that had the term "word" been left as Cranmer intended it, as a reference to the institution narrative rather than the incarnate Word, we might have a compromise form which would draw us close to the early Christian emphases' of a eucharistic prayer that was consecratory only in its entirety.[33]

The epiclesis in itself does not mention eschatological benefits or any other fruits of communion flowing from the epiclesis. However, the intercessions which immediately follow implicitly mention some common fruits of the Spirit desired through this partaking in the eucharistic meal, including unity among members of the Church through indwelling in Christ's body through the Spirit (without, however, mentioning the Spirit directly in this context). Compared to Eucharistic Prayer I, this prayer's vision of the ecclesial body is also somewhat more expansive, insofar as the 'petition for unity now includes the whole church, not just those communicating on this occasion'.[34]

THE EPICLESES OF THE HOLY EUCHARIST: RITE TWO

The four prayers of Rite Two are cast in contemporary language and have considerable range in terms of both theology and literary style. Eucharistic Prayer A is printed in full at the appropriate juncture in Rite Two (pp. 361–3) and – perhaps for this reason – is the most frequently used of these new prayers.[35] Prayers B, C and D (designated 'Alternative Forms of the Great Thanksgiving') are located several pages later in the book (pp. 367–75). All but the last of these originated in prior books prepared for trial use.[36] The accompanying reflections in the *BCP*

---

32 Porter, 'Episcopal Anaphoral Prayers', p. 66.

33 McKenna, 'Epiclesis Revisited', p. 182; cf. John H. McKenna, *The Eucharistic Epiclesis: A Detailed History from the Patristic to the Modern Era* (Chicago: Hillenbrand 2009, 2nd edn), pp. 68–70.

34 Hatchett, *Commentary*, p. 374.

35 Porter, 'Episcopal Anaphoral Prayers', p. 67.

36 Eucharistic Prayers A and C first appeared as part of the Second Service in *Services for Trial Use* (1971) and were maintained in *Authorized Services* (1973). Prayer B is a conflation of prayers A and B from the Order for Celebrating the Holy Eucharist from the aforementioned books. Prayer D, an adaptation of the Egyptian Anaphora of Basil

offer no guidance as to which prayers might be particularly appropriate to certain feasts and seasons or for other events within the life of the church. Like Rite One, Rite Two also features proper prefaces (totalling 22) that are very similar to those in Rite One.[37]

The epicleses of the four prayers are given in Table 6.1.

Table 6.1: Epicleses of The Holy Eucharist: Rite Two (Episcopal Church in the USA)

Eucharistic Prayer A (p. 363)	*Eucharistic Prayer B (p. 369)*
Sanctify them [i.e. 'these gifts'] by your Holy Spirit to be for your people the Body and Blood of your Son, the holy food and drink of new and unending life in him. Sanctify us also that we may faithfully receive this holy Sacrament, and serve you in unity, constancy, and peace; and at the last day bring us with all your saints into the joy of your eternal kingdom.	We pray you, gracious God, to send your Holy Spirit upon these gifts that they may be the Sacrament of the Body of Christ and his Blood of the new Covenant. Unite us to your Son in his sacrifice, that we may be acceptable through him, being sanctified by the Holy Spirit.
Eucharistic Prayer C (p. 371)	*Eucharistic Prayer D (p. 375)*
And so, Father, we who have been redeemed by him, and made a new people by water and the Spirit, now bring before you these gifts. Sanctify them by your Holy Spirit to be the Body and Blood of Jesus Christ our Lord.	Lord, we pray that in your goodness and mercy your Holy Spirit may descend upon us, and upon these gifts, sanctifying them and showing them to be holy gifts for your holy people, the bread of life and the cup of salvation, the Body and Blood of your Son Jesus Christ. Grant that all who share this bread and cup may become one body and one spirit, a living sacrifice in Christ, to the praise of your name.

---

prepared by an ecumenical committee of Roman Catholic, Episcopal, Presbyterian, Lutheran, and Methodist scholars, is the newest of the four. It was approved for trial use by the Episcopal Church in 1975 and incorporated into the *Draft Proposed Book* in 1976. Charles P. Price for the Standing Liturgical Commission of the Episcopal Church, *Introducing the Proposed Book: A Study of the Significance of the Proposed* Book of Common Prayer *for the Doctrine, Discipline, and Worship of the Episcopal Church*, Prayer Book Studies 29 (New York: Church Hymnal Corporation 1976, revised edn), p. 83.

37 Porter, 'Episcopal Anaphoral Prayers', p. 67. (The prefaces can be found on pp. 377–82 of the *BCP*.)

The epiclesis of Prayer A follows the anamnesis and resembles the epiclesis of Eucharistic Prayer I (which is not surprising, given that both of these are dependent to a greater or lesser degree on the prayer from 1928).[38] The inclusion of the phrases 'the holy food and drink of new and unending life in him' and 'the joy of your eternal kingdom' in this epiclesis (along with some other features of Prayer A) contribute to a strong eschatological orientation flowing from eucharistic communion.[39] There is also a renewed emphasis in this epiclesis on the participation of the communicating assembly (as *eating* and *drinking* are implied) and the Spirit's sanctification of the worshippers as well as the gifts.[40]

Eucharistic Prayer B incorporates material from earlier draft prayers, particularly the brief Eucharistic Prayers A and B in the order for informal celebrations which first appeared in *Services for Trial Use* (1971).[41] Some phrases of the prayer are borrowed directly from *Apostolic Tradition* 4,[42] although the epiclesis does not reflect influence from this prayer. The epiclesis again follows the anamnesis. Despite the close association between the Incarnation (highlighted in this prayer's post-Sanctus section) and the Spirit, the epiclesis does not take advantage of the potential opportunity to highlight this connection. The epiclesis asks God to send the Spirit on the eucharistic gifts so that they 'may be the Sacrament of the Body of Christ and his Blood of the new Covenant'. Kennedy designates this reference to sacrament as 'a creative use of a term that is central to Anglican formularies'.[43] In contrast to the direct

---

38 According to the official commentary on Rite Two, 'The actual wording of this particular prayer derives in large measures from the Eucharistic Prayer of *The Liturgy of the Lord's Supper, 1967*, which was, in turn, a shorter version of the one in the 1928 edition of the American Book of Common Prayer.' See Episcopal Church, *Liturgy of the Lord's Supper*, pp. 13–16 and Porter and Associated Parishes, *Holy Eucharist*, p. 15.
39 Hatchett, *Commentary*, pp. 374–5.
40 Porter, 'Episcopal Anaphoral Prayers', p. 68.
41 Porter, 'An American Assembly', p. 188. While no specific guidelines are provided in the *BCP* regarding when this prayer might be particularly appropriate, the *Commentary* asserts that, 'The Incarnation of our Lord is here strongly emphasized, making this prayer particularly appropriate for the Christmas Season and other feasts of the Incarnation.' Porter and Associated Parishes, *Holy Eucharist*, p. 16. Hatchett concurs, observing that, 'Reference to the prophets, emphasis on the incarnation, and the eschatological references at the conclusion make this prayer particularly suitable for use during Advent, Christmas, Epiphany, and on saints' days.' Hatchett, *Commentary*, p. 375. Here Hatchett notes some influences on various parts of the prayer, but he does not mention anything specific about the origin of the epiclesis.
42 Porter, 'Episcopal Anaphoral Prayers', p. 68.
43 Kennedy, *Eucharistic Sacramentality*, p. 175.

epiclesis on the gifts, the epiclesis on the people is phrased in passive form ('Unite us to your Son ... being sanctified by the Holy Spirit') and subsumed into a petition whose primary focus is the unity of the communicants.[44] Consumption of the gifts is not discussed, and the strength of the epiclesis' eschatological orientation depends upon the dividing line between the epiclesis and intercessions.[45]

Prayer C originated as a trial prayer intended for less formal eucharistic celebrations and was initially published in 1970. The approach and structure of Prayer C distinguish it from the other prayers in the Episcopal repertoire.[46] It begins with the expected Sursum corda, but then, in lieu of a proper preface, the fixed 'preface' of this prayer continues the back-and-forth exchange between presider and congregation throughout the pre-Sanctus section. After the Sanctus comes a brief post-Sanctus section (which includes an epiclesis); this is followed in turn by the institution narrative, anamnesis and intercessions, and doxology. Although not as frequent after the Sanctus, congregational acclamations play a prominent role throughout the prayer.[47]

---

44 Hatchett, *Commentary*, p. 375.

45 McKenna (see McKenna, 'Epiclesis Revisited', p. 170), Porter (see Porter, 'Episcopal Anaphoral Prayers', p. 68) and Kennedy (see Kennedy, *Eucharistic Sacramentality*, p. 176) consider all three of the imperative phrases following the request for the sanctification of the gifts ('Unite us to your Son in his sacrifice ... put all things in subjection under your Christ, and bring us to that heavenly country where, with [_____and] all your saints, we may enter the everlasting heritage of your sons and daughters') as part of the epiclesis. However, Senn (Frank C. Senn, 'Intercessions and Commemorations in the Anaphora' in Frank C. Senn (ed.), *New Eucharistic Prayers: An Ecumenical Study of Their Development and Structure* (Mahwah, NJ: Paulist Press 1987), p. 203) groups only the first of these (i.e. the petition for unity which explicitly mentions the Spirit) with the epiclesis and considers the remaining as belonging to the intercessions. (For example, Senn notes that the epiclesis in and of itself does not have strong eschatological overtones – although the petition immediately following, 'In the fullness of time ... the everlasting heritage of your sons and daughters', carries this eschatological sense in a position after the epiclesis (p. 203).) I follow Senn's division here.

46 Initially published in 1970, this prayer originated as a trial prayer intended for less formal eucharistic celebrations. Its author was Captain Howard Galley. The favourable reaction towards this prayer contributed to its eventual incorporation into the collection of prayers which comprised Rite Two. Porter, 'Episcopal Anaphoral Prayers', pp. 68–9, and Porter and Associated Parishes, *Holy Eucharist*, p. 17.

47 Porter reflects on the 'remarkable dramatic movement' conveyed through its 'litany-like exchange between priest and congregation' as well as the appeal to contemporary scientific concerns and environmental stewardship. See Porter, 'Episcopal Anaphoral Prayers', p. 69. Hatchett comments on the Eastern affinities of this prayer (in terms of the congregational responses and fixed preface which rehearses salvation history). 'There is special emphasis on the creation, more than in any of the other prayers, and reference to the fall within a penitential petition. The prayer reminds us of the Old Testament drama

Unlike the other Episcopal prayers examined so far, the epiclesis of the prayer concludes the post-Sanctus section and thus precedes the institution narrative rather than following it. This arrangement necessitates slight modification of other sections of the prayer with possible theological implications. The elements are presented or 'brought before' God prior to the pre-institution invocation of the Spirit; in the anamnesis 'this sacrifice of thanksgiving' (instead of bread and wine) is offered to God.[48] As with the other prayers, there is a rubric directing the celebrant to hold or lay a hand upon the bread and cup accompanying the words over bread and wine in the institution narrative. Consequently, the presence of this gesture *immediately following* the pre-institution epiclesis in the case of this prayer may give the initial epiclesis of Prayer C an additional consecratory valence that it does *not* have in the other Episcopal eucharistic prayers, despite the official stance of the Episcopal Church that the *entire* prayer (rather than a particular section within it) sanctifies the gifts.

Compared to the first two prayers of Rite Two, the epiclesis of Prayer C is quite succinct and direct. The sole action requested from the Father through the Spirit is the sanctification of the eucharistic gifts 'to *be* the Body and Blood of Jesus Christ'. The soon-to-be communicants are not mentioned at all in the epiclesis, even in the more limited sense of sharing in gifts that have been sanctified so that they might be 'for *us*' or 'for *your people*' as in some of the other eucharistic prayers. No other benefits are in view as fruits of communion (if the phrase from the intercessions quoted above is not considered as pertaining to the narrowly epicletic section of the prayer),[49] and the prayer lacks the eschatological note sounded by some of the other Episcopal epicleses. What this epiclesis does do, however, is emphasize a strong connection between entrance into full participation of the life of the Christian community through

---

of God's continuing effort to draw His people back to Himself. The recital of salvation history reaches its climax in the proclamation of the incarnation and atonement. The people's variable responses are largely in words from the Scriptures.' Hatchett, *Commentary*, pp. 375–6. The prominence of penitential themes makes this prayer particularly appropriate for use during Lent. Porter and Associated Parishes, *Holy Eucharist*, pp. 16, 17.

48 Porter, 'Episcopal Anaphoral Prayers', p. 69.

49 The intercessions contain a phrase whose themes echo those of some other epicleses in the post-anamnesis location: 'Let the grace of this Holy Communion make us one body, one spirit in Christ, that we may worthily serve the world in his name' (p. 372); however, the Holy Spirit is not explicitly connected with this 'grace' of communion that unites the community and strengthens it for service.

baptism ('made a new people by water and the Spirit') and its culmination in the Eucharist.[50]

Eucharistic Prayer D is not only ecumenical in orientation, based as it is on the shorter Egyptian form of the Anaphora of St Basil, but is also ecumenical in its more immediate compositional history. It grew out of the joint efforts of liturgical scholars representing seven major churches with a presence in North America to develop and promote a eucharistic prayer which would be acceptable for at least occasional use in worship within all of these denominations (and have potential for use at ecumenical services as well). The results of this ecumenical endeavour were published in 1975 as 'A Common Eucharistic Prayer'. The bulk of the text simply represents a fresh translation of the Latin text of Roman Catholic Eucharistic Prayer IV, with some exceptions.[51]

Consistent with its ancient predecessor, Eucharistic Prayer D features a single fixed preface, with the preface, Sanctus and post-Sanctus providing a comprehensive overview of salvation history. In classic West Syrian form, the institution narrative then leads to the anamnesis, epiclesis, intercessions and final doxology, lending a decided Trinitarian framework to the prayer as a whole. In addition to the epiclesis itself, the Spirit is mentioned twice in the post-Sanctus review of salvation history, in connection with the Incarnation and Pentecost. Some leeway was left in the precise wording of various sections to make the prayers suitable for use in the diverse congregations which were intended to be able to pray it

---

50 Cf. McKenna, 'Epiclesis Revisited', p. 171 and Hatchett, *Commentary*, pp. 375–6.
51 'A Common Eucharistic Prayer', © 1975 by Marion J. Hatchett for The Committee for a Common Eucharistic Prayer. For more details on this prayer, see Porter, 'Episcopal Anaphoral Prayers', pp. 69–70; Leonel L. Mitchell, 'The Alexandrian Anaphora of St Basil of Caesarea: Ancient Source of "A Common Eucharistic Prayer"', *AThR* 58.2 (1976), pp. 194–206 and Hatchett, *Commentary*. A more extensive discussion of the influences on the various parts of the prayer can be found in Hatchett: 'The text of the prayer up to the institution narrative is a translation of the Latin original of the Roman sacramentary. The institution narrative is that of Prayers A and B. The anamnesis, oblation, and epiclesis are basically those of the earliest known manuscript of the prayer, with the addition of the phrase, "the bread of life and the cup of salvation, the Body and Blood of your Son Jesus Christ," from later manuscripts. The petition for the communicants is based on the Roman Sacramentary Latin version; the petition for the church is from the earliest manuscript, and the bracketed intercessions are based on those of the Roman sacramentary. The final petition, that we may find our inheritance with the saints, contains phrases from the early manuscripts and from the old Roman prayer. The concluding expression of praise and the doxology are from the Latin version of the Roman sacramentary.' Hatchett, *Commentary*, pp. 377–8. For the story of how 'A Common Eucharistic Prayer' became part of the 1979 *BCP*, see Price for the Standing Liturgical Commission, *Introducing the Proposed Book*, p. 83.

separately or together.[52] In this way, the prayer is especially appropriate for ecumenical gatherings, in line with its original intent.

The epiclesis requests the Spirit's descent on both people and gifts, in that order, 'sanctifying and showing them to be holy gifts for your holy people'.[53] Terminology of bread and cup (with the additional qualifying phrases 'of life' and 'of salvation' associated with the bread and cup, respectively) is used alongside the designation 'Body and Blood of your Son Jesus Christ' to denote the sort of 'change' or 'result' of the Spirit's showing and sanctification. Eucharistic Prayer D includes some typical epicletic elements not found in Eucharistic Prayer C insofar as D includes an explicit pneumatic epiclesis on the people as well as the gifts, envisions further benefits of communion through the community's sharing in the gifts, and features a possible eschatological allusion in the request that the communicants might become 'a living sacrifice in Christ'. The chief benefit requested on behalf of the communicants is unity with one another ('*one* body and *one* spirit') in and through Christ, in whom they are to become a living sacrifice of praise to glorify God's name.

Whereas the language of the epiclesis is quite similar to that of Eucharistic Prayer IV of the *Roman Missal* (see above), the fact that the consecratory and communion dimensions of the epiclesis are left intact as a single unit rather than split among separate sections of the prayer enables the unity of these two dimensions of the epiclesis to emerge more clearly.[54] Furthermore, while the epiclesis is clearly connected with consecration or the 'fulfillment of consecration', this arrangement of the prayer places less emphasis on the particular 'moment' by not specifying when this fulfilment is imagined to occur.[55] On the other hand, a theological reading which sees the epiclesis as connected with both the offering which precedes it and the intercessions which follow draws

52 For example, the wording of the institution narrative can be determined by the usage of the church praying the prayer. (Accordingly, the Episcopal adaptation uses the same form of the narrative as in Prayers A–C of Rite Two.) Some phrases of the intercessions are considered optional and are designated as such by the use of brackets, for example the reference to 'the blessed Virgin Mary, with patriarchs, prophets, apostles, and martyrs'. The Episcopal form of the prayer also provides for the optional insertion of a saint's name, making the prayer easily customizable for use on saints' days. Porter, 'Episcopal Anaphoral Prayers', p. 70.

53 Porter comments that, 'The patristic concept of "showing" is not familiar to most American Christians, although in our secular speech "to show" is sometimes used to mean to effect, achieve or bring about.' Porter, 'An American Assembly', p. 193.

54 McKenna, 'Epiclesis Revisited', p. 171.

55 Porter, 'An American Assembly', p. 193.

attention to the role of the people as participants in and beneficiaries of the eucharistic action. Leonel Mitchell remarks that, 'The *epiclesis* is the invocation which accompanies the offering: "We offer you this bread and cup. Send your Holy Spirit upon them and upon us who offer them."' This view of the epiclesis, highlighted in Eucharistic Prayer D, represents something of an innovation for a church of the Anglican tradition.[56]

THE EPICLESES OF EPISCOPAL EUCHARISTIC PRAYERS: ANALYSIS AND CRITIQUE

In terms of theology and language, the Episcopal eucharistic prayers consistently represent a blend of tradition and innovation bound together within the pages of a single liturgical book. Compared to the epicleses of the Roman Catholic tradition and of *Lutheran Book of Worship* (published in 1978), the Episcopal epicleses exhibit more variation in content and structure. Regarding content, with the exception of Rite One, Prayer I, all of the prayers envision some change in the bread and wine through the Spirit's intervention such that the people might receive them as Christ's body and blood. The language of this request, addressed to God the Father, differs from prayer to prayer, but some version of 'be' or 'be for' (us, your people, etc.) is common. The Spirit's engagement with the communicants receives no further attention in the prayers of Rite One but is a focus of attention in all but one of the prayers of Rite Two.[57] (The exception is Prayer C which, as noted above, contains a pre-institution epiclesis and then a subsequent intercession that the *grace* of Holy Communion might make those who partake of the gifts 'one body, one spirit in Christ'.) Clear eschatological references in connection with the epiclesis are not present in the prayers of Rite One but are contained in some (but not all) of the prayers of Rite Two. Direct references to the people's sharing in the eucharistic gifts are mentioned in the epicleses of some of the prayers across both Rites.

---

56 Leonel L. Mitchell, 'The Theology of Eucharist' in H. B. Evans (ed.), *Prayer Book Renewal* (New York: Seabury Press 1978), p. 49. Highlighting the connection between the epiclesis and intercessions, Mitchell continues, '[The epiclesis] expands the "us" into a prayer for the Church in which the names of specific people may be mentioned, upon whom we ask that the Spirit may descend.'

57 Some eucharistic prayers in the supplemental Episcopal resource, *Enriching Our Worship*, envision the Spirit's action invoked in the epiclesis extending even beyond the immediate eucharistic encounter to shape the communicants' interaction with the larger world. For example, 'By your Holy Spirit may [this bread and wine] be for us the Body and Blood of our Savior Jesus Christ. Grant that we who share these gifts may be filled with the Holy Spirit and live as Christ's body in the world.' See *Enriching Our Worship I* (New York: Church Publishing 1998), p. 59.

The variation in the location of the epiclesis within the prayer may be more significant as this represents a departure from the Roman Catholic and Lutheran rites which had previously appeared in North America; both of these traditions had adopted a similar placement for the epiclesis in all of their eucharistic prayers. Porter notes that the pre-institution epiclesis of Prayer C (and Form 1) provides a connection between the practice of the Episcopal Church, some Anglican rites then extant and the historic practice of the Roman Catholic Church (if the Roman Canon is viewed as having an epicletic component located before the institution narrative) as well as the arrangements of the 'new' prayers of the Roman rite. He also views the varying location of the epiclesis as a sign of the flexibility of the Episcopal tradition. 'It marks a willingness on the part of the Episcopal Church to recognize that its own historic Nonjuror type of prayer is not the only acceptable pattern.'[58]

While not due to the epiclesis of this prayer per se, the adoption of 'A Common Eucharistic Prayer' into the official collection of eucharistic prayers of the Episcopal Church further attests to the openness of this tradition to inspiration of prayer patterns developed by others, both ancient and modern. This prayer was based on the form of the Anaphora of Basil which had appeared a few years previously in the Roman sacramentary – but was rooted in much older prayer forms from the East. 'A Common Eucharistic Prayer' has had ecumenical impact, having been authorized for use by the Inter-Lutheran Commission on Worship and by the United Methodist Church's Committee on Word and Table; it was also recommended by the worship committee of the Consultation on Church Union (COCU).[59] It has subsequently been incorporated into the Presbyterian *Book of Common Worship* (1993) and enjoys unofficial use in a number of other churches.

UNITED METHODIST EPICLESES IN *THE UNITED METHODIST BOOK OF WORSHIP* (1992)

Around the time that the Second Vatican Council was concluding in Europe, the Methodist Church was introducing new liturgical resources of its own in the United States. In 1964, the General Conference approved a new *Book of Worship* (published in 1965) and *Hymnal* (which appeared in 1966). However, the timing of the revision and publication was rather unfortunate. As was typical of the worship books of the Methodist and other traditions at the time, the book included just one

58 Porter, 'Episcopal Anaphoral Prayers', p. 69.
59 Hatchett, *Commentary*, p. 377.

eucharistic prayer.[60] Furthermore, the 1968 merger of the Methodist Church with the Evangelical United Brethren Church to form the United Methodist Church created a new denomination in need of liturgical resources which drew upon both of these traditions but created something new as well. Finally, both United Methodist and ecumenical liturgical scholars were aware that the United Methodist Sunday Services of the late 1960s were neither strikingly contemporary nor traditional. They had drifted over time from the vision of John and Charles Wesley and did not reflect recent scholarship on the origins of Sunday worship and eucharistic praying.[61]

The project of crafting new resources for this new denomination was delegated to its Commission on Worship.[62] Over the next 20 years, the United Methodists went beyond the reforms undertaken in many other denominations both in sheer number of prayers and by the significance of the break between the prayers produced in the course of these reforms and Methodist prayers of the past.[63] Until the publication of the Presbyterian *Book of Common Worship* in 1993 (with 26 Great Thanksgivings), the United Methodist tradition had the largest number of authorized eucharistic prayers of any Western church with 23 in the *United Methodist Book of Worship* alone.

'The Sacrament of the Lord's Supper: An Alternate Text' (1972)[64] introduced the word-and-table framework of Sunday worship to modern Methodists and featured a eucharistic rite (with epiclesis) along the fourfold lines (with epiclesis) imagined by Gregory Dix. This rite was more consistent with ecumenical liturgical developments around the

---

60 As James F. White recalled, 'indeed the idea of multiple eucharistic prayers was scarcely considered in Western churches at the time'. James F. White, 'United Methodist Eucharistic Prayers: 1965–1985' in Senn (ed.), *New Eucharistic Prayers*, p. 81.
61 See Hoyt L. Hickman, 'Word and Table: The Process of Liturgical Revision in the United Methodist Church, 1964–1992' in Karen B. Westerfield Tucker (ed.), *The Sunday Service of the Methodists: Twentieth-Century Worship in Worldwide Methodism: Studies in Honor of James F. White* (Nashville: Kingswood 1996), pp. 120–1. In the category of compromised Wesleyan heritage, Hickman notes a eucharistic theology dampened by rationalism and the infrequent celebration of the Lord's Supper contrary to John Wesley's hope of 'constant communion'.
62 For more on the revision process, see White, 'United Methodist Eucharistic Prayers', pp. 80–95; Robert B. Peiffer, 'How Contemporary Liturgies Evolve: The Revision of United Methodist Liturgical Texts (1968–1988)', PhD dissertation, University of Notre Dame 1992; Hickman, 'Word and Table'; and Karen B. Westerfield Tucker, *American Methodist Worship* (Oxford and New York: Oxford University Press 2001).
63 White, 'United Methodist Eucharistic Prayers', p. 80.
64 Commission on Worship, United Methodist Church, *The Sacrament of the Lord's Supper: An Alternate Text, 1972* (Nashville: United Methodist Publishing House 1972).

world up until that time than the prior revision of 1965, and it proved incredibly popular. A revised version of the 1972 rite was published (alongside texts for baptism, marriage and funerals) in *We Gather Together* (Supplemental Worship Resources #10) and also independently as *The Sacrament of the Lord's Supper: Revised Edition 1981.*[65] The 1972 alternative text also served as the foundation piece for a series of 'Supplemental Worship Resources' (SWR) that would appear over the next several years. Among these resources were over 25 eucharistic prayers for various feasts and seasons of the liturgical year and important events in the lives of individual Christians and congregations. These prayers, including material written in different styles and inspired by the texts of several eras, were concentrated especially in the collections *At the Lord's Table* (1981) and *Holy Communion* (1987).[66] Thus one eucharistic prayer provided the basic pattern that has been tweaked and adapted in many United Methodist eucharistic prayers developed subsequently.[67]

THE EPICLESES OF UNITED METHODIST PRAYERS

Like the majority of Western churches, the Methodists opted for a West Syrian or Antiochene structure in their 'new' eucharistic prayers (i.e. the ones not based on older, traditional Methodist models). The epiclesis is in the Antiochene location after the anamnesis, and the epiclesis is followed by just a nod towards intercession, since the weight of the intercessions in this tradition are carried by the intercessory prayers near the conclusion of the Service of the Word. In contrast to other traditions, the United Methodists opted to incorporate variability into their eucharistic prayers not by the use of variable prefaces but by the use of full eucharistic prayers with variable elements (mainly in the preface, post-Sanctus and epiclesis) intended for use for important feasts and seasons of the church year and for various occasions (including weddings, funerals and baptismal renewals).[68]

---

65 Consultation on Church Union, Commission on Worship, United Methodist Church, *Sacrament of the Lord's Supper* (Nashville: United Methodist Publishing House 1982).
66 See United Methodist Church, *At the Lord's Table: A Communion Service Book for Use by the Minister* (Nashville: Abingdon Press 1981); Hoyt L. Hickman, *Holy Communion: A Service Book for Use by the Minister* (Nashville: Abingdon Press 1987).
67 White, 'United Methodist Eucharistic Prayers', p. 82.
68 In terms of feasts and seasons, *The United Methodist Book of Worship* includes Great Thanksgivings for Advent; for Christmas Eve, Day or Season; for New Year, Epiphany, Baptism of the Lord or Covenant Reaffirmation; for Early in Lent; for Later in Lent; for

Despite the large number of eucharistic prayers included in *The United Methodist Book of Worship*, the epicleses fall into just three basic types. The first accounts for the majority of the epicleses in the new book and comprises a base text with two substantive changes in structure and content. The first type features the epiclesis of the standard Great Thanksgiving patterned after the one revised in 1972 and further in 1984; this wording also serves as the model for the prayers for certain seasons and occasions. This version of the epiclesis is identical to the form adopted by the General Conference of the United Methodist Church in 1984.[69] This text, with its accompanying rubrics, is as follows:

The pastor may hold hands, palms down, over the bread and cup.
Pour out your Holy Spirit on us gathered here, and on these gifts of bread and wine. Make them be for us the body and blood of Christ, that we may be for the world the body of Christ, redeemed by his blood.
The pastor may raise hands.
By your Spirit make us one with Christ, one with each other, and one in ministry to all the world, until Christ comes in final victory and we feast at his heavenly banquet.[70]

Holy Thursday Evening; for Easter Day or Season; for the Day of Pentecost; for the Season after Pentecost; for World Communion Sunday; for All Saints and Memorial Occasions; and for Thanksgiving Day or for the Gift of Food. See United Methodist Church, *The United Methodist Book of Worship* (Nashville: United Methodist Publishing House 1992), pp. 54ff. As far as occasions are concerned, in addition to the prayer for Covenant Reaffirmation mentioned above which is also associated with Epiphany, the book includes Great Thanksgivings for use with the sick or homebound (= 'A Service of Word and Table V', pp. 52–3), for Christian marriage (pp. 124–6), for Christian burial (pp. 152–3), for healing services (pp. 618–19), for ordination (pp. 679–81) and for consecration of bishops (pp. 706–8).
69 See United Methodist Church, *The Book of Services: Containing the General Services of the Church Adopted by the 1984 General Conference* (Nashville: United Methodist Publishing House 1985), pp. 24–5.
70 *UMBW*, p. 38. This same epiclesis also appears in 'A Service of Word and Table II'. The text is almost identical in 'A Service of Word and Table V with Persons who are Sick or Homebound'; the only change is that 'Pour out your Holy Spirit on us gathered here' has been shortened to 'Pour out your Holy Spirit upon us', likely reflecting the lack of anything other than a token presence of the gathered congregation which is likely to be present in eucharistic celebrations under such circumstances. In the seasonal prayers, this type of epiclesis appears in the Great Thanksgivings for Advent (p. 55); for Christmas Eve, Day or Season (p. 57); for New Year, Epiphany, Baptism of the Lord or Covenant Reaffirmation (p. 59); for early in Lent (p. 61); for later in Lent (p. 63), for Holy Thursday Evening (p. 65); for Easter Day or Season (p. 67); for the Season after Pentecost (Ordinary Time, or Kingdomtide) (p. 71); and for Thanksgiving Day or for the Gift of Food (p. 77).

There are two types of variants on this pattern. The first of these, present in just one Great Thanksgiving, introduces an extra interpolation of sorts highlighting the work of the Spirit on occasions in which this might be especially appropriate – in this instance, on the pre-eminent feast of the Spirit, that of Pentecost. the epiclesis of the Great Thanksgiving for the Day of Pentecost contains two such additions (in bold type below):

> Pour out your Holy Spirit on us gathered here, and on these gifts of bread and wine. Make them be for us the body and blood of Christ, that we may be for the world the body of Christ, redeemed by his blood **and empowered by the gifts of the Spirit.**
> By your Spirit make us one with Christ, one with each other, and one in ministry to all the world, **showing forth the fruit of the Spirit** until Christ comes in final victory, and we feast at his heavenly banquet.[71]

These additions serve to highlight the Spirit's role in animating the body of Christ at work in the world and identify the manifestation of the Spirit's gifts as a desired fruit of communion.

A second type of variation on the predominant pattern features an intervening intercession and is found in four of the Great Thanksgivings. Three of these follow an identical pattern (see Table 6.2).

The epiclesis of the Great Thanksgiving for World Communion Sunday has an intercession directed towards the unity of the church between the first and second parts of the epiclesis. In light of this insertion, the following request for unity takes on the specific overtones of a plea for the unity of the whole Church and a desire for the fullness of communion which the scandal of the separation of the churches has compromised.

The epiclesis for the Great Thanksgiving for All Saints and Memorial Occasions features an intercession highlighting the connection between the assembled community gathered to celebrate the Eucharist and the communion of saints. The additions in this text highlight the extension of the 'communion' achieved through this particular occasion of the community's sharing in the Eucharist to all those who have gone before and now dwell in God's presence. The combination of this extra petition for communion with all the saints and the references to Christ's final victory and participation in the heavenly banquet found in most of the

---

71 *UMBW*, p. 69, emphasis added.

Table 6.2: Intervening intercession in three Methodist Great Thanksgiving Prayers

Base text	Intervening intercession
The pastor may hold hands, palms down, over the bread and cup. Pour out your Holy Spirit on us gathered here, and on these gifts of bread and wine. Make them be for us the body and blood of Christ, that we may be for the world the body of Christ, redeemed by his blood. *The pastor may raise hands.* {Intercession} By your Spirit make us one with Christ, one with each other, and one in ministry to all the world, until Christ comes in final victory and we feast at his heavenly banquet.	**Great Thanksgiving for World Communion Sunday (***UMBW***, p. 73)** Renew our communion with your Church throughout the world, and strengthen it in every nation and among every people to witness faithfully in your name. **Great Thanksgiving for All Saints and Memorial Occasions (***UMBW***, p. 75)** Renew our communion with all your saints, especially those whom we name before you – *Names(s)* – *(in our hearts)*. [*Rubric: Silence may be kept for the remembrance of names.*] Since we are surrounded by so great a cloud of witnesses, strengthen us to run with perseverance the race that is set before us, looking to Jesus, the Pioneer and Perfecter of our faith. **Great Thanksgiving for A Service of Christian Marriage (***UMBW***, pp. 125–6)** *The pastor may extend hands over the husband and wife.* By the same Spirit bless *Name* and *Name*, that their love for each other may reflect the love of Christ for us and grow from strength to strength as they faithfully serve you in the world. Defend them from every enemy. Lead them into all peace. Let their love for each other be a seal upon their hearts, a mantle about their shoulders, and a crown upon their heads. Bless them in their work and in their companionship; in their sleeping and in their waking; in their joys and in their sorrows; in their lives and in their deaths. Finally, by your grace, bring them and all of us to that table where your saints feast for ever in your heavenly home. *The pastor may raise hands.*

United Methodist eplicleses contributes to the especially strong eschatological thrust of this invocation of the Spirit's action in the eucharistic context.

The intervening prayer in the Great Thanksgiving for A Service of Christian Marriage takes the form of a blessing of the newly married couple. The rubrical option for the pastor to extend hands in blessing over the newly married couple resembles the optional gesture immediately preceding over the bread and cup. The themes of unity and service found in the primary form of the epiclesis are transferred here into an emphasis on the unity of the couple and their faithful service of God in the world. The concluding reference to heavenly life is modified slightly for this occasion, the reference to 'table' linking domestic, ecclesial and eschatological life.

The Great Thanksgiving found in A Service of Death and Resurrection incorporates an intercession for the deceased into the text of the epiclesis, modifying the concluding eschatological petition of the standard form of the epiclesis to reflect a sense of remembrance and hope appropriate to the context of a funeral:

> *The pastor may hold hands, palms down, over the bread and cup.*
> Pour out your Holy Spirit on us gathered here, and on these gifts of bread and wine. Make them be for us the body and blood of Christ, that we may be for the world the body of Christ, redeemed by his blood.
> *The pastor may raise hands.*
> By your Spirit, make us one with Christ, one with each other, **and one in communion with all your saints, especially** *Name* **and all those most dear to us, whom we now remember in the silence of our hearts.**
> ***A time of silence for remembrance.***
> **Finally, by your grace, bring them and all of us to that table where your saints feast for ever in your heavenly home.**[72]

A second form of epiclesis is found in the two Great Thanksgivings designated for 'General Use'. 'An Alternative Great Thanksgiving for General Use' contains several phrases reminiscent of earlier draft versions of the United Methodist epiclesis en route to the 1972 text:

---

72 *UMBW*, p. 153, emphasis added.

The pastor may hold hands, palms down, over the bread and cup.
Pour out your Holy Spirit on us gathered here, and on these gifts, that
in the breaking of this bread and the drinking of this wine we may
know the presence of the living Christ and be renewed as the body of
Christ for the world, redeemed by Christ's blood.
The pastor may raise hands.
As the grain and grapes, once dispersed in the fields,
are now united on this table in bread and wine,
so may we and all your people be gathered from every time and place
into the unity of your eternal household
and feast at your table for ever.[73]

The idea of sharing in the gifts is conveyed through the phrase 'in the
breaking of this bread and the drinking of this wine', thereby highlighting
a common aspect of the epiclesis not found in the standard form that
serves as a model for most of the United Methodist texts. The image of
unity employed here, that of scattered grain and grapes now united under
the forms of bread and wine, contains a clear allusion to chapter 9 of the
Didache. The unity now present around this table is to be a foretaste of
the unity of the eschatological banquet, to which all of God's people are
invited and in which the communicants hope to share some day.

'A Brief Great Thanksgiving for General Use' begins the same way but
contains a shorter eschatological petition that constitutes a slight
variation of that of the United Methodist epicleses discussed above:

Pour out your Holy Spirit on us gathered here, and on these gifts, that
in the breaking of this bread and the drinking of this wine we may
know the presence of the living Christ and be renewed as the body of
Christ for the world, redeemed by Christ's blood, until Christ comes
in final victory and we feast at your table for ever.[74]

'A Service of Word and Table IV' preserves a third type of epiclesis. This
final Methodist epicletic pattern was inherited from the Evangelical
United Brethren heritage preceding the 1968 union of this denomination with the Methodist Church to form the United Methodist
Church.[75] The epiclesis features traditional Cranmerian–Wesleyan

---

73 *UMBW*, p. 79.
74 *UMBW*, p. 80. This prayer does not contain any rubrics denoting optional gestures to
accompany the epiclesis.
75 Westerfield Tucker, *American Methodist Worship*, p. 142.

Prayer Book language and, in contrast to all the other contemporary Methodist prayers in *The United Methodist Book of Worship*, it occurs in a pre-institution location. The text reads:

> Hear us, O merciful Father, we most humbly beseech thee; and bless and sanctify with thy Word and Holy Spirit these thy gifts of bread and wine, that we, receiving them according to thy Son our Savior Jesus Christ's holy institution, in remembrance of his passion, death, and resurrection, may be partakers of the divine nature through him.[76]

The text resembles that of the epiclesis in Thomas Cranmer's 1549 Book of Common Prayer, which also served as the model for Eucharistic Prayer I of the Episcopal Church. The major differences between the Episcopal version of the prayer and its Methodist incarnation are that the latter version includes reference not only to Christ's Passion and death but also to his resurrection – but lacks references to sharing in Christ's body and blood (replaced by the request that the communicants might share in Christ's divine nature). The reference to the resurrection combined with the hope of partaking in the divine nature may effectively introduce at least an eschatological allusion to this prayer, even if the eschatological orientation is not as direct as in the more recent Methodist compositions.

THE EPICLESES OF METHODIST EUCHARISTIC PRAYERS: ANALYSIS AND CRITIQUE

John McKenna observes that the epiclesis of the Great Thanksgiving officially adopted by the United Methodist Church in 1984, which serves as the model for the majority of the 1992 prayers, 'has a strong eschatological emphasis and is probably the most complete resumé of elements traditionally associated with the epiclesis. It also forcefully underlines the transformation of the gifts as well as the assembly.'[77] To this end, it is not surprising that the Spirit's presence is consistently invoked not only on the gifts but on the assembly as well. The fact that the Spirit is invoked upon the people first and the gifts second makes it slightly less clear that it is, in this context at least, in and through their

---

76 *UMBW*, p. 48. A rubric at the beginning of this service notes its origins: 'It is a traditional text from the rituals of the former Methodist and former Evangelical United Brethren churches' (p. 41). This prayer is essentially that of the 1662 Book of Common Prayer, with a few adaptations made during the twentieth century.
77 McKenna, 'Epiclesis Revisited', pp. 182–3.

consumption of the pneumaticized gifts that this transformation is expected to occur – in other words, that the gifts are first transformed *so that* those who subsequently receive them might be transformed in turn.

Nonetheless, this transformation of the gifts is requested in bold terms[78] – 'Make [these gifts] *be for us* the body and blood of Christ'; however, this language is also worded cautiously enough that those who wish to interpret this 'being for us' as experienced spiritually in the act of reception rather than as a literal change in the gifts could interpret the underlying theology of the text in this manner. However, the question of whether the scope of the epiclesis entails consumption of the eucharistic gifts seems even less clear. Save for the possible allusion to eucharistic communion couched in the request that the Spirit make the gifts be 'for us' the body and blood of Christ, there is no overt mention of consuming the gifts in the majority of the Methodist epicleses (save for those of the second and third types discussed above). The 1972 pattern, with its references to breaking bread and drinking wine, brought out this aspect of the Eucharist more clearly. Even so, the epicleses of these Methodist prayers do convey a deep connection between the eucharistic body of Christ and the ecclesial body of Christ in terms of the connection between *being* the body of Christ in the eucharistic context and being of service to the wider world in consciousness of the community's call to mission. E. Byron Anderson identifies this dimension as one of the greatest strengths of the Methodist epicleses.

> Our eucharistic epiclesis remains incomplete without the request that we be transformed and empowered by the Spirit for ministry in the world. The benefits we receive as participants in and partakers of the bread and wine are benefits to be shared, benefits not for our sake but 'for the life of the world.'[79]

In contrast to some other epicleses, ancient and modern, the dominant verb is neither 'come' nor 'send' but 'pour out', which suggests a dynamic (and somewhat anthropomorphic image) with scriptural resonances (e.g. God's promise to pour out the Spirit on all flesh, cf. Joel 2.28 and Acts 2.17). This represents a change from the epicleses of the Great Thanksgivings in *At the Lord's Table* (1981), most of which asked God to 'send' the 'power' of the Holy Spirit on gifts and people in order

---

78 McKenna, 'Epiclesis Revisited', p. 175.
79 E. Byron Anderson, 'A Body in the Spirit for the World: Eucharist, Epiclesis, and Ethics', *Worship* 85.2 (2011), p. 106.

that the breaking of bread and drinking of wine might lead to the communicants knowing the presence of Christ, with the additional benefit of unity.[80] In terms of the fruits of communion, unity is a benefit consistently emphasized, as is the theme of the presence of Christ empowering the community for ministry and mission whose concern encompasses not only the bounds of the Methodist denomination or the Christian communion but the entire human family: 'one with Christ, one with each other, and one in ministry to all the world'. Eschatology is another theme which regularly recurs in most of these epicletic texts. While the expression varies slightly, it remains prominent in all the prayers which follow the first two epicletic patterns described above, and may be implied in the third.

Most of the prayers which fall into the first two categories above with regard to the epiclesis contain a proleptic 'remembrance' of Christ's return in glory. This reference to the parousia relocates a feature typically found in the anamnesis of eucharistic prayers to a position just afterwards.[81] Mention of Christ's second coming is therefore not a feature of the anamnesis of most Methodist prayers, save for 'A Common Eucharistic Prayer' which was composed by an ecumenical committee and enjoys unofficial status within the denomination.[82]

Geoffrey Wainwright has expressed hope that the recovery of the intrinsic connection between celebrations of Word and Eucharist will contribute to a deeper appreciation of eucharistic theology among Methodists including, presumably, its pneumatic dimensions. Perhaps subsequent reforms of the eucharistic prayer in this denomination might more fully incorporate elements from this tradition's Wesleyan roots, such as the *Hymns on the Lord's Supper*.[83]

---

80 For a brief analysis of the epicleses of the prayers in *At the Lord's Table*, see McKenna, 'Epiclesis Revisited', pp. 173–5.

81 David Noel Power, 'The Anamnesis: Remembering, We Offer' in Senn (ed.), *New Eucharistic Prayers*, p. 149.

82 The official prayers currently in use by the denomination are those which appear in *The United Methodist Hymnal* (1989) and *The United Methodist Book of Worship*, although other prayers, such as those from the supplemental liturgical resources *At the Lord's Table* (1981) and *Holy Communion* (1987) may be used. 'A Common Eucharistic Prayer' was Great Thanksgiving 6 in *At the Lord's Table*.

83 Geoffrey Wainwright, 'The Ecumenical Scope of Methodist Liturgical Revision', *Centro Pro Unione Bulletin* 62 (2002), p. 26. This essay is available online at <http://www.prounione.urbe.it/pdf/f_prounione_bulletin_n62_fall2002.pdf> and reprinted in James F. Puglisi (ed.), *Liturgical Renewal as a Way to Christian Unity* (Collegeville, MN: Liturgical Press 2005). Wainwright draws a parallel between the Wesleyan eucharistic hymns and the American Methodist prayers insofar as both connect 'the self-offering of

EPICLESES IN THE CHURCH OF ENGLAND'S *COMMON WORSHIP* (2000)[84]

The Church of England, too, followed the trend of incorporating invocations of the Spirit into its eucharistic prayers during the last third of the twentieth century. The first of these epicleses were incorporated into official texts intended for use in the Church of England beginning in 1973, drawing inspiration in part from the experiences surrounding the unsuccessful 1927–8 Prayer Book and reflection during the intervening period on the role of the Holy Spirit in the Eucharist. Several prayers presented in modern English included a split epiclesis of the sort which had been introduced by recent Roman Catholic revisions of eucharistic prayers.[85] The petition for consecration before the institution narrative was expanded with the phrase 'by the power of your Spirit', and a prayer for the Spirit's action upon the communicants was included after the anamnesis.[86] These prayers were authorized for trial use and later incorporated into the *Alternative Service Book* (*ASB*) (1980), eventually influencing the eucharistic prayers in the Church of England's latest series of worship resources, those of *Common Worship* (2000).

The way for liturgical textual revision in the Church of England was cleared in 1965 with the passage of The Prayer Book (Alternative and Other Services) Measure which re-envisioned the channels of authority

---

Christ and the self-oblation of the believers'; the latter represent an innovation insofar as 'they include among the fruits of communion an active participation in Christ's redemptive mission and ministry in the world' (p. 26).

84 For a visual overview of the many influences on the books in the *Common Worship* series, see the chart 'Tracing the Roots of Common Worship' in Group for Renewal of Worship, *Common Worship Today: An Illustrated Guide to Common Worship* (London: HarperCollins, 2001), p. 93. The process that culminated in *Common Worship* is discussed in more detail in Jeremy Fletcher, *Communion in Common Worship: The Shape of Orders One and Two* (Cambridge: Grove Books 2000).

85 Paul F. Bradshaw, 'The Rediscovery of the Holy Spirit in Modern Eucharistic Theology and Practice' in Teresa Berger and Bryan D. Spinks (eds), *The Spirit in Worship – Worship in the Spirit* (Collegeville, MN: Liturgical Press 2009), p. 89. The Anglican–Roman Catholic International Commission's 'Windsor Statement' on the Eucharist from 1971, which addresses the issue of the Spirit's part in the eucharistic celebration, may have also provided some additional impetus for this development at this time. Kennedy, *Eucharistic Sacramentality*, p. 147.

86 David Kennedy reviews several reasons why the introduction of an epiclesis along these lines (i.e. 'by the power of your Holy Spirit') into Series Three and ultimately into the *ASB* caused relatively little controversy, especially when compared to the strident resistance a potential epiclesis in Anglican rites faced in the 1920s. See Kennedy, *Eucharistic Sacramentality*, p. 153.

needed to amend extant services or establish new ones, with the hope that gradual exposure to and introduction of revised services might avert situations like Parliament's refusal to approve the proposed 1928 BCP. While the 1662 Book of Common Prayer retained a privileged status and could only be altered with Parliament's permission, the Alternative Services Measure of 1965 made a place for new categories of worship materials which could be developed and used alongside those of the BCP. Three series of *Alternative Services* were published between the mid-1960s and the early 1970s, with Series Three representing the most radical departure in language and form compared to previous revisions.

The Series 3 revisions included two distinct epicleses – one on the bread and wine preceding the institution narrative and another on communicants located after the anamnesis. The stance established by the 1971 Agreed Statement on Eucharistic Doctrine of the Anglican–Roman Catholic International Commission – i.e. that bread and wine become Christ's body and blood through the action of the Holy Spirit – made epicleses on gifts *and* people, ironically, somewhat more tenable than they might have been before.[87] The first component of this split epiclesis asked 'that by the power of your Holy Spirit these gifts of bread and wine may be to us his body and blood' and the second aspect requested that 'as we eat and drink these holy gifts in the presence of your divine majesty, renew us by your Spirit'.[88] Kennedy notes that this adaptation 'was cleverly conceived; it falls short of an unambiguous invocation on the elements alone: the work of the Spirit could as easily be interpreted as relating to the "may be to us" clause'.[89] In other words, this form of epiclesis need not necessarily be read as implying consecration of the gifts associated with the Spirit's action in the eucharistic context, and this ambiguity made the text palatable to individuals across a wider range of the theological spectrum.

Revised forms of eucharistic prayers from Series 1, 2 and 3, plus a new prayer based on *Apostolic Tradition* 4, were included in the *ASB*. Considering the neuralgic legacy between Eastern and Western churches concerning the 'moment' of consecration and summing up the emerging

---

87 Paul F. Bradshaw, Gordon Giles and Simon Kershaw, 'Holy Communion' in Paul F. Bradshaw (ed.), *A Companion to Common Worship*, vol. 1, ACC 78 (London: SPCK 2001), p. 127.

88 See *Alternative Services Series 3: An Order for Holy Communion* (London: Cambridge University Press 1973).

89 Kennedy, *Eucharistic Sacramentality*, p. 150.

ecumenical view on the matter, the *ASB* presumes the view that 'there is now no solemnly identified formula or "moment of consecration". Rather, the whole giving of thanks sets the theological context within which we can confidently assert that this is the communion of the body and blood of the Lord.'[90]

The desire to provide more options, address the needs of diverse congregations and revisit the issue of liturgical language soon prompted another round of revisions.[91] The successor to the *Alternative Service Book 1980*, *Common Worship* is not a single book but a collection of worship resources designed for flexibility and ease of use.[92] This leaves users of *Common Worship* free to mix and match to customize resources for use in their congregations with their own particular needs. Unlike the *ASB*, the material in *Common Worship* presents options in both traditional and current English, juxtaposes authorized and commended material, and has no official 'expiration date' for its authorization.[93]

The eucharistic orders of service are clearly derived from their predecessors, as shown in Table 6.3, with the fourth form of service (not found in the *ASB*) coming from the BCP.

As indicated in the chart, Order One in *Common Worship* is a revised version of Rites A and B from the *ASB*. Of the two orders, this is the one most frequently used, perhaps in part because it is the more flexible and is better endowed with supplementary resources which can be used in

---

90 *The Alternative Service Book, 1980: A Commentary by the Liturgical Commission* (London: CIO 1980). This same commentary (p. 83, n. 53) takes pains to show that the Spirit is not invoked on the elements exclusively or even necessarily directly. See Kennedy, *Eucharistic Sacramentality*, p. 159, nn. 59, 60.

91 The trajectory of further reforms is summarized in Michael Perham, 'Liturgical Revision 1981–2000' in Bradshaw (ed.), *A Companion to Common Worship*, p. 22.

92 *Common Worship – Services and Prayers for the Church of England* is the primary volume featuring resources for Sunday worship services. Unlike the bound worship books of most traditions, *Common Worship* is available in a wider array of formats: in full 'printed volumes, in separate booklets of varying sizes, on congregational cards, as computer disks (both text-only disks and as the Church's *Visual Liturgy* service-composing programme) and on the Internet'. Perham, 'Liturgical Revision', p. 114; cf. Fletcher, *Communion*, p. 21. The texts are available online through the Church of England's official site: <http://www.churchofengland.org/prayer-worship/worship/texts.aspx>. Texts from *Common Worship* may be reproduced freely for local, non-commercial use provided that the conditions in the Archbishops' Council's booklet, *A Brief Guide to Liturgical Copyright*, are met. (These conditions can be found at <www.cofe.anglican.org/commonworship>.)

93 *Common Worship Today*, p. 115.

Table 6.3: Eucharistic orders of service in *ASB* and *Common Worship*

Antecedent service	Common Worship*'s adaptation*[94]
ASB Rite A	Order One
ASB Rite B	Order One in Traditional Language
BCP Holy Communion	Order Two
ASB Rite A 'According to the Pattern of the *Book of Common Prayer*'	Order Two in Contemporary Language

conjunction with its basic texts.[95] Order One presents eight eucharistic prayers (A–H).[96] Order One in Traditional Language represents a revision of Rite B and includes two eucharistic prayers (A and C of *Common Worship*) that came from Rite B.[97] The eight eucharistic prayers of Order One are 'recognizably distinct from one another in their overall style, imagery, language, and length'.[98] The first three have their roots in prayers from the *ASB* Rite A and have been adapted for *Common Worship* although their connection to their parent prayers remains clear; part of their similarity can be traced to a common dependence on Cranmer and/ or *Apostolic Tradition* 4 at various stages of their compositional history.[99] All feature an epicletic petition for consecration before the institution narrative and a post-anamnesis section requesting the fruits of communion. This latter section sometimes mentions the Holy Spirit again (as in

---

94 Table 6.3 is adapted from Fletcher, *Communion*, p. 3.
95 Fletcher, *Communion*, p. 3.
96 The full text of the eucharistic prayers is printed only at the end of the service whereas the main text, designed for ease of congregational use, provides only the responses pertinent to the assembly.
97 Fletcher, *Communion*, p. 4. Fletcher adds in a footnote: 'in fact they are versions of Prayers A and C in Order One, but their Rite B roots are recognizable'. For a discussion on how the versions of prayers A and C in traditional language differ from Order One, see Bradshaw, Giles and Kershaw, 'Holy Communion', p. 145. One point which is potentially significant for the discussion of the epiclesis is that, 'Both these prayers omit the directions for the manual acts which were in the *ASB* Rite B' (p. 145).
98 Bradshaw, Giles and Kershaw, 'Holy Communion', p. 122.
99 For a chart showing connections among Eucharistic Prayers A, B and C of Order One of *Common Worship*, the preceding interim liturgical resources, and ultimately Cranmer's texts of 1549 and 1552 (which directly or indirectly influenced Prayers A and C) and *Apostolic Tradition* 4 (which affected Prayers A and B), see the chart in *Common Worship Today*, p. 166. Eucharistic Prayers A, B and C all present a broad view of salvation history from the world's beginning in Creation to its final eschatological end. However, there are slight though discernible colourations of emphasis distinguishing them. 'A has an extra touch of Easter triumph, B has a slightly greater emphasis on the incarnation, whilst C, with its roots in Cranmer's texts, has a strong affirmation of Christ's sacrifice on the cross.' Bradshaw, Giles and Kershaw, 'Holy Communion', p. 167.

Prayers A and B) but does not consistently do so (e.g. a further reference to the Holy Spirit, outside of the final doxology, is absent from Prayer C). Since one of the criticisms which surfaced about the *ASB* eucharistic prayers was that they were too similar, the addition of five other eucharistic prayers reflecting different styles (including different patterns of interaction between the presider and the congregation in some cases), lengths and content make this less of a concern with *Common Worship*.

Order Two likewise appears in two forms – one in traditional language and one in contemporary English. Both of these forms follow the outline of the Prayer Book communion service.[100] Order Two in Contemporary Language is modelled after the *ASB*'s version of the 1662 BCP prayer; the difference is that the service in its entirety (rather than just the portion following the exchange of peace in Rite A) is now aligned with the pattern of the BCP service. Its overall structure conforms closely to that of Order Two (with provision for a bit more flexibility),[101] and the language is a mix of traditional and contemporary.

The variety of treatments of the epiclesis in *Common Worship*, especially in Order One, may reflect a shift in Anglican circles to the idea that it is the *whole* eucharistic prayer that accomplishes the consecration rather than any particular part of it, and that the fundamental theological point is thanksgiving, not consecration as an end in itself.[102] In fact Order One does not use the designation 'Prayer of Consecration' – derived from the Prayer Book Tradition – in its rubrics at all, thereby distancing itself from the idea that consecration is achieved through a particular petition or formula.[103] In terms of the epiclesis Prayers A and B follow the split epiclesis approach of the *ASB*. Prayers C and E fit a single, pre-narrative pneumatic epiclesis into the general framework of the 1552/1662 Prayer Book pattern. On the other hand, Prayers D, F, G and H have a single epiclesis located *after* the institution narrative and anamnesis 'implying an Eastern rather than a Western view of

100 The 1662 BCP order, unadapted, is *not* included in *Common Worship* but nonetheless remains an official authorized form of worship in the Church of England; however, Order Two does denote additions to the 1662 text by placing them along the right margin. Bradshaw, Giles and Kershaw, 'Holy Communion', pp. 145–6. Order Two does contain rubrics for the manual acts in connection with the eucharistic prayer.

101 Some of this flexibility affects the shape of the eucharistic prayer, which may be 'modified so that it conforms to that of the Interim Rite' (i.e. the Prayer of Humble Access may be relocated before the Sursum corda (or Salutation, if used) such that the Sanctus may be followed immediately by the Prayer of Consecration, then the Prayer of Oblation and Lord's Prayer. Bradshaw, Giles and Kershaw, 'Holy Communion', p. 146.

102 See *Common Worship Today*, p. 157.

103 *Common Worship Today*, p. 166.

consecration'.[104] Whereas Episcopal churches in Scotland and the United States had adopted this pattern much earlier, the official inclusion of prayers of this type represents a new step for the Church of England.[105] Thus the Prayers of the Church of England, perhaps more than those of any other worship book considered here, may represent a diversity of views on the role of the epiclesis vis-à-vis eucharistic 'consecration'. Since the eight prayers of Order One are the most distinctive in comparison to the prayers that have been discussed previously, only the corresponding eight epicleses will be considered in detail below, divided according to their structure.

THE EPICLESES OF EUCHARISTIC PRAYERS A–H OF COMMON WORSHIP

Eucharistic Prayers A and B: a split epiclesis

The epicletic material of these prayers is given in Table 6.4.

Table 6.4: Epicletic material of *Common Worship* Eucharistic Prayers A and B

Eucharistic Prayer A	*Eucharistic Prayer B*
Accept our praises, heavenly Father, through your Son our Saviour Jesus Christ, and as we follow his example and obey his command, grant that by the power of your Holy Spirit these gifts of bread and wine may be to us his body and his blood …	Lord, you are holy indeed, the source of all holiness; grant that by the power of your Holy Spirit, and according to your holy will, these gifts of bread and wine may be to us the body and blood of our Lord Jesus Christ …
Accept through him, our great high priest, this our sacrifice of thanks and praise, and as we eat and drink these holy gifts in the presence of your divine majesty, renew us by your Spirit, inspire us with your love and unite us in the body of your Son, Jesus Christ our Lord. [*All* To you be glory and praise for ever.][106]	Send the Holy Spirit on your people and gather into one in your kingdom all who share this one bread and one cup, so that we, in the company of [N and] all the saints, may praise and glorify you for ever, through Jesus Christ our Lord …[107]

104 Bradshaw, Giles and Kershaw, 'Holy Communion', p. 127.
105 Bradshaw, 'Rediscovery', p. 89.
106 Text from <http://www.churchofengland.org/prayer-worship/worship/texts/principal-services-and-resources/holy-communion/epsforonefront/prayera.aspx>.
107 See <http://www.churchofengland.org/prayer-worship/worship/texts/principal-services-and-resources/holy-communion/epsforonefront/prayerb.aspx>.

In Prayer A, 'a conflation and mild revision of the first and second eucharistic prayers from the *ASB*',[108] the Spirit is invoked, in a general way, on the gifts in the first part of the epiclesis and on the people in the second; however, the language is vague enough that other interpretations are plausible. For example, the Spirit is not necessarily invoked upon the gifts alone in the first section; the power of the Holy Spirit at work could be imagined as operative in contributing to the possibility that the gifts 'may be to us' Christ's body and blood rather than acting directly on the eucharistic elements themselves to work some sort of change in them. However, the epiclesis seems to imagine some sort of consecration or 'change' in the gifts in the direction of Christ's body and blood at least insofar as the bread and wine could be perceived by faith as such at the moment of communion. In the second part of the epiclesis, the fruits of communion are to be realized through consuming the gifts (i.e. 'as we eat and drink . . .'). Furthermore, it is while 'in the presence of [God's] divine majesty' that this partaking occurs and the fruits of communion are requested. This seems to reflect a theological emphasis which Bryan Spinks describes as 'High Calvinism' – if heaven is regarded as the proper dwelling place of God's divine majesty, and, by extension, of the risen humanity of Christ whose body the communicants hope to become.[109] The fruits of communion include renewal through the Spirit and inspiration through God's love – as well as unity in the body of Christ. There is an implicit request for the Holy Spirit to come upon the communicants through their sharing in the eucharistic gifts but no explicit invocation of the Spirit upon the community as such. Clear eschatological references are not present in this prayer.

Prayer B is a slightly revised version of the third eucharistic prayer from the *ASB*. The text and imagery are ultimately dependent upon *Apostolic Tradition* 4, although the structure of the prayer most

---

108 Bradshaw, 'Rediscovery', p. 139.

109 Bryan D. Spinks, *News of Liturgy* 183 (March 1990), p. 6. Elsewhere, Spinks presents Calvin's understanding of the Spirit's presence and power in the Eucharist as follows: 'Communion in the Lord's Supper is also due to the Spirit; we are by the Holy Spirit made partakers of him, and the Spirit effects this since he is the virtue of the living God proceeding from the Father and the Son. Appealing to Cyril of Alexandria, Calvin insists that the faithful communicate in the flesh and blood of Christ and at the same time enjoy participation of life: this comes about by the Spirit which "truly unites things separated by space".' Bryan D. Spinks, 'The Ascension and the Vicarious Humanity of Christ: The Christology and Soteriology behind the Church of Scotland's Anamnesis and Epiklesis' in J. Neil Alexander (ed.), *Time and Community: In Honor of Thomas J. Talley* (Washington, DC: Pastoral Press 1990), pp. 196–7, as quoted in Kennedy, *Eucharistic Sacramentality*, pp. 157–8.

immediately resembles that of Roman Catholic Eucharistic Prayer II – a derivative of *Apostolic Tradition* which contains a split epiclesis.[110] Therefore, Eucharistic Prayer B expresses a traditional *Western* theology of eucharistic consecration. The prayer also includes the Sanctus (a feature not found in *Apostolic Tradition*). The first epicletic component occurs in the post-Sanctus section of the prayer which immediately precedes the institution narrative, and the second part of the epiclesis follows the institution narrative and anamnesis, and, as in *Apostolic Tradition*, leads into the prayer's concluding doxology. The pre-institution epiclesis more closely follows the text of the Roman Catholic adaptation of *Apostolic Tradition* as it cannot follow the ancient text at this point. Curiously, the corollary to the Holy Spirit in relation to the gifts being for the community Christ's body and blood is the 'holy will' – presumably of God the Father as the addressee of this prayer. This seems to connect to a phrase in the preface of Eucharistic Prayer B that is derived from *Apostolic Tradition*, denoting Christ as the one who 'fulfilled your will and won for you a holy people'.[111] As in Prayer A, the Spirit is not sent or otherwise invoked overtly on the gifts. Therefore, the result that the gifts of bread and wine 'be to us' Christ's body and blood *may* be read as implying consecration of the gifts; however, this is not the only possible theological conclusion. Once again, the community may encounter Christ's body and blood in the act of communion rather than in the transformation of the gifts.

Unlike Prayer A, however, Prayer B does contain a specific request for the Holy Spirit to come upon the people. The beginning of the request for God to 'send' the Spirit seems to follow the ancient text rather than the recent Roman Catholic prayer (which requests the community's unity through the Spirit at this point). However, whereas the breadth of the 'offering' upon which this Spirit is sent in *Apostolic Tradition* is rather ambiguous, the people are the clear object of the Spirit's sending in Eucharistic Prayer B. The following eschatological references are additions to the core of the ancient text. The unity which is requested as a fruit of communion is to be fully realized in God's kingdom, where the communicants hope to share for ever in the fullness of the

---

110 Bradshaw, Giles and Kershaw, 'Holy Communion', p. 140.

111 The 'savior and redeemer and angel of your will' mentioned in the preface of *Apostolic Tradition* is God's 'beloved child Jesus Christ' and 'inseparable Word'. If such allusions are intended in this case as well, the reference in the prayer from *Common Worship* seems to have shifted slightly. While the will in either case is, in the end, God's will, the immediate connection to Christ's saving action in the world is attenuated in the contemporary version for those who do not know the reference to the ancient text.

Table 6.5: The pre-narrative epiclesis in *Common Worship* Eucharistic Prayers C and E

Eucharistic Prayer C	Eucharistic Prayer E
Hear us, merciful Father, we humbly pray, and grant that, by the power of your Holy Spirit, we receiving these gifts of your creation, this bread and this wine, according to your Son our Saviour Jesus Christ's holy institution, in remembrance of his death and passion, may be partakers of his most blessed body and blood; who, in the same night that he was betrayed . . .[112]	We praise and bless you, loving Father, through Jesus Christ, our Lord; and as we obey his command, send your Holy Spirit, that broken bread and wine outpoured may be for us the body and blood of your dear Son. On the night before he died . . . [113]

communion of saints. Therefore, the phrase 'all who share in this one bread and one cup' could extend beyond the boundaries of the immediate congregation to include all who profess faith in Christ in all times and places.

Eucharistic Prayers C and E: a pre-narrative epiclesis

Eucharistic Prayer C (see Table 6.5) is a modified version of the fourth prayer from the *ASB*, whose remote origin is the prayer from the 1662 BCP. Like its model, this prayer shares a focus on salvation through Christ's sacrifice on the cross.[114] The pre-institution epiclesis emphasizes the fruits of communion – here presented as remembering Christ's Passion and sharing in Christ's body and blood in receiving the gifts. Although the bread and wine are the vehicle through which communion in Christ's body and blood occurs (which again, may or may not imply that the gifts themselves are transformed), the thrust of this epiclesis seems to fall squarely on the impact of the Eucharist upon the communicants. The immediate epicletic context does not specify any expected change in the communicants as a consequence of their sharing

---

112 <http://www.churchofengland.org/prayer-worship/worship/texts/principal-services-and-resources/holy-communion/epsforonefront/prayerc.aspx>.

113 <http://www.churchofengland.org/prayer-worship/worship/texts/principal-services-and-resources/holy-communion/epsforonefront/prayere.aspx>.

114 Commentators have noted that this theme 'is stressed even more in this revision, which reinstates some of the earlier wording, especially in the paragraph after the *Sanctus* and *Benedictus*, "who made there by his one oblation of himself once offered a full, perfect, and sufficient sacrifice, oblation and satisfaction for the sins of the whole world"'. Bradshaw, Giles and Kershaw, 'Holy Communion', p. 140.

in Christ's body and blood. However, a prayer after the institution narrative and anamnesis (and preceding the concluding doxology) requests that God might 'fill us all who share in this holy communion with your grace and heavenly blessing'.[115] What this might entail is not specified. While the orientation of this petition somewhat resembles an epiclesis in its content (and in its original inspiration as well), it does not mention the Holy Spirit.

Prayer E (see Table 6.5) is a new composition for *Common Worship* and casts the prayer in the form of a story featuring dramatic (albeit strongly scriptural) imagery. However, unlike some of the other new prayers, its overall shape or structure is quite similar to the prayers from the *ASB* (and thus also to Prayers A, B and C from *Common Worship*).[116] The prayer has a single epiclesis, located between an allusion to the warrant for the celebration and the institution narrative.

The current text contains no specificity concerning upon what or whom the Spirit is expected to be sent.[117] The purpose of the sending, however, is clearly stated, i.e. that bread and wine may be for the communicants the body of Christ, although transformation of the gifts is once again not indicated very strongly, if it is envisioned at all. On the one hand, mention of the Holy Spirit only after a reference to the preceding institution narrative ('as we obey his command') could be read as subordinating the role of the epiclesis to that of the narrative. On the other hand, the request for the Spirit to come *as* the community remembers Christ's saving action broadly understood could also be interpreted as an attempt to view the whole eucharistic action, rather than any one moment within it, as having a consecratory orientation towards the bread and wine and/or the worshipping community.

Eucharistic Prayer E contains a less direct reference to consuming the gifts than some of the Church of England's other prayers do. However, broken bread and outpoured wine are typically meant to be eaten and drunk, and 'be for us' could be read as belonging to the context of

---

115 This prayer is modelled after the prayer for fruitful reception of communion from the 1662 BCP and ultimately a reworking of the epiclesis from Cranmer's 1549 BCP text.
116 It may be especially appropriate in the following contexts: 'When children are present, as it is short and direct. At an evening or midweek Eucharist. As the "standard" Eucharistic prayer in a parish (with seasonal prefaces being used throughout the year to add variety).' Bradshaw, Giles and Kershaw, 'Holy Communion', p. 170.
117 In contrast, an earlier draft for trial use contained the phrase 'send your Holy Spirit on us and on these gifts', but ultimately such a request was deemed inconsistent with the Church of England's eucharistic theology. See Kennedy, *Eucharistic Sacramentality*, p. 160 and *Common Worship Today*, p. 170.

consumption as well. Beyond the gifts being 'for us' Christ's body and blood, no further fruits of communion are requested, and no eschatological references are found in this epiclesis.

Eucharistic Prayers D, F, G and H: a post-anamnesis epiclesis

Prayer D (see Table 6.6) is new to the Anglican repertoire of eucharistic prayers. It is deliberately constructed in a narrative style focused on the drama of salvation history culminating in Christ. There was a desire to

Table 6.6: The post-anamnesis epiclesis in *Common Worship* Eucharistic Prayers D, F, G and H

Eucharistic Prayer D	*Eucharistic Prayer F*	*Eucharistic Prayer G*	*Eucharistic Prayer H*
Send your Spirit on us now that by these gifts we may feed on Christ with opened eyes and hearts on fire. May we and all who share this food offer ourselves to live for you and be welcomed at your feast in heaven where all creation worships you, Father, Son and Holy Spirit . . .[118]	As we recall the one, perfect sacrifice of our redemption, Father, by your Holy Spirit let these gifts of your creation be to us the body and blood of our Lord Jesus Christ; form us into the likeness of Christ and make us a perfect offering in your sight. [All: Amen. Come, Holy Spirit.][119]	Pour out your Holy Spirit as we bring before you these gifts of your creation; may they be for us the body and blood of your dear Son. As we eat and drink these holy things in your presence, form us in the likeness of Christ, and build us into a living temple to your glory.[120]	. . . send your Holy Spirit that this bread and this wine may be to us the body and blood of your dear Son. All: As we eat and drink these holy gifts make us one in Christ, our risen Lord. With your whole Church throughout the world we offer you this sacrifice of praise and lift our voice to join the eternal song of heaven . . . [121]

118 <http://www.churchofengland.org/prayer-worship/worship/texts/principal-services-and-resources/holy-communion/epsforonefront/prayerd.aspx>.

119 <http://www.churchofengland.org/prayer-worship/worship/texts/principal-services-and-resources/holy-communion/epsforonefront/prayerf.aspx>.

120 <http://www.churchofengland.org/prayer-worship/worship/texts/principal-services-and-resources/holy-communion/epsforonefront/prayerg.aspx>.

121 <http://www.churchofengland.org/prayer-worship/worship/texts/principal-services-and-resources/holy-communion/epsforonefront/prayerh.aspx>.

include in *Common Worship* new eucharistic prayers that were 'short, responsive, suitable for both adults and children, and usable when both were together, [and] full of vivid, concrete images [many of them from Scripture] rather than abstract phrases'.[122] One of the more distinctive features of this prayer is its use of a set of responses with familiar cue texts, facilitating the participation of the congregation without excessive reliance on a printed text.[123]

The epiclesis is located near the end of the prayer, sandwiched between the anamnesis and doxology. The simple request, 'Send your Spirit on us now', is followed by a purpose clause that contains a clear allusion to the Emmaus account (Luke 24.30–32) when two disciples on the road to Emmaus recognized Christ in the breaking of the bread, realizing that their hearts had been burning within them as Christ spoke to them on the way about the Scriptures. The initial focus of the invocation is again on the community ('us') with no mention of a separate sending of the Spirit upon the gifts. The Spirit's sending on the gifts could be implied through the phrase that 'by these gifts' Christ may be recognized and consumed by the community – at least by those who might be theologically inclined to read the text in this way. If 'high Calvinism' was potentially implicit in Eucharistic Prayer A, it seems quite blatant in this prayer, with its reference to 'feeding' on Christ. Whether or not the bread and wine are transformed through this prayer, there is a definite hope that the congregation will make living for God its mission. Hope of sharing in the heavenly banquet introduces an eschatological note. Clear references to partaking of the gifts are laced throughout the prayer, building on the meal imagery of the Emmaus account. The phrase 'may we *and all who share* this food' hints at the desire for unity in the body of Christ, suggesting that this body may be larger than the collection of communicants immediately gathered around this particular table. There is also a sense of a common Christian mission flowing from communion.

---

122 *Common Worship Today*, p. 168. The need for such prayers was perceived as early as 1981 in the report *Children on the Way* (The National Society/Church House Publishing 1981) and in view of the fact that the Roman Catholic Church had developed eucharistic prayers intended for congregations consisting exclusively or primarily of children.

123 *Common Worship Today*, p. 168. For a discussion of the controversy over call and response during the prayer's development and trial use, see *Common Worship Today*, p. 169. The 'cue line' for the response starts out as 'This is his story' and then changes to 'This is *our* story' partway through, leading the congregation to respond, 'This is our song: Hosanna in the highest.'

Prayer F (see Table 6.6) is based upon the Egyptian anaphora of St Basil, although the English translation is not as literal as the adapted forms of Egyptian Basil which can now be found in the Roman rite (as Eucharistic Prayer IV), in the 1979 American *Book of Common Prayer* (as Eucharistic Prayer D), and in the Presbyterian *Book of Common Worship* (as Great Thanksgiving F).[124] However, the inherent Trinitarian structure of the prayer is maintained: thanksgiving to the Father for Creation, remembrance of the Son's work of redemption (including the institution of the Eucharist), and the invocation of the Spirit upon those gathered in light of the Spirit's continuing work in the world. It is fitting that the epiclesis appears in this third section of the prayer, after the anamnesis. Whereas the ancient text petitions the Father that the 'Holy Spirit may descend upon us and upon these gifts that have been set before you, and may sanctify them and make them holy of holies',[125] the Church of England's rendition of Basil is much more circumspect concerning how the Spirit is to be made manifest, the focus of the Spirit's activity and the Spirit's impact upon the gifts. The Spirit is not asked to 'descend' in order to sanctify the gifts, but rather the prayer expressed is that 'by your Spirit' the gifts may 'be' to the community Christ's body and blood (although the optional congregational acclamation does ask the Spirit to 'come'). This request that the gifts might 'be' Christ's body and blood could be interpreted in a narrow consecratory sense or as a broader understanding of spiritual communion at the moment of reception of the gifts. (The idea of reception is likewise implicit rather than explicit in the text of Eucharistic Prayer F – especially when compared to the Basilian text which implores God that the communicants might be found worthy to share in the 'holy things'.) The prayer does not direct the Spirit's action specifically towards either the eucharistic gifts or the assembly. The fruits of communion requested are not holiness of soul and body, unity as one body and one Spirit (in Christ) or a share in the inheritance of the saints (as in Egyptian Basil). The request that the community might be formed in the 'likeness of Christ' and thus be a perfect offering to God *may* hint at the dimension of unity, but the clear eschatological reference conveyed by the community's sharing in the communion of saints is absent from Eucharistic Prayer F.

---

124 Bradshaw, Giles and Kershaw, 'Holy Communion', p. 141.
125 ET of the Sahidic Coptic text from R. C. D. Jasper and G. J. Cuming (eds), *Prayers of the Eucharist: Early and Reformed* (Collegeville, MN: Liturgical Press 1990, 3rd edn, revised and enlarged), p. 71.

Eucharistic Prayer G (see Table 6.6) is a revised version of a prayer first published in 1984 by ICEL (the Roman Catholic Church's International Commission on English in the Liturgy) with the title 'Original Eucharistic Prayer, Text 1' but never authorized for use in that tradition.[126] Changes included minor tweaking of the language of the epiclesis and the inclusion of a prayer for fruitful reception derived from the *ASB*'s Prayer 2 ('build us into a living temple to your glory') that was not incorporated into Eucharistic Prayer A.[127] In this epiclesis, the Spirit seems to be called not upon gifts or people per se but rather on the eucharistic action in its entirety ('as we bring before you these gifts . . . may they be for us'). The prayer does contain references to the body and blood of Christ, although the Spirit is not explicitly connected to transforming the gifts of creation into Christ's body and blood. The phrase 'be for us' may hint at partaking of the gifts, but the petition for fruitful reception mentions eating and drinking directly.

The aspects associated with fruitful reception in this prayer (being formed into Christ's likeness and built into a living temple) have something in common with elements of traditional epicleses (e.g. unity and sanctification of the communicants). The prayer for fruitful reception in the BCP tradition originated through a modification of the epiclesis to make it more in line with the prevailing trends of Anglican theology at the time; the addition of this prayer from the *ASB* to the epiclesis of Prayer G thus represents a combination of a current ecumenical trend with a unique strand from the Anglican tradition. The 'living temple' which the communicants hope to become *may* be read in an eschatological sense, but the text itself does not demand this interpretation. Aside from this ambiguous possibility, there are no other eschatological references in the prayer.

Prayer H, the final eucharistic prayer in *Common Worship*'s collection (see Table 6.6), is innovative in terms of general structure for a modern eucharistic prayer and also especially in terms of the extensive use of congregational responsorial participation. 'It does not simply include

---

126 This text was taken up by the Church of England's Liturgical Commission and a modified version of it was included in *Patterns for Worship* (1989). It was among the six prayers which failed to win final approval in the Synod in 1996. A portion of the prayer was then considered as a preface for Eucharistic Prayer F, but a revised version of the entire prayer was eventually brought before the Synod for approval. See *Common Worship Today*, pp. 173–4.

127 Bradshaw, Giles and Kershaw, 'Holy Communion', p. 142. See the same article, pp. 142–3, for an overview of other noteworthy features of this prayer that do not pertain to the epiclesis.

dialogue between president and people, it *is* dialogue from beginning to end.'[128] It emerged fairly late in the revision process to meet the demand for an 'interactive' text.[129] The prayer contains all the components of a typical eucharistic prayer, but many of them appear in an extremely truncated form. While satisfactory as one option for the eucharistic prayer among many, it was not imagined that this would become any community's primary eucharistic prayer text.[130] Prayer H employs a single epiclesis separated from the institution narrative by a concise anamnesis[131] – 'As we proclaim his death and celebrate his rising in glory . . .'

The language of the epiclesis is similar to that found in the other epicleses of *Common Worship*. The prayer asks God to send the Spirit, but further specificity concerning upon whom or what the Spirit is to be sent is absent. The purpose of the sending is that the bread and wine might 'be' for the community the body and blood of Christ – a phrase which is yet again capable of being read in either a realistic, consecratory sense or in the spiritual sense of communing with Christ in a more abstract way through reception of the elements. The congregational acclamation which follows the presider's prayer resembles especially the second part of the split epiclesis of Eucharistic Prayer A. Although the epiclesis is very brief, the congregational response brings in themes common to many epicleses – i.e. partaking in the gifts through eating and drinking and unity in Christ – that are not present in the presider's part. There are no eschatological references in the epiclesis proper, but the transition to the Sanctus (which concludes this eucharistic prayer) that immediately follows the epiclesis does contribute an eschatological

---

128 *Common Worship Today*, p. 176, emphasis added.
129 'Thus, the congregational texts are not solely acclamation or refrain but integral to the "forward movement" of the prayer.' Bradshaw, Giles and Kershaw, 'Holy Communion', p. 143. 'However, the role of the president as the focus of the unity of the congregation is maintained: in each section of the prayer, the first part is spoken by the president, and the second by the congregation, so that the president initiates the dialogue.' 'Holy Communion', p. 143.
130 Bradshaw, Giles and Kershaw, 'Holy Communion', p. 143. For other unique features of this prayer, see the same article. *Common Worship Today* notes that this prayer was 'deliberately drafted for informal and intimate occasions . . . That does not mean it cannot be or should not be used on more formal occasions, it merely means that its central or mainstream use is in less formal contexts.' *Common Worship Today*, pp. 176–7.
131 Prayers F and H in particular have a very brief anamnesis section, with a hint of remembrance forming a link between the anamnesis and epiclesis. The anamnesis of Prayer H is the shortest of all. Bradshaw, Giles and Kershaw, 'Holy Communion', p. 125.

theme to the end of the prayer as a whole: '. . . we offer you this sacrifice of praise and lift our voice to join the eternal song of heaven . . .'.

THE EPICLESES OF THE CHURCH OF ENGLAND'S EUCHARISTIC PRAYERS: ANALYSIS AND CRITIQUE

As an explicit pneumatic eucharistic epiclesis has become a regular component of most modern eucharistic prayers, so too such epicleses have made their way into modern Anglican eucharistic prayers reflected by the texts of the Church of England. However, while the fact of an epiclesis is no longer a point of contention as it was in the early twentieth century, some of the minor details have continued to be controversial. For example, should the Spirit's activity be invoked upon bread and wine, on the members of the gathered assembly, or should the object(s) of pneumatic engagement be left unspecified? This quandary ties into the broader question of how best to articulate the anticipated presence and power of the Holy Spirit on the eucharistic action in a eucharistic prayer.[132]

The epicleses of Order One of *Common Worship* have dealt with this question by providing some variety concerning the object of invocation, but also by being vague enough in many instances that the epicleses could be open to a variety of possible interpretations. Those who envision something like a transformation of bread and wine could read that into many of the epicleses with only a minimal stretch of the imagination; likewise, those who view communion as a more spiritual presence of the body and blood of Christ could find something amenable to that reading in the Anglican epicleses as well. To a certain degree, such a stance reflects humility in the face of the eucharistic mystery – humility towards human incapacity to know the details about what transpires in bread and wine and people during the eucharistic action from the preparation of the table through the moment of communion and beyond. However, at least some of the ambiguity seems to be a deliberate choice, perceived as theologically advantageous in the current climate. Vague epicleses can be interpreted in a variety of ways such that people with a broader range of theological opinions about the Eucharist might be more likely to celebrate together without doctrinal unease becoming an issue. In this way the current language of the Church of England's epicleses may facilitate, for the moment at least, the sort of unity in the body of Christ for which many epicleses ask God.

---

132 *Common Worship Today*, p. 173.

The importance of sharing in the blessed bread and wine is a consistent concern of many of the epicleses considered above, and this may partially explain the lack of emphasis on the object of the Spirit's invocation prior to this climactic act of communion. As one commentary introducing *Common Worship* explains:

> Anglican epicleses have stressed the importance of the reception of the elements. Thus epicleses are not written in an absolute form, looking only to the consecration of the elements, but also connect the Eucharistic action to the reception of the bread and wine. In the *Common Worship* Eucharistic prayers these questions are addressed in different ways, using a number of slightly different expressions. Proposals to invoke the Spirit directly on the bread and wine have been resisted by General Synod. Some prayers invoke the Spirit on us, and all pray that by the Spirit the bread and wine may be to us Christ's body and blood.[133]

Some of the new prayers (particularly Prayers A and B, and to a lesser extent C with its single post-Sanctus epiclesis) perpetuate the issue of the 'double' or 'split' epiclesis in Western churches, with a consecratory petition located before the institution narrative and a 'communion' petition after the institution narrative and anamnesis. As has been mentioned before, the root of this issue can be traced to the Western insistence since the time of Ambrose and Augustine on 'the power of the word to bear Christ's presence'.[134] On a related issue, the Lutheran scholar Frank Senn has critiqued the 'ecumenically beloved consortium of "Word and Holy Spirit," first proposed by Thomas Cranmer in the 1549 Prayer Book of King Edward VI' as a form of compromise on this point that is 'ontologically confusing, if not implausible'.[135] As contemporary theologians continue to ponder the essential roles of the incarnate Word and the life-giving Spirit in the eucharistic mystery, the eucharistic prayers of *Common Worship*'s Order Two (and, to a lesser extent, Eucharistic Prayers A, C and E of Order One) at the very least perpetuate a long-standing tension in the Western tradition by placing the epiclesis (or part of it) in very close temporal and textual conjunction with the words of the institution narrative. Since the underlying agenda of *Common Worship* is a

---

133 *Common Worship Today*, p. 173.
134 Frank C. Senn, 'Toward a Different Anaphoral Structure', *Worship* 58.4 (1984), p. 348.
135 Senn, 'Toward a Different Anaphoral Structure', p. 349.

bit more subtle than that of its predecessor, the *Alternative Service Book*, the theological and textual rationale may emerge more clearly as the book is used, raising points for praise and critique that can be taken into account in further liturgical revisions in the Church of England.[136]

The three Anglican traditions discussed in this chapter have done much in recent years to articulate a fuller understanding of the Spirit's role in the Eucharist through the inclusion of explicit pneumatic epicleses in their eucharistic prayers. Any critiques about the scope of the epicleses in these traditions, however, should be balanced by the comparatively extensive attention to the Spirit elsewhere in the eucharistic liturgy. As E. Byron Anderson points out for the United Methodist prayers, the eucharistic epiclesis is by no means the sole euchological attestation of the community's consciousness of its 'vocation' in the Spirit; 'rather this invocation of the Holy Spirit occurs in the context of a fuller celebration of the saving work of the Holy Trinity'.[137] In the United Methodist prayers, for example, the epiclesis extends references to the Spirit's role in salvation history raised in the anamnesis concerning Christ's anointing in the Spirit at his baptism for the sake of ministry.[138] In the Episcopal tradition, the third preface provided for use on Sundays after Epiphany and Pentecost emphasizes the role of the Holy Spirit in baptism, noting that it is God 'Who by water and the Holy Spirit hast made us a new people in Jesus Christ our Lord, to show forth thy glory in all the world'.[139]

Those praying the prayers of *Common Worship* likewise are reminded of the Spirit's role in salvation history more broadly, emphasized especially in the pre-Sanctus sections of Eucharistic Prayers A and B of Order One. Congregations using the second option for the preface dialogue proclaim at the outset of the prayer: 'The Lord is here. / His Spirit is with us.' 'Amen. Come, Holy Spirit' is an optional acclamation for use with Prayer F. The Prayer of Preparation at the beginning of the Order One service requests the Spirit's inspiration, and one option for the Prayer after Communion concludes with an epicletic petition: 'Send us out in the power of your Spirit to live and work to your praise and glory.'[140] Those who hear and pray these words regularly cannot help but be formed in their vocation to participate in the life of the Trinity, inspired by the Spirit.

136 Fletcher, *Communion*, p. 6.
137 Anderson, 'A Body in the Spirit', p. 107.
138 Anderson, 'A Body in the Spirit', p, 108.
139 Episcopal Church, *The Book of Common Prayer*, pp. 344–9.
140 See <http://www.churchofengland.org/prayer-worship/worship/texts/principal-services/holy-communion/orderone.aspx>.

Chapter 7

The epiclesis in contemporary Presbyterian and Lutheran eucharistic prayers

Both in terms of the superficial arrangement of components and the underlying theological structure, eucharistic services developed in recent decades are strikingly parallel to one another. Horace T. Allen Jr, the inaugural director of the Presbyterian Joint Office of Worship, has remarked, 'Were I to bind all those rites in brown paper and put them on a table, you would probably have some difficulty in sorting them out as to denominational origin. They are astonishingly similar in conception.'[1] The new books in these various traditions (and the eucharistic prayers and eucharistic epicleses they contain) reflect the ecumenical liturgical activity which has been a prominent feature of Roman Catholic, Anglican and Protestant traditions in the English-speaking world in the second half of the twentieth century. This chapter will continue the exploration begun in the previous two chapters by exploring a representative sample of eucharistic epicleses from two North American Protestant traditions.

EPICLESES IN THE PRESBYTERIAN CHURCH (USA)'S *BOOK OF COMMON WORSHIP* (1993)

Before devoting attention to the eucharistic prayer in general and the epiclesis in particular, the American Presbyterian tradition first had to grapple with the concept of a service book and the normativity of the Eucharist as an integral part of Sunday worship. The story outlined

---

1 Horace T. Allen Jr, 'The Ecumenical Context of the Proposed Book' in H. B. Evans (ed.), *Prayer Book Renewal: Worship and the New Book of Common Prayer* (New York: Seabury Press 1978), p. 101.

for other traditions applies broadly to the Presbyterians as well, that is to say, 'by virtue of the liturgical movement and influences from other churches, the eucharist of praise, with its classical elements of anamnesis and epiclesis, becomes generally accepted in the celebration of the Lord's Supper' in contemporary Reformed and Presbyterian churches.[2] Unlike some of the other traditions considered here, however, an official worship book (even granting that its use was by no means mandatory) was a relatively new development for American Presbyterians.[3] A new Directory for Worship was approved by the General Assembly in 1961 that advocated regular celebration of the Lord's Supper, 'as frequently as on each Lord's Day'.[4] During the remainder of that decade, a new kind of book was developed for the Presbyterian tradition: *The Worshipbook* (1970), that presented the Reformed word-and-table pattern as the paradigm for Sunday worship and contributed, directly and indirectly, to more frequent eucharistic celebrations among American Presbyterians.[5]

The Worshipbook was the first Protestant service book published in North America after Vatican II, and as such its strengths and limitations soon became apparent. While it contributed to ongoing liturgical reform, especially the recovery of the tradition of eucharistic praying in some Protestant denominations, it included only one eucharistic prayer and its 'modern' language quickly seemed dated as ecumenical work on common English liturgical texts progressed rapidly. Beginning in 1980, several Presbyterian groups collaborated on a series of Supplemental Liturgical Resources (SLR).[6] SLR 1, *The Service for the Lord's Day*

---

2 Bruno Bürki, 'The Celebration of the Eucharist in Common Order (1994) and in the Continental Reformed Liturgies' in Bryan D. Spinks and Iain R. Torrance (eds), *To Glorify God: Essays on Modern Reformed Liturgy* (Grand Rapids, MI: Eerdmans 1999), p. 228.

3 For a concise overview of worship in the Reformed tradition – with particular attention to its articulation in the American context to *c.*1970 – see Fred R. Anderson, '*Book of Common Worship* (1993): A Pastoral Overview', *PSB* 16.2 (1995), pp. 121–4.

4 'Directory for the Worship of God', *The Constitution of the United Presbyterian Church in the United States of America, Part II: The Book of Order* (New York: Office of the General Assembly of the United Presbyterian Church in the United States of America 1961), para. 21.01.

5 Joint Committee on Worship, *The Worshipbook* (Philadelphia: Westminster Press 1970). See also Harold M. Daniels, 'Weekly Eucharist among Presbyterians', *RefLitM* 19.1 (1985), p. 18.

6 For more background about the reform process culminating in the *Book of Common Worship* (1993), see Harold M. Daniels, 'The Story of the Process Leading to a New Service Book', *RefLitM* 26.3 (Summer 1992), pp. 146–52 and Arlo D. Duba,

(1984),[7] contained eight eucharistic prayers, but, with weekly eucharistic celebrations becoming more typical – at least in some congregations – than they had been circa 1980 when the reform process formally began, it was soon recognized that more variety and more options were desirable in the final form of the revised worship book.[8]

The *Book of Common Worship* (1993)[9] contains 24 full Great Thanksgivings plus two additional 'prayers' which consist of guidelines for developing or extemporizing a text, one with some sample texts included (= Prayer I) and another which amounts to a bare framework of components (= Prayer J). These Great Thanksgivings are not all located in the same place but rather are dispersed in three separate locations in *BCW*. Prayers A–J are situated within the 'Service for the Lord's Day' section (pp. 31–161, A within the full text version of the service and B to J together in a separate section of additional Great Thanksgivings), 14 prayers are located in the 'Resources for the Liturgical Year' (pp. 163–400) and the remaining two are placed in context within the marriage and funeral services, respectively. Many of these prayers (22 of 26) are revised versions of prayers that had appeared previously in various Supplemental Liturgical Resources – six from *Service for the Lord's Day* (SLR 1), one from *Christian Marriage: The Worship of God* (SLR 3), one from *The Funeral: A Service of Witness to the Resurrection* (SLR 4) and 14

'Presbyterian Eucharistic Prayers' in Frank C. Senn (ed.), *New Eucharistic Prayers: An Ecumenical Study of their Development and Structure* (Mahwah, NJ: Paulist Press 1987), pp. 98ff.

7 The Joint Office of Worship for the Presbyterian Church (USA) and the Cumberland Presbyterian Church, *The Service for the Lord's Day: The Worship of God* (Philadelphia: Westminster Press 1984). Related resources included an introductory essay, Harold M. Daniels, 'An Overview of a Major Liturgical Resource: The Service for the Lord's Day', *ReflLitM* 18.4 (1984), pp. 181–4 and a study guide, *Study Guide to the Service of the Lord's Day* (Louisville, KY: Office of Worship of the Presbyterian Church (USA) 1987).

8 For a discussion of the background and an assessment of the contents of the eucharistic prayers in *Service for the Lord's Day*, see Duba, 'Presbyterian Eucharistic Prayers'. For more on the reform of eucharistic prayers in the Presbyterian tradition, see Karen B. Westerfield Tucker, 'The Eucharist in the *Book of Common Worship (1993)*', *PSB* 16.2 (1995), (referenced above in n. 3), pp. 138–49; Anderson, '*Book of Common Worship* (1993): A Pastoral Overview', pp. 121–37; Horace T. Allen Jr, '*Book of Common Worship* (1993): The Presbyterian Church (USA), "Origins and Anticipations"' in Spinks and Torrance (eds), *To Glorify God*, pp. 13–29; and Harold M. Daniels, 'The Making of the *Book of Common Worship* (1993)' in Spinks and Torrance (eds), *To Glorify God*, pp. 31–53.

9 Presbyterian Church (USA) and Cumberland Presbyterian Church, *Book of Common Worship* (Louisville, KY: Westminster John Knox Press 1993). Further references to this worship book will be given in parentheses in the text above.

from *Liturgical Year* (SLR 7).[10] Two prayers (Great Thanksgivings A and E) and the two 'outline prayers' (I and J) are new to Presbyterian Books.[11]

Horace T. Allen speculates that the plethora of options in the Sunday service may compromise the extensive use of any but the most basic rites and that the provision of so many options may reflect some continued unease surrounding the use of fixed liturgical texts for the church's Sunday worship.[12] In addition to the texts provided, there are guidelines at a number of points 'as to how given services or portions thereof may be done in an entirely extemporaneous way', aiming towards the Presbyterian ideal of 'integrating form and freedom'.[13] Among these options is a skeletal form of the components which should be included in a eucharistic prayer (Great Thanksgiving J), including a rich range of possible references for the epiclesis as part of this prayer.

The eucharistic prayers in the *Book of Common Worship* consistently conform closely to the West Syrian or Antiochene shape.[14] Exceptions to this general rule can be found in Prayer G, which contains neither the Sanctus nor intercessions in imitation of *Apostolic Tradition* 4, the model text upon which it was based. In Prayer D, which is based on an older American Presbyterian prayer, the 'oblation' section follows the epiclesis instead of flowing from the anamnesis where it would normally be expected.[15] The intercessions are another traditional anaphoral component that may or may not be a part of all these Presbyterian prayers, representing another departure

---

10 See The Office of Worship for the Presbyterian Church (USA) and the Cumberland Presbyterian Church, *Christian Marriage: The Worship of God*, SLR 3 (Philadelphia: Westminster Press 1986); *The Funeral: A Service of Witness to the Resurrection*, SLR 4 (Philadelphia: Westminster Press 1986), and *Liturgical Year*, SLR 7 (Louisville, KY: Westminster John Knox Press 1992).

11 For an overview of the sources of the prayers, see Daniels, 'Making of the *Book of Common Worship*', p. 38 and Westerfield Tucker, 'Eucharist in the *Book of Common Worship*', pp. 141–2.

12 Allen, '*Book of Common Worship* ... "Origins and Anticipations"', pp. 25–6.

13 Allen, '*Book of Common Worship* ... "Origins and Anticipations"', p. 27.

14 The option for this West Syrian shape seems to have been cemented by the choices made in the previous resource, *Service for the Lord's Day*. See Duba, 'Presbyterian Eucharistic Prayers', p. 106.

15 Westerfield Tucker suspects that this pattern 'may reflect a Reformed stress on pneumatology and the necessary work of the Holy Spirit to produce a human offering'. Westerfield Tucker, 'Eucharist in the *Book of Common Worship*', p. 145.

from the traditional West Syrian pattern.[16] Some of the prayers have a fixed preface of their own, but 20 variable prefaces are presented as options for use with Prayers B and C. Prayer D presents seven short prefaces for major seasons and feasts as optional additions to the very brief initial pre-Sanctus thanksgiving section. Between them, these prefaces for various liturgical seasons and pastoral occasions (i.e. baptism, reaffirmation of the baptismal covenant, ordination and funeral/memorial services) allow the prayers which can accommodate variable prefaces to be adapted to diverse situations.[17]

Eighteen of the 26 Great Thanksgivings (among them Prayers A and B, all the seasonal prayers, and the eucharistic prayers for the celebration of marriages and funerals) share a common structure insofar as they consist of a blend of fixed and variable components. The outline form, Prayer I, also reflects this structure and, due to its brevity, makes it readily apparent (see Table 7.1).

In these prayers, the epiclesis is among the components which remain relatively fixed; the variation among the epiclesis of these prayers largely consists of alternation between two basic texts expressing similar themes.[18]

In contrast to the prayers of other traditions, the institution narrative does not have a consistent place in Presbyterian prayers. With the exception of Great Thanksgivings E, F and G (which include the narrative as an integral part of the prayer), the institution narrative is not (in the case of H) or need not (for the remaining prayers) be included as

---

16 The rubrics of Prayers A and B state that the intercessions included as part of these prayers *may* be prayed at this point (see pp. 72 and 129); alternatively, such intercessions may occur at a prior location in the Sunday service, preceding the Great Thanksgiving. Intercessions are included in Prayer F (which is based on the Egyptian form of the Anaphora of Basil and thus contained intercessions in the original) as a bracketed option that may be omitted if desired. The remaining prayers, in contrast to the classic Antiochene shape, contain no intercessions at all save for a concluding eschatological petition that serves as a transition to the final doxology.

17 Marney Ault Wasserman, 'The Shape of Eucharistic Thanksgiving', *RefLitM* 29.3 (1995), p. 143. The Spirit is mentioned in several of the proper prefaces for Great Thanksgivings B and C – i.e. those for the Baptism of the Lord, Pentecost, Trinity Sunday, Baptism, and Reaffirmation of the Baptismal Covenant (see *BCW*, pp. 135–7) as well as in the proper preface for the Day of Pentecost to accompany Great Thanksgiving D (*BCW*, p. 139).

18 Commenting on the interaction between fixed and variable components in these prayers, Marney Ault Wasserman notes that the epicletic invocation typically begins the same way and that the phrase, 'As this bread is Christ's body for us, send us out to be the body of Christ in the world', is present in nearly all of the prayers. See Wasserman, 'Shape of Eucharistic Thanksgiving', p. 143.

Table 7.1: Relation of *BCW* Great Thanksgiving I to traditional anaphoras

Description of prayer elements from BCW *Great Thanksgiving I*[19]	*Traditional anaphoral component (bracketed components are considered optional in at least some of the prayers)*
The prayer begins with thankful praise to God …	Preface
The 'Holy, Holy, Holy Lord' may be included.	Sanctus
The prayer continues with thankful recalling of the acts of salvation in Jesus Christ: redemption; Christ's birth, life, and ministry; Christ's death and resurrection; his present intercession for us and the promise of his coming again; the gift of the Sacrament [which may include the words of institution if not otherwise used]:	Post-Sanctus [Institution Narrative]
The thankful recalling of God's saving work in Christ concludes with these or similar words:	Anamnesis
The people may sing or say one of the following memorial acclamations:	
The Holy Spirit is called upon …	Epiclesis
Petitions are offered … [20]	[Intercessions]
The prayer concludes with doxological praise …	Doxology

19 See *BCW*, pp. 153–5. The *BCW* does not label these discursive descriptions in terms of categories representing traditional components of the anaphora.

20 The description of the Sunday service on pp. 42–3 does *not* mention intercessions, but rather moves directly from invocation of the Spirit to final praise of the triune God. Rubrics in many of the individual prayers, however, make it clear that intercessions *may* be prayed at this point – but are not mandatory.

part of the Great Thanksgiving at all, rendering the question of a pre- or post-institution narrative location for the epiclesis somewhat moot in this tradition.[21] Unless a particular prayer directs otherwise, the institution narrative may be included before the Great Thanksgiving as a warrant for the celebration, within the eucharistic prayer or at the fraction.[22]

In addition to the language used in the prayers, Daniels notes that the Reformed heritage of this worship book is also apparent insofar as it presents texts laced with scriptural language in a diverse collection of liturgical options which may be employed as is or taken as inspiration for more spontaneous forms of prayer. Evangelical components are also present in the book as well; among these elements, Daniels notes the guidelines for free prayer for the eucharistic prayer (see pp. 153–6, i.e. Great Thanksgivings I and J) and in other contexts throughout the book.[23] With this view of variety in mind, the epicleses of Great Thanksgivings A–J will now be examined in more detail.

THE EPICLESES OF GREAT THANKSGIVINGS A–J

Prayers A and B (see Table 7.2) represent the two basic variations on the epiclesis noted above.[24]

Both of these epicleses follow the institution narrative (if included in the prayer) and anamnesis. Prayer A is one of the two 'new' complete

---

21 John Calvin had used the words of institution as a separate 'proclamation and warrant for the sacrament'. J. Dudley Weaver Jr, *Presbyterian Worship: A Guide for Clergy* (Louisville, KY: Geneva Press 2002), p. 60. Harold Daniels explains that there was a difference of opinion among the members of the task force that prepared the eucharistic prayers in *Service for the Lord's Day* regarding whether provision should be made for the institution narrative as an optional component of the eucharistic prayer proper. Consequently both the test draft of *Service for the Lord's Day* and its final form presented the narrative in relation to the eucharistic prayer in various ways. See Daniels, 'Making of the *Book of Common Worship*', pp. 38–9.
22 *BCW*, p. 84. Donald Wilson Stake states that the third of these options, the recitation of the institution narrative accompanying the fraction, is the most common, and the inclusion of suggested alternative words to accompany the fraction rite if the words of institution have already been recited previously seems to bear this out (see *BCW*, p. 74) – whereas if the words of institution are not used in positions 1 and 2 they are simply omitted. See Donald Wilson Stake, 'Gestures, Postures, and Movements at the Eucharist', *RefLM* 29.3 (1995), pp. 161–2.
23 Daniels, 'Making of the *Book of Common Worship*', p. 40. Other contexts in which recommendations/guidelines for free prayer appear include the Prayers of the People (*BCW*, pp. 66, 99), the Prayer of Confession (*BCW*, p. 89) and the Prayer Over the Water in baptism (*BCW*, p. 412).
24 These two variations recur in the Great Thanksgivings for various feasts and seasons and for Christian marriage and funerals.

Table 7.2: Epicleses of *BCW* Great Thanksgiving Prayers A and B

Great Thanksgiving A (p. 72)	*Great Thanksgiving B (p. 129)*
Gracious God,	Gracious God,
pour out your Holy Spirit upon us	pour out your Holy Spirit upon us
and upon these your gifts of bread and wine,	and upon these your gifts of bread and wine,
that the bread we break	that the bread we break
and the cup we bless	and the cup we bless
may be the communion of the body and blood of Christ.	may be the communion of the body and blood of Christ.
By your Spirit make us one with Christ,	By your Spirit unite us with the living Christ
that we may be one with all who share this feast,	and with all who are baptized in his name,
united in ministry in every place.	that we may be one in ministry in every place.
As this bread is Christ's body for us,	As this bread is Christ's body for us,
send us out to be the body of Christ in the world.	send us out to be the body of Christ in the world.

prayers in the *Book of Common Worship* (1993); it is featured in the section entitled 'Service for the Lord's Day – Order with Text'.[25] Prayer B is a rather significant reworking of Prayer B from SLR 1.[26] As in all the prayers which follow, the epiclesis is addressed to God (the Father). These prayers feature an epiclesis upon both the people and the gifts; however, by inverting the traditional order of these two requests (i.e. first gifts, then people) the sense that it is most immediately through their consumption of the 'pneumaticized' gifts in the eucharistic context that

25 It originated not in *Service for the Lord's Day* (SLR 1, 1984) but rather in the resources designed for *The Liturgical Year* (SLR 7, 1992). Daniels indicates that it 'was prepared as a prototype of those [prayers] designated for seasons and festivals'. Daniels, 'Making of the *Book of Common Worship*', p. 38. The prominence of this prayer (printed as it is within the full text of the Sunday service) suggests that Prayer A is intended to have a 'normative' status among the eucharistic prayers of *BCW*; additional credence might be lent to this position by the fact that the two outline forms of the prayer (i.e. I and J) both conform closely to the structure of Prayer A. (In the case of Prayer I, which includes some text as well, the text which is chosen is from Prayer A with minor variations in the congregational responses.) Westerfield Tucker, 'Eucharist in the *Book of Common Worship*', p. 141.

26 Westerfield Tucker, 'Eucharist in the *Book of Common Worship*', p. 142. This prayer was written for that resource chiefly by the Rev. Dr Ross MacKenzie, with the goal that it would meet the prevailing standards for gender-inclusive language. Accordingly, the drafters prescinded from gendered language applied to either God or God's people and steered clear of the terminology of 'Father' and 'Son' – but did use some masculine pronouns where Christ was concerned. Duba, 'Presbyterian Eucharistic Prayers', p. 101.

the people's unity in the Spirit is strengthened is dampened somewhat. These aspects just mentioned *are* indeed present in the prayer (namely the request for the Spirit's coming on the gifts of bread and wine *that* the bread and cup 'may be the communion of the body and blood of Christ' and the sense of unity with Christ through the Spirit).

However, the preliminary request for the Spirit's sending on the people before mentioning the gifts, and the sentence break between the reference to sharing in the gifts and the community's union with Christ in the Spirit, set these phrases apart from those which do apply more specifically to the eucharistic celebration at hand. (For example, it might be equally appropriate in any other context of Christian prayer to ask God to 'pour out your Holy Spirit upon us . . . [and] by your Spirit make us one with Christ'.) Nonetheless, as a whole, this is clearly a eucharistic epiclesis, and the Spirit's sending on the gifts as well as the people and the extension of unity in the Spirit to 'all who share this feast' (Prayer A) make this fact readily apparent.

The request that the in-Spirited bread and cup 'may be the communion of the body and blood of Christ' leaves the question of the transformation of the gifts (i.e. *how* the elements are related, if at all, to communion in Christ's body and blood) open, and does not necessarily imply consecration of the gifts, through the Spirit's action or otherwise. It is possible that the language was left deliberately vague so as to be amenable to a variety of theological interpretations on this point. Unless unity 'with all who share this feast' extends to the eschatological banquet, there is not a strong eschatological orientation within the epiclesis itself, although some eschatological themes do arise in the optional intercessions which follow the epiclesis and in the concluding petition before the final doxology that God might act to fulfil God's purpose not only in the assembled congregation but in the whole world.[27]

The idea that the broken bread and blessed cup are to be a 'communion of the body and blood of Christ' alludes to 1 Corinthians 10.16–17 and points to the community's sharing in these holy gifts through eating and drinking. Unity is the sole fruit of communion mentioned in this epiclesis, but it is a unity very broadly conceived. The hope expressed is that this unity will extend beyond the immediate

---

27 In Prayer A, the text of this final petition, which follows the optional intercessions, reads: 'In union with your church in heaven and on earth, we pray, O God, that you will fulfill your eternal purpose in us and in all the world. Keep us faithful in your service until Christ comes in final victory, and we shall feast with all your saints in the joy of your eternal realm' (*BCW*, pp. 72–3).

assembly which is presently celebrating the Eucharist (i.e. 'us') but also to 'all who share this feast' (Prayer A). This certainly refers to members of other Presbyterian and Reformed congregations; however, given the ecumenical outlook of the *BCW* as a whole, a broader frame of reference is likely in view as well. This communion may extend not only to members of other churches but perhaps even to the communion of saints who have gone before. The desired unity articulated in Prayer B is even broader – unity with 'all who are baptized in his name'. This links the celebration of Eucharist to baptism and more clearly expresses the conviction that this unity and common mission extends across ecumenical boundaries. Furthermore, 'all who are baptized in [Christ's] name' must certainly include not only the living members of the Christian community gathered around this or any table to celebrate the Eucharist but also those who have gone before and since fallen asleep in Christ, making the implicit eschatological overtones of Prayer A more explicit.

There is also a missionary aspect to the unity envisioned through this epiclesis in the sense that this broad category of all those who are one in Christ may be 'united' (Prayer A) or 'one' (Prayer B) 'in ministry in every place'. The dimensions of this ministry are spelled out in the final sentence of the epiclesis. The community that is about to receive the body of Christ expresses its desire to '*be* the body of Christ in the world'.

The epiclesis of Great Thanksgiving C is quite similar to the two prayers discussed previously:

> Gracious God, pour out your Holy Spirit upon us
> and upon these your gifts of bread and wine.
> Make them be for us the body and blood of Christ
> that we may be for the world the body of Christ, redeemed by his
>   blood.
> Send us out in the power of the Spirit
> to live for others, as Christ lived for us,
> announcing his death for the sins for the world,
> and telling his resurrection to all people and nations.
> By your Spirit draw us together into one body
> and join us to Christ the Lord,
> that we may remain his glad and faithful people
> until we feast with him in glory.

Again, the request is for an outpouring of the Spirit upon people and gifts, in that order. The result of the Spirit's sending upon the gifts is expressed more forcefully than in Prayers A and B ('*Make* them be for us the body and blood of Christ' (as opposed to the passive 'may be the communion of the body and blood of Christ'). The expected fruits of communion manifest themselves in ministry and mission according to the pattern of the paschal mystery. The idea of unity and a sense of eschatological participation in the heavenly banquet are evident again, but the implications of unity for evangelism and mission in this world on the one hand and as anticipation of eternal union with Christ on the other are developed more extensively.

The epiclesis of Great Thanksgiving D is quite brief:

> Merciful God,
> by your Holy Spirit bless and make holy
> both us and these your gifts of bread and wine,
> that the bread we break may be a communion in the body of Christ,
> and the cup we bless may be a communion in the blood of Christ.[28]

Once again, the epiclesis in this prayer is addressed to God (the Father), and the Holy Spirit is invoked upon the people and the gifts (in that order) so that both might be blessed and made holy.[29] The epiclesis of this prayer leads into a statement of offering, which 'may reflect a Reformed stress on pneumatology and the necessary work of the Holy Spirit to produce a human offering'.[30] Perhaps at least partly for this reason, there is no mention of the fruits of sharing in communion in this prayer. The only change in the epiclesis of Great Thanksgiving D relative to its immediate predecessor, Prayer C in SLR 1, is that the earlier version read: '. . . that the bread we break may be *the* communion *of* the body of Christ, and the cup we bless may be *the* communion *of* the blood of Christ'.[31] The difference between 'the communion of' and 'a communion in' (as in

---

28 Like Great Thanksgiving C, this prayer too is an adaptation of an earlier American Presbyterian prayer, in this case that of the 1946 *Book of Common Worship*. Harold M. Daniels composed the first version of the revised prayer which – along with a few minor changes originating from field-testing feedback – was incorporated into SLR 1 as Prayer C. The language of the prayer was updated between the 1946 and 1984 texts (e.g. the verb 'sanctify' has been replaced with the more colloquial term 'make holy', 'Thy' has been rendered as 'your'); however, the overall content of the prayer has remained intact. See Westerfield Tucker, 'Eucharist in the *Book of Common Worship*', p. 142 and Duba, 'Presbyterian Eucharistic Prayers', p. 102.
29 Cf. John H. McKenna, 'The Epiclesis Revisited' in Frank C. Senn (ed.), *New Eucharistic Prayers: An Ecumenical Study of Their Development and Structure* Mahwah, NJ: Paulist Press 1987), p. 176.
30 Westerfield Tucker, 'Eucharist in the *Book of Common Worship*', p. 145.
31 SLR Great Prayer of Thanksgiving C (no. 185), p. 105; emphasis added.

the 1993 version) need not be that significant, but it may reflect a desire to emphasize that the Eucharist is one of many means of achieving communion with Christ rather than *the* exclusive way in a paramount sense.

Prayer E is the other 'new' prayer in *Book of Common Worship* (1993). The text is from an original prayer published by the International Commission on English in the Liturgy in 1986.[32] Karen B. Westerfield Tucker considers its inclusion a 'testimony to modern liturgical scholarship and continuing efforts toward Christian unity'.[33] Unlike most of the other Presbyterian prayers, the narrative is an important component of this prayer, as an accompanying rubric states: 'Since the words of institution are included in this prayer, they are not said in the invitation to the Lord's table, or in relation to the breaking of the bread.'[34]

The epiclesis follows the anamnesis in the version which appears in the *Book of Common Worship* (1993):

> Eternal God,
> let your Holy Spirit move in power over us
> and over these earthly gifts of bread and wine,
> that they may be the communion of the body and blood of Christ,
> and that we may become one in him.

Again addressed to God (the Father), the request for the Spirit to move 'in power' over the assembly and the 'earthly gifts of bread and wine' conveys a sense of the dynamism of the Spirit in the biblical record, from creation through Pentecost to the eschatological outpouring of the Spirit

---

32 *BCW* itself says: 'This great thanksgiving was prepared by the International Committee on English in the Liturgy' (p. 142). This prayer has been substituted for an ecumenical prayer text from *The Sacrament of the Lord's Supper: A New Text – 1984* prepared by the Commission on Worship of COCU which appeared in the previous Presbyterian resource as Prayer F of SLR 1.

33 Westerfield Tucker, 'Eucharist in the *Book of Common Worship*', p. 143. She regards the use of this prayer (along with prayers F and G which are derived from the common heritage of the ancient Christian tradition) as 'particularly appropriate on occasions for celebrating and praying for Christian unity', and, because of their ecumenical and catholic character, ideal candidates for communion services involving Christians from multiple denominations. Other overtly 'ecumenical' components of the Presbyterian Great Thanksgivings include the collection of four memorial acclamations included in prayers A, B, C, D, E and I. The first, second and fourth acclamations are derived from the Roman Sacramentary and the third from Eastern liturgical traditions (via the intermediary of the Episcopal *Book of Common Prayer*). See Westerfield Tucker, 'Eucharist in the *Book of Common Worship*', pp. 143–4.

34 *BCW*, p. 142.

on all people in the last days. Again, the invocation of the Spirit first on the people and then on the gifts makes it unclear what additional benefit to the people is expected from the Spirit's action in relation to the gifts – at least when this first request is considered in isolation. The concluding result clause details the purpose of this request – that the people may receive these gifts as 'the communion of' Christ's body and blood and that they all might be united in Christ. No further benefits associated with communion are mentioned besides unity, and this epiclesis need not be read as implying any change whatsoever in the gifts as a result of the Spirit's movement over them. There is no explicit eschatology in this epiclesis, although some of the eschatological connotations associated with the Spirit, as noted above, may be implied between the lines.

Great Thanksgiving F in the *Book of Common Worship* (1993) is 'A Common Eucharistic Prayer' published by the Consultation on Church Union, printed with the sorts of adaptations proposed by the prayer's framers which would make it suitable for use in a Presbyterian context. A rubric in the *BCW* notes the prayer's remoter origins and the implications of the prayer's structure for its use in Presbyterian worship: 'This eucharistic prayer is adapted from the Alexandrine Liturgy of St. Basil (fourth century). Since the words of institution are included in this prayer, they are not said in the invitation to the Lord's table, or in relation to the breaking of the bread.'[35] Except for the use of lowercase letters in reference to Christ's 'body' and 'blood' (as opposed to capital letters in the Episcopal version), the text of this epiclesis is otherwise identical to that of Eucharistic Prayer D in the Episcopal *Book of Common Prayer* (1979), which has been analysed already.[36]

Great Thanksgiving G is an adaptation and translation of the sample eucharistic prayer presented for the occasion of a bishop's ordination in *Apostolic Tradition* 4. The perception that it was the 'earliest known text of a eucharistic prayer', attributed to Hippolytus of Rome and dating to the early third century,[37] likely contributed to its inclusion in SLR 1 as Prayer D and its later incorporation into the 1993 *BCW* as a prayer which was, in various versions, enjoying wide ecumenical use.[38] The post-anamnesis epiclesis is:

---

35 *BCW*, p. 146.
36 See pp. 194–6.
37 *BCW*, p. 150.
38 The Rev. Dr Horace Allen did the first draft translation of the prayer from *Apostolic Tradition*, and then this translation was refined for use in SLR 1. Duba, 'Presbyterian Eucharistic Prayers', p. 102. Duba also notes here that, 'In addition to the work done on this prayer by Horace Allen and Harold Daniels of the task force, the significant work of

We ask you to send your Holy Spirit
upon the offering of the holy church.
Gather into one all who share these holy mysteries,
filling them with the Holy Spirit
and confirming their faith in the truth,
that together we may praise you and give you glory,
through your Servant, Jesus Christ.

Like the prayer as a whole, the epiclesis bears recognizable connections with its model text, *Apostolic Tradition.*[39] However, Great Thanksgiving G is unique among the English-language renditions of *Apostolic Tradition* considered in this study insofar as it is the only version to translate *oblationem* into English as 'offering'. The meaning of 'offering' in the ancient Latin text and in this prayer is ambiguous and open to a variety of interpretations. 'The offering of the holy church may be interpreted as the church itself in its sacrifice of praise and thanksgiving, but it may also be the offering of the bread and the wine.'[40] This prayer also adopts a literal translation of the designation of Christ as servant or child (Latin *puerum* or Greek *pais*) in the concluding statement of the epiclesis which sets up the final doxology. Otherwise the themes and content of this epiclesis are quite similar to those of Great Thanksgiving XI in *Evangelical Lutheran Worship*. No change in the 'offering' is requested as a result of the Spirit's sending. The desired benefits of communion (i.e. of sharing in the 'holy mysteries', which presumably includes the eucharistic bread and wine but may have a broader intent as well) are unity, an infusion of the Holy Spirit, and strengthening of faith in truth *so that* the community might praise and glorify God through Christ.[41] The alternation of first-person and third-person pronouns in Great Thanksgiving G makes it unclear whether by '*all* who share these holy mysteries' the reference is to all those present at that particular eucharistic celebration or to all who are sharing now and have shared in

---

Professor Gordon Lathrop should be mentioned as should Father Patrick Byrne and other members of the Eucharistic Prayer Group of the NAAL.' It received further minor modifications prior to its publication in the 1993 *BCW*.

39 Since the prayer's structure follows that of *Apostolic Tradition* 4 in including the institution narrative, this element is to occur within the prayer rather than at another location, as a rubric states: 'Since the words of institution are included in this prayer, they are not said in the invitation to the Lord's table, or in relation to the breaking of the bread.' *BCW*, p. 150.

40 Duba, 'Presbyterian Eucharistic Prayers', p. 115.

41 Cf. McKenna, 'Epiclesis Revisited', p. 176, commenting on Prayer D in SLR 1.

the past. The latter interpretation would insert a possible eschatological aspect not otherwise present in this epicletic text.

Great Thanksgiving H is the last of the 'letter-labelled' options in the *BCW* to present the full text of a eucharistic prayer.[42] Compared to those that have come before, this prayer is quite short and, although its use for the Sunday service is not expressly prohibited, an accompanying rubric states that it is intended for informal celebrations and for pastoral care of the sick.[43] This prayer does not include the Sanctus or the institution narrative; an opening dialogue 'may be added' to the prayer but is not printed in the book.[44] Following a very brief anamnesis section, the epiclesis reads:

> Pour out your Holy Spirit upon us
> that this meal may be
> a communion in the body and blood of our Lord.
> Make us one with Christ
> and with all who share this feast.
> Unite us in faith,
> encourage us with hope,
> inspire us to love,
> that we may serve as your faithful disciples
> until we feast at your table in glory.   (*BCW*, p. 152)

---

42 This prayer is a modified version of Prayer H from SLR 1. Westerfield Tucker, 'Eucharist in the *Book of Common Worship*', pp. 138–49. Concerning its origins and intent, Duba recalls that, 'This brief prayer for small, informal celebrations was drafted by Ross MacKenzie and revisions were made in consultation with Professor John Burkhart. In twenty-three brief lines this prayer seeks to cover what is necessary in eucharistic praying.' Duba, 'Presbyterian Eucharistic Prayers', p. 103.

43 This rubric states, 'This prayer may be used when serving Communion in the home or hospital, or in other informal celebrations.' *BCW*, p. 152. A slightly modified version of Prayer H, which includes optional opening dialogue and Sanctus (with a brief introduction), is located elsewhere in the book in the section 'Holy Communion with Those Unable to Attend Public Worship'; see *BCW*, pp. 998–1000. On this latter version, Anderson observes, 'The title itself gives witness to the sensitivity of the book and its understanding of how the sacrament's multivalent nature takes on a unique pastoral dimension as communion rather than as eucharist. Provision is made for participation by elders or deacons, as those who both read scripture and join in the laying on of hands. An abbreviated great thanksgiving is both eucharistic and proclamatory, providing for acclamations as people are able.' See Anderson, '*Book of Common Worship* (1993): A Pastoral Overview', p. 134.

44 Whereas the words of institution accompanied the fraction in the SLR 1 version, the rubric of *BCW* presents both locations outside the prayer as options: 'When this prayer is used, the words of institution are said in the invitation to the Lord's table, or in relation to the breaking of the bread.' *BCW*, p. 152.

Here God is asked to 'pour out' the Holy Spirit, replicating the verb used in Great Thanksgivings A, B and C. The Spirit's outpouring is expressly requested only in relation to the people, although the final result is that the meal may be a communion in Christ's body and blood. This prayer effectively inverts traditional epicletic language – i.e. language which asks God to send the Spirit on the *gifts* so that *people* might be transformed. Other benefits requested include unity (with Christ and with 'all who share this feast'), faith, hope and love – with a clear eschatological orientation. The parallel themes of service and eschatological hope may be especially appropriate for informal celebrations in the first instance and for those who are sick and suffering in the second instance.

Prayers I and J, as noted above, are not full texts of the eucharistic prayer but rather provide guidance for free prayer. None of the prayers in the *Book of Common Worship* need be prayed exactly as written by the one presiding at eucharistic worship; however, these two skeletal prayers provide a loose framework around which spontaneous prayer may be constructed. Prayer I supplies a 'form … for praying the great thanksgiving in a free and spontaneous style'[45] through sketching the general contours of a eucharistic prayer according to the West Syrian pattern. The suggested epiclesis of Prayer I, which is to follow the anamnesis (i.e. 'the thankful recalling of God's saving work in Christ'), is an abbreviated version of that of Great Thanksgiving A:

> Gracious God,
> pour out your Holy Spirit upon us
> and upon these your gifts of bread and wine,
> that the bread we break
> and the cup we bless
> may be the communion of the body and blood of Christ.[46]

This text has already been discussed above; the epiclesis text is identical except that the concluding request of Prayer A, highlighting unity and

---

45 *BCW*, p. 153. The prayer includes sample text for the opening dialogue, transition to the Sanctus, Sanctus, institution narrative, anamnesis, memorial acclamation, epiclesis and concluding doxology which may be prayed 'in these or similar words' – and, in the case of the opening dialogue, Sanctus, institution narrative and memorial acclamation, need not be included as part of the prayer at all.

46 *BCW*, p. 154.

service, and perhaps at least alluding to eschatology, has been omitted.[47] Therefore, as written, the epiclesis of Great Thanksgiving I simply requests the Spirit's outpouring on the people and the gifts with the more immediate act of communion as sharing in Christ's body and blood being the primary focus.

Unlike the previous prayer, Great Thanksgiving J consists entirely of a rubrical outline with no sample texts at all: 'The outline below is provided to guide those who desire to pray the great thanksgiving in a free style.'[48] The section on the epiclesis is the longest section of this outline prayer. The epiclesis follows thanksgiving to God for salvation in Christ (a section which might conceivably include the institution narrative, especially if thanksgiving for the Eucharist is involved). The 'prayer' suggests a number of elements which might be incorporated into the epiclesis:

The Holy Spirit is called upon

to lift all who share in the feast into Christ's presence;
to make the breaking of the bread and sharing of the cup a
    participation in the body and blood of Christ;
to make us one with the risen Christ and with all God's people;
to unite us in communion with all the faithful in heaven and on earth;
to nourish us with the body of Christ so that we may mature into the
    fullness of Christ;
to keep us faithful as Christ's body, representing Christ in ministry in
    the world,
in anticipation of the fulfillment of the kingdom Christ proclaimed.[49]

While it would not be expected that *all* of these ideas would be treated comprehensively in any one prayer, the broad scope of themes which *could* be treated in an epiclesis is impressive. The addressee of the prayer is not specified, nor is the intended object (thus bread and wine, people, both gifts and people, or no object specified would seem to be possibilities). The prayer focuses instead on a range of potential fruits of communion: (1) Christ's presence, (2) communion in Christ's body and

---

47 The epiclesis of Great Thanksgiving A concludes thus: 'By your Spirit make us one with Christ, that we may be one with all who share this feast, united in ministry in every place. As this bread is Christ's body for us, send us out to be the body of Christ in the world.' *BCW*, p. 72.
48 *BCW*, p. 156.
49 *BCW*, p. 156.

blood through the community's sharing of the eucharistic gifts, (3) unity with Christ and with one another that (4) extends to the communion of saints, (5) growth in maturity and faith in conformity to Christ (cf. Eph. 4.13), (6) faith that manifests itself in Christian service in the world, and, finally, (7) eschatological hope oriented towards sharing in the full realization of the kingdom of God. Therefore, the four aspects which John McKenna identified as typical of ancient versions of the fully fledged epiclesis (i.e. some notion of explicit or implicit change in the bread and wine so that the people may receive it as Christ's body and blood, partaking of the gifts, additional fruits of communion and eschatology) are at least potentially present in a prayer prepared according to the model provided by Great Thanksgiving J.[50]

THE EPICLESIS OF PRESBYTERIAN EUCHARISTIC PRAYERS: ANALYSIS AND CRITIQUE

As the previous discussion has amply demonstrated, the Spirit's activity in the eucharistic context is indeed stressed in the epicleses of current American Presbyterian prayers, as befits the descendants of this Scottish Reformed tradition. As Craig Douglas Erickson notes, 'The Reformed *epiclesis* is typically a dual one, in which the Holy Spirit is invoked upon both the eucharistic elements and the body of believers, or a communion *epiclesis*, in which the Holy Spirit is invoked upon the Church'[51] – and both of these alternatives are present in the *BCW*.

Nevertheless, the role of the Spirit is not articulated consistently and unequivocally in these texts. For example, while many of the prayers in *BCW* request that the Spirit be poured out on both people and gifts, in that order (e.g. Great Thanksgivings A–F),[52] Prayer H expressly requests the Spirit's outpouring on the people alone, and the object of the epiclesis in Prayer G depends on how 'the offering of the holy church' from *Apostolic Tradition* is to be interpreted.

---

50 John H. McKenna, 'Eucharistic Prayer: Epiclesis' in A. Heinz and H. Rennings (eds), *Gratias Agamus: Studien zum eucharistischen Hochgebet. Für Balthasar Fischer* (Freiburg: Herder 1992), p. 288.
51 Craig Douglas Erickson, 'Reformed Eucharistic Theology', *RefLitM* 29.4 (1995), p. 224.
52 Given this concern for the Spirit's action on the people, Westerfield Tucker remarks, 'Surprisingly, no specific anaphoras are provided using language and imagery for the circumstances of baptism (though the Baptism of the Lord text is suggested) or a congregational service of wholeness and healing (form H or a variation is recommended).' See Westerfield Tucker, 'Eucharist in the *Book of Common Worship*', p. 141.

Some of this ambiguity of address may be related to the status of the Spirit's activity vis-à-vis the relationship between Christ's presence in the Eucharist and the status of the eucharistic bread and wine – a relationship which is itself somewhat nebulous in the American Presbyterian tradition. The prayers of the *Book of Common Worship* (1993) continue the trajectory of their predecessor ritual book, *Service for the Lord's Day*, insofar as they

> avoid localizing the presence of Christ in the bread and the wine, but the bread and the wine are an indispensable accompaniment of the service in which the presence of Christ is experienced and received. The Constitution of the Presbyterian Church, in its 'Directory for the Service of God,' lists a number of components: 'the Words of Institution ... the prayer and the responses ... the invocation of the Holy Spirit ... the breaking of the bread and the pouring of the wine ... (and) the distribution and partaking of the elements show the reality of the believers' union with Christ by faith and their willingness that Christ's presence should abide in them.'[53]

The role of the Spirit in the church as a dynamic presence that imparts life and blessing is emphasized well in the epicleses of these Presbyterian prayers. Nearly all of the Presbyterian prayers enumerate several 'fruits' of communion flowing from the Spirit's action on the people and/or the eucharistic gifts. Most of the prayers include some reference to sharing in the gifts – frequently as 'the communion of' Christ's body and blood. While the prayers do not overtly associate any transformation in the gifts with the Spirit's outpouring upon them, there is nonetheless some connection made between the elements of bread and wine and feeding on Christ, even if the elements are an accompaniment rather than the direct vehicle of the community's 'consumption' of Christ so that they may be his body in and for the world. While the aspect of the community's service-oriented mission flowing from communion is mentioned in many of the Presbyterian epicleses, the eschatological orientation of the Eucharist is present only in some of the epicleses – and, in many cases, only if phrases such as 'all who are baptized in his name'

---

53 Duba, 'Presbyterian Eucharistic Prayers', p. 113. The list quoted above is from the Directory for the Service of God, 3.05, p. 176. The Directory similarly notes that Christ is present (3.01, p. 170) in the Eucharist without going far in the direction of specifying the mode of this presence.

and 'all who share this feast' are interpreted in the broadest possible sense.

McKenna notes that the option in many Presbyterian prayers to recite the institution narrative during the invitation to the Lord's Table or during the fraction represents 'a significant variation from the ancient pattern'.[54] Wasserman puts the relative status of the institution narrative and epiclesis in context in the Presbyterian tradition by emphasizing that eucharistic praying is ultimately about thanksgiving – *eucharist* – and not consecration.[55] Nonetheless, Westerfield Tucker points out that the many options for the placement of the institution narrative have theological implications for the status of the epiclesis in these prayers as well. Conceding that the entire Great Thanksgiving rather than any one component within it should properly be viewed as consecratory, despite the strong eucharistic pneumatology that has characterized the Reformed tradition, 'the epikleses in these prayers are not strong enough to carry the notion of "consecration" without the words of institution'.[56]

It would have been possible to make these prayers more characteristically Reformed had some options been exercised which were not. Westerfield Tucker laments this loss:

> Unfortunately, what was probably the most 'Reformed' of all the SLR I anaphoras did not survive the transition to the new publication: prayer G, which was Calvin's communion exhortation of 1542 reworked into the form of a short eucharistic prayer. Although this prayer may not have found widespread use, such vividly Calvinistic phrases as 'we remember how Jesus invites us to his table, imprinting on our hearts his sacrifice on the cross,' 'pour out your Holy Spirit

---

54 McKenna, 'Epiclesis Revisited', p. 183.

55 Consequently, the purpose of the Great Thanksgiving 'is not to make the feast holy (only God can do that), but to speak our thanks to God who has provided it . . . In the end, the gifts are consecrated, not with specific words of consecration, but by the God whom we thank for them and for the redemption to which they point.' Wasserman, 'Shape of Eucharistic Thanksgiving', p. 139.

56 Westerfield Tucker, 'Eucharist in the *Book of Common Worship*', p. 147. She goes on to question the omission of the words of institution from the eucharistic prayer proper on ecumenical grounds, given that the majority of ancient prayers (with the exception of Addai and Mari and possibly that described in the *Mystagogical Catecheses*) did contain the narrative and the general Protestant stress (outside the Reformed tradition) on the significance of the institution narrative as a component of a eucharistic prayer. 'A solution may be eventually to place the words of institution invariably in the anaphora, but many congregations and pastors may not be ready for such an absolutist decision and the loss of what has been a distinctive emphasis in the Reformed tradition' (p. 147).

upon us that as we receive bread and wine we may be assured that Christ's promise in these signs will be fulfilled,' and 'lift our hearts and minds on high where, with Christ your only Son, and with the Holy Spirit, all glory is yours' could have been incorporated into some of the other prayers.[57]

Erickson identifies the tension inherent in the Reformed position on the epiclesis as due to the conviction that the Eucharist is God's free gift but also the congregation's expectation of the Spirit's blessing on the church's meal, concluding that:

> Reformed eucharistic theology could profitably reflect more deeply upon the contemporary understanding of the sacrament as an act of prayer empowered by the Holy Spirit praying through the gathered community, 'a sacrifice of praise and thanksgiving, which we offer in union with Christ's sacrifice for us as a living and holy surrender of ourselves.' The understanding of Christ praying through the church in the Eucharist by the power of the Holy Spirit challenges the legitimacy of the altar/table, meal/sacrifice dichotomies and the polemics upon which they are based.[58]

The expectation of the Spirit's blessing on the meal comes out in the frequent request in these epicleses that sharing in the gifts might be the communion of Christ's body and blood. The sense that the community's celebration of the Eucharist involves Christ praying through the Church in the power of the Spirit may explain the invitation of the Spirit's outpouring on the people before the gifts in cases where the Spirit is

---

57 Westerfield Tucker, 'Eucharist in the *Book of Common Worship*', p. 142. The middle of the three phrases quoted above constitutes the epiclesis of Great Prayer of Thanksgiving G of SLR 1: 'Almighty God, pour out your Holy Spirit upon us, that as we receive bread and wine we may be assured that Christ's promise in these signs will be fulfilled.' See *Service for the Lord's Day*, p. 117. About this very short epiclesis text, McKenna writes, 'The request is simply that, through the outpouring of the Spirit upon the people, those receiving the bread and wine be assured of the fulfilment of Christ's promise in these signs. No mention is made of any transformation (although this may be implied) or of any further themes often connected with epicleses.' See McKenna, 'Epiclesis Revisited', p. 177. Since the institution narrative accompanies the breaking of the bread in this context, the epiclesis, by virtue of belonging to the prayer at all, precedes the institution narrative.
58 Erickson, 'Reformed Eucharistic Theology', p. 223. For a more extended discussion of the connections between the Holy Spirit and the Lord's Supper in Reformed theology, see Erickson, 'Reformed Eucharistic Theology', p. 224.

invoked on both. The epiclesis text would then serve as a reminder to the people that they can receive the Eucharist only as God's free gift and not as a product of their own action in relation to God. However, it may also reflect a residual uneasiness in the Reformed tradition with invoking the Holy Spirit upon objects – a characteristic which can be traced back to Calvin himself.[59]

THE EPICLESES OF ELCA/ELCIC'S *EVANGELICAL LUTHERAN WORSHIP* (2006)

By the mid-1960s, Lutherans in North America (and elsewhere) had already been contemplating and experimenting with liturgical reforms for nearly two decades. However, in some ways Lutherans had to traverse more territory than some other traditions in recovering the eucharistic epiclesis as they first had to accept the *concept* of a complete eucharistic prayer before incorporating an epiclesis into it.[60] In the middle decades of the twentieth century, American Lutherans saw several attempts at the restoration of a full eucharistic prayer, sometimes including an epiclesis in either a pre- or post-institution narrative location. In 1946, Paul Zeller Strodach published a eucharistic prayer he had assembled in part from excerpts derived from ancient sources including the Liturgies of St James, St John Chrysostom, St Basil, Gaul and the 1549 Book of Common Prayer.[61] Luther D. Reed, in *The Lutheran Liturgy* (first edition, 1947), presented the text of a eucharistic prayer drawing upon early liturgies and Lutheran theology which included a communion-type epiclesis.[62] The 1958 *Service Book and Hymnal of the Lutheran Church in America* contained a prayer of 'thanksgiving' – a eucharistic prayer – which built upon these two prayers by Strodach and Reed and included an epiclesis

---

59 Duba, 'Presbyterian Eucharistic Prayers', p. 115.
60 The Lutheran World Federation's Commission on Liturgy officially accepted the use of a eucharistic prayer in the 1950s. Philip H. Pfatteicher, *Commentary on the Lutheran Book of Worship: Lutheran Liturgy in Its Ecumenical Context* (Minneapolis: Augsburg Fortress 1990).
61 For the text, see Paul Zeller Strodach, *A Manual on Worship* (Philadelphia: Muhlenberg Press 1946, revised edn), pp. 253–4. It is also reproduced as 'Addendum I' in Pfatteicher, *Commentary*, pp. 199–200. The text of the epiclesis appears there on p. 199. The presence of this prayer in the liturgy of the Federation of Lutheran Churches in India (1936) suggests that it was composed some time before 1936 – or at least before the publication of this latter text.
62 Luther Dotterer Reed, *The Lutheran Liturgy: A Study of the Common Liturgy of the Lutheran Church in America* (Philadelphia: Muhlenberg Press 1959, revised edn), pp. 336–7. This text is reprinted as 'Addendum II' in Pfatteicher, *Commentary*, pp. 336–7.

in the Antiochene position. Arthur Carl Piepkorn composed an anaphora whose outlines resemble the Alexandrian structure with a pre-institution epiclesis inspired in part by Cranmer's 1549 Book of Common Prayer.[63]

In February 1967, the Inter-Lutheran Commission on Worship (ILCW) initiated the process that would culminate in the production of the *Lutheran Book of Worship* in 1978.[64] In terms of eucharistic prayers, preliminary steps involved the preparation of trial supplements that would complement extant worship resources; these included the booklets *Contemporary Worship 2* (1970) and *The Great Thanksgiving* (1975).[65] The second stage of the ILCW's work on eucharistic prayers involved a second committee retooling the draft prayers produced by the first committee into the six options for eucharistic praying which, after further testing and revision, eventually appeared in *Lutheran Book of Worship* (1978).[66]

Unlike the *Service Book and Hymnal* (1958) and *The Lutheran Hymnal* (1941) of the Lutheran Church–Missouri Synod, *Lutheran Book of Worship* (1978) presents Holy Communion as the default rite for congregational worship on Sundays and feasts rather than as something additional.[67] *LBW* included four optional eucharistic prayers of the West Syrian pattern, each containing a single epiclesis following the

---

63 A. C. Piepkorn, 'The Eucharistic Prayer', *Una Sancta* 7.3 (1947), pp. 10–12.

64 Ralph W. Quere, 'Liturgy, Unity, and Disunity: The Context and Legacy of *LBW*', *Currents in Theology and Mission* 30.5 (2003), p. 349. The Lutheran Church–Missouri Synod would eventually pull out of the process and ended up producing its own worship book, *Lutheran Worship* (1982), using many of the same materials.

65 Quere, 'Liturgy, Unity, and Disunity', p. 350. Unlike previous and some subsequent Lutheran resources, *Contemporary Worship 2* presented a eucharistic prayer for use in Lutheran worship without providing alternatives consisting of a prayer followed by the Verba or the use of the Verba alone. Pfatteicher notes that this arrangement raised no objections for the duration of its use as a trial prayer, suggesting implicit approval for the idea of a eucharistic prayer in Lutheran worship. See Pfatteicher, *Commentary*, p. 175. *The Great Thanksgiving* contained eight trial prayers.

66 Gail Ramshaw-Schmidt, 'Toward Lutheran Eucharistic Prayers' in Senn (ed.), *New Eucharistic Prayers*, p. 74.

67 This is indicated by a rubric following the Creed: 'when there is no Communion, the service continues on page 75'; Inter-Lutheran Commission on Worship *et al.*, *Lutheran Book of Worship* (Minneapolis: Augsburg 1978, Minister's Desk edn), p. 65. In contrast, in the *Service Book and Hymnal*, the Lord's Prayer and Benediction are printed at the conclusion of the Sunday Service of the Word with the option to proceed instead to Thanksgiving and communion, should that be desired. For more on the development of *Lutheran Book of Worship*, see Quere, 'Liturgy, Unity, and Disunity', pp. 349–65; and Ralph W. Quere, *In the Context of Unity: A History of the Development of Lutheran Book of Worship* (Minneapolis: Lutheran University Press 2003).

anamnesis.[68] Consequently, while the prayers have a clear Trinitarian structure, focusing on the Father, Son and Spirit in turn, the entire prayer is addressed to God the Father (through the Son and in the Holy Spirit).

Thus the epiclesis is not precisely an invocation of the Spirit, a prayer addressing the Spirit directly to come. It is addressed rather to the Father asking for the gift of the Spirit promised by the risen Christ to guide the church into all truth in order to continue his redeeming work.[69]

None of the epicleses is explicitly consecratory.

Evangelical Lutheran Worship (2006)[70] multiplies the options by incorporating prayers from additional sources, without, however, introducing any substantial innovations in either structure or substance as far as the epiclesis is concerned. Despite the examples of prayers with alternative structures to be found in the Church of England's *Common Worship* (2000) and even within the Lutheran tradition itself in recent Swedish eucharistic prayers, the prayers of *ELW* without exception continue to follow the Antiochene pattern, with not a single example to be found from the Alexandrian tradition, an oversight which Maxwell Johnson calls 'surprising and lamentable'.[71]

---

68 *LBW* presents the complete post-Sanctus prayers of Antiochene shape first, which, given the history of the canon in the Lutheran tradition, could represent something of a statement in itself regarding a shift in theology. While only two of the full eucharistic prayers are featured in the pew edition of *LBW*, all four are printed in full in the Minister's Edition. The two other options for the 'Great Thanksgiving' presented in *LBW* respect the hesitance of some Lutherans to include the institution narrative within the framework of a prayer addressed to God and are carried over from Lutheran resources from earlier in the twentieth century. *LBW*'s rubric 32 also makes a concession for using the institution narrative alone, to accommodate Lutherans 'who did not find the historical, confessional, and theological reasons for a eucharistic prayer persuasive'. However, 'the danger of using the words of institution alone is that they come to be regarded as effecting the consecration, the very thing which the Formula of Concord, Article VII, rejects'. Walter R. Bouman, 'Worship and the Means of Grace' in Ralph R. Van Loon (ed.), *Encountering God: The Legacy of Lutheran Book of Worship for the 21st Century* (Minneapolis: Kirk House 1998), p. 29.

69 Pfatteicher, *Commentary*, p. 167.

70 Evangelical Lutheran Church in America and Evangelical Lutheran Church in Canada, *Evangelical Lutheran Worship* (Minneapolis: Augsburg Fortress 2006, Leader's Desk edn). Subsequent references to specific pages will be given in parentheses in the text above.

71 Maxwell E. Johnson, 'The Holy Spirit and Lutheran Liturgical-Sacramental Worship' in Teresa Berger and Bryan D. Spinks (eds), *The Spirit in Worship – Worship in the Spirit* (Collegeville, MN: Liturgical Press 2009), p. 170.

Several of the prayers from *LBW* are reprinted virtually unchanged in this resource. For example, the epiclesis of Great Thanksgiving I seems to be a slight modification of that of Eucharistic Prayer III from *LBW*, and the epiclesis of Great Thanksgiving XI is identical to that of *LBW* Eucharistic Prayer IV (Gordon Lathrop's translation of *Apostolic Tradition* 4). New additions include seasonal prayers such as Great Thanksgivings III and IV (for the Advent–Christmas and Lent–Easter seasons, respectively), and several prayers from other Lutheran resources developed between *LBW* and *ELW*, including Great Thanksgivings VI from *This Far by Faith* (1999) – whose epiclesis draws on aspects of that of *LBW*'s Eucharistic Prayers I and II) – and VII from *Libro de Liturgia y Cántico* (1998). The texts of the epicleses found in the prayers of *ELW* will now be considered in turn.

GREAT THANKSGIVINGS I–XI

Great Thanksgiving I (*ELW*, p. 195)

Comparing the epiclesis of the *LBW*'s Eucharistic Prayer III and *ELW*'s Great Thanksgiving I side by side suggests that the latter largely represents an updating of the former using slightly more contemporary language.[72] The epiclesis in *ELW* is:

> We ask you mercifully to accept our praise and thanksgiving and with your Word and Holy Spirit to bless us, your servants, and these your own gifts of bread and wine, so that we and all who share in the body and blood of Christ may be filled with heavenly blessing and grace, and, receiving the forgiveness of sin, may be formed to live as your holy people and be given our inheritance with all your saints.

This prayer is ultimately derived from the thanksgiving found in the 1958 *Service Book and Hymnal*. Its considerable biblical resonances as well as general fondness for the prayer among Lutherans led to its inclusion in the *LBW*, with the most noticeable revision being an updating of the prayer's language; for example, 'thee' and 'thou' have been replaced by the more contemporary address of 'you'.[73] This prayer draws upon early Eastern and Western sources as well as Cranmer's 1549

---

72 For example, *LBW*'s 'we implore' has become 'we ask' in *ELW*; 'may be sanctified in soul and body' is changed to 'may be formed to live as your holy people' (which has less individualistic and more communal overtones); and 'have our portion' is modified to 'be given our inheritance'.

73 Ramshaw-Schmidt, 'Toward Lutheran Eucharistic Prayers', p. 76.

BCP.[74] Cranmer is the ultimate source of the phrase 'with your Word and Holy Spirit', although the uppercase 'Word' does not come from Cranmer.[75] The words '. . . bless us, your servants, and these your own gifts of bread and wine' are from the Liturgy of St John Chrysostom; '. . . that we and all who share . . .' is again from the 1549 BCP; '. . . with heavenly peace and joy' comes from the Roman Canon as translated into English in the Lutheran Church–Missouri Synod's 1969 *Worship Supplement*; ' . . . and, receiving the forgiveness of sin . . .' comes from the Jerusalem Liturgy of St James and Paul Zeller Strodach.

In terms of content, the prayer asks that God's 'Word and Spirit' might 'bless' the people and the gifts, in that order. This raises the question about the ordering of the epicletic elements – as the more typical order in ancient prayers is to request God's blessing of bread and wine *so that* the people receiving them might be transformed. No transformation of the gifts is specifically sought, but several benefits are requested for those sharing in the gifts – blessing and grace, forgiveness of sins, formation as God's holy people. An eschatological aspect emerges in the prayer that communicants might be 'given our inheritance with all your saints'.

Great Thanksgiving II (see *ELW*, pp. 194, 206) consists of only the opening dialogue, preface, Sanctus and institution narrative before moving to the Lord's Prayer; it does not contain an epiclesis.

Great Thanksgivings III and IV

As mentioned above, Great Thanksgivings III and IV are seasonal prayers, intended for use from the beginning of Advent through Epiphany and from Ash Wednesday to Pentecost, respectively. Both prayers blend seasonal imagery with pneumatic themes.

Great Thanksgiving III (see Table 7.3) highlights a longing for the coming of God's Spirit (which also introduces an eschatological note appropriate for the Advent and Christmas seasons), alludes to the

---

74 See Pfatteicher, *Commentary*, pp. 179–80 for what follows; cf. Reed, *Lutheran Liturgy*, p. 357.

75 While this phrase was present already in the thanksgiving of the *Service Book and Hymnal*, its inclusion here had possible ecumenical implications given that Eucharistic Prayers I and II of Rite One of the Episcopal *Book of Common Prayer* likewise contained this phrase. The *BCP* was not officially published until 1979, but it had existed in proposed form since 1976. The ILCW had access to this resource while developing the *LBW* prayers. (See Philip H. Pfatteicher, 'The Blood in Our Veins' in Ralph Van Loon (ed.), *Encountering God: The Legacy of Lutheran Book of Worship for the 21st Century* (Minneapolis: Kirk House 1998), p. 65.)

Table 7.3: *ELW* Great Thanksgiving Prayers III and IV

Great Thanksgiving III (ELW, p. 196)	*Great Thanksgiving IV (ELW, p. 197)*
Holy God,	O God of resurrection and new life:
we long for your Spirit.	Pour out your Holy Spirit on us
Come among us.	and on these gifts of bread and wine.
Bless this meal.	Bless this feast.
May your Word take flesh in us.	Grace our table with your presence.
Awaken your people.	*Come, Holy Spirit.*
Fill us with your light.	
Bring the gift of peace on earth.	
Come, Holy Spirit.	

Incarnation (and the desire that it become a current reality in the life of the community as a result of the eucharistic celebration) and refers to awakened people who desire to be filled with God's light and receive the gift of God's peace. The primary addressee of the prayer is God (the Father), but the concluding congregational acclamation assumes the form of a direct invocation for the Spirit's coming. While both people ('us') and the gifts (implied in 'this meal') are mentioned, there is no direct request for the Spirit to do anything in particular beyond coming and blessing the meal. If the phrase 'bless this meal' were excised, the rest of the prayer would be equally applicable to nearly *any* context of Christian prayer (particularly during the Advent and Christmas seasons). Even as written, this portion of Great Thanksgiving III would not seem out of place in meal settings that were not eucharistic.

Much of the imagery encapsulated in Great Thanksgiving IV (see Table 7.3) is particularly associated with the Easter season – resurrection, new life, the outpouring of the Spirit at Pentecost (which could also be read as a sign inaugurating the last times and thus introducing an eschatological note to this prayer) and the presence of God among God's people in a festal meal setting. The numerous references to meals – 'bread and wine', 'feast', 'table' – make the eucharistic imagery of this epiclesis stronger than that of Great Thanksgiving III, as do the biblical accounts of Christ's meal ministry (including the Last Supper and the presence of the risen Christ feasting with disciples in the Emmaus account and elsewhere) and the imagery of the heavenly banquet which were likely in the minds of the framers of this prayer. It would seem that specific mention of the community's sharing in the eucharistic gifts would have been a natural extension of this theme, although this is not specifically mentioned here. This prayer asks more explicitly than Great Thanksgiving III for the Spirit's outpouring on the people and the gifts (in that order) without requesting any further specific effect in either.

Great Thanksgiving V

Great Thanksgiving V (*ELW*, p. 198) connects a brief anamnesis section with the concluding doxology via a similarly concise epiclesis:

> Pour out upon us
> the Spirit of your love, O Lord,
> and unite the wills
> of all who share this heavenly food,
> the body and blood
> of Jesus Christ, our Lord.

The Spirit imagined here is 'the Spirit of [the Lord's] love'. While the end of the epiclesis makes it clear that Christians recognize Christ as Lord, the Lord whose Spirit is invoked is more likely God the Father in the first instance. God has been the addressee of the prayer throughout, and earlier in the prayer God is addressed as Lord in a context where only God the Father makes logical sense (i.e. after the Sanctus: 'Holy, mighty, and merciful Lord, heaven and earth are full of your glory. In great love, you sent to us Jesus, your Son ...'). The Spirit's outpouring is here invoked upon the people only. A bit later, 'heavenly food', presumably the eucharistic gifts as a foretaste of the heavenly banquet, is mentioned. The description of this food as 'the body and blood of Jesus Christ' cements the eucharistic nature of this epiclesis, although the food is here identified (already) with Christ's body and blood in a way that does not imply that the Spirit now requested is to participate in any sort of transformation of this food. The verb 'share' suggests eating or partaking of these gifts, making this epiclesis much more specific in terms of envisioning the act of communion which is to follow than the previous two epicleses in *ELW*. The benefit of this sharing is the unity of all who partake, although the phrase 'unite the wills' could be understood in individualistic terms.

Great Thanksgiving VI

The epiclesis of Great Thanksgiving VI (*ELW*, p. 199) combines elements from Eucharistic Prayers I and II of *LBW* (see Table 7.4).

The opening phrase, 'Send now, we pray, your Holy Spirit', is common to all three of these prayers. The absence of the relative clause

Table 7.4: Epiclesis of *ELW* Great Thanksgiving Prayer VI

LBW *Eucharistic Prayer I*	LBW *Eucharistic Prayer II*	ELW *Great Thanksgiving VI*
Send now, we pray, your Holy Spirit, the spirit of our Lord and of his resurrection, that we who receive the Lord's body and blood may live to the praise of your glory and receive our inheritance with all your saints in light.	Send now, we pray, your Holy Spirit, that we and all who share in this bread and cup may be united in the fellowship of the Holy Spirit, may enter the fullness of the kingdom of heaven, and may receive our inheritance with all your saints in light.	Send now, we pray, your Holy Spirit, that we who share in Christ's body and blood may live to the praise of your glory and receive our inheritance with all your saints in light. *Amen. Come, Holy Spirit.*

and the phrasing 'that we who share in' more closely resembles *LBW*'s Eucharistic Prayer II. It is curious that, whereas Eucharistic Prayer II reads 'we *and all* who share', this phrase has been condensed in Great Thanksgiving VI to 'we who share', suggesting a possible narrowing of focus to the immediate context of the community celebrating the Eucharist at the particular time and place the prayer is used. However, whereas Eucharistic Prayer II continues with 'this bread and cup', Great Thanksgiving VI reads 'Christ's body and blood' at this point, making this part of the prayer somewhat broader in focus than Eucharistic Prayer II. The latter's use of the demonstrative adjective 'this' puts the present eucharistic celebration in view whereas the group sharing Christ's body and blood could extend beyond the bounds of the gathered community, or perhaps even denominational boundaries. The concluding phrase, 'may live to the praise of your glory and receive our inheritance with all your saints in light', seems to borrow its eschatological reference directly from Eucharistic Prayer I.

Great Thanksgiving VII

The epiclesis of Great Thanksgiving VII (*ELW*, p. 201) is:

> Holy God,
> holy and merciful,
> holy and compassionate,
> send upon us and this meal
> your Holy Spirit,
> whose breath revives us for life,

whose fire rouses us to love.
Enfold in your arms
all who share this holy food.
Nurture in us
the fruits of the Spirit,
that we may be a living tree,
sharing your bounty
with all the world.
Amen. Come, Holy Spirit.

This prayer features more extensive descriptions of the attributes of both God and the Spirit while requesting that God send the Spirit upon the people ('us') and the gifts ('this meal'). Whereas the attributes of God express who God is by virtue of being God, the extended descriptions of the Spirit pertain to the Spirit's effects within the Christian community – a Spirit 'whose breath revives us for life' and 'whose fire rouses us to love'. The references to 'this meal' and sharing in 'holy food' place the prayer in a eucharistic (or at least a meal) context, but these references could be excised to yield a more general epiclesis without much additional compositional effort. However, when used in a eucharistic context, 'Nurture in us the fruits of the Spirit' alludes to the fruits of communion. The 'fruit' envisioned – that the communicants may in turn *be* a tree bearing good fruit for the world – while not a traditional way of expressing the fruits of communion, does introduce a missionary thrust to the epiclesis that is not present in the epicleses of most of the other Lutheran prayers.

Great Thanksgiving VIII

The epiclesis of Great Thanksgiving VIII (*ELW*, p. 202), shares some of the outward-looking dimensions of that of Great Thanksgiving VI:

Send your Holy Spirit, our advocate,
to fill the hearts of all
who share this bread and cup
with courage and wisdom
to pursue love and justice
in all the world.
Come, Spirit of freedom!
And let the church say, Amen.
Amen.

Unlike some of the preceding prayers, the Spirit's sending is asked upon the people only (to fill their hearts) but not specifically on the gifts. However, sharing in the gifts is presented as the condition for receiving hearts filled with courage and wisdom, leading to lives characterized by love and justice – thus mentioning directly or indirectly some of the traditional gifts and fruits of the Holy Spirit intended here as fruits of communion. The pursuit of 'love and justice in all the world' calls the community to conform its conduct to that expected of Spirit-filled people. The epiclesis concludes with a direct, *maranatha*-like invocation to the Spirit to which the community assents with, 'Amen.'

Great Thanksgiving IX

The epiclesis of Great Thanksgiving IX (*ELW*, p. 203) is quite concise:

> We pray for the gift of your Spirit:
> in our gathering;
> within this meal;
> among your people;
> throughout the world.

This epiclesis would seem to be equally at home at the beginning of a eucharistic service or at the final dismissal as within the eucharistic prayer itself. In context, the 'meal' reference suggests the eucharistic meal, but there is little beyond this to make this a eucharistic epiclesis in the limited sense. There is no verb (e.g. 'come' or 'send') associated with the request for the gift of the Spirit and no further specification regarding what the Spirit is expected to do in the context of the gathering, meal, people or world. The Spirit is not invoked on either people or gifts explicitly but, through the references to 'gathering' and 'meal', an implicit request could be read between the lines.

Great Thanksgiving X

Great Thanksgiving X (*ELW*, p. 204) casts the epiclesis in metaphorical language:

> O God, you are Breath:
> send your Spirit on this meal.
> O God, you are Bread:
> feed us with yourself.
> O God, you are Wine:
> warm our hearts and make us one.

This epiclesis contains some resonances of a typical eucharistic epiclesis (for example, 'feeding' alludes to communion and 'make us one' to unity). However, of the three major metaphors (God as Breath, Bread and Wine), the only one that is specifically associated with the Spirit is the first one, and there in a rather vague way (since God is asked to send the Spirit on the meal but the Spirit is not described as doing anything further beyond, perhaps, pervading the atmosphere like an inspiring breath). While Spirit as breath or wind is a familiar biblical image (e.g. Gen. 1.2; John 3.6–8; 20.22), it is more difficult to find parallels for the imagery of bread and wine used to designate the divine. God gives manna to the Israelites wandering in the wilderness, for example, but there God *gives* bread rather than *is* bread. John 6.35 describes Jesus as 'the bread of life', and this christocentric image may be imagined here. God *as* wine is likewise an unusual reference in both the biblical milieu and the realm of epicletic texts.

Great Thanksgiving XI

Great Thanksgiving XI (*ELW*, p. 205) is Gordon Lathrop's translation of the model anaphora for an episcopal ordination presented in *Apostolic Tradition* 4 which appeared in *LBW* as Eucharistic Prayer IV.[76] The epicleses of these two prayers are identical:

> Send your Spirit upon these gifts of your church;
> gather into one
> all who share this bread and wine;
> fill us with your Holy Spirit
> to establish our faith in truth,
> that we may praise and glorify you
> through your Son Jesus Christ . . .

The Spirit is invoked *first* upon the gifts for the sake of the unity of the communicants (presumably including those who are present at that

---

76 Philip H. Pfatteicher, Carlos R. Messerli and Inter-Lutheran Commission on Worship, *Manual on the Liturgy: Lutheran Book of Worship* (Minneapolis: Augsburg 1979), p. 241. *Apostolic Tradition* had first come into use in Lutheran circles through the 1969 *Worship Supplement* of the Lutheran Church–Missouri Synod. (See *Worship Supplement*, pp. 46–7.) The version in *LBW* and *ELW* follows the structure of *Apostolic Tradition* closely, and therefore contains neither a preface nor Sanctus, and provides no place for congregational acclamations. This prayer is 'recommended for use especially on weekdays or whenever a simple service is desired'. See *Lutheran Book of Worship*, Minister's Desk edn, p. 29, no. 31.

particular celebration, but the 'all' may envision a larger group united in eucharistic fellowship as well), followed by a parallel request that the communicants ('us') be filled with the same Spirit so that their faith might be established in truth and that they may praise and glorify God. The confluence of concerns expressed here – unity and the foundation of the community's faith in truth – reflects those of *Apostolic Tradition* without introducing any new elements.

THE EPICLESES OF LUTHERAN EUCHARISTIC PRAYERS: ANALYSIS AND CRITIQUE

Overall, *Evangelical Lutheran Worship* continues the trend begun in *Lutheran Book of Worship*, incorporating many positive insights of contemporary scholarship on eucharistic praying available to the committees that worked on these books. In terms of the epicleses in particular, these Lutheran prayers introduce a robust eschatological anticipation in connection with the Spirit's activity in the eucharistic context.[77] Many of the prayers of *ELW* also feature a strong sense of the community's awareness of its mission in the larger world as Spirit-filled people, flowing from the eucharistic encounter. Through the use of these prayers in ELCA and ELCIC, Lutheran liturgies in North America certainly have a more explicit expression of the function and activity of the Spirit in eucharistic rites than they did several years ago.

Unlike, however, the fully fledged Antiochene epiclesis that emerged by the late fourth century, which typically asked God:

1 to send the Holy Spirit (on us and) on the offered gifts,
2 to make the bread and wine the body and blood of Christ by the power of the Holy Spirit,
3 so that they might be unto salvation for those who receive them in communion,[78]

the Lutheran epicleses considered here, which all conform to the Antiochene pattern, are completely lacking any language of transformation or change in the bread and wine in the direction of Christ's body and blood and do not uniformly request the Spirit's sending on the gifts (although some reference to the Spirit's sending on the people is present

---

77 McKenna, 'Epiclesis Revisited', p. 182.
78 Robert F. Taft, 'From Logos to Spirit: On the Early History of the Epiclesis' in Andreas Heinz and Heinrich Rennings (eds), *Gratias Agamus: Studien zum eucharistischen Hochgebet: Für Balthasar Fischer* (Freiburg: Herder 1992), p. 490.

in most of these epicleses). John McKenna wonders whether the absence of such references in Lutheran prayers is 'due to an emphasis on the institution narrative as "consecratory" or a desire to avoid the implications of certain terms – or both?'[79]

Others have noted this discrepancy as well. For example, Johnson comments that:

> The Spirit-epicleses in the prayers from all of the modern Lutheran books … with some exceptions here and there, are ambiguous both liturgically and theologically. In many it is not clear what role, if any, the epiclesis actually plays in the particular sacramental event in question, or even upon what or whom the Holy Spirit is being invoked … It could be argued that with phrases like 'Come, Holy Spirit,' without specifying any place, person, or thing, Lutherans are in touch with a very archaic epicletic theology … [in which] 'the epiclesis was primarily a prayer for communion, not for consecration.' At the same time, in light of contemporary ecumenical liturgical scholarship, one must ask whether Lutheran theology and liturgy might not be in a position today to embrace a more explicit form of consecratory epiclesis as well.[80]

Some of the ambiguity in the Lutheran epicleses is consistent with descriptions in the books themselves or commentaries upon them concerning how the epiclesis in these texts is to be interpreted. Pfatteicher's *Commentary on the Lutheran Book of Worship*, under the heading 'The Epiclesis of the Holy Spirit', notes that 'The prayer is for the sending of the Spirit to the meal, so that it and all God's acts and promises may come to fulfillment.'[81] The hope that the meal might come to fulfilment in the context of God's promises is specifically eucharistic, but the second part is so only by extension, insofar as those who receive the Eucharist will be transformed according to God's promises.

But Johnson's question deserves further attention: 'must Lutheran liturgy be characterized by epicletic texts that remain theologically and liturgically somewhat ambiguous?' If the Spirit of the crucified and risen

---

79 McKenna, 'Epiclesis Revisited', p. 182.
80 Johnson, 'Holy Spirit', p. 161. The Taft quote to which Johnson refers is in Taft, 'From Logos to Spirit', pp. 492–3. See Johnson's article for references to controversy over a eucharistic epiclesis in Lutheran circles during the twentieth century.
81 Pfatteicher, *Commentary*, p. 177.

Christ makes redeeming encounter with this same Christ possible today, 'then why not say so liturgically by petitioning the Spirit to do that sacramentally?'[82] Bryan Spinks has recently commented that 'an epiklesis may not be so difficult for Lutheran theology as some have maintained'.[83]

Spinks' claim that recent liturgical reforms have tended, in practice if not in theory, to treat the West Syrian pattern of eucharistic praying as 'the perfect and only paradigm for authentic eucharistic prayer'[84] is particularly apt when considering the eucharistic prayers of *LBW* and *ELW* which uniformly place the eucharistic epiclesis in the West Syrian, post-anamnesis position.[85] Johnson contends that, 'Prior to LBW and ELW a strong theological position was developing in favor of a pre-Institution Narrative location for such a Spirit invocation.'[86]

Furthermore, contemporary precedent now exists within the Lutheran tradition for structuring eucharistic prayers in a different way. The current prayers of the Church of Sweden conform not only with classical Lutheran doctrine along the lines sketched in the Pfalz-Neuberg Church Order (1543), the *Kassel Agenda* (1896) and the *Agenda* of the Lutheran Church in Bavaria (1879), but also with twentieth-century theology articulated by theologians such as Peter Brunner.[87] In contrast to the prayers featured in *LBW* and *ELW*, the Lutheran Church of Sweden's eucharistic prayers are not limited to a single anaphoral form and also exhibit variety in terms of the placement of the epiclesis within the prayer. In this way, they resemble some of the options chosen in the Church of England's *Common Worship* (2000).[88] Of the Lutheran Church of Sweden's seven alternative texts, five have a pre-institution

---

82 Johnson, 'Holy Spirit', p. 163.

83 Bryan D. Spinks, 'Berakah, Anaphoral Theory and Luther', *LQ* 3.3 (1989), p. 277.

84 Spinks, 'Berakah, Anaphoral Theory and Luther', p. 277.

85 Johnson, 'Holy Spirit', p. 177.

86 Johnson, 'Holy Spirit', p. 177.

87 See Peter Brunner, 'Zur Lehre vom Gottesdienst der im Namen Jesu versammelten Gemeinde', *Leiturgia* 1 (1954), esp. pp. 290–311 (ET Peter Brunner, *Worship in the Name of Jesus*, trans. M. H. Bertram (St Louis: Concordia 1968)).

88 Johnson, 'Holy Spirit', p. 170. One half (four of eight) of the prayers in *Common Worship*'s 'Use One' have a pre-institution epiclesis. Johnson comments further: 'What is intriguing about these Church of Sweden and Church of England eucharistic prayers, together with the theological position of Brunner and the small but significant Lutheran heritage in this context, is how close all of this is to the often maligned structure of the eucharistic prayers of the Missal of Paul VI, where the emphasis on a pre-Institution epiclesis is so strong that it influenced the way texts like the anaphora from the *Apostolic Tradition* 4 and the anaphora called "Egyptian Basil" were used to compose Eucharistic Prayers 2 and 4, respectively' (Johnson, 'Holy Spirit', pp. 170–1).

epiclesis; some of these (for example, that of Prayer G) are unreservedly consecratory in orientation and some feature language of offering (e.g. Prayers A and D) which resembles the prayers for the Preparation of the Gifts in the Missal of Paul VI.[89] Incorporating a wider variety of epicletic prayer patterns into the eucharistic prayers of North American Lutherans in the future will likely require revisiting the status of the epiclesis relative to the institution narrative in light of Luther's theology of eucharistic consecration, which clearly seems to provide some role for the Spirit in the eucharistic action.[90]

The last two chapters have provided some indication of the tremendous diversity of epicleses present in several Western churches which ultimately trace their roots, directly or indirectly, to the Protestant and Anglican Reformations of the sixteenth century: the Episcopal Church in the United States of America, the United Methodist Church, the Church of England, the Presbyterian Church (USA), and the Evangelical Lutheran Churches in America and Canada. The language of the prayers often sounds quite similar – and in some cases this is due to various churches collaborating on eucharistic prayer texts (as was the case for 'A Common Eucharistic Prayer' based on the Anaphora of Basil) or jointly borrowing from an ancient liturgical text that is part of the common stream of early Christian tradition that continues to nourish members of the body of Christ that is the Church today. Some of the different pneumatological, eucharistic, ecclesiological and eschatological resonances that emerge in the epicleses of denominations considered here are attributable to unique insights in the theological heritage of each of these traditions, while others reflect the results of compromises negotiated in church committees. The final chapter will review the movement of the Spirit through the traditions and eucharistic prayers discussed thus far and point out a few ways in which the Spirit might be invited to move more freely in the texts of Western traditions and the lives of communicants nourished and sent out into the world by this same Spirit.

---

89 Johnson, 'Holy Spirit', pp. 168–9. See <http://www.svenskakyrkan.se/gudstjanstbanken/service_book/14gudstjanstens_alternativamoment.htm> for the text of these Swedish prayers. ETs of the epicleses of Eucharistic Prayers A, D, E, F and G are provided in Johnson, 'Holy Spirit', pp. 169.
90 Johnson, 'Holy Spirit', p. 168.

Conclusion: reflections and future directions

Historical liturgical scholarship treating the 'epiclesis question' during the early and middle decades of the twentieth century exposed the complexity underlying this pneumatological element of early Christian eucharistic prayers. The development of the eucharistic epiclesis prior to the emergence of a request for the sending (or coming) of the Spirit for consecration and/or communion in anaphoras of the late fourth and early fifth centuries remained an open question. It was also unclear whether all living Christian traditions had incorporated an explicit pneumatic epiclesis into their eucharistic prayers at some point when this anaphoral element with uncertain origins became more widespread (perhaps inspired by the pneumatological debates of the fourth century) – or whether the prayers of some traditions, such as the Roman rite, represented a period of less developed Trinitarian eucharistic theology. When historians and theologians took pains to avoid reading later theological convictions into earlier texts, it was unclear whether early Christian authors understood the eucharistic epiclesis in a consistent way. What did seem clear, however, was that different traditions of eucharistic praying (East Syrian, West Syrian, Alexandrian, etc.) adopted diverse approaches towards the epiclesis in their eucharistic prayers, and that the developed epiclesis sought a much wider array of benefits flowing from communion (as opposed to a narrow focus on the consecration of the elements).[1]

While many of these conclusions still stand, some other conclusions have been challenged by more recent studies of the early epiclesis such as those discussed in Chapter 1. Gabriele Winkler's treatment of the

---

1 Richard Albertine, 'Problem of the (Double) Epiclesis in the New Roman Eucharistic Prayers', *EL* 91 (1977), pp. 192–202.

epicleses in the apocryphal *Acts of the Apostles* has challenged the idea that a pneumatic eucharistic epiclesis would have been an unlikely occurrence before the mid-fourth century and also the idea that pneumatic epicleses developed out of invocations for the presence of the Logos in the eucharistic celebration (the former arising in an age when the identities of the second and third persons of the Trinity were not clearly differentiated). The idea that the consecratory dimension of the eucharistic epiclesis was a relatively early concern (whatever other purposes the epiclesis may have had) is less clear now than it was a generation ago. Likewise, the conviction that the eucharistic epiclesis had a *single* point of origin from which it was subsequently dispersed is less firmly held now than it once was.

While the overall shape of liturgical prayers proved very important to twentieth-century liturgical revisers, this does not seem to have been the case – at least not to the same degree – in the late fourth century. While one tradition borrowed elements freely from the texts of another, there does not seem to have been the same sort of concern that components from a host rite were transposed into the corresponding section of texts where these newly introduced components initially resided as guests. Even after the exchange of elements in the fourth century, regional diversity in the overall structure of eucharistic rites persisted even while the *content* of eucharistic rites became more similar.[2] In contrast, the twentieth century has seen a considerable homogenization of structure and some similarity in content; however, this superficial similarity sometimes belies, upon further examination, some significant differences in eucharistic pneumatology rooted in the theological commitments of particular Western churches.

All of the Roman prayers feature a 'split epiclesis' with a prayer for the Spirit's action on the gifts preceding the institution narrative and a prayer for the Spirit's action upon the communicants after the anamnesis. Aside from lacking a precedent in ancient texts (unless the Roman Canon is taken as evidence for this form), at least two theological issues arise from this arrangement.[3] First, separating the 'consecration' and 'communion' orientations of the epiclesis by relegating them to discrete sections of the

---

2 Paul F. Bradshaw, 'The Homogenization of Christian Liturgy – Ancient and Modern: Presidential Address', *SL* 26.1 (1996), p. 7.
3 See John H. McKenna, 'Eucharistic Prayer: Epiclesis' in Andreas Heinz and Heinrich Rennings (eds), *Gratias Agamus: Studien zum eucharistischen Hochgebet: Für Balthasar Fischer* (Freiburg: Herder 1992) and *The Eucharistic Epiclesis: A Detailed History from the Patristic to the Modern Era* (Chicago: Hillenbrand 2009, 2nd edn), pp. 224ff.

prayer limits the epiclesis' ability to highlight the connection between the transformation of the gifts as being *for the sake of* the fruits associated with sharing in communion. Second, placing the appeal for the Spirit's transformation of the gifts before the institution narrative could contribute to the perception that it is the words of institution that are ultimately or at least primarily responsible for achieving this transformation which serves the eventual fulfilment of the eucharistic action in the consumption of the consecrated elements such that the *communicants* might be transformed into the body and blood of Christ for the life of the world.

The eucharistic prayers of the Episcopal Church USA's *Book of Common Prayer* (1979), with one exception (Prayer C), locate the epiclesis after the institution narrative and invoke the Spirit's action upon both the eucharistic gifts and the people, although in the prayers based on the *BCP* this action is somewhat indirect, mediated through the community's sharing in the eucharistic gifts. For example, Eucharistic Prayer II (*BCP* in contemporary language) reads:

> And we most humbly beseech thee, O merciful Father, to hear us, and, with thy Word and Holy Spirit, to bless and sanctify these gifts of bread and wine, that they may be unto us the Body and Blood of thy dearly-beloved Son Jesus Christ.

Communicants hope to receive the gifts as Christ's body and blood, and most prayers articulate further graces expected as a result of the Spirit's participation in the eucharistic action.

Great Thanksgivings in the *United Methodist Book of Worship* (1992) similarly favour locating the epiclesis after the institution narrative and do this consistently in almost all of the prayers. The epiclesis which, with minor variations and additions suited to particular seasons (e.g. Pentecost) or occasions in the life of the church (e.g. All Saints and Memorial Occasions), forms the basis for many of the prayers in this book is quite comprehensive in terms of requesting the Spirit's action on the people and the gifts in the eucharistic action conceived very broadly. As a result of the Spirit's outpouring on the people and the gifts, those who pray these texts expect communion in Christ's body and blood that they might *be* Christ's redeemed body, living in service to the wider world until they receive a dinner invitation to the eschatological banquet.

The Great Thanksgivings in the Presbyterian Church (USA)'s *Book of Common Worship* (1993) prayers locate the epiclesis after the institution narrative in all instances in which the institution narrative is part of the prayer. The institution narrative does not form a part of Great Thanksgiving H, and in many other instances there is an option to recite the institution narrative during the fraction rather than as part of the eucharistic prayer proper – or even as part of the 'Invitation to the Lord's Table' just before the Great Thanksgiving, if Option B of this invitation is used, in which case the words of institution are not repeated later. The words of institution are necessarily included in the prayer only in cases where the texts adapt ancient prayers whose final form included the narrative and/or in texts prepared by ecumenical committees (i.e. Great Thanksgivings E, F and G). As with the Methodist prayers, most of the Presbyterian prayers are quite concerned about the Spirit's impact on the gathered people as well as the gifts and take a broad view of the eucharistic action.

Of the eight eucharistic prayers in the Church of England's *Common Worship* (2000), many possible patterns of the epiclesis are represented. Two of the prayers (A and B) have a 'split' epiclesis with a consecratory petition before the institution narrative and a 'communion' petition afterwards. Two of the prayers (C and E) mention the Holy Spirit before the institution narrative but not afterwards (outside of the concluding doxology). Prayer E in particular seems to lack anything approaching a 'communion' dimension of the epiclesis, whether the Holy Spirit is mentioned or not. The rest of the prayers (D, F, G and H) situate both the consecratory and communion dimensions of the epiclesis after the institution narrative. The content of these epicleses is also quite diverse, although communion with Christ and further benefits flowing from this frequently emerge as central themes.

The prayers in *Evangelical Lutheran Worship* uniformly place the epiclesis after the institution narrative (with the exception of Great Thanksgiving II, which does not contain an epiclesis). While most of the prayers request some clear action of the Spirit with respect to the communicants and the act of sharing in communion, only Great Thanksgivings I, III and IV explicitly request the Spirit's interaction with the gifts at this point: to 'bless' the bread and wine in I, the 'meal' in III and the 'feast' in IV. The results of the Spirit's sending and/or blessing are not defined more clearly; nowhere is a change or transformation of the gifts from bread and wine to Christ's body and blood associated with the action of the Holy Spirit. Great Thanksgiving VI requests the sending of the Spirit without further specification, and Great Thanksgiving IX requests the 'gift of the Spirit' upon the eucharistic action in its entirety.

LOOKING BACK AS A WAY FORWARD

In an article entitled 'Toward a Different Anaphoral Structure', Frank Senn notes the theological difficulties Western churches have encountered with respect to the location and language of the epiclesis of early Eastern anaphoras of the West Syrian type, such as the Egyptian Anaphora of Basil, concluding that

> it would be problematic in this tradition for the church to petition the Holy Spirit to do what the authoritative and creative words of Christ do with regard to the gifts, notwithstanding a generally appreciative regard for the role of the Holy Spirit in the Eastern eucharist on the part of Western theologians since the sixteenth century.[4]

Some of the solutions adopted in current Western eucharistic prayers do not respect the integrity or internal logic of West Syrian prayers. An epiclesis preceding the institution narrative disrupts the account of salvation history located in the post-Sanctus of prayers of the West Syrian type. On the other hand, leaving the epicleses in their traditional post-anamnesis location – while excising language which might be interpreted as asking the Spirit to sanctify the gifts at this point in the prayer – results in an attenuated epiclesis in which the inherent unity of the consecration and communion dimensions is lost. Furthermore, the epiclesis itself becomes a minor component whose purpose is reduced to little more than a transition between the anamnesis and intercessions. For the most part, 'it is evident that the Western churches are not yet prepared to import Eastern anaphoras without altering them to suit Western stylistic and theological preferences'.[5]

However compelling reasons for favouring the West Syrian structure may have been for liturgical reformers of the late twentieth century, alternative models of eucharistic praying (some derived from very early prayers and some from later Western models) might profitably be tapped to enrich the euchological repertoire of Western churches in the future – without selectively appropriating Eastern frameworks which happen to be amenable to accommodating Western concerns. The first (and simplest) solution with regard to the epiclesis would be to take a cue from very early texts, no matter what the precise location of the epiclesis in the prayer. Brock and Winkler have argued that the most primitive form of

---

4 Frank C. Senn, 'Toward a Different Anaphoral Structure', *Worship* 58.4 (1984), pp. 348–9.
5 Senn, 'Toward a Different Anaphoral Structure', p. 349.

the epiclesis simply asked that the Holy Spirit 'come' without any further specificity regarding the objects and/or persons who might benefit from this coming or even any elaboration about the effects which this coming might have on anyone or anything; there was certainly no petition for 'consecration' contained in such epicleses.[6] Maxwell Johnson highlights the potential of such a solution to address discomfort in ecumenical dialogue with a high degree of specificity regarding how or when the Spirit acts in the context of the eucharistic action. 'Indeed, such an "epiclesis," such an invocation of the Holy Spirit in the liturgical assembly, is an ancient petition merely for the Spirit's divine presence and, as such, transcends the confession-specific concerns about theories of consecration.'[7]

Senn also suggests that Western Christians might look to the bipartite anaphoral structure of praise and supplication (which is perhaps even more ancient than the tripartite praise–thanksgiving–supplication structure which received its fullest expression in the West Syrian anaphoras) as a way around the Western theological impasse with West Syrian structure. This bipartite pattern can be found in ancient texts as diverse as *Didache* 10, *Apostolic Tradition* 4 and the *Mar Esha'ya* text of the anaphora of Addai and Mari – and possibly also in the Roman Canon if the Sanctus is considered as the division between the two main sections of the prayer. Some of the first examples of reformed liturgies from the sixteenth century adopted a bipartite structure as well, including Martin Luther's *Formula Missae et Communionis* (1523), Diebold Schwarz's German Mass (1524–5), the Brandenburg Church Order (1540) and Thomas Cranmer's first Book of Common Prayer (1549).

It is noteworthy that these examples, progenitors of the Reformed, Lutheran, and Anglican eucharistic traditions respectively, still followed the pattern of the Roman canon even though the reformers

---

6 However, Robert F. Taft provides a helpful caveat, noting that 'any prayer for the power of God to come upon something in order that it be unto salvation for those who partake of it or participate in it as God intended, necessarily implies that God do something by his coming to make that object salvific'; one should not therefore infer that 'a more primitive, less explicit epicletic prayer is not, in fact implicitly consecratory' since considerations of this kind reveal more about the structure of a text than its theology. See Taft, 'From Logos to Spirit' in Heinz and Rennings (eds), *Gratias Agamus*, p. 493.
7 Maxwell E. Johnson, 'The Origins of the Anaphoral Use of the Sanctus and Epiclesis Revisited: The Contribution of Gabriele Winkler and Its Implications' in Hans-Jürgen Feulner, Elena Velkovska and Robert F. Taft (eds), *Crossroad of Cultures: Studies in Liturgy and Patristics in Honor of Gabriele Winkler* (Rome: Pontifical Oriental Institute 2000), p. 435.

eschewed the use of the Roman canon itself. This is significant because the reformers were increasingly familiar with editions and translations of the Greek anaphoras.[8]

Senn's proposed anaphoral structure introduces the congregational acclamation, 'Amen. Come, Lord Jesus', in imitation of the ancient *maranatha* as a division between the praise and supplication sections of the prayer, followed by an epiclesis (although not necessarily a pneumatic one) and a petition for the fruits of communion.[9]

John McKenna's reflections on whether or not an 'epiclesis proper' (i.e. an explicit petition for the Holy Spirit to sanctify the gifts and/or the faithful) is an absolutely necessary component of eucharistic prayers suggest a third potential alternative to the West Syrian pattern that could open Western churches to a greater degree of structural flexibility in their official eucharistic prayer texts. Of course, historical evidence from the early centuries (and the practice of many major Western Christian traditions until relatively recently) and hesitance to elevate *any* prayer formula (whether the institution narrative or the epiclesis) into a sort of liturgical *sine qua non* argue against the view that an epiclesis proper is necessary. Nonetheless, a case could be made for the necessity of an 'epiclesis attitude' whether an explicit epiclesis is present in a community's eucharistic prayers or not.

> It is a practical necessity for the eucharistic assembly to express its awareness, for instance, of the necessary intervention of the Holy Spirit and of its own need for a praying or 'epiclesis' attitude ... an epiclesis proper is a *practical* necessity in the realization of the Eucharist.[10]

Granting that the epiclesis, conceived in this way, is a practical necessity, it may not be necessary for a particular praying community to include an explicit pneumatic epiclesis in *all* of its eucharistic prayers or to frame all

---

8 Senn, 'Toward a Different Anaphoral Structure', p. 352. Greek editions of the Liturgies of St John Chrysostom and St Basil were published in Europe in 1526, and occasional allusions and citations from Greek anaphoras can be found in Reformation liturgies. Senn discusses in some detail the Liturgy of King Johan III of Sweden (1576), which borrows phrases from Book 8 of the *Apostolic Constitutions* and the Anaphora of St John Chrysostom – while nonetheless maintaining the twofold pattern of praise and supplication found in the Roman Canon.

9 See Senn, 'Toward a Different Anaphoral Structure', pp. 357–8.

10 See McKenna, *Eucharistic Epiclesis*, pp. 224–7, quote from pp. 225–6.

of its epicleses in a similar way (in terms of location within the prayer, benefits requested, etc.).

Yet another option would be to focus less on either the words of institution or the epiclesis as consecratory, and instead emphasize that the *whole* eucharistic prayer is consecratory, once again along the lines of the early Church's emphasis on the sacrifice of praise and thanksgiving. For, as Senn has written elsewhere,

> The early liturgical tradition was simply uninterested in pinpointing a 'moment of consecration' and identifying that with either the words of institution or with the invocation of the Holy Spirit. There are early Christian traditions that had neither an institution narrative nor a consecratory epiclesis, without thereby losing a sense of communion with Christ in, with, and through the bread and cup.[11]

However, even though concerns about the 'moment of consecration' were not an issue for the framers of early eucharistic prayers, it may represent an insurmountable obstacle in practice to expect this sort of second naivety from modern liturgical revisers. As W. Jardine Grisbrooke notes, once such concerns arose, 'even the attempt to abandon such a concept by saying that the whole prayer consecrates merely results, in practice, in regarding the conclusion of the prayer as that moment'.[12]

Employing some of these strategies may result in prayers with a greater range and nuance of epicletic patterns than those presently printed in current official liturgical books. Meanwhile, it should also be emphasized that considerable diversity in terms of the epicleses themselves already exists among Western eucharistic prayers, although the influence of more contemporary theological concerns makes this diversity of a different sort from that which is characteristically found in early eucharistic prayers. Even the correspondence of two prayers based on the same ancient text cannot be presumed.

MINING AND MULTIPLYING METAPHORS

When speaking of the Spirit, the multiplication of metaphor may hold more promise than the deductive speech of rational discourse. While

---

11 Frank C. Senn, *Christian Liturgy: Catholic and Evangelical* (Minneapolis: Fortress Press 1997), p. 79.
12 W. J. Grisbrooke, 'Anaphora' in J. Gordon Davies (ed.), *A New Dictionary of Liturgy and Worship* (London: SCM Press 1986), p. 20.

ancient texts might be considered as models and appreciated for their theological resonance, another avenue for incorporating a more expansive pneumatology into Western eucharistic prayers might be to turn to the resources found *within* these traditions in the realm of metaphor and imagery to articulate the place of the Spirit in Christian life and worship. There are many metaphors for the Spirit that have not been dominant in recent tradition or applied to the eucharistic context. Nonetheless, well-loved or even long-dormant images and metaphors for the Spirit might be given new life in contemporary eucharistic prayers seeking to put Christians in touch with the roots of their own traditional modes of prayer and worship.

Scripture could provide a common starting point and a common source. Pondering what is needed in eucharistic prayers today, first on Gail Ramshaw's list of suggested criteria was 'more biblical inspiration in imagery for God and about the sacramental life'.[13] Hearing of the Holy Spirit as fire, breath or wind moving through an epicletic invocation in a eucharistic prayer might rouse worshippers to a sense that the Spirit is a force beyond their control that challenges and compels. The Spirit as inspiration for life or anointing for ministry could connect what happens in the eucharistic action with what happens in the lives of believers always sent back out into the world at the liturgy's conclusion. The Spirit's coming as both the Paraclete, promise of Christ's presence, and the eschatological sign of the final age could comfort the burdened and rouse the complacent.

Language about the Spirit coined within particular Christian traditions could continue to speak to contemporary worshippers who find life through the pneumatic richness of the Roman rite's *Veni Creator Spiritus* or Calvin's theological treatises or the Wesleys' hymns, for example. What might emerge from reflection on Catherine of Siena's image of the Holy Spirit as a waiter who serves the food of the incarnate Word at the table of God, both in this life and in the heavenly banquet to come, against the backdrop of the eucharistic epiclesis? Bernard of Clairvaux conceived of the Holy Spirit as a 'kiss' that enabled the Church as bride of Christ and its members to carry out their appointed mission in the world.[14] In an epicletic context, this metaphor could capitalize on the relational nature of the Eucharist in terms of its role of incorporating

---

13 Gail Ramshaw, 'A Look at New Anglican Eucharistic Prayers', *Worship* 86.2 (2012), p. 167.
14 These metaphors are drawn from Elizabeth A. Dreyer, *Holy Power, Holy Presence: Rediscovering Medieval Metaphors for the Holy Spirit* (New York: Paulist Press 2007).

believers into the Trinitarian life and inviting others to participate in this life through their witness in the world.

Beyond the explicitly Christian tradition, another source of metaphors might be sought in the riches of the world's cultures. A few brief examples will suffice to illustrate the potential for inculturation of the eucharistic epiclesis. Jung Young Lee, in *The Trinity in Asian Perspective*, describes the Holy Spirit as a feminine principle, as a mother who sustains the world. One image Lee emphasizes would be especially apt in the context of a eucharistic epiclesis – the maternal metaphor of the kettle. Lee observes:

> The kettle is for cooking, and is the symbol of nourishment. Here, spiritual nurture is not separate from the nourishment of the body ... Because food is cooked in the kettle, the kettle represents the nurture and transformation of all things.[15]

Applied to the eucharistic context, the Spirit could be seen as contributing divine 'transforming power' that helps to change ordinary bread and wine into spiritual food that provides nourishment for eternal life and also empowers Christians to become nourishment for the world in which they live. As a mother's meal brings her family together around the table, so the pneumaticized body of Christ which the Christian community is called to receive and become in the Eucharist unites those who share in the meal and forms them for a common mission. Thus an epiclesis that plays up the metaphor of Eucharist as kettle could highlight both the change in the eucharistic gifts and the essential role of partaking in those gifts for spiritual nourishment.

Moving to a Latin American context and the perspective of liberation theology, José Comblin observes that:

> The Spirit is the one who gathers the poor together so as to make them a new people who will challenge all powers of the earth. The Spirit is the strength of the people of the poor, the strength of those who are weak. Without the Spirit, the poor would not raise their voices and conflict would not raise its head ... The people of the poor cries out for liberation.[16]

---

15 Jung Young Lee, *The Trinity in Asian Perspective* (Nashville: Abingdon Press 1996), p. 104.
16 José Comblin, *The Holy Spirit and Liberation*, trans. Paul Burns (Maryknoll, NY: Orbis Books 1989), p. 99.

Without uncritically 'baptizing' all aspects of liberation theology, the concept of the Spirit as the divine spokesperson for the poor, the creator of unity among people and of a more just community, and the agent of empowerment for change of unjust structures could be included among the list of graces flowing forth as fruits of communion for which epicleses typically pray.

In African Christian theology, the Holy Spirit is sometimes perceived as the 'Grand Ancestor' who sustains and guides the people. As the 'ancestor par excellence', explains Nigerian theologian Caleb Oladipo, the Holy Spirit

> sustains the entire line of humanity by embracing the beginning as well as the end of human spiritual destiny . . . This means that the eminent assumption of the spiritual destiny which African ancestors seek to guarantee to their earthly descendants is obtainable through an indigenous Christian definition of the Holy Spirit.[17]

Thus it would seem that paying attention to the eschatological implications of eucharistic participation might bear fruit in African epicleses that underscore the Spirit as the enabler of unity among the members of the body of Christ across time and space; as the facilitator of ongoing communion with the 'living dead'; and as the Ancestor whose mission is the present and future spiritual welfare of the entire community. Obviously, conceiving of the Spirit as a kettle, a liberator or an ancestor would make little sense in the prayers of cultures unfamiliar with these metaphors, and incorporating such imagery into an epiclesis would require a more radical rethinking of the surrounding content of the eucharistic prayer as a whole. However, in an age when more and more Christians who pray in 'Western' traditions live in cultural contexts that are *not* shaped primarily by Indo-European influences, an openness to indigenous expressions of the Spirit's activity in the Eucharist could create new possibilities for speaking of the Spirit.

MOVING BEYOND EPICLETIC TEXTS

This work has highlighted some of the diversity found in contemporary Western eucharistic prayers in terms of both structure and language. However, the focus throughout has been on eucharistic prayer *texts*.

---

17 Caleb Oluremi Oladipo, *The Development of the Doctrine of the Holy Spirit in the Yoruba (African) Indigenous Christian Movement*, American University Studies, Series 2: Theology and Religion 185 (Frankfurt: Peter Lang 1996), pp. 104, 107–8.

While examining the location of a pneumatic epiclesis within an anaphora, the addressee of the petition (God the Father, the Logos, the Spirit), the verb(s) used (come, let come, send, etc.) and the variety of additional benefits requested as a result of the Spirit's coming or sending can provide a useful starting point for analysis of the epiclesis, it is only a starting point. The wider context of eucharistic celebration (framed by postures of the assembly and gestures of the assembly and presider, the architectural environment, the musical setting, the cultural context, etc.) would provide a fuller picture of the implicit and explicit pneumatology of an assembly actively engaged in praying these prayers. The narrow focus of this study on the textual aspects of the epiclesis certainly overlooks important aspects of the Spirit's engagement of particular worshipping communities.

Even within the textual realm, this study has not examined how pneumatology (or other aspects traditionally associated with the epiclesis such as unity and eschatology) is incorporated into *other* aspects of a community's eucharistic prayers. Pneumatology, for example, may be a subtle or overt component of variable prefaces for certain feasts (such as Pentecost or the Baptism of the Lord) or seasons (relating to the incarnational focus of the Advent–Christmas season or the eschatological orientation of Easter). If the desired fruits of communion conveyed by some epicleses have at their core a concern that the celebrating community find itself immersed more deeply in the paschal mystery, bringing this hope to more conscious awareness in the minds and hearts of the assembly may be achieved through other means than paying conscious attention to the epicletic texts of the prayers. Furthermore, some aspects which frequently accompany the developed Antiochene form of the epiclesis (such as eschatological benefits as fruits of sharing in communion) are carried by Western traditions in other parts of their eucharistic prayers (such as an eschatological focus to the intercessions in the Roman Catholic tradition). Focusing too narrowly on the articulation of the Spirit's presence and activity in epicletic texts may lead to overlooking its presence and activity elsewhere in a tradition's rites and prayers – and its movement in the lives of its members.

Finally, in focusing on a subset of denominations in the English-speaking world that have official liturgical books, this study overlooks the movement of the Holy Spirit in the eucharistic celebrations of traditions which favour extemporaneous prayer inspired by this same Spirit. Pentecostal, Baptist, evangelical and charismatic traditions, which also have a presence and roots within the same Western heritage as the churches considered here, have traditionally attended more strongly to the pneumatological aspects of Christian theology and worship. Attention to the place of the Spirit in the eucharistic worship of traditions such as these could provide a valuable complement to the sort of work undertaken here – and a fuller picture of the movements of the Spirit in eucharistic celebrations today.

FINAL WORDS

As this study has indicated, the role of the epiclesis in a specifically eucharistic context is not understood in the same way in every tradition. Major differences include location of the epiclesis within the eucharistic prayer as a whole (particularly in relation to the institution narrative) and the language used to articulate how the community requests the Holy Spirit to act on the people, the gifts, or both. Reconsidering the epicleses of ancient anaphoras will not necessarily provide easy solutions to more modern dilemmas. However, reflection on the diversity of early epicleses might inspire openness towards a greater variety of prayer patterns and a broader range of theological resonance within which eucharistic epicleses might legitimately be interpreted.

All this is not to suggest that insights from ancient anaphoras should not be adapted for modern liturgies. Through their continued use in changing contexts, early traditions and texts can connect contemporary Christian congregations with the wider tradition of their faith as past reality, present participation and future hope. Ancient examples should not, however, be used as uncritical justification for positions which these very texts cannot be read as supporting. While the emphases of modern epicleses could be viewed as perfectly acceptable within their own denominational frameworks, they do not necessarily represent unbroken continuity with any one particular 'ancient tradition' of eucharistic praying. As Paul Bradshaw has noted, some degree of tension between tradition and innovation seems to be essential to ongoing liturgical development:

> Quite clearly what is required is . . . some sort of 'creative tension' between adhering to tradition and following contemporary trends, in order to avoid the extremes of either position . . . But we have to risk letting liturgy go wrong if it is to develop naturally at all, if it is to have any real chance of getting it right. For, in the end, the only real test of good liturgy is the test of time.[18]

---

18 Paul F. Bradshaw, 'The Liturgical Use and Abuse of Patristics' in Kenneth W. Stevenson (ed.), *Liturgy Reshaped* (London and Garden City, NY: SPCK/Anchor Press 1982), p. 145.

Perhaps one fruit of such tension in the realm of eucharistic praying will be the incorporation of a more diverse and robust pneumatology into the eucharistic prayers of Western traditions in the future, both within the epiclesis proper and elsewhere in the prayers.

In debating whether a eucharistic epiclesis is permissible or problematic, desirable or necessary, the role of the Holy Spirit in creating and maintaining the Church's unity is stressed again and again. Unfortunately, even if the recovery of the epiclesis *has* been a sign of unity and renewal in recent Western Christian tradition, it has not led to the visible unity among separated Christian churches that ecumenists such as Vischer hoped for in the 1960s and 1970s. Until such time as greater actual agreement on the place of the Spirit in the eucharistic prayer can be achieved, perhaps *less* specificity in the eucharistic epiclesis rather than more might provide a way for Christians of different denominations to pray together and express their hope of one day sharing a common table in cases where this seems like more of an eschatological hope than an impending reality. If the early epicleses may have simply invited the Spirit to 'come' or be 'sent' without much further elaboration, perhaps the Spirit's presence in the eucharistic encounter will be able to achieve more for those who desire unity than much theological reflection on the role of pneumatology.

In any case, the use of the epiclesis in the liturgies of the early Church sets a precedent for the desirability (although not the necessity) of incorporating an explicit pneumatic epiclesis into at least some eucharistic prayers as an option which serves to highlight the mission and power of the Spirit in Christian worship and life. The long-standing use of the epiclesis in Eastern churches and its recent recovery in the West may be signs of growing convergence in eucharistic practice that may provide a trace of the Spirit's work in the world. Citing Luke 11.13,[19] Albert Curry Winn concludes that prayer for the Spirit in the eucharistic context is 'clearly permissible ... There are no qualifying clauses in that promise [that the Father will give the Spirit to those who ask]. On any occasion, under any circumstances, we may pray for the Holy Spirit.'[20]

This points to the deeper theological rationale for invoking the Spirit in the eucharistic context or any other context of Christian life. The

---

19 'If you then, who are evil, know how to give good gifts to your children, how much more will the heavenly Father give the Holy Spirit to those who ask him!'
20 Albert Curry Winn, 'The Role of the Holy Spirit in Communion', *RefLitM* 29.4 (1995), p. 229.

reason that the Church prays *for* the Spirit is so that its members might live *in* the Spirit – and so participate in the life of the triune God as children of the Father and siblings of the Son. The goal of Christian life is nothing less than doxology. Whether or not the Holy Spirit is directly invoked on the eucharistic gifts and/or the people so that pneumaticized people might live eucharistic lives, the Holy Spirit has long been named in almost every tradition alongside the Father and the Son in the concluding doxology of the eucharistic prayer. Robert Taft highlights the theological importance of this euchological moment, saying, 'It brings out the truth that our glorification of God is his gift to us, not ours to him: he is glorified in us insofar as we receive and live the life he offers us in the Spirit.'[21] The epiclesis is a prayer for the Spirit's coming *so that* we might come to share in this life.

---

21 Robert F. Taft, 'The Fruits of Communion in the Anaphora of St John Chrysostom' in Ildebrando Scicolone (ed.), *Psallendum: Miscellanea di studi in onore del Prof. Jordi Pinell i Pons, O.S.B.* (Rome: Pontificio Ateneo S. Anselmo 1992), p. 283.

Bibliography

Albertine, Richard. 'Problem of the (Double) Epiclesis in the New Roman Eucharistic Prayers', *Ephemerides Liturgicae* 91 (1977), pp. 192–202.

Allen, Horace T., Jr. '*Book of Common Worship* (1993): The Presbyterian Church (USA), "Origins and Anticipations"' in Bryan D. Spinks and Iain R. Torrance (eds), *To Glorify God: Essays on Modern Reformed Liturgy* (Grand Rapids, MI: Eerdmans 1999), pp. 13–29.

Allen, Horace T., Jr. 'The Ecumenical Context of the Proposed Book' in H. B. Evans (ed.), *Prayer Book Renewal: Worship and the New Book of Common Prayer* (New York: Seabury Press 1978), pp. 99–111.

Allmen, Jean-Jacques von. *Essai sur le Repas du Seigneur*, Cahiers Théologiques 55 (Neuchâtel: Delachaux et Niestlé 1966).

Allmen, Jean-Jacques von. *The Lord's Supper*, Ecumenical Studies in Worship 19 (Richmond, VA: John Knox Press 1969).

Alternative Services Series 3: An Order for Holy Communion (London: Cambridge University Press 1973).

The Alternative Service Book, 1980: A Commentary by the Liturgical Commission (London: C10 1980).

Amon, Karl. 'Gratias Agere: Zur Reform des Messcanons', *Liturgisches Jahrbuch* 15 (1965), pp. 79–98.

Anderson, E. Byron. 'A Body in the Spirit for the World: Eucharist, Epiclesis, and Ethics', *Worship* 85.2 (2011).

Anderson, Fred R. '*Book of Common Worship* (1993): A Pastoral Overview', *Princeton Seminary Bulletin* 16.2 (1995), pp. 121–37.

Atchley, E. G. Cuthbert F. 'The Epiclesis: A Criticism', *Theology* 29 (1934), pp. 28–35.

Atchley, E. G. Cuthbert F. *On the Epiclesis of the Eucharistic Liturgy and in the Consecration of the Font*, Alcuin Club Collections 31 (London: Oxford University Press, H. Milford 1935).

Backus, Irena Dorota. *The Reception of the Church Fathers in the West: From the Carolingians to the Maurists* (Leiden and New York: Brill 1997).

Baldovin, John F. *Liturgy in Ancient Jerusalem*, Alcuin/GROW Liturgical Study 9; Grove Liturgical Study 57 (Bramcote: Grove Books 1989).

Barnes, Michel René. *The Power of God:* Δύναμις *in Gregory of Nyssa's Trinitarian Theology* (Washington, DC: Catholic University of America Press 2001).

Baumstark, Anton. 'Die Anaphora von Thmuis und ihre Überarbeitung durch den h.l. Serapion', *Römische Quartalschrift* 18 (1904), pp. 134–5.

Baumstark, Anton. *Comparative Liturgy* (Westminster, MD and London: Newman Press 1958).

Baumstark, Anton. *Vom geschichtlichen Werden der Liturgie*, Ecclesia Orans 10 (Freiburg and Breisgau: Herder 1923).

Baumstark, Anton. 'Zu den Problemen der Epiklese und des römischen Messkanons', *Theologische Revue* 15 (1916), pp. 337–50.

Bell, George Kennedy Allen. *Randall Davidson, Archbishop of Canterbury* (London and New York: Oxford University Press 1952).

Bellah, Robert N. *Beyond Belief: Essays on Religion in a Post-Traditional World* (New York: Harper & Row 1976).

Berger, Teresa. '*Veni Creator Spiritus*: The Elusive Real Presence of the Spirit in the Catholic Tradition' in Teresa Berger and Bryan D. Spinks (eds), *The Spirit in Worship – Worship in the Spirit* (Collegeville, MN: Liturgical Press 2009), pp. 141–54.

Berger, Teresa with Bryan D. Spinks. 'Introduction' in Teresa Berger and Bryan D. Spinks (eds), *The Spirit in Worship – Worship in the Spirit* (Collegeville, MN: Liturgical Press 2009), pp. xi–xxv.

Berger, Teresa and Bryan D. Spinks (eds). *The Spirit in Worship – Worship in the Spirit* (Collegeville, MN: Liturgical Press 2009).

Bishop, Edmund. 'The Moment of Consecration' in R. H. Connolly (ed.), *The Liturgical Homilies of Narsai*, Texts and Studies: Contributions to Biblical and Patristic Literature 8.1 (Cambridge: Cambridge University Press 1909).

Bishop, W. C. 'Liturgical Comments and Memoranda II', *Journal of Theological Studies* 10 (1909), pp. 592–603.

Bishop, W. C. 'The Primitive Form of Consecration of the Holy Eucharist', *Church Quarterly Review* 66 (1908), pp. 385–404.

Bishops' Committee on the Liturgy. *BCL Report: The Directory for Masses with Children and Eucharistic Prayers for Children* (Washington, DC: Bishops' Committee on the Liturgy 1979).

Black, Matthew. 'The Maranatha Invocation and Jude 14, 15 (1 Enoch 1:9)' in Barnabas Lindars and Stephen S. Smalley (eds), *Christ and Spirit in the New Testament: In Honour of Charles Francis Digby Moule* (Cambridge: Cambridge University Press 1973), pp. 189–96.

Boggis, Robert James Edmund. *Revision of the Book of Common Prayer from the Point of View of a Parish Priest* (Canterbury: Cross & Jackman 1914).

Botte, Bernard. 'L'épiclèse dans les liturgies syriennes orientales', *Sacris Erudiri* 6 (1954), pp. 48–72.

Boulton, Matthew Myer. 'The Adversary: Agony, Irony, and the Liturgical Role of the Holy Spirit' in Teresa Berger and Bryan D. Spinks (eds), *The Spirit in Worship – Worship in the Spirit* (Collegeville, MN: Liturgical Press 2009), pp. 59–77.

Bouman, Walter R. 'Worship and the Means of Grace' in Ralph R. Van Loon (ed.), *Encountering God: The Legacy of Lutheran Book of Worship for the 21st Century* (Minneapolis: Kirk House 1998), pp. 22–39.

Bouyer, Louis. *Eucharist: Theology and Spirituality of the Eucharistic Prayer*, trans. C. U. Quinn from the 2nd French edition (1968) (Notre Dame, IN: University of Notre Dame Press 1968).

Bradshaw, Paul F. 'Baptismal Practice in the Alexandrian Tradition: Eastern or Western?' in Maxwell E. Johnson (ed.), *Living Water, Sealing Spirit: Readings on Christian Initiation* (Collegeville, MN: Liturgical Press 1995), pp. 82–100.

Bradshaw, Paul F. 'The Barcelona Papyrus and the Development of Early Eucharistic Prayers' in Maxwell E. Johnson (ed.), *Issues in Eucharistic Praying in East and West: Essays in Liturgical and Theological Analysis* (Collegeville, MN: Liturgical Press 2011), pp. 129–38.

Bradshaw, Paul F. *Eucharistic Origins* (London: SPCK 2004).

Bradshaw, Paul F. 'God, Christ, and the Holy Spirit in Early Christian Praying' in Bryan D. Spinks (ed.), *The Place of Christ in Liturgical Prayer: Trinity, Christology, and Liturgical Theology* (Collegeville, MN: Liturgical Press/Pueblo 2008), pp. 51–64.

Bradshaw, Paul F. 'The Homogenization of Christian Liturgy – Ancient and Modern: Presidential Address', *Studia Liturgica* 26.1 (1996), pp. 1–15.

Bradshaw, Paul F. 'The Liturgical Use and Abuse of Patristics' in Kenneth W. Stevenson (ed.), *Liturgy Reshaped* (London and Garden City, NY: SPCK/ Anchor Press 1982), pp. 134–45.

Bradshaw, Paul F. 'The Rediscovery of the Holy Spirit in Modern Eucharistic Theology and Practice' in Teresa Berger and Bryan D. Spinks (eds), *The Spirit in Worship – Worship in the Spirit* (Collegeville, MN: Liturgical Press 2009).

Bradshaw, Paul F. *The Search for the Origins of Christian Worship: Sources and Methods for the Study of Early Liturgy* (New York: Oxford University Press 2002).

Bradshaw, Paul F., Gordon Giles and Simon Kershaw. 'Holy Communion' in Paul F. Bradshaw (ed.), *A Companion to Common Worship*, vol. 1, Alcuin Club Collections 78 (London: SPCK 2001).

Bradshaw, Paul F., Maxwell E. Johnson and L. Edward Phillips. *The Apostolic Tradition: A Commentary* (Minneapolis: Fortress Press 2002).

Brand, Eugene L. 'An Ecumenical Enterprise' in Ralph R. Van Loon (ed.), *Encountering God: The Legacy of Lutheran Book of Worship for the 21st Century* (Minneapolis: Kirk House 1998), pp. 9–21.

Brightman, F. E. 'Correspondence: Eucharistic Invocation', *Theology* 9.49 (1924), pp. 33–40.

Brightman, F. E. *The English Rite, Being a Synopsis of the Sources and Revisions of the Book of Common Prayer, with an Introduction and an Appendix* (London: Rivingtons 1915).

Brightman, F. E. *Liturgies, Eastern and Western; Being the Texts, Original or Translated, of the Principal Liturgies of the Church* (Oxford: Clarendon Press 1896).

Brinktrine, Johannes. 'Zur Entstehung der morgenländischen Epiklese', *Zeitschrift für Katholische Theologie* 42 (1918), pp. 301–26, 483–518.

Brock, Sebastian P. 'The Epiklesis in the Antiochene Baptismal Ordines', *Symposium Syriacum 1972*, Orientalia Christiana Analecta 197 (Rome: Pontifical Oriental Institute 1974), pp. 183–218.

Brock, Sebastian P. 'Invocations to/for the Holy Spirit in Syriac Liturgical Texts: Some Comparative Approaches' in Robert F. Taft and Gabriele Winkler (eds), *Comparative Liturgy Fifty Years after Anton Baumstark (1872–1948)* (Rome: Pontifical Oriental Institute 2001), pp. 377–406.

Brock, Sebastian P. 'Towards a Typology of the Epicleses in the West Syrian Anaphoras' in Hans-Jürgen Feulner, Elena Velkovska and Robert F. Taft (eds), *Crossroad of Cultures: Studies in Liturgy and Patristics in Honor of Gabriele Winkler* (Rome: Pontifical Oriental Institute 2000), pp. 173–92.

Brunner, Peter. *Worship in the Name of Jesus*, trans. M. H. Bertram (St Louis: Concordia 1968).

Buchwald, Rudolph. *Die Epiklese in der römischen Messe* (Vienna: Verlag der Leo-Gesellschaft 1907).

Bugnini, Annibale. *The Reform of the Liturgy, 1948–1975* (Collegeville, MN: Liturgical Press 1990).

Bürki, Bruno. 'The Celebration of the Eucharist in Common Order (1994) and in the Continental Reformed Liturgies' in Bryan D. Spinks and Iain R. Torrance (eds), *To Glorify God: Essays on Modern Reformed Liturgy* (Grand Rapids, MI: Eerdmans 1999), pp. 227–39.

Burn, A. E. 'Invocation in the Holy Eucharist', *Theology* 9 (1924), pp. 317–21.

Cabrol, F. 'Épiclèse' in F. Cabrol, H. Leclercq and H. Marrou (eds), *Dictionnaire d'Archéologie Chrétienne et de Liturgie*, vol. 5.1 (Paris: Letouzey et Ané 1922), cols 142–84.

Chan, Simon. 'The Liturgy as the Work of the Spirit' in Teresa Berger and Bryan D. Spinks (eds), *The Spirit in Worship – Worship in the Spirit* (Collegeville, MN: Liturgical Press 2009), pp. 41–57.

Chauvet, Louis Marie. *Symbol and Sacrament: A Sacramental Reinterpretation of Christian Existence*, trans. Patrick Madigan and Madeleine Beaumont (Collegeville, MN: Liturgical Press 1995).

Church of England. *A Revised Liturgy: Being the Order of the Administration of the Lord's Supper According to the Use of the Church of England: With Divers Enrichments and Alterations* (London and Milwaukee: Mowbray/Young Churchman 1914).

Clements, R. E. *et al. Eucharistic Theology Then and Now* (London: SPCK 1968).

Comblin, José. *The Holy Spirit and Liberation*, trans. Paul Burns (Maryknoll, NY: Orbis Books 1989).

Commission on Worship, United Methodist Church. *The Sacraments of the Lord's Supper: An Alternative Text, 1972* (Nashville: United Methodist Publishing House 1972).

Congar, Yves. 'Pneumatologie ou "Christomonisme"' dans la tradition latine?', *Ecclesia a Spiritu Sancto Edocta: Mélanges Théologiques: Hommage à Mgr. Gérard Philips*, Bibliotheca Ephemeridum Theologicarum Lovaniensium 27 (Gembloux: J. Duculot, 1970), pp. 41–63.

Crehan, Joseph H. 'Eucharistic Epiklesis: New Evidence and a New Theory', *Theological Studies* 41.4 (1980), pp. 698–712.

Crichton, J. D. *Christian Celebration: The Mass* (London: G. Chapman 1971).

Crichton, J. D. 'A Theology of Worship' in Cheslyn Jones, Geoffrey Wainwright, Edward Yarnold and Paul Bradshaw (eds), *The Study of Liturgy* (London and New York: SPCK/Oxford University Press 1992, revised edn), pp. 3–31.

Crockett, William R. *Eucharist: Symbol of Transformation* (New York: Pueblo 1989).

Cuming, Geoffrey J. 'The Anaphora of St. Mark: A Study in Development', *Le Muséon* 95 (1982), pp. 115–29.

Cuming, Geoffrey J. 'Egyptian Elements in the Jerusalem Liturgy', *Journal of Theological Studies* 24 (1974), pp. 117–24.

Cuming, Geoffrey J. *The Liturgy of St. Mark*, Orientalia Christiana Analecta 234 (Rome: Pontifical Oriental Institute 1990).

Cuming, Geoffrey J. 'ΔΙ΄ ΕΥΧΗΣ ΛΟΓΟΥ (Justin, *Apology* i.66.2)', *Journal of Theological Studies* 31.1 (1980), pp. 80–2.

Cutrone, Emmanuel J. 'Anaphora of the Apostles: Implications of the Mar Esa'ya Text', *Theological Studies* 34.4 (1973), pp. 624–42.

Cutrone, Emmanuel J. 'Cyril's Mystagogical Catecheses and the Evolution of the Jerusalem Anaphora', *Orientalia Christiana Periodica* 44 (1978), pp. 52–64.

Cyril of Jerusalem. *Catéchèses Mystagogiques [par] Cyrille de Jérusalem*, Sources Chrétiennes 126, trans. Pierre Paris, ed. Auguste Piédagnel (Paris: Cerf 1966).

Daniels, Harold M. 'The Making of the *Book of Common Worship (1993)*' in Bryan D. Spinks and Iain R. Torrance (eds), *To Glorify God: Essays on Modern Reformed Liturgy* (Grand Rapids, MI: Eerdmans 1999), pp. 31–53.

Daniels, Harold M. 'An Overview of a Major Liturgical Resource: The Service for the Lord's Day', *Reformed Liturgy and Music* 18.4 (1984), pp. 181–4.

Daniels, Harold M. 'The Story of the Process Leading to a New Service Book', *Reformed Liturgy and Music* 26.3 (Summer 1992), pp. 146–52.

Daniels, Harold M. 'Weekly Eucharist among Presbyterians', *Reformed Liturgy and Music* 19.1 (1985).

Davis, Carl Judson. *The Name and Way of the Lord: Old Testament Themes, New Testament Christology*, Journal for the Study of the New Testament Supplement Series 129 (Sheffield: Sheffield Academic Press 1996).

Denysenko, Nicholas. *The Blessing of Waters and Epiphany: The Eastern Liturgical Tradition* (Burlington, UT and Farnham: Ashgate 2012).

Detscher, Alan F. 'The Eucharistic Prayers of the Roman Catholic Church' in Frank C. Senn (ed.), *New Eucharistic Prayers: An Ecumenical Study of Their Development and Structure* (Mahwah, NJ: Paulist Press 1987), pp. 15–52.

Dinesen, Palle. 'Die Epiklese im Rahmen altkirchlicher Liturgien: Eine Studie über die eucharistische Epiklese', *Studia Theologica* 16.1 (1962), pp. 42–107.

'Directory fot the Worship of God', *The Constitution of the United Presbyterian Church in the United State of America, Part II: The Book of Order* (New York: Office of the General Assembly of the United Presbyterian Church in the United States of American 1961).

Dix, Gregory. *The Shape of the Liturgy* (Westminster, MD and London: Dacre Press 1945).

Dix, Gregory. *The Shape of the Liturgy*, ed. and with additional notes by Paul V. Marshall (New York: Seabury Press 1982, reprint of 2nd (1945) edn).

Doresse, Jean and Emmanuel Lanne. *Un Témoin Archaique de la Liturgie Copte de S. Basile* (Louvain: Publications Universitaires 1960).

Doval, Alexis James. *Cyril of Jerusalem, Mystagogue: The Authorship of the Mystagogic Catecheses*, Patristic Monograph Series 17 (Washington, DC: Catholic University of America Press 2001).

Dreyer, Elizabeth A. *Holy Power, Holy Presence: Rediscovering Medieval Metaphors for the Holy Spirit* (New York: Paulist Press 2007).

Duba, Arlo D. 'Presbyterian Eucharistic Prayers' in Frank C. Senn (ed.), *New Eucharistic Prayers: An Ecumenical Study of Their Development and Structure* (Mahwah, NJ: Paulist Press 1987), pp. 96–123.

Duchesne, Louis. *Christian Worship: Its Origin and Evolution: A Study of the Latin Liturgy up to the Time of Charlemagne*, trans. M. L. McClure (London: SPCK 1956, 5th edn).

Dunphy, Walter. 'Maranatha: Development in Early Christianity', *Irish Theological Quarterly* 37 (1970), pp. 294–308.

Elliott, J. K. *The Apocryphal New Testament: A Collection of Apocryphal Christian Literature in an English Translation* (Oxford and New York: Clarendon Press/ Oxford University Press 1993).

Episcopal Church. *The Book of Common Prayer and Administration of the Sacraments and Other Rites and Ceremonies of the Church: Together with the Psalter or Psalms of David: According to the Use of the Episcopal Church* (New York: Church Hymnal Corporation 1979, Pew edn).

Episcopal Church. *The Liturgy of the Lord's Supper: The Celebration of the Holy Eucharist and Ministration of Holy Communion* (New York: Church Pension Fund 1967).

Erickson, Craig Douglas. 'Reformed Eucharistic Theology', *Reformed Liturgy and Music* 29.4 (1995), pp. 223–8.

Evangelical Lutheran Church in America and Evangelical Lutheran Church in Canada. *Evangelical Lutheran Worship* (Minneapolis: Augsburg Fortress 2006, Leader's Desk edn).

Evans, H. B. *Prayer Book Renewal: Worship and the New Book of Common Prayer* (New York: Seabury Press 1978).

Evdokimov, Paul. 'Eucharistie – mystère de l'Église', *La Pensée Orthodoxe* 2 (1968), pp. 53–69.

Every, George. 'Edmund Bishop and the Epiclesis' in A. H. Armstrong and E. J. B. Fry (eds), *Re-discovering Eastern Christendom: Essays in Commemoration of Dom Bede Winslow* (London: Darton, Longman & Todd 1963), pp. 77–89.

Farag, Mary K. 'A Shared Prayer over Water in the Eastern Christian Traditions' in Teresa Berger (ed.), *Liturgy in Migration: From the Upper Room to Cyberspace* (Collegeville, MN: Liturgical Press 2012).

Farag, Mary K. 'Δύναμις Epicleses: An Athanasian Perspective', *Studia Liturgica* 39.1 (2009), pp. 63–79.

Fenwick, John R. K. *The Anaphoras of St. Basil and St. James: An Investigation into Their Common Origin*, Orientalia Christiana Analecta 240 (Rome: Pontifical Oriental Institute 1992).

Fenwick, John R. K. *Fourth-Century Anaphoral Construction Techniques*, Grove Liturgical Study 45 (Bramcote: Grove Books 1986).

Fenwick, John R. K. *'The Missing Oblation': The Contents of the Early Antiochene Anaphora*, Alcuin/GROW Liturgical Study 11 (Bramcote: Grove Books 1989).

Fenwick, John R. K. and Bryan D. Spinks, *Worship in Transition: The Liturgical Movement in the Twentieth Century* (New York: Continuum 1995).

Flannery, Austin (ed.). *Vatican Council II: The Basic Sixteen Documents: Constitutions, Decrees, Declarations: A Completely Revised Translation in Inclusive Language* (Northport, NY: Costello 1996).

Fletcher, Jeremy. *Communion in Common Worship: The Shape of Orders One and Two*, Grove Worship Series W159 (Cambridge: Grove Books 2000).

Fortescue, Adrian. *The Mass: A Study of the Roman Liturgy* (London and New York: Longmans, Green and Co. 1917).

Fossum, Jarl. 'Jewish-Christian Christology and Jewish Mysticism', *Vigiliae Christianae* 37.3 (1983), pp. 260–87.

Frere, Walter Howard. *The Anaphora, or Great Eucharistic Prayer: An Eirenical Study in Liturgical History* (London and New York: SPCK /Macmillan 1938).

Frere, Walter Howard. *The Primitive Consecration Prayer: A Lecture Given at the Annual Meeting of the [Alcuin] Club, June 7, 1922*, Alcuin Club Prayer Book Revision Pamphlets 8 (London and Milwaukee: Mowbray/Morehouse 1922).

Frere, Walter Howard. *Some Principles of Liturgical Reform: A Contribution towards the Revision of the Book of Common Prayer* (London: John Murray 1911).

Fuchs, Lorelei F. and Lawrence C. Brennan. 'The Spirit in the Worship and Liturgy of the Church' in William R. Barr and Rena M. Yocum (eds), *The Church in the Movement of the Spirit* (Grand Rapids, MI: Eerdmans 1994), pp. 51–73.

Gelston, Anthony. *The Eucharistic Prayer of Addai and Mari* (Oxford and New York: Clarendon Press/Oxford University Press 1992).

Gelston, Anthony. 'The Relationship of the Anaphoras of Theodore and Nestorius to that of Addai and Mari' in G. Karukaparampil (ed.), *Tuvaik: Studies in Honour of Rev. Jacob Vellian*, Syrian Churches Series 16 (Kottayam: Mad'naha Theological Institute 1995), pp. 20–6.

Gelston, Anthony. 'ΔΙʹ ΕΥΧΗΣ ΛΟΓΟΥ (Justin, *Apology* i.66.2)', *Journal of Theological Studies* 33.1 (1982), pp. 172–5.

Gore, Charles. *A Prayer-Book Revised: Being the Services of the Book of Common Prayer, with Sundry Alterations and Additions Offered to the Reader* (London and Milwaukee: Mowbray/Young Churchman 1913).

Gray, Donald. *The 1927–28 Prayer Book Crisis, Vol. 1: Ritual, Royal Commissions, and Reply to the Royal Letters of Business*, Joint Liturgical Studies 60 (Norwich: SCM-Canterbury Press 2005).

Gray, Donald. *The 1927–28 Prayer Book Crisis, Vol. 2: The Cul-de-sac of the 'Deposited Book' . . . Until Further Order Be Taken*, Joint Liturgical Studies 61 (Norwich: SCM-Canterbury Press 2006).

Grisbrooke, W. Jardine. 'Anaphora' in J. G. Davies (ed.), *A New Dictionary of Liturgy and Worship* (London: SCM Press 1986), pp. 13–21.

Grisbrooke, W. Jardine. *Anglican Liturgies of the Seventeenth and Eighteenth Centuries* (London: SPCK 1958).

Group for Renewal of Worship. *Common Worship Today: An Illustrated Guide to Common Worship* (London: HarperCollins 2001).

Gummey, Henry Riley. *The Consecration of the Eucharist: A Study of the Prayer of Consecration in the Communion Office from the Point of View of the Alterations and Amendments Established Therein by the Revisers of 1789* (Philadelphia and London: H. F. Anners Press/De la More Press 1908).

Halliburton, R. J. 'The Patristic Theology of the Eucharist' in Cheslyn Jones, Geoffrey Wainwright, Edward Yarnold and Paul Bradshaw (eds), *The Study of Liturgy* (London and New York: SPCK/Oxford University Press 1992, revised edn), pp. 245–51.

Hänggi, Anton, Irmgard Pahl, Louis Ligier, Albert Gerhards and Heinzgerd Brakmann. *Prex Eucharistica* (Freiburg: Universitätsverlag 1998).

Hatchett, Marion J. *Commentary on the American Prayer Book* (New York: Seabury Press 1980).

Hebert, A. G. 'Anaphora and Epiclesis', *Theology* 37 (1938), pp. 89–94.

Hefling, Charles C. '*Gratia*: Grace and Gratitude: Fifty Unmodern Theses as Prolegomena to Pneumatology', *Anglican Theological Review* 83.3 (2001), pp. 473–91.

Heintz, Michael. 'δί εὐχῆς λόγου τοῦ παρ᾿ αὐτοῦ: (Justin, *Apology* 1.66.2): Cuming and Gelston Revisited', *Studia Liturgica* 33.1 (2003), pp. 33–6.

Hickman, Hoyt L. *Holy Communion: A Service Book for Use by the Minister* (Nashville: Abingdon Press 1987).

Hickman, Hoyt L. 'Word and Table: The Process of Liturgical Revision in the United Methodist Church, 1964–1992' in Karen B. Westerfield Tucker (ed.), *The Sunday Service of the Methodists: Twentieth-Century Worship in Worldwide Methodism: Studies in Honor of James F. White* (Nashville: Kingswood 1996), pp. 117–35.

Höller, Josef. *Die Epiklese der griechisch-orientalischen Liturgien: Ein Beitrag zur Lösung der Epiklesisfrage*, Studien und Mitteilungen aus dem kirchen-geschichtlichen Seminar der theologischen Fakultät der k.k. Universität in Wien 9 (Vienna: Mayer 1912).

Houssiau, Albert. 'The Alexandrine Anaphora of St. Basil' in Lancelot C. Sheppard (ed.), *The New Liturgy: A Comprehensive Introduction to the New Liturgy as a Whole and to Its New Calendar, Order of Mass, Eucharistic Prayers, the Roman Canon, Prefaces and the Sunday Lectionary* (London: Darton, Longman & Todd 1970), pp. 228–43.

Hughes, Kathleen. 'Original Texts: Beginnings, Present Projects, and Guide-lines' in Peter C. Finn and James M. Schellman (eds), *Shaping English Liturgy: Studies in Honor of Archbishop Denis Hurley* (Washington, DC: Pastoral Press 1990), pp. 219–55.

Inter-Lutheran Commission on Worship, Lutheran Church in America, American Lutheran Church, Evangelical Lutheran Church of Canada and Lutheran Church–Missouri Synod. *Lutheran Book of Worship* (Minneapolis: Augsburg 1978, Minister's Desk edn).

Jasper, R. C. D. and G. J. Cuming (eds), *Prayers of the Eucharist: Early and Reformed* (Collegeville, MN: Liturgical Press 1990, 3rd edn, revised and enlarged).

Johnson, Caroline. 'Ritual Epicleses in the Greek Acts of Thomas' in François Bovon, Ann Graham Brock and Christopher R. Matthews (eds), *Apocryphal Acts of the Apostles: Harvard Divinity School Studies* (Cambridge, MA: Harvard University Center for the Study of World Religions 1999), pp. 171–204.

Johnson, Maxwell E. 'The Archaic Nature of the Sanctus, Institution Narrative, and Epiclesis of the Logos in the Anaphora Ascribed to Sarapion of Thmuis' in Paul F. Bradshaw (ed.), *Essays on Early Eastern Eucharistic Prayers* (College-ville, MN: Liturgical Press 1997), pp. 73–107.

Johnson, Maxwell E. 'The Holy Spirit and Lutheran Liturgical-Sacramental Worship' in Teresa Berger and Bryan D. Spinks (eds), *The Spirit in Worship – Worship in the Spirit* (Collegeville, MN: Liturgical Press 2009), pp. 155–77.

Johnson, Maxwell E. *Living Water, Sealing Spirit: Readings on Christian Initiation* (Collegeville, MN: Liturgical Press 1995).

Johnson, Maxwell E. 'The Origins of the Anaphoral Use of the Sanctus and Epiclesis Revisited: The Contribution of Gabriele Winkler and its Implica-tions' in Hans-Jürgen Feulner, Elena Velkovska and Robert F. Taft (eds), *Crossroad of Cultures: Studies in Liturgy and Patristics in Honor of Gabriele Winkler* (Rome: Pontifical Oriental Institute 2000), pp. 405–42.

Johnson, Maxwell E. *The Prayers of Sarapion of Thmuis: A Literary, Liturgical, and Theological Analysis* Orientalia Christiana Analecta 249 (Rome: Pontifical Oriental Institute 1995).

Joint Committee on Worship, *The Worshipbook* (Philadelphia: Westminster Press 1970).

The Joint Office of Worship for the Presbyterian Church (USA) and the Cumberland Presbyterian Church. *The Service for the Lord's Day: The Worship of God*, Supplemental Liturgical Resource 1 (Philadelphia: Westminster Press 1984).

Jungmann, Josef A. *The Mass of the Roman Rite*, trans. Francis A. Brunner (New York: Benziger 1951).

Kaczynski, Reiner. 'Direktorium und Hochgebetstexte für Messfeiern mit Kindern', *Liturgisches Jahrbuch* 29 (1979), pp. 157–75.

Kavanagh, Aidan. 'Thoughts on the New Eucharistic Prayers', *Worship* 43.1 (1969), pp. 2–12.

Kennedy, David J. 'The Epiclesis and the Role of the Holy Spirit in the Eucharistic Prayer' in David R. Holeton (ed.), *Revising the Eucharist: Groundwork for the Anglican Communion: Studies in Preparation for the 1995 Dublin Consultation*, Alcuin/GROW Liturgical Study 27 (Bramcote: Grove Books 1994), pp. 43–4.

Kennedy, David J. *Eucharistic Sacramentality in an Ecumenical Context: The Anglican Epiclesis*, Ashgate New Critical Thinking in Religion, Theology and Biblical Studies (Aldershot and Burlington, VT: Ashgate 2008).

Kilmartin, Edward J. 'The Active Role of Christ and the Holy Spirit in the Sanctification of the Eucharistic Elements', *Theological Studies* 45.2 (1984), pp. 225–53.

Kilmartin, Edward J. *Christian Liturgy: Theology and Practice, Vol. 1: Systematic Theology and Liturgy* (Kansas City, MO: Sheed & Ward 1988).

Kilmartin, Edward J. 'Sacrificium Laudis: Content and Function of Early Eucharistic Prayers', *Theological Studies* 35.2 (1974), pp. 268–87.

Klauser, Theodor. *The Western Liturgy and Its History* (London: Mowbray 1952).

Klijn, A. F. J. (ed.), *The Acts of Thomas: Introduction, Text, and Commentary* (Leiden and Boston: Brill 2003, 2nd revised edn).

Küng, Hans. 'Das Eucharistiegebet: Konzil und Erneuerung der römischen Liturgie', *Wort und Wahrheit* 18 (1963), pp. 102–7.

Lathrop, Gordon W. 'Conservation and Critique: Principles in Lutheran Liturgical Renewal as Proposals toward the Unity of the Churches' in James F. Puglisi (ed.), *Liturgical Renewal as a Way to Christian Unity* (Collegeville, MN: Liturgical Press 2005), pp. 87–100.

Lee, Jung Young. *The Trinity in Asian Perspective* (Nashville: Abingdon Press 1996).

Lietzmann, Hans. *Mass and Lord's Supper: A Study in the History of the Liturgy*, trans. Dorothea H. G. Reeve (Leiden: Brill 1953).

Ligier, Louis. 'De la cène de Jésus à l'anaphore de l'Église', *La Maison-Dieu* 87 (1966), pp. 7–51.

Ligier, Louis. 'From the Last Supper to the Eucharist' in Lancelot C. Sheppard (ed.), *The New Liturgy: A Comprehensive Introduction to the New Liturgy as a Whole and to Its New Calendar, Order of Mass, Eucharistic Prayers, the Roman Canon, Prefaces and the Sunday Lectionary* (London: Darton, Longman & Todd 1970), pp. 113–50.

Lipsius, Richard Adelbert and Maximilian Bonnet (eds). *Acta Apostolorum Apocrypha* (Hildesheim: G. Olms 1959).

McGoldrick, Patrick. 'The Holy Spirit and the Eucharist', *Irish Theological Quarterly* 50 (1983), pp. 48–66.

McGowan, Anne Vorhes. 'The Basilian Anaphoras: Rethinking the Question' in Maxwell E. Johnson (ed.), *Issues in Eucharistic Praying in East and West: Essays in Liturgical and Theological Analysis* (Collegeville, MN: Liturgical Press 2010), pp. 221–8.

McKenna, John H. 'The Epiclesis Revisited' in Frank C. Senn (ed.), *New Eucharistic Prayers: An Ecumenical Study of Their Development and Structure* (Mahwah, NJ: Paulist Press, 1987), pp. 169–94.

McKenna, John H. 'The Epiclesis Revisited: A Look at Modern Eucharistic Prayers', *Ephemerides Liturgical* 99 (1985), pp. 314–36.

McKenna, John H. *Eucharist and Holy Spirit: The Eucharistic Epiclesis in Twentieth-Century Theology (1900–1966)* (Great Wakering: Mayhew-McCrimmon (for the Alcuin Club) 1975).

McKenna, John H. *The Eucharistic Epiclesis: A Detailed History from the Patristic to the Modern Era* (Chicago: Hillenbrand 2009, 2nd edn).

McKenna, John H. 'Eucharistic Epiclesis: Myopia or Microcosm?' *Theological Studies* 36.2 (1975), pp. 265–84.

McKenna, John H. 'Eucharistic Prayer: Epiclesis' in Andreas Heinz and Heinrich Rennings (eds), *Gratias Agamus: Studien zum eucharistischen Hochgebet: Für Balthasar Fischer* (Freiburg: Herder 1992), pp. 283–91.

Macleod, Donald. 'Calvin into Hippolytus?' in Bryan D. Spinks and Iain R. Torrance (eds), *To Glorify God: Essays on Modern Reformed Liturgy* (Grand Rapids, MI: Eerdmans 1999), pp. 255–67.

McManus, Frederick R. 'Back to the Future: The Early Christian Roots of Liturgical Renewal', *Worship* 72.5 (1998), pp. 386–403.

McManus, Frederick R. 'Preface' in Cipriano Vagaggini, *The Canon of the Mass and Liturgical Reform*, ed. and trans. Peter Coughlan (Staten Island, NY: Alba House 1967).

Macomber, W. F. 'The Oldest Known Text of the Anaphora of the Apostles Addai and Mari', *Orientalia Christiana Periodica* 32 (1966), pp. 335–71.

McPartlan, Paul. *The Eucharist Makes the Church: Henri de Lubac and John Zizioulas in Dialogue* (Edinburgh: T. & T. Clark 1993).

Marshall, Paul V. (ed.). *Prayer Book Parallels: The Public Services of the Church Arranged for Comparative Study* (New York: Church Hymnal Corporation 1989).

Mazza, Enrico. *The Eucharistic Prayers of the Roman Rite*, trans. Matthew J. O'Connell (New York: Pueblo 1986).

Mazza, Enrico. *The Origins of the Eucharistic Prayer*, trans. Ronald E. Lane (Collegeville, MN: Liturgical Press 1995).

Meyers, Ruth. 'Liturgy and Society: Cultural Influences on Contemporary Liturgical Revision' in Paul Bradshaw and Bryan Spinks (eds), *Liturgy in Dialogue: Essays in Memory of Ronald Jasper* (Collegeville, MN: Liturgical Press 1994), pp. 154–75.

Miller, R. H. *Study Guide for the Holy Eucharist (Proposed Book of Common Prayer)* (Wilton, CT: Morehouse-Barlow 1977).

Mingana, Alphonse. *Commentary of Theodore of Mopsuestia on the Lord's Prayer and on the Sacraments of Baptism and the Eucharist* (Cambridge: W. Heffer & Sons Ltd 1933).

Mitchell, Leonel L. 'The Alexandrian Anaphora of St Basil of Caesarea: Ancient Source of "A Common Eucharistic Prayer"', *Anglican Theological Review* 58.2 (1976), pp. 194–206.

Mitchell, Leonel L. *Praying Shapes Believing: A Theological Commentary on* The Book of Common Prayer (Harrisburg, PA: Morehouse 1991).

Mitchell, Leonel L. 'The Theology of Eucharist' in H. B. Evans (ed.), *Prayer Book Renewal* (New York: Seabury Press 1978), pp. 45–52.

Montgomery, Kevin Andrew. 'When Sacraments Shall Cease: Toward a Pneumatological and Eschatological Approach to the Eucharist', MA thesis, Graduate Theological Union 2006.

Myers, Susan E. *Spirit Epicleses in the* Acts of Thomas, Wissenschaftliche Untersuchungun zum Neuen Testament 2, Reihe 281, ed. Jörg Frey *et al.* (Tübingen: Mohr Siebeck 2010).

Nichols, Bridget and Alistair MacGregor. *The Eucharistic Epiclesis*, Ushaw Library Publications 4 (Durham: Ushaw College Library 2001).

Nocent, Adrien. *A Rereading of the Renewed Liturgy*, trans. Mary M. Misrahi (Collegeville, MN: Liturgical Press 1994).

O'Brien, Thomas C. (ed.). *Documents on the Liturgy, 1963–1979: Conciliar, Papal, and Curial Texts*, trans. Thomas C. O'Brien (Collegeville, MN: Liturgical Press 1982).

The Office of Worship for the Presbyterian Church (USA) and the Cumberland Presbyterian Church. *Christian Marriage: The Worship of God*, SLR 3 (Philadelphia: Westminster Press 1986).

The Office of Worship for the Presbyterian Church (USA) and the Cumberland Presbyterian Church. *The Funeral: A Service of Witness to the Resurrection*, SLR 4 (Philadelphia: Westminster Press 1986).

The Office of Worship for the Presbyterian Church (USA) and the Cumberland Presbyterian Church. *The Liturgical Year*, SLR 7 (Philadelphia: Westminster Press 1986).

Oladipo, Caleb Oluremi. *The Development of the Doctrine of the Holy Spirit in the Yoruba (African) Indigenous Christian Movement*, American University Studies, Series 2: Theology and Religion 185 (Frankfurt: Peter Lang 1996).

Peiffer, Robert B. 'How Contemporary Liturgies Evolve: The Revision of United Methodist Liturgical Texts (1968–1988)', PhD dissertation, University of Notre Dame 1992.

Perham, Michael. 'Liturgical Revision 1981–2000' in Paul F. Bradshaw (ed.), *A Companion to Common Worship*, vol. 1, Alcuin Club Collections 78 (London: SPCK 2001).

Pfatteicher, Philip H. 'The Blood in Our Veins' in Ralph Van Loon (ed.), *Encountering God: The Legacy of Lutheran Book of Worship for the 21st Century* (Minneapolis: Kirk House 1998).

Pfatteicher, Philip H. *Commentary on the Lutheran Book of Worship: Lutheran Liturgy in Its Ecumenical Context* (Minneapolis: Augsburg Fortress 1990).

Pfatteicher, Philip H., Carlos R. Messerli and Inter-Lutheran Commission on Worship, *Manual on the Liturgy: Lutheran Book of Worship* (Minneapolis: Augsburg 1979).

Piepkorn, A. C. 'The Eucharistic Prayer', *Una Sancta* 7.3 (1947), pp. 10–12.

Piil, Mary Alice. 'The Local Church as the Subject of the Action of the Eucharist' in Peter C. Finn and James M. Schellman (eds), *Shaping English Liturgy: Studies in Honor of Archbishop Denis Hurley* (Washington, DC: Pastoral Press 1990).

Porter, Harry Boone. 'An American Assembly of Anaphoral Prayers', *Sacrifice of Praise* (Rome: CLV – Edizioni Liturgiche 1981), pp. 181–96.

Porter, Harry Boone. 'Episcopal Anaphoral Prayers' in Frank C. Senn (ed.), *New Eucharistic Prayers: An Ecumenical Study of Their Development and Structure* (Mahwah, NJ: Paulist Press 1987), pp. 63–73.

Porter, Harry Boone and Associated Parishes. *The Holy Eucharist: Rite Two: A Commentary* (Alexandria, VA: Associated Parishes 1976).

Power, David Noel. 'The Anamnesis: Remembering, We Offer' in Frank C. Senn (ed.), *New Eucharistic Prayers: An Ecumenical Study of Their Development and Structure* (Mahwah, NJ: Paulist Press, 1987), pp. 146–68.

Power, David N. *Sacrament: The Language of God's Giving* (New York: Crossroad 1999).

Presbyterian Church in the United States of America. *The Book of Common Worship* (Philadelphia: Published for the Office of the General Assembly of the Publication Division of the Board of Christian Education of the Presbyterian Church in the United States of America 1946).

Price, Charles P. *Introducing the Draft Proposed Book*, Prayer Book Studies 29 (New York: Church Hymnal Corporation 1976).

Price, Charles P. for the Standing, Liturgical Commission for the Episcopal Church. *Introducing the Proposed Book: A Study of the Significance of the Proposed* Book of Common Prayer *for the Doctrine, Discipline, and Worship of the Episcopal Church*, Prayer Book Studies 29 (New York: Church Hymnal Corporation 1976, revised edn).

Puglisi, James F. (ed.). *Liturgical Renewal as a Way to Christian Unity* (Collegeville, MN: Liturgical Press 2005).

Quere, Ralph W. *In the Context of Unity: A History of the Development of Lutheran Book of Worship* (Minneapolis: Lutheran University Press 2003).

Quere, Ralph W. 'Liturgy, Unity, and Disunity: The Context and Legacy of *LBW*', *Currents in Theology and Mission* 30.5 (2003), pp. 349–65.

Ramshaw, Gail. 'A Look at New Anglican Eucharistic Prayers', *Worship* 86.2 (2012).

Ramshaw-Schmidt, Gail. 'Toward Lutheran Eucharistic Prayers' in Frank C. Senn (ed.), *New Eucharistic Prayers: An Ecumenical Study of Their Development and Structure* (Mahwah, NJ: Paulist Press 1987).

Reed, Luther Dotterer. *The Lutheran Liturgy: A Study of the Common Liturgy of the Lutheran Church in America* (Philadelphia: Muhlenberg Press 1959, revised edn).

Regan, Patarick. 'Quenching the Spirit: The Epiclesis in Recent Roman Documents', *Worship* 79.5 (2005), pp. 386–404.

Richardson, Cyril Charles. 'The Origin of the Epiclesis', *Anglican Theological Review* 28.3 (1946), pp. 148–53.

Roberts, Alexander and James Donaldson (eds). *The Ante-Nicene Fathers: Translations of the Writings of the Fathers down to A.D. 325, Vol. 1: The Apostolic Fathers with Justin Martyr and Irenaeus* (Edinburgh and Grand Rapids MI: T. & T. Clark/Eerdmans 1996, reprint of the 1926 edn).

Robinson, J. Armitage. 'Invocation in the Holy Eucharist', *Theology* 8 (1924), pp. 89–100.

Roman Catholic Church. *Missale Romanum: Ex Decreto Sacrosancti Oecumenici Concilii Vaticani II Instauratum: Auctoritate Pauli PP. VI Promulgatum* (Civitas Vaticana: Libreria Editrice Vaticana 1975, editio typica altera edn).

Roman Catholic Church. *Missale Romanum: Ex Decreto Sacrosancti Oecumenici Concilii Vaticani II Instauratum: Auctoritate Pauli PP. VI Promulgatum: Ioannis Pauli PP. II Cura Recognitum* (Civitate Vaticana: Typis Vaticanis 2002).

Roman Catholic Church. *The Sacramentary* (New York: Catholic Book Publishing Co. 1985).

The Roman Missal: Study Edition (Collegeville, MN: Liturgical Press 2012).

Rouwhorst, Gerard. 'La célébration de l'eucharistie selon les Actes de Thomas' in Herman A. J. Wegman and Charles Caspers (eds), *Omnes Circumadstantes: Contributions towards a History of the Role of the People in the Liturgy* (Kampen: J. H. Kok 1990, pp. 51–77.

Russo, Nicholas V. 'The Validity of the Anaphora of *Addai and Mari*: Critique of the Critiques' in Maxwell E. Johnson (ed.), *Issues in Eucharistic Praying in East and West: Essays in Liturgical and Theological Analysis* (Collegeville, MN: Liturgical Press 2011), pp. 21–62.

Ryan, John Barry. 'Eucharistic Prayers for Masses with Children' in Frank C. Senn (ed.), *New Eucharistic Prayers: An Ecumenical Study of Their Development and Structure* (Mahwah, NJ: Paulist Press 1987), pp. 53–62.

Salaville, Séverien. 'Épiclèse eucharistique' in A. Vacant, E. Mangenot and E. Amann (eds), *Dictionnaire de Théologie Catholique*, vol. 5.1 (Paris: Letouzey et Ané 1913), cols 194–300.

Schmidt-Lauber, Hans. *Die Eucharistie als Entfaltung der Verba Testamenti*, Lutherischen Gottesdienstes und seiner Liturgie (Kassel: Stauda 1957).

Seasoltz, R. Kevin. *God's Gift Giving: In Christ and through the Spirit* (New York and London: Continuum 2007).

Seasoltz, R. Kevin. 'Non-Verbal Symbols and the Eucharistic Prayer' in Frank C. Senn (ed.), *New Eucharistic Prayers: An Ecumenical Study of Their Development and Structure* (Mahwah, NJ: Paulist Press 1987), pp. 214–36.

Senn, Frank C. *Christian Liturgy: Catholic and Evangelical* (Minneapolis: Fortress Press 1997).

Senn, Frank C. 'Intercessions and Commemorations in the Anaphora' in Frank C. Senn (ed.), *New Eucharistic Prayers: An Ecumenical Study of Their Development and Structure* (Mahwah, NJ: Paulist Press 1987), pp. 195–209.

Senn, Frank C. 'Introduction' in Frank C. Senn (ed.), *New Eucharistic Prayers: An Ecumenical Study of Their Development and Structure* (Mahwah, NJ: Paulist Press 1987).

Senn, Frank C. 'Toward a Different Anaphoral Structure', *Worship* 58.4 (1984), pp. 346–58.

Shepherd, Massey Hamilton. 'The Patristic Heritage of the American Book of Common Prayer of 1979', *Historical Magazine of the Protestant Episcopal Church* 53 (1984), pp. 221–34.

Shults, F. LeRon and Andrea Hollingsworth. *The Holy Spirit*, Guides to Theology (Grand Rapids, MI: Eerdmans, 2008).

Smit, G. C. 'Épiclèse et théologie des sacrements', *Mélanges de Science Religieuse* 15 (1958), pp. 95–136.

Smyth, Matthieu. 'The Anaphora of the So-Called "Apostolic Tradition" and the Roman Eucharistic Prayer' in Maxwell E. Johnson (ed.), *Issues in Eucharistic Praying in East and West: Essays in Liturgical and Theological Analysis* (Collegeville, MN: Liturgical Press 2010), pp. 71–97.

Spinks, Bryan D. 'The Ascension and the Vicarious Humanity of Christ: The Christology and Soteriology behind the Church of Scotland's Anamnesis and Epiklesis' in J. Neil Alexander (ed.), *Time and Community: In Honor of Thomas J. Talley*, NPM Studies in Church Music and Liturgy (Washington, DC: Pastoral Press 1990), pp. 185–201.

Spinks, Bryan D. 'Berakah, Anaphoral Theory and Luther', *Lutheran Quarterly* 3.3 (1989), pp. 267–80.

Spinks, Bryan D. 'A Complete Anaphora? A Note on Strasbourg Gr. 254', *Heythrop Journal* 25 (1984), pp. 51–9.

Spinks, Bryan D. 'The Consecratory Epiklesis in the Anaphora of St. James', *Studia Liturgica* 11.1 (1976), pp. 19–38.

Spinks, Bryan D. 'The Epiclesis in the East Syrian Anaphoras', *Worship: Prayers from the East* (Washington, DC: Pastoral Press 1993), pp. 89–96.

Spinks, Bryan D. 'The Jerusalem Liturgy of the Catecheses Mystagogicae: Syrian or Egyptian?' *Studia Patristica* 2 (1989), pp. 391–6.

Spinks, Bryan D. *Mar Nestorius and Mar Theodore the Interpreter: The Forgotten Eucharistic Prayers of East Syria, with Introduction, Translation and Commentary by Bryan D. Spinks* (Cambridge: Grove Books 1999).

Spinks, Bryan D. 'Mis-shapen: Gregory Dix and the Four-Action Shape of the Liturgy', *Lutheran Quarterly* 4.2 (1990), pp. 161–77.

Spinks, Bryan D. 'Review of Gabriele Winkler, *Das Sanctus: Über den Ursprung und die Anfänge des Sanctus und sein Fortwicken*', *Journal of Theological Studies* 55.1 (2004), pp. 365–8.

Spinks, Bryan D. *Sacraments, Ceremonies and the Stuart Divines: Sacramental Theology and Liturgy in England and Scotland, 1603–1662* (Aldershot and Burlington, VT: Ashgate 2002).

Spinks, Bryan D. *The Sanctus in the Eucharistic Prayer* (Cambridge and New York: Cambridge University Press 1991).

Stake, Donald Wilson. 'Gestures, Postures, and Movements at the Eucharist', *Reformed Liturgy and Music* 29.3 (1995), pp. 160–4.

Standing Liturgical Commission of the Episcopal Church. *Alternative Texts for Trial Use, 1975–76: At the Ordination of a Bishop, Confession of Sin, Alternative Eucharistic Prayer for Rite I, Two Alternative Eucharistic Prayers for Rite II, The Ten Commandments* (New York: Church Hymnal Corporation 1975).

Standing Liturgical Commission of the Episcopal Church. *The Holy Eucharist*, Prayer Book Studies 21 (New York: Church Hymnal Corporation 1970).

Stanton, Graham N., Bruce W. Longnecker and Stephen Barton (eds). *The Holy Spirit and Christian Origins: Essays in Honor of James D. G. Dunn* (Grand rapids, MI: Eerdmans 2004).

Steven, James. 'The Spirit in Contemporary Charismatic Worship' in Teresa Berger and Bryan D. Spinks (eds), *The Spirit in Worship – Worship in the Spirit* (Collegeville, MN: Liturgical Press 2009), pp. 245–59.

Stevenson, Kenneth W. *Gregory Dix – Twenty-Five Years On*, Grove Liturgical Study 10 (Bramcote: Grove Books 1977).

Strodach, Paul Zeller. *A Manual on Worship* (Philadelphia: Muhlenberg Press 1946, revised edn).

Stuckwisch, D. Richard. 'The Basilian Anaphoras' in Paul F. Bradshaw (ed.), *Essays on Early Eastern Eucharistic Prayers* (Collegeville, MN: Liturgical Press 1997), pp. 109–30.

Taft, Robert F. 'The Authenticity of the Chrysostom Anaphora Revisited: Determining the Authorship of Liturgical Texts by Computer', *Orientalia Christiana Periodica* 56.1 (1990), pp. 5–51.

Taft, Robert F. *Beyond East and West: Problems in Liturgical Understanding* (Rome: Edizioni Orientalia Christiana, Pontifical Oriental Institute 1997, 2nd revised and enlarged edn).

Taft, Robert F. 'From Logos to Spirit: On the Early History of the Epiclesis' in Andreas Heinz and Heinrich Rennings (eds), *Gratias Agamus: Studien zum eucharistischen Hochgebet: Für Balthasar Fischer* (Freiburg: Herder 1992), pp. 489–502.

Taft, Robert F. 'The Fruits of Communion in the Anaphora of St. John Chrysostom' in Ildebrando Scicolone (ed.), *Psallendum: Miscellanea di studi in onore del Prof. Jordi Pinell i Pons, O.S.B.* (Rome: Pontificio Ateneo S. Anselmo 1992), pp. 275–302.

Taft, Robert F. 'The Interpolation of the Sanctus into the Anaphora: When and Where? A Review of the Dossier', *Orientalia Christiana Periodica* 57.2 (1991), pp. 281–308.

Taft, Robert F. 'The Interpolation of the Sanctus into the Anaphora: When and Where? A Review of the Dossier, Part II', *Orientalia Christiana Periodica* 58.1 (1992), pp. 83–121.

Taft, Robert F. 'Mass without the Consecration? The Historic Agreement on the Eucharist between the Catholic Church and the Assyrian Church of the East Promulgated 26 October 2001', *Worship* 77.6 (2003), pp. 482–509.

Taft, Robert F. 'Some Structural Problems in the Syriac Anaphora of the Twelve Apostles', *Aram* 5 (1993), pp. 505–20.

Taft, Robert F. 'St. John Chrysostom and the Byzantine Anaphora that Bears His Name' in Paul F. Bradshaw (ed.), *Essays on Early Eastern Eucharistic Prayers* (Collegeville, MN: Liturgical Press 1997), pp. 195–226.

Taft, Robert F. 'The Structural Analysis of Liturgical Units: An Essay in Methodology', *Beyond East and West: Problems in Liturgical Understanding* (Rome: Pontifical Oriental Institute 1997, 2nd revised and enlarged edn), pp. 187–202.

Taft, Robert F. and Gabriele Winkler (eds). *Comparative Liturgy Fifty Years after Anton Baumstark (1872–1948)* (Rome: Pontifical Oriental Institute 2001).

Talley, Thomas Julian. 'The Literary Structure of the Eucharistic Prayer', *Worship* 58.5 (1984), pp. 404–20.

The Theology and Worship Ministry Unit for the Presbyterian Church (USA) and the Cumberland Presbyterian Church. *The Book of Common Worship* (Louisville, KY: Westminster John Knox Press 1993).

Thompson, William E. 'The Epiclesis and Lutheran Theology', *Logia* 4.1 (1995), pp. 31–5.

Thraede, Klaus. 'Ursprünge und Formen des "Heiligen Kusses" im frühen Christentum', *Jahrbuch für Antike und Christentum* 11/12 (1968–9), pp. 124–80.

Tidner, Erik (ed.). *Didascaliae Apostolorum Canonum Ecclesiasticorum Traditionis Apostolicae Versiones Latinae*, Texte und Untersuchungen zur Geschichte der altchristlichen Literatur 75 (Berlin: Akademie-Verlag 1963).

Tillard, J.-M. R. 'L'Eucharistie et le Saint-Esprit', *Nouvelle Revue Théologique* 90 (1968), pp. 363–87.

Tyrer, J. W. *The Eucharistic Epiclesis* (London and New York: Longmans, Green 1917).

United Methodist Church. *At the Lord's Table: A Communion Service Book for Use by the Minister* (Nashville: Abingdon Press 1981).

United Methodist Church. *The Book of Services: Containing the General Services of the Church Adopted by the 1984 General Conference* (Nashville: United Methodist Publishing House 1985).

United Methodist Church. *The United Methodist Book of Worship* (Nashville: United Methodist Publishing House 1992).

Vadakkel, Jacob. *The East Syrian Anaphora of Mar Theodore of Mopsuestia: A Critical Edition, English Translation and Study*, Oriental Institute of Religious Studies India Publications 129 (Kottayam: Oriental Institute of Religious Studies India 1989).

Vagaggini, Cipriano. *The Canon of the Mass and Liturgical Reform*, ed. and trans. Peter Coughlan (Staten Island, NY: Alba House 1967).

Vagaggini, Cipriano. *Theological Dimensions of the Liturgy: A General Treatise on the Theology of the Liturgy* (Collegeville, MN: Liturgical Press 1976).

Vajta, Vilmos. 'Renewal of Worship: De Sacra Liturgia' in George A. Lindbeck (ed.), *Dialogue on the Way: Protestants Report from Rome on the Vatican Council* (Minneapolis: Augsburg 1965).

Varghese, Baby. 'The Theological Significance of the Epiklesis in the Liturgy of Saint James' in István Perczel, Réka Forrai and György Geréby (eds), *Eucharist in Theology and Philosophy: Issues of Doctrinal History in East and West from the Patristic Age to the Reformation*, Ancient and Medieval Philosophy, Series 1, vol. 35 (Leuven: Leuven University Press 2005), pp. 363–80.

Vischer, Lukas. 'The Epiclesis: Sign of Unity and Renewal', *Studia Liturgica* 6.1 (1969), pp. 30–9.

Vööbus, Arthur. *Liturgical Traditions in the Didache* (Stockholm: ETSE 1968).

Wainwright, Geoffrey. *Doxology: The Praise of God in Worship, Doctrine, and Life: A Systematic Theology* (London and New York: Epworth/Oxford University Press 1980).

Wainwright, Geoffrey. 'The Ecumenical Scope of Methodist Liturgical Revision', *Centro Pro Unione Bulletin* 62 (2002), pp. 16–26.

Wainwright, Geoffrey. *Eucharist and Eschatology* (Peterborough: Epworth 2003, 3rd edn).

Wasserman, Marney Ault. 'The Shape of Eucharistic Thanksgiving', *Reformed Liturgy and Music* 29.3 (1995), pp. 139–45.

Weaver, J. Dudley, Jr. *Presbyterian Worship: A Guide for Clergy* (Louisville, KY: Geneva Press 2002).

West, Fritz. *The Comparative Liturgy of Anton Baumstark* (Bramcote: Grove Books 1995).

Westerfield Tucker, Karen B. *American Methodist Worship* (Oxford and New York: Oxford University Press 2001).

Westerfield Tucker, Karen B. 'The Eucharist in the *Book of Common Worship (1993)*', *Princeton Seminary Bulletin* 16.2 (1995), pp. 138–49.

Westerfield Tucker, Karen B. *The Sunday Service of the Methodists: Twentieth-Century Worship in Worldwide Methodism: Studies in Honor of James F. White* (Nashville: Kingswood 1996).

White, James F. *Introduction to Christian Worship* (Nashville: Abingdon Press 2000, 3rd edn, revised and expanded).

White, James F. *Protestant Worship: Traditions in Transition* (Louisville, KY: Westminster John Knox Press 1989).

White, James F. 'United Methodist Eucharistic Prayers: 1965–1985' in Frank C. Senn (ed.), *New Eucharistic Prayers: An Ecumenical Study of Their Development and Structure* (Mahwah, NJ: Paulist Press 1987), pp. 80–95.

Winkler, Gabriele. *Das armenische Initiationsrituale: Entwicklungsgeschichtliche und liturgievergleichende Untersuchung der Quellen des 3. bis 10. Jahrhunderts* (Rome: Pontifical Oriental Institute 1982).

Winkler, Gabriele. 'Further Observations in Connection with the Early Form of the Epiklesis', *Le Sacrement de l'Initiation: Origines et Prospective*, Patrimoine Syriaque Actes du colloque III (Antélias, Lebanon: Centre d'Études et de Recherches Pastorales 1996), pp. 66–80.

Winkler, Gabriele. 'Nochmals zu den Anfängen der Epiklese und des Sanctus im Eucharistischen Hochgebet', *Theologische Quartalschrift* 174.3 (1994), pp. 214–31.

Winkler, Gabriele. 'The Original Meaning of the Prebaptismal Anointing and Its Implications', *Worship* 52.1 (1978), pp. 24–45.

Winkler, Gabriele. 'Weitere Beobachtungen zur frühen Epiklese (den Doxologien und dem Sanctus): Über die Bedeutung der Apokryphen für die Erforschung der Entwicklung der Riten', *Oriens Christianus* 80 (1996), pp. 177–200.

Winkler, Gabriele. 'Zur Erforschung orientalischer Anaphoren in liturgievergleichender Sicht, I: Anmerkungen zur Oratio post Sanctus und Anamnese bis Epiklese', *Orientalia Christiana Periodica* 63.2 (1997), pp. 363–420.

Winn, Albert Curry. 'The Role of the Holy Spirit in Communion', *Reformed Liturgy and Music* 29.4 (1995), pp. 229–31.

Wood, Susan K. 'Participatory Knowledge of God in the Liturgy' in James Joseph Buckley and David S. Yeago (eds), *Knowing the Triune God: The Work of the Spirit in the Practices of the Church* (Grand Rapids, MI: Eerdmans 2001), pp. 95–118.

Woolley, Reginald Maxwell. *The Liturgy of the Primitive Church* (Cambridge: Cambridge University Press 1910).

World Council of Churches. *Baptism, Eucharist and Ministry*, Faith and Order Paper 111 (Geneva: World Council of Churches 1982).

Wright, William. *Apocryphal Acts of the Apostles* (Amsterdam: Philo Press 1968, reprint of 1871 London edn).

Zheltov, Michael. 'The Anaphora and the Thanksgiving Prayer from the Barcelona Papyrus: An Underestimated Testimony to the Anaphoral History in the Fourth Century', *Vigiliae Christianae* 62.5 (2008), pp. 467–504.

Index of modern authors

Index of subjects and ancient authors

Printed and bound by CPI Group (UK) Ltd, Croydon, CR0 4YY

28/07/2024

14533185-0002